W9-BBQ-744

THE LUXURY GUIDE TO

DISNEY VACATIONS

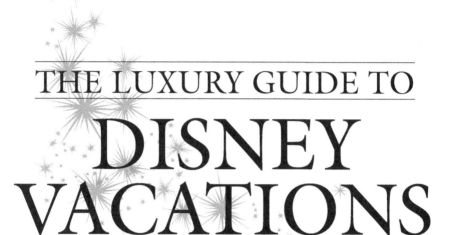

THE LUXURY GUIDE TO
DISNEY VACATIONS

HOW TO GET THE MOST
OUT OF THE BEST
DISNEY HAS TO OFFER

Cara Goldsbury

Bowman Books

All information in this guidebook is subject to change.
Call ahead for up-to-date and totally current information.

Copyright © 2014 by Cara Goldsbury

ALL RIGHTS RESERVED. No part of this book may be reproduced or
transmitted in any form by any means, electronic or mechanical, including
photocopying and recording, or by any information storage and retrieval
system, except as may be expressly permitted in writing from the publisher.
Requests for permission should be addressed to Bowman Books, 249 E.
Summit Ave, San Antonio, TX 78212.

ISBN 978-0-9726972-0-0

Printed in the United States of America
10 9 8 7 6 5 4 3 2 1

CONTENTS

SECTION FOUR: ADVENTURES BY DISNEY

SECTION FIVE: AULANI

INTRODUCTION

Disney. The word instantly fills the mind with images of Mickey Mouse, Peter Pan, Cinderella, and Snow White. It's a word that sends the imagination soaring to places only dreamed of in our wildest fantasies, a trip back to the idyllic innocence of childhood when nothing was unattainable and the world was filled with unlimited possibilities. It's a place where grown-ups can leave their responsibilities behind, at least for a little while, and have permission to be a kid again. Disney Destinations are so varied that they could fill your vacation schedule for years to come.

But is it really possible for sophisticated travelers to truly enjoy themselves at a Disney Destination? Of course! Simply allow this guidebook to step in and show you the *luxury* way to *Walt Disney World*® Resort, *Disneyland*® Resort, *Disney Cruise Line*®, *Adventures By Disney*®, and Aulani, A Disney Resort & Spa. This unique travel guide overflows with tips and techniques for all kinds of splendid Disney vacations designed for those who wish to reside in luxurious resorts and staterooms, dine at many of Disney's best restaurants, and enjoy the trip of a lifetime. I'm uniquely prepared to advise you in planning a visit in which each day comes with the best Disney has to offer. Helpful tips throughout can make the difference between a mediocre trip and a fantastic one.

Let's get going!

WALT DISNEY WORLD®
RESORT

At Walt Disney World Resort the four theme parks are so totally unique that it's almost like taking a different vacation each day of your visit. Enhancing the experience are exciting, themed resorts, a cornucopia of great restaurants, recreation galore, and special events throughout the year. Only a small percentage of its 30,000 acres are fully developed offering endless choices of lush grounds dotted with lakes, wetlands, and stunningly landscaped resorts and parks

With so many delightful diversions it's difficult to know where to begin. Together we will decide the most convenient time of year to visit, which resort best fits your personality, what rooms or suites are perfect for you, where to dine, and much, much more. Allow me to show you the way.

PLANNING YOUR WALT DISNEY WORLD VACATION

Planning a successful and stress-free vacation requires some fore-thought. And believe it or not the planning can sometimes be almost as fun as the vacation itself. Walt Disney World offers endless possibilities for all types of travelers. Begin by reading this book cover to cover and visiting WDWLuxuryGuide.com or CaraGoldsbury.com, the companion website to this guidebook with menus, photos, and information on Disney Destinations where you can also sign up for our newsletter and blog for up-to-date information. Have a look around at Disneyworld.disney.go.com. And remember, the help of a travel advisor who specializes in Disney Destinations may be the key to your best vacation ever.

There's nothing quite like a *true* Disney expert when it comes to choosing a travel advisor. An Authorized Disney Vacation Planner agency can make the difference between a mediocre vacation and an excellent one. For your Disney travel needs call Glass Slipper Concierge at (866) 725-7595 or go online at GlassSlipperConcierge.com. Glass Slipper Concierge is the brainchild of this book's author, Cara Goldsbury, originating from a desire to offer a client-centric option to those who want an exceptional and unforgettable Disney vacation. Cara has gathered an exclusive team of luxury concierge advisors whose knowledge of Disney Destinations can only be matched by their passion for delivering white-glove service.

When Should I Travel?

This can be a tough decision. Each season has its ups and downs. Summer seems to be the logical time to visit during the school break, but it's also a hot and steamy time of year when parks can be very crowded. Busier seasons come with congested parks, long lines, and higher resort rates but also greatly extended park hours. The slower seasons bring half-filled parks, shorter waits in line, and lower resort rates along with later opening times, earlier closing times, and attractions that are closed for rehab. For me, a slower season can't be beat. If you are able to do so avoid the busiest times of the year. If not the summer months or holidays are certainly better than nothing and, with a bit of planning and a lot of energy, can be equally enjoyable.

The following guidelines may not be exact since each year comes with different Florida resident offers, special celebrations, conventions, and so forth that affect crowd size. Use them as a general guide to avoiding the parks at their worst.

Busiest: President's Day week; mid-March through the week after Easter (staggered spring break around the country); the second week of June to mid-August; Thanksgiving Day through the weekend; the week of Christmas to New Year's Day.

Busy: The last two weeks of February (avoid President's Day week) to the first part of March before the onset of spring break; the second week after Easter until the second week of June; the month of October (a big convention month, the PGA Golf Classic, and Halloween celebrations at the Magic Kingdom); the first two weeks of December.

Least busy: Just after New Year's Day to the first week of February (avoiding the marathon weekend in early January and the Martin Luther King holiday weekend), but do expect huge school groups of South American teenagers; the third week of August to the beginning of October; the month of November excluding Thanksgiving weekend; just after Thanksgiving and again the week preceding Christmas week, a special time when the parks and resorts are festively decorated for the holidays.

Important Walt Disney World Resort Phone Numbers:

Glass Slipper Concierge—Travel Advisors (866) 725-7595

Advance Dining Reservations (407) WDW-DINE or (407) 939-3463

Behind-the-Scenes tours (407) WDW-TOUR or (407) 939-8687

Boating and tennis (407) WDW-PLAY or (407) 939-7529

Children's Activity Center reservations (407) WDW-DINE or (407) 939-3463

Fishing information and reservations (407) WDW-BASS or (407) 939-2277

General information (407) 824-4321

Golf tee times (407) WDW-GOLF or (407) 939-4653

Language Line (407) 824-7900

Park tickets (407) 566-4985

Switchboard (407) 824-2222

Transportation information (407) 939-7433

What Is the Weather Like in Orlando?

Because Orlando is a year-round vacation destination you probably won't encounter bitter cold weather. Winter has many days of sunshine along with the occasional cold snap, while summer brings uncomfortably muggy and warm days with almost daily afternoon showers. Peak hurricane season begins in August and runs through October, so be prepared for a washout (just about every store in the parks sells inexpensive Mickey-motif rain ponchos for that afternoon shower). The best months of the year—with delightfully mild and low-humidity weather, relatively small amounts of rainfall, and little or no danger of hurricanes—are October, November, April, and early May. Before leaving, call (407) 824-4104 for daily weather information or check one of the many weather sites on the Internet.

Month	Average High Temp (°F)	Average Low Temp (°F)	Average Rainfall (inches)
January	71	49	2.35
February	74	52	2.47
March	78	56	3.77
April	83	60	2.68
May	88	66	3.45
June	91	72	7.58
July	92	74	7.27
August	92	74	7.13
September	90	73	6.06
October	85	66	3.31
November	79	59	2.17
December	73	52	2.58

What Should I Pack?

Think casual! Park attire is appropriate throughout Walt Disney World with the exception of the more stylish resort restaurants (for dress codes see individual restaurant descriptions), but (with the exception of Victoria & Albert's) there isn't a suit or tie in site. In the warmer months of April through October bring shorts, light-colored short-sleeved or sleeveless shirts (darker colors really attract the heat), comfortable walking shoes (bring two pairs to switch off), cushy socks, sunglasses, hat, bathing suit and cover-up, water-resistant footwear, and a rain jacket. Women should bring a light purse or backpack; nothing is worse than lugging a heavy bag around the parks. For evenings away from the park at one of the more sophisticated dining venues dress is resort casual: women should plan on wearing a simple dress, dress shorts, or casual pants or jeans with a stylish blouse and sandals; men will be comfortable in khakis, nice jeans or dress shorts, and a short or long-sleeved collared shirt with loafers or sandals. Only at Victoria & Albert's is a jacket required for men (tie is optional).

The remaining months are anyone's guess. The weather is usually mild, but bring an assortment of casual clothing in the form of shorts and comfortable long pants along with short- and long-sleeved shirts, a sweater, hat, sunglasses, bathing suit and cover-up (pools are heated), rain jacket, light jacket for morning's cool air, and, of course, comfortable walking shoes and socks. For evenings away from the parks, women should wear smartly casual transitional clothing, and men casual pants and long-sleeved shirts. Florida is known (particularly November through February) for unexpected cold fronts that will find you in shorts one day and a winter jacket the next, although it never gets uncomfortably hot. Don't get caught off guard or you'll find yourself with, what might be, an unwanted Mickey Mouse motif wardrobe. Check the Internet for a weather forecast before beginning your packing.

How Long Should I Plan on Staying?

With four major theme parks and two water parks a long weekend will barely give you a taste of Disney's many attractions. Staying at least five or more nights provides a good taste of each theme park and perhaps one day at a Disney water park. Stay a week and there will be time to relax by the pool and rest your feet each afternoon for a few hours. Of course if all you can spare is a long weekend go for it, but you will have some tough decisions to make. With only a few days for touring go when the parks are not as crowded and plan on visiting the *Magic Kingdom*®, *Epcot*®, and either the *Animal Kingdom*® Theme Park or *Disney's Hollywood Studios*® with a trip in mind for another year to pick up all you've missed.

Should I Rent a Car?

Does driving in an unknown place make you uneasy? Will you be staying at a resort serviced by the monorail or a more isolated one? Would you like to dine at other resorts, or do you see yourself eating at the parks or simply staying put at your hotel for dinner? All these factors play a large part in your decision.

The drive from the airport on the Central Florida GreeneWay (SR 417) is a no-brainer, and finding your way around Disney is fairly easy because of the excellent signage. However, if driving a car in new situations tends to be a nerve-racking experience use Disney's more-than-adequate transportation system of buses, monorail, and water launches to make your way around.

If your plans include a stay at Disney's Animal Kingdom Lodge and Villas or Disney's Wilderness Lodge and Villas, renting a car provides you with many more options. No matter the plan a car is perhaps a more convenient option for traveling to Disney's Animal Kingdom Theme Park (not serviced by the monorail or by boat), the water parks, or evening restaurant hopping at Disney's excellent resort dining spots. Think about trying Disney transportation for a day or two and, if that doesn't work for you, then rent a car. Alamo has free shuttle service from the Disney resorts to its Car Care Center location near the Magic Kingdom making it almost hassle-free.

Those who would like to sample some of Disney's excellent resort restaurants will find it time-consuming, not to mention complex, to resort-hop using Disney transportation. It requires a trip to an open park or *Downtown Disney*® Area and then another bus to the resort and the same thing back again (of course you can always simplify things and take a cab). A stay at one of the Magic Kingdom Area resorts offers easy monorail access to the Magic Kingdom, other Magic Kingdom resorts, and Epcot. The Epcot Resorts are just a walk or water launch away from Epcot, *Disney's BoardWalk* Entertainment District, and Disney's Hollywood Studios, greatly expanding your restaurant choices.

In short, you will probably be using a combination of Disney transportation and a car for added convenience. And if you're like me who hates waiting for public transportation, rent a car to save hours of frustration.

Do remember that if your plans include a rental car, parking will be a factor. Parking at Disney's theme parks is complimentary to registered guests of *Official Walt Disney World*® Hotels, but instead of being dropped off in front by bus, those with a car will need to catch a shuttle from the parking lots. Self-parking is complimentary at the Disney resorts, but will set you back $15 per day (if you pay to valet park at a Disney resort the price includes valet park at other Disney resorts that same day, something that comes in quite handy when resort-hopping for dinner). This does not include the Walt Disney World Swan and Dolphin where it's $15 per day for self-parking and $23 for valet or the Waldorf Astoria where there's valet parking only for $24 per day.

TIPS FOR WALT DISNEY WORLD FIRST-TIMERS

- Slow down and enjoy the magic. Resist the urge to see everything at breakneck speed, and take time to enjoy the many amenities offered at your resort. You can't possibly see everything, so think of this as your first trip to Disney not your last. There will be time to pick up what you missed on the next go-round.

- Think ahead. Decide your priorities before your vacation begins and plan out each day beforehand.

- Get to the parks early! It's amazing, particularly in busy season, how many of the popular rides you can knock off before half the "World" gets out of bed.

- Plan for a rest in the middle of the day particularly if you have children in tow or the parks are open late. Stay at one of the Magic Kingdom or Epcot resorts, allowing an easy return to your room in the middle of the day for a nap or a plunge in the pool.

- Call or go online exactly 180 days prior at 7:00 a.m. Orlando time (Eastern time) for dining reservations if a meal at Cinderella's Royal Table or Be Our Guest in the Magic Kingdom is tops on your list. You might get away with sleeping in and booking a bit later but only when traveling during extremely slow seasons.

- Come prepared for an afternoon shower during the rainy summer months even if the sky looks perfectly clear in the morning. Rent a locker to store your rain gear, circling back if skies start to look threatening. If you're caught unprepared just about every store in the parks sells inexpensive rain ponchos.

- Arrive at the water parks at opening time if a lounge chair is a priority, or, better yet, pre-reserve one of the private cabanas or premium beach chair space. And remember that in the busy summer months, water parks are sometimes filled to capacity by midmorning with new guests kept from entering until late afternoon.

- Use *Disney's FastPass+*® option which allows up to three Fast-Pass+ attractions per day to be pre-reserved 60 days prior to arrival.

- Make Advance Dining Reservations, especially in the busier times of year (see the Dining In Style at Walt Disney World Resort chapter for a more detailed explanation), to save hours of waiting and frustration.

- Allow plenty of time to reach the theme parks each morning. It's easy to miss your breakfast reservations when enough time has not been allocated.

- Be selectively spontaneous. If something catches your eye, even if it's not on your daily list of things to do, be ready to stop and explore or you may miss something wonderful.

- Be attuned to the limitations of your children. If they're tired take a break; if their feet hurt get them a stroller (forget that they outgrew one years ago); if a ride seems scary to them don't force the issue. It will make your day and the day of other park visitors much less stressful.

- Wear broken-in, comfortable footwear. Better yet, bring several pairs and rotate them. Nothing is worse than getting blisters on your first day and then having to nurse them for the remainder of your vacation.

ARRIVAL AT WALT DISNEY WORLD

Getting to Walt Disney World Resort

Orlando Airports

Travelers will want to arrive at the Orlando International Airport (MCO), approximately a 25-minute drive from Walt Disney World. Private jets will want to land at Kissimmee (ISM), the closest airport to Walt Disney World.

By Car

Walt Disney World is located off Interstate 4, about 25 miles southwest of Orlando and west of the Florida Turnpike. From Interstate 95 or U.S. Highway 1 from the Florida Turnpike, take I-4 west and follow the signs to the correct Walt Disney World exit for your resort or theme park destination. Those traveling south on the Florida Turnpike will want to shorten their travel time by taking the Walt Disney World's Western Way—look for 429 West Toll Road (Tampa) to exit the turnpike and in 14 miles take the Walt Disney World exit. Those traveling northbound on the turnpike should take the Osceola Parkway that will lead directly to Walt Disney World.

Once inside Walt Disney World excellent signage will direct you to all destinations; however, you'll need to know what area your resort belongs to in order to find your way. *Disney's Contemporary* Resort, *Bay Lake Tower at Disney's Contemporary* Resort, *Disney's Grand Floridian* Resort & Spa, *The Villas at Disney's Grand Floridian* Resort & Spa, *Disney's Polynesian* Resort, and *Disney's Wilderness* Lodge and Villas are located in the *Magic Kingdom* Resort Hotels area. *Disney's BoardWalk* Inn, *Disney's Yacht and Beach Club* Resorts, and the Walt Disney World Swan and Dolphin Hotels are in the Epcot Resort Hotels area. *Disney's Animal Kingdom* Lodge and *Disney's Animal Kingdom* Villas–Kidani Village sit in the Animal Kingdom Theme Park area.

Airport Transportation

For personalized service book private car or limousine transfers prior to your arrival with Garden Tours & Transportation (GardenToursAndTransportation.com or 866-534-6217). Town car rates to and from Walt Disney World one-way are $94.50, SUVs $104.50, and limousines $164.50 including gratuities and taxes. Your driver will meet you as you exit the escalator downstairs at baggage claim. Reservations are mandatory.

Disney's Magical Express® Transportation, a motor coach service provided by Mears Transportation, allows registered guests of Official Walt Disney World Hotels to check bags at their hometown airport and bypass baggage claim at the Orlando (MCO) airport before heading to their resort. Buses stop at up to four resorts so plan on spending plenty of time on your bus before arriving at your destination (those short on patience should book private car transfers). Bags are delivered to the room, but may take up to four hours to reach you; guests arriving at the airport after 10:00 p.m. need to pick up their luggage at baggage claim and take it with them to the *Magical Express* motor coach.

On departure day avoid airport lines by checking luggage and receiving boarding passes through the Resort Airline Check-In Service located at each Disney resort (available only to passengers of AirTran Airways, Alaska Airlines, American Airlines, Delta Air Lines, JetBlue Airways, Southwest Airlines, United Airlines, and US Airways). You need not necessarily be utilizing Disney's Magical Express Transportation to make use of this handy service. Those with a flight departure time before 8:00 a.m. must check-in at the airport. This service is complimentary (individual airline baggage fees still apply) and available only to registered guests of an Official *Walt Disney World* Hotel (not available at the Walt Disney World Swan and Dolphin).

Car Rental

Alamo Rent-A-Car, the official car rental company of Walt Disney World, is located at the Orlando airport. They have an additional location at the AAA Car Care Center near the Magic Kingdom with free shuttle service provided to and from your Disney resort. For convenience stick with car companies located on airport property—Alamo, Avis, Budget, Dollar Car Rental, Enterprise Rent-A-Car, E-Z Rent-A-Car, Hertz Car Rental, L&M Car Rental, National, and Thrifty—whose cars are parked a quick walk away from the baggage claim area.

For something more luxurious try the Hertz Prestige and Dream Collection offering Infiniti QX56 and G37, Mercedes C Class, GL 450, and GLK350, and Porsche Boxter, 911, and Panamera. Specific models may be reserved, and Sirius/XM and a complimentary NeverLost GPS system are included. Avis has Signature Series rentals including a BMW 528.

Excellent signage and a great toll road from the airport make for an easy twenty-five-minute drive. Take the South exit out of the airport to toll road State Route 417 South, also known as the Central Florida GreeneWay and follow the signage to Walt Disney World and your resort or theme park destination. The drive is approximately 22 miles. Another slightly shorter option is the north route out of the airport to toll Highway 528, also known as the Bee Line Expressway, then to I-4, but it's best to avoid it as a route during rush-hour traffic.

Walt Disney World Transportation

Disney's complimentary transportation system designed for the exclusive use of Disney resort guests (although only on the busiest days do they require an ID to ride) is in most cases efficient, particularly the monorail. In addition, taxis can be found at every resort, all four theme parks, and Downtown Disney. For more information call (407) WDW-RIDE or (407) 939-7433.

Bus Transportation

Disney has an extensive and reliable system of clean, air-conditioned buses traversing the extent of the property. Designed for the exclusive use of Disney's registered guests, buses depart approximately every twenty minutes carrying guests to all four theme parks, both water parks, Downtown Disney, and all resort hotels. However, it takes more time than a car, as multiple stops are made at several resorts in what sometimes seems like a roundabout direction. Some buses are direct (to the theme parks and Downtown Disney) while others require a change at Downtown Disney or a stop at an additional resort. Buses operate as early as 6:30 a.m. for those with before park hours breakfast reservations until one and a half hours after park closing time. One advantage of bus transportation is the convenient drop-off directly in front of the park entrance, translating into no parking hassles and no waiting for a tram. The downside occurs after park closing when quite a line can form; consider leaving just a few minutes before the fireworks finale or hanging out to shop at one of the stores near the exit.

Getting easily from one resort to another is a different story altogether. Those staying at a Magic Kingdom or Epcot resort have many choices within walking distance or a monorail ride away, but those utilizing bus transportation find the only way to accomplish this feat is to take the quickest form of transportation to the nearest open theme park and then a bus to the resort of choice. After park hours it's necessary to bus to Downtown Disney and then to the resort. For example, it takes a good hour or more to travel between, say, Disney's Yacht Club Resort and Disney's Wilderness Lodge. If you want to resort-hop I strongly encourage renting a car or utilizing a taxi for optimum convenience.

Monorail

With over 13 miles of track at up to 40 mph, three lines service the Walt Disney World Resort: the Epcot Monorail travels between Epcot and the Transportation and Ticket Center (TTC); the Express Monorail travels nonstop and counterclockwise between the TTC and the Magic Kingdom; and the Magic Kingdom Resorts monorail travels clockwise from the TTC with stops at Disney's Polynesian Resort, Disney's Grand Floridian Resort, Magic Kingdom, and Disney's Contemporary Resort. All use the TTC as their central hub. The monorail system operates from one hour prior to earliest park opening until one hour after the latest park closing. Monorail service is not offered during evening *Extra Magic Hours* Benefit; resort guests should use the Disney bus or water launch service instead.

Boat Service

Ferryboats found at the TTC are a fun form of transportation for Magic Kingdom visitors. The Magic Kingdom is also accessible by water launch from Disney's Polynesian Resort, Disney's Grand Floridian Resort & Spa, Villas at Grand Floridian Resort & Spa, and Disney's Wilderness Lodge and Villas. Both Epcot and Disney's Hollywood Studios are accessible by water launch from Disney's BoardWalk Inn, Disney's Yacht and Beach Club, and the Walt Disney World Swan and Dolphin.

Walt Disney World Reference Guide

Alcoholic beverages. Alcohol is served at every park and resort on Disney property, except at the Magic Kingdom (the one exception being Be Our Guest restaurant and only at dinner). The legal drinking age in Florida is twenty-one, however, Disney's lounges allow minors as long as they do not drink alcohol or sit at the bar. Bottled liquor, wine, and beer can be purchased in at least one shop in every *Walt Disney World* Resort Hotel and/or from In-Room Dining.

ATMs. Chase automated teller machines (ATMs) are located at each park, at *Downtown Disney*, at the TTC, and in or near the lobby of each resort.

Business centers. Ricoh Business Centers operate at Disney resorts with convention center facilities (Disney's Yacht and Beach Club Resort, Disney's BoardWalk Inn, Disney's Contemporary Resort, Disney's Grand Floridian Resort & Spa) and offer a complete office environment including imaging services, high-speed Internet access, fax, shipping and postal services, notary public, and office supplies. In addition, The Walt Disney World Swan and Dolphin each have a business center in their main lobby areas.

Car care and gasoline. Hess Express has three stations at Walt Disney World Resort open twenty-four hours: on Floridian Way near the Magic

ROMANCE IS IN THE AIR

Even in the land of Mickey Mouse there are many opportunities for romance to be had at Walt Disney World. Here are just a few:

- Plan for date night at a romantic restaurant (Victoria & Albert's is certainly the most intimate dining choice). Leave the kids at one of Disney's excellent resort Children's Activity Centers, or if your child is under age three or not potty trained call Kid's Nite Out for in-room service.

- Consider two guest rooms. Disney guarantees connecting rooms for families with children in most categories as long as there are only two adults in the party.

- Enjoy a bottle of wine on your room balcony. A small selection of wine can be found at Disney's resort shops, with the widest range and best selection of vintages available from In-Room Dining.

- Relax and enjoy a candlelit couples massage at *Senses—A Disney Spa at Disney's Grand Floridian* Resort, a perfectly shared experience.

- Stroll Epcot's World Showcase in the evening when all the countries are beautifully lit by twinkling lights. Pick up a glass of wine from a kiosk in France or Italy and just enjoy!

- Watch the evening fireworks spectacular from the beach at either Disney's Polynesian Resort or Disney's Grand Floridian Resort & Spa.

- Sail away for a fireworks cruise from one of the Magic Kingdom or Epcot resorts and don't forget to pre-order a bottle of champagne from In-Room Dining. If it's true luxury you want rent the 52-foot *Grand I* yacht for a moonlight spin around the Seven Seas Lagoon.

- Plan a *Disney's Fairy Tale Wedding*® Service or Vow Renewal at Walt Disney World for the ultimate in romance. It's a dream come true!

Kingdom, across from Downtown Disney, and near Disney's Board-Walk Entertainment District entrance. For car repair go to the AAA Car Care Center (407-824-0976) adjoining the Hess station near the Magic Kingdom open Monday through Friday from 7:00 a.m. to 7:00 p.m. and Sunday 7:00 a.m. to 4:00 p.m. If your car becomes disabled while on Disney property, AAA has complimentary towing to the Car Care Center; after hours call Disney security at (407) 824-4777.

Childcare. Disney's Children's Activity Centers include the Cub's Den at Disney's Wilderness Lodge, the Sandcastle Club at Disney's Yacht and Beach Club Resort, Simba's Cubhouse at Disney's Animal Kingdom Lodge, and the Never Land Club at Disney's Polynesian Resort (closed through the end of 2014), all offering childcare services for potty-trained children ages three through twelve. Cost is $11.50 per hour per child including a meal; minimum of two hours. See individual resort descriptions for detailed information. Reservations should be made at least twenty-four hours in advance by calling (407) WDW-DINE or (407) 939-3463. At the Walt Disney World Dolphin Hotel it's Camp Dolphin. Call (407) 934-4241 for reservations and information.

For in-room childcare, nanny, or mother's/father's helper services use Kid's Nite Out. Call (800) 696-8105, extension 0, or (407) 828-0920 at least seventy-two hours in advance; four-hour minimum charge.

Dietary requests. Dietary requests such as kosher, no sugar added, low-sodium, low-fat as well as special requests regarding allergies to gluten or wheat, shellfish, soy, lactose or dairy, peanuts, tree nuts, fish, eggs, corn, or other foods can be accommodated at table-service restaurants. Advance notice is not required but you can indicate your food allergy when making online or phone dining reservations. Those with metabolic disorders and multiple allergies require that a 14-day advance notice be requested by emailing to Special.Diets@DisneyWorld.com. Kosher dietary needs can be accommodated at most table-service restaurants with a 24-hour advance notice by calling (407) 939-3463; quick-service kosher meals can be found at Cosmic Ray's Starlight Café at the Magic Kingdom, ABC Commissary at Disney's Hollywood Studios, Liberty Inn and Electric Umbrella at Epcot, and Pizzafari at the Animal Kingdom with no advance notice necessary. Most table-service and many quick-service restaurants offer at least one vegetarian choice, which I have tried to reflect in my entrée examples in the dining chapter.

Flowers and such. Flowers and gourmet food baskets can be delivered and magical experiences created anywhere on Disney property. Welcome, Romantic, Princess, Pirate, and Birthday In-room Celebrations as well as Holiday, Character, and Special Occasion items add that special touch for your loved ones. Call (407) 827-3505 or DisneyFlorist.com.

Groceries. The closest full-service grocery store to Walt Disney World is a twenty-four-hour Goodings located in the Crossroads Shopping Center of Lake Buena Vista near Downtown Disney; or you can order online at Goodings.com for resort delivery (minimum $50 per order plus a $25 service charge). Just north of Goodings is a Winn Dixie at 11957 South Apopka-Vineland Rd. You can also shop online ahead of time at GardenGrocer.com from a large selection of grocery items that can be delivered to your resort with a minimum $40 per order plus a $14 service fee (only a $2 fee with an order of $200 or more). A small selection of groceries is also available at each Disney Deluxe Villa Resort.

Guests with disabilities. Vehicles equipped with lifts to accommodate wheelchairs and most electric-controlled vehicles (ECVs) service all bus routes. Watercraft access varies according to the type of craft and water levels. All monorails, many park attractions, and most restrooms are wheelchair accessible. Special parking areas are available at all four theme parks. Wheelchairs and ECVs may be rented in limited quantities at each theme park; no advance reservations available. Another ECV rental option is with Buena Vista Scooter Rentals who will deliver and pick up from your resort; www.buenavistascooters.com or 866-484-4797.

Each Disney resort offers special equipment and facilities for guests with disabilities. Features vary by resort but may include wider bathroom doors, roll-in showers, shower benches, handheld showerheads, accessible vanities, portable commodes, bathroom and bed rails, bed shaker alarm, text typewriter, strobe-light fire alarm, and phone amplifier. Other features include double peepholes in doors, closed-captioned television, and braille on signage and elevators.

Most theme park attractions provide access through the main queue while others have auxiliary entrances for wheelchairs and service animals along with up to five members of your party. Certain attractions require guests to transfer from their wheelchair to a ride system. For detailed information the helpful Guide For Guests With Disabilities is available at Guest Services at each park or at the front desk of each Disney Resort.

Handheld receivers are available to read captions at more than twenty park attractions. Each park offers assistive listening devices, video captioning, braille guidebooks, and audio taped tours, all available for a refundable $25 deposit; handheld captioning is available with a $100 deposit. Reflective captioning can be found at many theater-type attractions. A sign language interpreter for live shows can be made available with one week's notice on certain days of the week (see each individual park for details). Additional information can be found at Disneyworld.disney.go.com or by calling (407) 824-4321 (voice) or (407) 827-5141 (TTY).

Hair salons. Full-service salons are located at Disney's Grand Floridian Resort, Disney's Yacht and Beach Club Resort, and Walt Disney World Dolphin as well as the Waldorf Astoria. An old-fashioned barber haircut can be had on *Main Street U.S.A®* in the Magic Kingdom.

International travelers. Visitors who speak languages other than English may ask at Guest Services in each theme park for a park guide versed in that language. Guides are available in more than a dozen languages. Also available at Guest Services for a $100 refundable deposit are complimentary language translation headsets with wireless technology that provide synchronized narration in Spanish, French, German, Japanese, or Portuguese for more than thirty attractions. Interpreters are available by calling the Foreign Language Center at (407) 827-7900. Many restaurants offer menus in several languages. Foreign currency may be exchanged at any Disney resort.

Internet services. In-room high-speed Internet access is complimentary at all Disney resorts and theme parks. Additional access can be found at the business centers of all resorts offering convention services.

Laundry and dry cleaning. Self-service, coin-operated washers and dryers are located at every Disney resort in addition to same-day dry cleaning and laundry service.

Lockers. Lockers can be found in all four Walt Disney World theme parks, Downtown Disney, most resorts near the main pool area, both water parks, and the Transportation and Ticket Center (TTC).

Lost and found. Lost item claims may be made at each individual park's Lost and Found. The central Lost and Found is located at the TTC, where items not claimed the previous day at each individual park are sent; call (407) 824-4245.

Mail. Stamps may be purchased and letters mailed at all four theme parks, Downtown Disney, and all Disney resorts. All shops and business centers offer worldwide shipping for a fee.

Medical care. All Walt Disney World theme parks offer first aid during park hours. For 24-hour, non-emergency, in-room medical care call Physician Room Service (407-238-2000). Florida Hospital Centra Care Walk-In Urgent Care Centers (407-934-2273) has a Lake Buena Vista location at 12500 South Apopka Vineland Road near Downtown Disney, with complimentary transportation available and most insurance plans accepted. Emergency medical needs are met by Florida Hospital Celebration Health located at 400 Celebration Place in Kissimmee (407) 764-4000.

Money matters. Walt Disney World accepts cash, traveler's checks, Disney Dollars (available by calling (407) 566-4985, at your Disney resort hotel front desk or concierge, and Guest Relations at each Disney theme park and water park), and six types of credit cards: American Express, MasterCard, Visa, Discover, Japanese Credit Bureau, and Diners Club.

Guests of a Disney-owned resort may use their MagicBand to charge throughout Walt Disney World as long as a credit card is given at check-in. ATMs are readily available with locations at each resort, each theme park, Downtown Disney, and the TTC.

Parking. Parking at Disney theme parks is free to all registered guests of Official Walt Disney World Hotels and Annual Passport holders. All others pay $15 per day. Make sure you make a note of what section and aisle you have parked in; lots are enormous. Save your receipt if you plan on park hopping; it allows you to park for that day only at any of the other Disney theme parks for no additional fee.

All Disney resorts charge $15 per day for valet parking; no charge for self-parking. Be forewarned that after 11:00 p.m. most resorts have only one valet parking attendant on duty, not a grand welcome after returning from dinner or a late night at the parks.

Pets. Only service dogs for guests with disabilities are allowed inside Disney's theme parks and resorts. Disney's pet kennel, run by Best Friend Pet Care, is located across from *Disney's Port Orleans Riverside* Resort at 2510 Bonnet Creek Parkway. For more information go to BestFriendsPetCare.com.

Rider Switch Service. Parents traveling with young children who don't meet height restrictions should consider utilizing the Rider Switch program. One parent waits with the child while the other rides, then the second parent hands off the child and goes to the head of the line. Just speak to the cast member on duty.

Safety. Walt Disney World is a relatively safe environment but caution must still be taken. Be alert at all times, particularly at night. Always lock your guest room door, and make sure you verify who is knocking before allowing anyone entry. Use the safe provided in your room to store money and valuables. Park in well-lit areas, lock your car and be aware of your surroundings when leaving the car, and take extra care when traveling to Orlando and places outside *Walt Disney World* Resort where security is less stringent.

Security. All bags are checked prior to entering the theme parks by uniformed Security Cast Members; allow extra time if you've booked Advance Dining Reservations inside the theme parks.

Smoking. All Walt Disney World Resort guest rooms (including room balconies), restaurants, lounges, and public areas are smoke-free environments. Tobacco products are not sold in the theme parks and water parks where smoking is limited to designated areas; look for the smoking symbol on the guide maps.

Strollers and wheelchairs. Strollers, wheelchairs, and electric-controlled vehicles (ECVs) may be rented at all four theme parks and Downtown Disney. Retain your receipt for a replacement at any other Disney theme park for that day only. A limited number of wheelchairs are also available at all Disney resorts. Another great option is Orlando Stroller Rentals at

OrlandoStrollerRentals.com. Strollers are delivered to your hotel's bell service/luggage room and picked up upon checkout.

Taxi service. Taxis can be found in front of all resorts, theme parks, and at Downtown Disney. You'll find many van options that hold up to seven riders. Call directly for a taxi at (407) 699-9999.

Telephone calls. Orlando has a ten-digit calling system, meaning you must dial the area code of 407 followed by the number when making a local call.

Walt Disney World Weddings

Bride's magazine lists Walt Disney World among the top ten U.S. wedding destinations. In fact, Walt Disney World hosts over 2,700 weddings a year. Countless couples have taken their wedding vows in Disney's storybook atmosphere, and even more have picked Disney as their choice for a dream honeymoon. Imagine being escorted to your wedding in Cinderella's glass coach with horses and footmen in attendance or perhaps a Hollywood Grandeur Wedding at Disney's Hollywood Studios, even a Beauty and the Beast Ball. Everything can be arranged—from the flowers to the photographer, the waiters to the music. To speak to Disney's Fairy Tale Weddings Service team, call (321) 939-4610 or go to DisneyWeddings.disney.go.com.

Wedding Locations

Although weddings are allowed just about anywhere on Disney property, there are several very popular sites. If you want a theme park wedding, expect the price to skyrocket. On an island surrounded by the Seven Seas Lagoon is Disney's Wedding Pavilion at Disney's Grand Floridian Resort & Spa offering a magical view of Cinderella Castle. The Swan Boat Landing fronting Cinderella Castle at the Magic Kingdom is another top pick. At Epcot choose any of the romantic World Showcase pavilions—perhaps a sunrise wedding in Japan or a ceremony among the koi ponds in China. Sea Breeze Point at Disney's BoardWalk Inn offers a white gazebo overlooking Crescent Lake. Or you may want to consider the wedding gazebo in Disney's Yacht Club Resort's serene rose garden. You can even have your marriage ceremony on Disney Cruise Line's private island, Castaway Cay.

Wedding Themes

Choose from a traditional wedding to a variety of Disney-themed receptions. Some theme ideas include a Beauty and the Beast Ball Wedding or a Winter Wonderland Wedding. How about an Animal Kingdom Safari reception or an Under the Sea Theme in *The Seas With Nemo & Friends*® Attraction at Epcot? What about inviting Mickey to your cake cutting? Just about anything is possible at Walt Disney World Resort.

Wedding Packages

Disney's Memories Weddings are very small and intimate with up to four guests, including the bride and groom, at one of three locations. Prices start at $2,495 and includes flowers, wedding cake and bottle of champagne, violinist, limousine, photographer and portraits, wedding coordinator, and personalized wedding website; various enhancements can be added such as a bridal bouquet and ceremony decorations.

Disney's Escape Weddings are just a bit larger with eighteen or fewer guests at one of five locations at Walt Disney World Resort. Prices start at $4,925 and include bouquet and boutonniere, wedding cake and champagne, limousine transportation, violinist or organist depending on the venue, photographer and photo album, wedding coordinator, annual passes, and a personalized wedding website. Many alternative arrangements can be planned for an additional price such as videography, enhanced entertainment, flowers, transportation in Cinderella's Coach or a vintage car, or Disney characters to join in your celebration. Since a reception is not included in the basic cost consider a post-wedding dinner at a romantic restaurant, an *Illuminations: Reflections of Earth* dessert party, or perhaps tea at Disney's Grand Floridian Resort & Spa.

More elaborate weddings with a minimum of 18 guests can be completely customized and are considered a Wishes Wedding with prices beginning at $12,000. Ceremonies can take place just about anywhere on property but think about a dream-come-true option at the Magic Kingdom's Swan Boat Landing with Cinderella Castle as a backdrop, a fanfare trumpeter, a horse-drawn coach, and transportation down Main Street U.S.A. for your guests in motorized cars.

Disney has teamed up with celebrity wedding planner David Tutera to create glamorous Couture Weddings starting at $65,000. These grand affairs begin with Save the Date as well as wedding invitations created by David. For your ceremony the stage is dressed in sophistication and your reception is chosen from four heavenly styles that include shimmering fabrics, floral arrangements, props, furniture, elegant flatware, stemware, and table settings. What about a Cocktail Soiree in contemporary colors like ice blue and chocolate brown and a custom lounge area with illuminated bar and floor-to-ceiling draped walls? Or perhaps a Classic Elegance look with crystal chandeliers, gold drapery and candelabras, and gilded mirrors and pedestals? Specialty drinks can even be created that match your color scheme, your bridesmaid's dresses, or flowers.

ANNUAL WALT DISNEY WORLD CALENDAR OF EVENTS

January: Walt Disney World Marathon the second weekend of the month.

March: Ten-week *Epcot*® International Flower & Garden Festival begins.

April: Epcot International Flower & Garden Festival continues.

May: Epcot International Flower & Garden Festival continues; Star Wars Weekends at Disney's Hollywood Studios begins.

June: Star Wars Weekends at Disney's Hollywood Studios continues.

September: Night of Joy at the Magic Kingdom; *Mickey's Not So Scary Halloween* Party at the Magic Kingdom begins.

October: Six-week *Epcot*® International Food & Wine Festival begins; *Mickey's Not So Scary Halloween* Party at the Magic Kingdom continues; PGA golf tournament at Disney's Magnolia and Palm Golf Courses.

November: Epcot International Food & Wine Festival; Festival of the Masters at Downtown Disney; *Mickey's Very Merry Christmas* Party at the Magic Kingdom begins; Osborne Family Spectacle of Dancing Lights at Disney's Hollywood Studios begins.

December: *Mickey's Very Merry Christmas* Party at the Magic Kingdom continues; Osborne Family Spectacle of Dancing Lights at Disney's Hollywood Studios continues; Epcot's Holidays Around the World.

WALT DISNEY
WORLD LUXURY
ACCOMMODATIONS

Walt Disney World is rich in choices for the deluxe traveler, but which resort is truly best for you? Let's try to narrow down the field of possibilities by pinpointing your party's personality and preferences.

Those traveling with small children will find themselves spending quite a bit of time at the Magic Kingdom. They should strongly consider choosing one of the Magic Kingdom Resorts where the park is just a short monorail hop away and easily accessible for a quick afternoon nap or a dip in the pool.

Adults traveling without children or with older children will probably enjoy being closer to Epcot and Disney's Hollywood Studios. It's just a short walk or boat ride away to both parks from any of the Epcot resorts. You'll also find a world of possibilities in nearby dining and entertainment.

Those who enjoy nature and prefer a quiet, more isolated resort should opt for Disney's Animal Kingdom Lodge where hundreds of animals roam just below your room balcony. Or you could try Disney's

Wilderness Lodge surrounded by the pine forest fronting Bay Lake. If the convenience and comfort of a living area and kitchen are appealing think about one of the Disney Deluxe Villa Resorts located throughout Walt Disney World.

Also, consider room type preferences. Is a view of the water or pool important, or would you rather pay less and have a view of the resort's gardens? Will a standard room be all that you need, or should you consider one on the concierge level or maybe a roomy suite? Suites in each of the deluxe resorts come in virtually all shapes and sizes, some as large as 2,000 or more square feet, certainly the most luxurious option if your pocketbook allows. Of course budget together with how much time will be spent in your room are major considerations and will play a large part in your decision.

If hanging out at your resort sounds appealing the concierge rooms are a smart idea. These accommodations, usually located on a keyed-access floor, come with the use of a private lounge with complimentary continental breakfast, snacks throughout the day, before dinner hors d'oeuvres and cocktails, and late evening cordials and desserts. These amenities are in addition to private check-in and checkout and the assistance of a concierge staff ready to help you with Advance Dining Reservations, recreation, show tickets, or anything else within their power. It's definitely a nice plus to your vacation.

Walt Disney World Resorts

Although Disney offers a nice range of resorts in every price category, we will consider only the Deluxe Resorts and a few of the nicer Disney Deluxe Villa Resorts. The Moderate and Value Resorts, while interesting and well themed, do not fit this book's designation of luxury.

Deluxe Resorts

Disney's deluxe properties are graced with impressive lobbies, painstakingly landscaped grounds, first-rate restaurants, elaborately themed pools, and lovely, though not 5-star accommodations. These properties include Disney's Grand Floridian Resort & Spa, Disney's Polynesian Resort, Disney's Contemporary Resort, Disney's Wilderness Lodge, Disney's Animal Kingdom Lodge, Disney's BoardWalk Inn, and Disney's Yacht and Beach Club. Disney's Wilderness Lodge as well as Disney's

BENEFITS OF STAYING AT A WALT DISNEY WORLD RESORT

- Complimentary and convenient Disney transportation by monorail, bus, and water launch

- Complimentary parking at Disney's theme parks

- Easy access to the parks, making midday breaks and naps possible plus allowing parties to effortlessly split up to go their independent ways

- Charge privileges to your resort account for purchases throughout Disney

- Guaranteed entry to at least one Disney theme park, particularly important during busy holiday periods when filled-to-capacity parks often close to non-Disney resort guests

- *Extra Magic Hours* Benefit whereby one of Disney's theme parks opens an hour early or up to two hours later than regular park hours exclusively for registered guests of a Walt Disney World Resort

- Disney Dining Plans can save you up to 30 % per adult if purchased as part of your *Magic Your Way* Package, with dining at over 100 select restaurants

- Package delivery from anywhere on-property directly to your resort

- Access to Disney's childcare facilities available only to registered resort guests

- Complimentary airport transportation via Disney's Magical Express Transportation motorcoach

- The magic of Disney twenty-four hours a day

Animal Kingdom Lodge represent a slightly different level of deluxe. Standard rooms here are smaller than at other deluxe resorts; however, what they lack in room space they more than make up for in atmosphere.

Those who frequent five-star properties such as the Ritz-Carlton or Four Seasons should not expect the same amenities at Disney (although a Four Seasons 5-star resort is slated to open summer 2014 on Disney property). While I love Disney's resort theming, and I absolutely adore the wonderful atmosphere, they do tend to rest on their laurels a bit and there is definitely room for improvement. You'll find somewhat smallish guest rooms, and the pool areas have lounge chairs so tightly packed that you can forget about peace and quiet. Please don't expect butlers, marble baths (except in Disney's suites), Pay Per View movies, HBO and Showtime, and your choice of one hundred TV channels. But really, the point is to just enjoy the unparalleled theming and friendly service in the four-star-rated rooms at "the Most Magical Place on Earth."

For those choosing to stay off-property I recommend the Waldorf Astoria Orlando, a beauty of a resort sitting right in the middle of Disney property on a 300-acre parcel of land not owned by Disney. You won't be able to take advantage of the benefits of Disney resort guests, but you will be close to the action ensconced in 5-star luxury.

Deluxe Villas Resorts

Disney's Bay Lake Tower at the Contemporary Resort, Disney's Animal Kingdom Villas–Kidani Village (and some villas located in the next-door Jambo House), and The Villas at Disney's Grand Floridian Resort & Spa are the most luxurious Disney Vacation Club choices (called Disney's Deluxe Villa Resorts). It's a great way to enjoy Disney with all the conveniences of home, including a full kitchen, a living room, and a bathroom for each bedroom.

Disney's Bay Lake Tower at the Contemporary Resort and The Villas at Disney's Grand Floridian Resort & Spa have the advantage of being on the monorail with super access to the Magic Kingdom and Epcot as well as the other monorail resorts and their exceptional restaurants. Disney's Animal Kingdom Villas–Kidani Village, while remote, do have access to three very good restaurants and the advantage of some of Disney's best theming. I do feel, however, that the Disney Deluxe Villa Resort studio accommodation's sole benefit is the mini-kitchen consisting of a microwave, small refrigerator, and sink. A better choice for just about the same price is a guest room at one of the deluxe hotels.

Check-in and Checkout

Check-in time is 3:00 p.m. at all Disney Deluxe Resorts and 4:00 p.m. at all Disney Deluxe Villa Resorts. If arriving early in the day go straight to your resort to register and have your luggage stored until check-in time (if arriving on Disney's Magical Express luggage will be delivered directly to your room), then head off to a park or spend time exploring the property. In slower seasons it's sometimes possible to access your room or suite early so definitely give it a try.

Re-request any preferences at registration and be sure to have your room pointed out on a resort map. If the location is undesirable say so before leaving the desk. And if you've booked the concierge level or a suite remember to identify yourself as a concierge guest to the bellhop or valet on arrival so you'll be escorted directly to your private check-in.

Checkout time is 11:00 a.m. at both the Deluxe Resorts and Villas. If you're taking a late plane home on checkout day store your luggage at Bell Services and head out to the parks. Those traveling on participating airlines can simply check their bags and pick up boarding passes at the Resort Airline Check-in Service desk, making it a cinch at the airport. If you're resort hopping and staying at more than one Disney property Bell Services will transfer your luggage between resorts free of charge with luggage arriving by 3:00 p.m.

Walt Disney World Resort Discounts

Yes, this book is about a Disney deluxe vacation but even the biggest spenders like a discount. And specials and promotions are as easily available at the deluxe resorts as they are at the value ones. Better yet, opportunities to save on everything from dining to entertainment to behind-the-scenes tours abound. With the many discounts available, only in the busiest seasons or when reserving a top suite should anyone pay full price for a Disney resort. Following are some of the many ways to save:

Seasonal discounts. Rooms at Walt Disney World are priced using a season system that varies according to resort type. Remember, the busier the season the more expensive the room rate.

Annual Pass rates. This is one of Disney's better bargains. With the purchase of an Annual Pass you'll not only receive unlimited park admission with park hopping for one year but also excellent resort rates. Only one person in the room need be a pass holder to obtain room discounts available throughout most of the year. Also included: a quarterly Mickey Monitor newsletter; discounted admission to *Disney's Blizzard Beach* Water Park, *Disney's Typhoon Lagoon* Water Park, *DisneyQuest*® Indoor Interactive Theme Park, AMC Theater at Downtown Disney, Cirque du Soleil, and special ticketed events; free parking at the theme parks; discounts on selected dining, merchandise, car rentals, behind-the-scenes tours, spa treatments, water sports, boat rentals, golf, fishing excursions, and Richard Petty Driving Experience. Room discounts aren't typically available until two to three months in advance and are, of course, limited. A good strategy is to hold a room at the regular price just to be safe and continue calling periodically until hopefully an Annual Passholder discount becomes available at which point the reservation agent will lower your rate (or book with a travel advisor specializing in Disney who always is in the know about Disney's discounted room rates; they will keep an eye out for any discounts and apply them when available).

Disney Promotions. Throughout the year Disney offers great promotions associated with special discount codes. Have your travel advisor who specializes in Disney, always on top of the discount game, keep an eye out for you.

AAA/CAA discounts. Receive a discounted room price of 10 to 20 percent with AAA or CAA memberships for all but the busiest times of year.

Florida residents. Residents of Florida receive great Disney benefits particularly during the slower times of the year. Go to Disneyworld.disney.go.com/florida-residents or call your travel advisor for special prices on resort rooms and theme park tickets.

Military Discounts. For much of the year discounted rooms and park tickets are available to active and retired military.

Resort Reservations

Before calling for reservations narrow the field down to two or three resorts that best suit your needs. Reserve as soon as possible, particularly for travel during major holidays, to ensure that your preferred resort and room type are available. Again, decisions need to be made:

Is it best to go with a package deal or book a "room only" reservation and treat your air, park tickets, and car as separate elements? Is it wiser to make reservations yourself or call a travel advisor? How about booking your trip on the Internet? All good questions. With such a wide array of booking choices on the market there is no substitute for a good travel advisor, particularly one that specializes in Disney Destinations. This professional can certainly save you a lot of time, headaches, and usually money.

So remember, when it comes to finding a good travel advisor, an Authorized Disney Vacation Planner agency can make the difference between a mediocre vacation and an excellent one. For your Disney travel needs call Glass Slipper Concierge at (866) 725-7595 or go online at GlassSlipperConcierge.com. Glass Slipper Concierge is the brainchild of this book's author, Cara Goldsbury, originating from a desire to offer a client centric option to those who want an exceptional and unforgettable Disney vacation. Cara has gathered an exclusive team of luxury concierge advisors whose knowledge of Disney Destinations can only be matched by their passion for delivering white-glove service.

Considerations

When considering a concierge-level room, take into account the schedule you will more than likely keep during your vacation. If you plan on spending most of the day and into the evening at the parks the additional price for concierge service will not be worth the expense. You'll probably only have the time to take advantage of the continental breakfast and perhaps the late-night cordials and dessert, with the remaining offerings wasted. If returning to your resort to relax before dinner or for an afternoon swim at the pool sounds more to your liking the concierge level can't be beat. The almost continuous food and beverages, the attentive service, and that special feeling of staying in a small hotel within a larger complex certainly go a long way in making your vacation extra special.

It's always a good idea to inquire when a resort has last been renovated. If it's been over five years pick another resort. Disney does seem to stretch room renovations about two years too long resulting in overpriced and underwhelming accommodations that are not up to par. This is where a good travel advisor specializing in Disney will come in handy, someone who has that information at their fingertips.

Inquire whether any major construction will be in progress at your resort of choice during your visit. If so, book another property. No matter how nicely they try to cover up a pool reconstruction or an all-encompassing face-lift, it most certainly will affect your overall resort experience. Take my word for it.

At the time of booking request anything special or important to you, such as a desire to be far from the elevator or pool, or a certain bed type. Remember that these requests are never guaranteed unless you are reserving a suite with an assigned room number (usually only the Presidential or Vice Presidential Suites). The only guarantee Disney will make is connecting rooms for families with children for most room types as long as there are only two adults traveling.

Remember to take advantage of any discounts such as those described earlier in this chapter. Consider reserving tee times, childcare, special dinner shows, or Advance Dining Reservations when making your resort reservations (available up to 180 days prior to arrival).

Airlines Servicing Orlando

Airlines servicing Orlando include AirTran, Alaska Airlines, American Airlines, Delta Air Lines, Frontier Airlines, JetBlue, Southwest Airlines, Spirit Airlines, Sun Country Airlines, United Airlines, US Airways, Virgin America, and WestJet. International carriers include Aer Lingus, Aeromexico, Air Canada, Air France, Avianca, Bahamas Air, British Airways, CanJet, Caribbean Airlines, Copa Airlines, GOL Airlines, LAN, Lufthansa, Taca Airlines, Tam Airlines, Viva Aerobus, Volaris Airlines, and Virgin Atlantic. Check such websites such as Expedia, Orbitz, and Travelocity for the best fare, or have your travel advisor reserve air in conjunction with your Disney resort reservation. No one should ever expect to pay full fare for a coach-class seat unless booking at the last minute. Most important—shop, shop, shop! Fares to Orlando tend to be quite the bargain.

Walt Disney World Vacation Package Plans

In addition to The Walt Disney World Travel Company, travel agencies also offer Disney's special package plans. The more elaborate ones are a good buy only if you think you'll use all of the additional features. Beware of purchasing a plan with elements you do not want or need.

Disney also has land/sea vacations. Those who love cruising should consider three or four nights on the Disney Cruise Line out of Port Canaveral combined with several days at a Disney resort, the best of both worlds (see the Disney Cruise Line section of this book for more information).

Disney's package plans, including *Magic Your Way* tickets, are as follows:

Magic Your Way Package: Resort accommodations and Magic Your Way Base Tickets.

Magic Your Way Package Plus Quick Service Dining: Resort accommodations, Magic Your Way Base Tickets, and a Disney dining plan that includes two quick service meals and one snack per person per night plus a resort refillable mug per person.

Magic Your Way Package Plus Dining: Resort accommodations, Magic Your Way Base Tickets, and a Disney dining plan at more than one hundred on-property restaurants including per-person, per-night the following: one table-service meal (entrée, dessert, and nonalcoholic beverage, or one full buffet or character meal), one quick-service meal (entrée, dessert, and nonalcoholic beverage), and one snack plus a resort refillable mug per person. Two table-service meals can be exchanged for Private Dining, a Disney Dinner Show like Hoop-Dee-Doo Revue or Spirit of Aloha, or a Signature Dining experience (appetizer, entrée, dessert, and a nonalcoholic beverage) such as California Grill, Citricos, Flying Fish, and Cinderella's Royal Table.

Magic Your Way Package Plus Deluxe Dining: Resort accommodations, Magic Your Way Base Tickets, and a Disney dining plan at more than one hundred on-property restaurants including per-person, per-night the following: three meals at either a quick-service spot (entrée, dessert, and non-alcoholic beverage; or one complete combo meal) or a table-service restaurant (appetizer, entrée, dessert, and one non-alcoholic beverage; or one full buffet or character meal) as well as two snacks plus a resort refillable mug per person. Two dining credits will be needed for Signature Dining experiences, Disney Dinner Shows, and Private Dining.

Magic Your Way Premium Package: Resort accommodations, Magic Your Way Base Tickets, breakfast, lunch, dinner, and two snacks per person per night including In-Room Dining, Dinner Shows, Signature Dining, and Cinderella's Royal Table, plus a resort refillable mug per person, unlimited use of select recreation including golf, golf lessons, guided fishing excursions, water sports, boating, horseback riding, admission to Cirque du Soleil, unlimited childcare in the resort Children's Activity Centers, preferred fireworks viewing, and unlimited admission to theme park tours. 3-night minimum stay required.

Magic Your Way Platinum Package: Resort accommodations, Magic Your Way Base Tickets, breakfast, lunch, dinner (including Victoria & Albert's), and In-Room Dining, Dinner Shows, and Signature Dining, plus a resort refillable mug per person, unlimited recreation including golf, guided fishing excursions, water sports, boating, and horseback riding, unlimited select tours, preferred fireworks viewing, reserved seating for the *Fantasmic!* Show, private golf lessons, one selected spa treatment per adult, tickets for Cirque du Soleil, unlimited childcare in the resort Children's Activity Centers, in-room childcare, a fireworks cruise, unlimited theme park tours, *Disney's MemoryMaker®* Service CD, and a Richard Petty Ride Along Experience. 3-night minimum stay required.

THE BEST OF WALT DISNEY WORLD

Best Resort Pools

Disney's Yacht and Beach Club's Storm-along Bay, a three-acre miniature water park; the Nanea Volcano Pool at Disney's Polynesian Resort with its luxuriant waterfall, smoking peak, and perfect views of Cinderella Castle; and the boulder-strewn Silver Creek Springs Pool at Disney's Wilderness Lodge with its own erupting geyser.

Best Deluxe Resort

On Disney property it's Disney's Grand Floridian Resort's public areas with its upscale Victorian ambience and lagoon side setting facing the Magic Kingdom (guest rooms here need a redo, something that is scheduled to begin January 2014). Off-property it is the Waldorf Astoria Orlando where you may be tempted never to leave the resort. And stay tuned for the new Four Seasons Resort Orlando at Walt Disney World Resort, sure to be tops on this list!

Best Disney Deluxe Villa Resort

The Villas at Disney's Grand Floridian Resort & Spa, the newest Disney Deluxe Villa Resort in its repertoire. Second runner up is Bay Lake Tower at Disney's Contemporary Resort with is hip, modern look, monorail access, and spectacular views of the Magic Kingdom.

Best Atmosphere

Disney's Animal Kingdom Lodge, where hundreds of animals roam the savanna and the air is pulsating to the beat of African drums.

Best Lobby

How to choose? Three make the cut: Disney's Wilderness Lodge, Disney's Grand Floridian Resort & Spa, and Disney's Animal Kingdom Lodge, all eye-popping in their grandeur.

Best Access to the Parks

Disney's Contemporary Resort with not only monorail access to the Magic Kingdom but a walking path as well. Disney's Polynesian Resort where there is direct monorail access with no transfer required to reach both Epcot and the Magic Kingdom (a short stroll is required to reach the Transportation & Ticket Center and the direct Epcot Monorail). And any of the Epcot Resorts within walking distance to Epcot and a boat ride or long stroll to Disney's Hollywood Studios.

Best for Romance

Disney's Polynesian Resort whose lush tiki torch-lit grounds and white-sand beaches with views of Cinderella Castle are simply dreamy.

Best for Nature Lovers

Disney's Wilderness Lodge for its rushing waterfalls, spouting geysers, and bubbly creeks, all surrounded by stately pine trees and sparkling Bay Lake.

Best Resort Lounges

California Grill Lounge at Disney's Contemporary Resort with its splendid location on the 15th floor and unrivaled views of the Magic Kingdom, the Seven Seas Lagoon, and the *Wishes* fireworks show (you'll need to check in first at the second-floor podium). Blue-zoo Lounge at the Walt Disney World Dolphin, the snazziest place around. And Il Mulino Lounge at the Walt Disney World Swan's where a lively bar scene is to be had with live music on Friday and Saturday evenings.

Best Suite Views

Walt Disney World Dolphin's Two-Story Presidential Suites whose all-encompassing views just can't be beat; Disney's Contemporary Resort's 14th floor suites overlooking either Bay Lake or, better yet, the Magic Kingdom, views that will flat-out blow your mind; the Royal Assante Presidential and Royal Kuba V.P. Suites at Disney's Animal Kingdom Lodge with sweeping views of the resort's exotic savanna; Disney's Grand Floridian Resort's Grand Suite where fireworks can be viewed from four of five balconies; the Steeplechase Presidential Suite and Sonora V.P. Suite at Disney's BoardWalk Inn whose deep balconies overlook Crescent Lake and Epcot; and Disney's Wilderness Lodge's Yellowstone Presidential and Yosemite V.P. Suites overlooking the resort's lovely courtyard pool and sparkling Bay Lake.

Best Guest Room Views

Theme Park View rooms at Disney's Contemporary Resort, the higher up the better (reserve an Atrium Club concierge room on the 12th floor), with up-close views of the Seven Seas Lagoon, the Magic Kingdom, the Castle, and the Wishes fireworks show; Savanna View rooms at Disney's Animal Kingdom Lodge where exotic animals roam right below your balcony; Theme Park View rooms at Disney's Polynesian Resort overlooking the Seven Seas Lagoon, a lovely white sand beach, and the Castle and fireworks in the distance; and Deluxe Club Rooms at Disney's BoardWalk Inn with divine Crescent Lake and Epcot views.

Best Concierge Lounge

Disney's Grand Floridian Resort's Royal Palm Club where there's a great spread of appetizers and pleasant music wafting up from the Grand Lobby below.

Best Suites

The Royal Assante Presidential Suite at Disney's Animal Kingdom Lodge with its thatch roof ceiling, hand-carved furnishings, African textiles, and sweeping views of the resort's savanna; the Walt Disney World Dolphin's Two-Story Presidential Suites decorated in a divine contemporary style with views stretching for miles; and Disney's Polynesian Resort's two-story King Kamehameha Suite decked out in a contemporary Asian style with South Seas paddle fans cooling the open loft living area.

Magic Kingdom Area Resorts

This is the most enchanting area in all of Walt Disney World Resort with resorts hugging the shoreline of two bodies of water, the Seven Seas Lagoon and Bay Lake, all accessible by either monorail or water launch to the Magic Kingdom. Disney's Contemporary Resort, Bay Lake Tower at Disney's Contemporary Resort, Disney's Grand Floridian Resort & Spa, The Villas at Disney's Grand Floridian Resort & Spa, and Disney's Polynesian Resort all surround the Seven Seas Lagoon and feature magical views of Cinderella Castle; all connect to one another as well as to the Magic Kingdom and Epcot (via the Transportation and Ticket Center, or TTC) by monorail. Disney's Wilderness Lodge is not connected by monorail to the Magic Kingdom. However, it is accessible to the park by water launch with the plus of a pristine setting smack-dab in the middle of a pine forest fronting beautiful Bay Lake.

Those driving for the first time to the Magic Kingdom Resorts may feel confused when the signage seems to be leading straight into the Magic Kingdom parking lot. Drive up to the second window on the right, advise the parking lot attendant that you're checking in, and he or she will wave you past. Stay to your right and follow the signs to your resort.

Bay Lake Tower at Disney's Contemporary Resort

428 units. 4600 North World Drive, Lake Buena Vista, FL 32830; phone (407) 824–1000, fax (407) 824–3539. Check-in 4:00 p.m., checkout 11:00 a.m. For reservations contact your travel advisor or call (407) 939-3476.

Claim To Fame. Disney's first Deluxe Villa Resort on the monorail.

Room To Book. A theme park view villa overlooking the Magic Kingdom and the Seven Seas Lagoon with their superb fireworks view. The Grand Villas here are Disney's most spectacular three-bedroom option.

The Wow Factor! The up-close-and-personal Wishes fireworks show seen from the balcony of your Magic Kingdom view villa.

This sixteen-story Disney Deluxe Villa Resort linked by pedestrian sky bridge to Disney's Contemporary Resort offers dramatic views of the Magic Kingdom, the Seven Seas Lagoon, and Bay Lake. Its crescent shaped tower even has access to the monorail and all the Magic Kingdom area has to offer. The resort's small, circular lobby is bright and sunny due to huge glass windows with ultra contemporary seating, tropical palm trees, and a flirty glass bubble chandelier hanging overhead. Just outside the lobby is an outdoor area faintly Asian in design with dramatically lofty bamboo and a sparkling fountain that leads to the pool area and Bay Lake.

REST

Villas. Villas here are impressive with modern furnishings that are soothing to the eye. Contemporary artwork adorns the walls, and stylish charcoal gray carpeting (beginning to show wear) adds a soft look to the rooms. An iPod docking station, electronic safe, DVD player, iron and ironing board, Pack 'n' Play, coffeemaker, vacuum, and hairdryer are extra amenities included in each. One irritation is that ice machines are found on only three of the fifteen floors, what I consider to be an unbelievable inconvenience. On the plus side check-in is now located in Bay Lake Tower's lobby area instead of next-door at Disney's Contemporary Resort. The caveat is that you'll have to wait for a bellman to arrive from the next-door Contemporary Resort in order to store luggage if your villa isn't ready when you arrive, yet another frustrating inconvenience.

While *Studios* are pleasant they are a bit small at 356 square feet. Decorating the room is a queen bed topped with a soft white duvet and a gold and pumpkin-hued bed runner along with a sky blue leather ottoman coffee table, two-person dining table, full-size bureau over which is a located a wall-mounted, flat-screen TV, and a beige sofa sleeper with celery-colored throw pillows. In some units, off the entry hall is an open, somewhat cramped room where on one side is the mini-kitchen with wet bar, pullout pantry, under-counter refrigerator, and microwave, and, strangely enough, on the other side a bathroom vanity with a single sink (you're never sure whether to wash the dishes or wash your face), with the commode and tub down the hallway. Other units have the bath and sink in one area with a separated mini kitchen in another. A balcony adjoins the living area (first-floor units come with a patio instead).

Striking *One-bedroom Villas* are 727 square feet. The kitchen has contemporary, dark wood cabinets, sea blue backsplash, and taupe granite countertops with stainless steel refrigerator, dishwasher, stove, and microwave. A granite island features two yellow leather bar stools and just opposite is booth dining seating four. An adjoining living area is furnished with a dove gray sleeper sofa (also starting to show wear due to the light color) adorned with bright yellow pillows, blue leather oversized ottoman/coffee table, a sand-colored leather sleeper chair, chocolate brown occasional chair, and a bureau over which is mounted a flat-screen TV (turn on channel 20 to hear the accompanying Wishes fireworks show music). A sliding door leads to a balcony or patio also accessed from the bedroom. Off the foyer is a full-size bonus bath with a smallish corner single sink. You'll also find a stacked washer/dryer in the hallway.

In the bedroom is a king-sized bed with an interesting black and white woven leather headboard intermixed with dark wood. A kiwi green runner tops a white duvet with a punch of nautical blue in the bolster, and two glass-topped black side tables flank the bed. A dark wood bureau with a white cabinet front holds another flat-screen TV and built-in luggage rack, and there is a very small closet near the bath. You'll also find a vanity-style marble desk and a leather and chrome occasional chair.

One area of the marble master bath has a whirlpool tub and single sink set in a taupe granite vanity backed by a wall of shimmering glass tile; in the other is the commode and a frameless glass shower with chic hardware and splashes of glass tile. The only thing lacking is a makeup mirror. A *Two-bedroom Villa* is simply a combination of the One-bedroom and a Studio at 1,080 square feet. Some are dedicated units with the second bedroom offering two queen beds and no mini-kitchen.

With 2,044 square feet the spectacular *Grand Villas* offer magical views from the top floors (fourteen in all with six Magic Kingdom and eight Bay Lake views). Although these are the exact same layout as the Grand Villas at Disney's Animal Kingdom Villas–Kidani Village, the Bay Lake Tower villas seem larger because of the sunny interior and lighter décor. The very first thing you notice as you walk into the villas is the amazing view, so heavenly that you'll simply refuse to lower the shades. There are three bedrooms and four baths on two levels. The kitchen, dining area, living room, master bedroom, laundry room, and extra bath are on the 1st floor. Two bedrooms, two baths, and a TV loft are on the 2nd floor (entry doors are found on both floors). The kitchen is open to the living area with a small island, and there's an adjoining eight-person dining table with a balcony found off the kitchen. The soaring, two-story living area has hardwood flooring topped with a colorful, contemporary rug, sleeper sofa, two occasional chairs, ottoman-style coffee table, and entertainment center with TV and stereo system. A master, similar to those found in One-bedroom Villas, is just off the living area with its own balcony. Climb the stainless steel cable railing staircase to the 2nd floor where two identical bedrooms, each with two queen beds and balcony, flank the loft TV room with sleeper sofa. Sleeps 12.

Villa view choices range from a *Standard* one with a look at either the parking area or the pool, a *Bay Lake View*, or a *Theme Park View*. But like at the next-door Contemporary Resort Magic Kingdom views also offer a not-so-nice look of the resort's parking lot below.

CARA'S TIP: Those with a Magic Kingdom view villa should request a location on the north side of the building closest to the park which affords a superb vista of Space Mountain® and the Castle. On the Bay Lake side request floors nine and above for a distant view of Epcot's Spaceship Earth. A few bonus type villas on the far north side are considered Bay Lake View villas and actually have a view of the Magic Kingdom from their balconies only.

Be forewarned that the resort's Top of the World Lounge on the 16th floor is available only to Disney Vacation Club owners (an absolutely ridiculous concept for paying guests not to have access!).

DINE

Cove Bar. Located poolside. Caesar salad with chicken, hummus and chips, sushi, turkey BLT, Italian stacked sandwich, hot dog, cheeseburger, and vegetarian sandwich; specialty cocktails, frozen drinks, and wine.

In-Room Dining. Available 24/7 from the Contemporary Resort.

PLAY

Bay Lake Tower at Disney's Contemporary Resort shares all recreation with the adjacent Disney's Contemporary Resort. See the subsequent entry for Disney's Contemporary Resort.

Children's Activities. Duck races, chalk art, temporary tattoos, Disney trivia, dance parties, water relays, water basketball, and bingo. Movie Under the Stars nightly on the grassy area between Disney's Contemporary Resort and Bay Lake Tower.

Bocce Ball and Shuffleboard. Courts are located just outside the lobby; pick up equipment at Community Hall.

Community Hall. Located just off the lobby area offering recreation for the entire family; DVD rentals, foosball, video games, arts and crafts.

Jogging. A jogging path loops around the two resorts for just under one mile.

Swimming. Zero entry Bay Cove Pool fronting Bay Lake with a 148-foot fun tower water slide and interactive water feature; whirlpool; kid's splash pool; BBQ/picnic area; lovely, usually deserted beach accented with Spanish moss-dripping trees.

Tennis. Two lighted courts with nice views of Bay Lake are located on the north side of the property; complimentary equipment at Community Hall.

WORK, MOVE, SOOTHE

Bay Lake Tower at Disney's Contemporary Resort shares all services with the adjacent Disney's Contemporary Resort. See the subsequent entry for Disney's Contemporary Resort.

GO

Walk the 5th-floor Skyway Bridge over to Disney's Contemporary Resort's 4th floor to catch the monorail, or take the pathway to the Magic Kingdom. The monorail stops at the Transportation and Ticket Center where you can transfer to the Epcot Monorail. Buses run to Disney's Hollywood Studios, Animal Kingdom Theme Park, *Disney's Blizzard Beach* Water Park, Downtown Disney, and *Disney's Typhoon Lagoon* Water Park. Take the monorail to Disney's Polynesian Resort and Disney's Grand Floridian Resort & Spa.

To reach other Disney resorts during park operating hours take the monorail or walk to the Magic Kingdom, and from there pick up a bus to your resort destination. After park hours take the bus to Downtown Disney to transfer to your resort destination. Disney's Wilderness Lodge and *Disney's Fort Wilderness* Resort & Campground are reachable via the Blue Flag Launch found at Disney's Contemporary Resort's Bay Lake marina area.

Disney's Contemporary Resort

655 rooms. 4600 North World Drive, Lake Buena Vista, FL 32830; phone (407) 824-1000, fax (407) 824-3539. Check-in 3:00 p.m., checkout 11:00 a.m. For reservations contact your travel advisor or call (407) 939-3476.

Claim To Fame. What other resort anywhere has a monorail running through it?

Room To Book. A Theme Park View room overlooking the Magic Kingdom with its perfect vista of the Wishes fireworks spectacular.

The Wow Factor! The 15th-floor California Grill with the best views in all of Walt Disney World Resort.

The fifteen-story, A-frame Contemporary Resort has long been a familiar landmark. What used to be considered a modern façade is now pretty darn austere with its soaring, open interior and its sharp edges and angles. Love it or not, its accessibility to the Magic Kingdom can't be beat. Of course, the sight of the monorail silently gliding through its core is simply magical. The property consists of a high-rise tower, a three-story wing, and a next-door convention center, making it a favorite choice for groups.

Wacky trees cut in futuristic forms line the entrance leading to a marble lobby with sleek, chocolate colored, chenille sofas, and woven grass chairs. To feel the grandeur of the resort you'll want to head to its centerpiece, the fourth-floor Grand Canyon Concourse whose soaring space boasts floors of guest rooms surrounding the vast atrium. At its heart stands a charming 90-foot mosaic mural of Native American children surrounded by shops, restaurants, and the monorail station, all constantly buzzing with traffic. High above it all sits the fifteenth-floor California Grill, one of Disney's best restaurants, with a bird's-eye view of the Magic Kingdom.

REST

Guest rooms. Dark, rich wood furnishings, beds covered in white duvets, and black and white bed runners in a graphic design make these some of the nicer rooms in Disney's repertoire if only it weren't for the dated, low ceilings. Recently refreshed guest rooms offer attractive touches including a cream-toned, fabric-covered headboard stretching to the ceiling, a flip-over single sofa bed in an unexciting beige, a sleek frosted-glass-topped desk, and contemporary pendant lighting. Carpeting and wall color are a lovely shade of taupe, and the 39-inch LCD flat-screen TV, set in a shallow wall unit, is a bonus. Blasts of color in dandelion yellow, seen in the desk's ergonomic desk chair and round bed pillows monogramed with an animated Mickey head, brighten the neutral tone of the room. However, mattresses and pillows are in need of replacement.

Baths are elegant with chocolate brown and cream marble floors, but, while chic, vanities with elongated, contemporary sinks are quite impractical; you find yourself setting your toiletries in the wet sink instead of on the tiny stainless steel and frosted glass countertop. And while the built-in mirror lighting is nice, the overhead canned lights cause an overwhelming shadow that is irritating when trying to apply makeup. A bath/shower adjoins the two sinks with the commode in a separate area. The foyer's two closets are designed with frosted glass panels, trimmed in rich wood, with a granite alcove that hides a refrigerator and coffeemaker. Amenities include a laptop-size electronic safe, fluffy towels, non-lighted makeup mirror, hairdryer, iron and ironing board, iPod clock radio, H2O Grapefruit Bergamot bath products, and morning newspaper.

Tower rooms, all with balconies, are the ticket here and worth the additional cost with knockout views of either the Magic Kingdom and glorious sunsets on one side (for a higher price), or beautiful Bay Lake on the other. The higher the floor, the quieter the room and the better the view. Rooms tend to be noisy due to their suspended position over the Grand Canyon Concourse where the clamor of Chef Mickey's character breakfast begins in the wee hours of the morning. Request a room on the opposite side of the tower if you prefer to sleep in.

The three-story *Garden Wing* guest rooms offer the same decor and basic configuration as Tower rooms, but they come with a bit of a walk to the main building and the monorail. Bottom-floor rooms have a patio but the top two floors lack balconies. Spend a bit more for a Garden View with vistas of the gardens, the marina, the pools, or Bay Lake instead of a parking lot.

Garden Wing Deluxe Rooms sit in the corner of the building making them angular in shape with both the king bed and the living area all in one large space. The living area holds modern furnishings including a sleeper sofa, chair with ottoman, coffee table, entertainment center, and desk. The bath is slightly oversize with two areas: two sinks and tub in one area; shower and toilet apart. A wet bar is in the foyer.

CARA'S TIP: Although Tower rooms on the Magic Kingdom side have a marvelous view they also come with a not-so-marvelous view of the parking lot. Still, it's worth it for front-row seats of the nighttime fireworks display.

Concierge rooms. The Contemporary Resort has two concierge levels: one on the 12th floor and another on the 14th floor.

The relaxing *Atrium Club* on the resort's 12th floor is one of Disney's standout concierge lounges where you'll find continental breakfast, afternoon snacks, evening appetizers and wine, and after-dinner desserts and cordials as well as private check-in/checkout, turndown service, DVD players, and the services of a concierge staff. The best part is its lengthy balcony and unbeatable views of the Magic Kingdom and Seven Seas Lagoon including the Wishes fireworks show accompanied by music, perfect for those with only a Bay Lake View guest room. At breakfast are the usual suspects of fruit, juice, pastries, cereal, toast, croissants, mini-muffins, oatmeal, and bagels; afternoon snacks are gummy bears, cookies, house-made potato chips, goldfish, yogurt-covered pretzels, nuts, fruit, coffee, iced tea, and sodas. In the evening two hot items are offered such as macadamia nut chicken, prosciutto flatbread, conch fritters with spicy remoulade, mini blue crab cheesecakes with chipotle mayo, crunchy chicken lollipops, prosciutto wrapped scallops, beef flatbreads with caramelized onions and goat cheese, duck confit with apple slaw, spring rolls, and pot stickers with soy glaze along with cold items such as American artisanal cheeses, smoked tomato jam bruschetta with fresh mozzarella, vegetable crudités with ranch dip, sun-dried tomato pesto, and PB&J sandwiches. Canyon Road Merlot, BV Century Cellars Chardonnay, and Beringer White Zinfandel are the wines of choice along with a nice variety of beer. After dinner dessert consists of cookies, mini strawberry cheesecake, mini-tarts, chocolate chip mousse, chocolate-covered strawberries, and petit fours with cordials.

Fourteenth-floor rooms, suites, and lounge have recently had a complete re-do in a light modern and organic look. Most accommodations on the 14th floor are suites, but regular guest rooms (called Standard Club Rooms) on this floor are larger than the rest and have deep balconies, larger baths, and spectacular views of either the Magic Kingdom or Bay Lake (view is on request only). All have the exclusive use of the *Tower Club* concierge lounge offering the same amenities as the Atrium Club but in a more intimate setting. And because it is the only guest room floor not suspended over the Grand Concourse you won't be awakened in the early morning hours by the sound of Chef Mickey's, although those on the Magic Kingdom side might hear noise in the evening from the California Grill above them.

Suites. All of the following suites are located on the 14th floor. Recently renovated they are now in tip-top shape.

One-bedroom Suites have 1,428 square feet and come with either a Bay Lake or a Magic Kingdom view. Enter through a foyer with a metal wall hanging into the living room filled with creamy white furnishings including a sofa, coffee table, desk, and two occasional chairs with, strangely enough, tree stump side tables. Mounted on the wall is a flat-screen TV, and outside is a nice, deep balcony. A sofa table and contemporary floor lighting visually divides the living area with the dining room where you'll find a round, six-person table and buffet over which hangs a large piece of modern art in gray and green hues. The dove gray and white-hued contemporary carpeting is a standout. A small, open kitchen offers a full-size refrigerator, microwave, and sink, and a full bath with single sink and shower sits off the entry hall.

The suite's bedroom is similar to a standard-type guest room with two queens or one king bed covered in white duvets adorned with gray and white graphic bed runners and bolsters and fronted by an upholstered bench. Blond wood furnishings include a small nightstand and bureau/desk combination with a wall-mounted flat-screen TV. Its bath, slightly larger than a standard with tub and sink set in a white vanity in one room and a commode and sink in another area, has gray and white tile flooring. A king-bedded guest room can be added to make this a two-bedroom suite with 1,892 square feet.

The resort's *Presidential Suite* has two bedrooms, three baths in

2,061 square feet. Five deep and spacious balconies span its length and afford spectacular Magic Kingdom views. A spacious living room decorated in the same color scheme as the One-Bedroom suite comes with a wet bar and microwave, sofa bed, easy chairs, large flat-screen TV, and six-person dining table. Off the dining area is a two-person bar that opens into the suite's kitchen with full-size refrigerator, wet bar sink, and microwave. Guests love the huge king-bedded master bedroom with its large sitting area, TV, easy chairs with ottomans, and full-size working desk, as well as a mammoth whirlpool bathtub, separate marble shower, double sinks, two closets, and vanity desk inside the walk-in closet. The second bedroom comes with two queen-size beds and single-sink bath. An additional full bath is off the marble entry hall.

The *Vice Presidential Suite* has two bedrooms, three baths in 1,985 square feet and again the same color scheme as the 1-bedroom. Off the foyer is a single-sink full bath with shower, and in the living area (believe it or not it's smaller than the living area in a one-bedroom suite) is a six-person dining table, wet bar and microwave, easy chairs, sleeper sofa, oversized flat-screen TV, and deep balconies spanning the length of the suite with views of Bay Lake and, in the far distance, Epcot's Spaceship Earth. There are two queen-size beds and working desk in the sizable master bedroom. The master bath's tub lacks a whirlpool, but its two-part bath has one side with a shower, bidet, commode, and vanity desk; the other side is basically a standard size bath. A king bed, two-person table, and single sink bath are in the second bedroom.

DINE

California Grill. Popular fifteenth-floor restaurant open for dinner only with innovative cuisine accompanied by sweeping views of the Magic Kingdom and the Seven Seas Lagoon. (See full description in Dining In Style at Walt Disney World Resort.)

Chef Mickey's. Breakfast and dinner home-style buffet with Chef Mickey and friends Goofy, Pluto, Minnie, and Donald Duck. *Breakfast buffet:* fruit, yogurt, cereal, oatmeal, garden vegetable quiche, scrambled eggs with toppings, sausage quiche, cheesy potatoes, bacon and sausage links, challah French toast, pancakes, buttermilk biscuits and country gravy, turkey and corned beef hash, breakfast pizza, Mickey waffles, assorted pastries, croissants. *Dinner buffet:* soup and salad bar, spiced-rubbed sirloin of beef, oven roasted turkey breast or ham, Thai curry or chipotle BBQ chicken, salmon filet with mango chutney or dill aioli, parmesan mashed potatoes, stir-fry vegetables, broccoli with cheese sauce, baked or scalloped potatoes, glazed carrots, ice cream sundae bar, assorted desserts.

The Contempo Café. 24/7 quick-service dining. *Breakfast:* oatmeal, grits, waffles, grilled breakfast sandwich, French toast, breakfast burrito, egg platter. *Lunch:* marinated beef, cheese, pepperoni, vegetable, or chicken and artichoke flatbreads, chicken Caesar or chopped salad, roasted curried vegetable salad, steakhouse salad with goat cheese and tomatoes, multigrain turkey BLT sandwich, Italian stacked sandwich, Angus bacon cheeseburger, hot sandwich choices of smoked turkey, spice-crusted mahi-mahi, or grilled chicken. *Dinner* adds pasta with marinara, chicken basil pasta, beef pot roast, and a vegetable bake. *Children's menu:* pepperoni or cheese pizza, chicken nuggets, burger, turkey sandwich, mahi-mahi sandwich, tuna salad platter, turkey pasta marinara.

Sand Bar and Grill. Pool bar; specialty drinks, beer, and sangria; sushi, Angus bacon cheeseburger, chili cheese dog, Italian stacked sandwich, BLT sandwich, Caesar salad with chicken, Asian salad with chicken.

The Wave of American Flavors. Healthy American cuisine serving breakfast, lunch, and dinner. *Breakfast:* egg white frittata, make-your-own muesli, multigrain French toast, spinach, tomato, and feta cheese scrambled eggs. *Lunch:* bison burger, soft flour tortilla with fajita seasoned tofu and poblano chili, Rueben sandwich, seared herb ahi tuna salad. *Dinner:* braised lamb shank, curry vegetable stew, sustainable fish with edamame stew, whole grain penne pasta with shrimp, scallops, clams, and roasted garlic-tomato broth.

In-Room Dining. Available 24/7.

SIP

California Grill Lounge. Fifteenth-floor lounge in the California Grill restaurant with spectacular views of the Magic Kingdom and Seven Seas Lagoon. Sophisticated wine and cocktail list, pristine sushi and sashimi, and full menu available. Check-in at the 2nd floor podium for lounge access.

Contemporary Grounds. Lobby coffee bar with pastries and cookies, specialty coffees, iced tea and coffee, and frozen drinks.

Outer Rim. Downsized and glaringly bright fourth-floor lounge with sweeping views of Bay Lake; specialty drinks, martinis, wine, and beer.

The Wave Lounge. Glowing blue bar, the largest at any Disney Deluxe Resort offering wine, beer flights, and cocktails including organic choices. Appetizers: grass fed beef burger flatbread with smoked Tillamook cheddar, mozzarella flatbread with Roma tomatoes and pesto, soft pretzels and dips, sustainable fish taco with avocado gelato, lump crab Florida rock shrimp cakes with fennel slaw and apple cider dressing.

PLAY

Arcade. The Game Station, a super-sized arcade located on the 4th floor concourse.

Beach. Small white-sand beach dotted with hammocks located near the marina.

Boating. The Boat Nook Marina offers boating options on miles of Bay Lake and the adjoining Seven Seas Lagoon; Sea Raycers, Sun Tracker Pontoons, Boston Whaler Montauks, specialty cruises. Call (407) WDW-PLAY or (407) 939-7529 for reservations.

Children's Activities. Disney trivia, Goofy bingo, chalk art, water relays, balloon twisting, hula hoop games, giant board games, rubber duck races, contemporary crafts, Name That Tune. Campfire and Movie Under the Stars on the lawn between Disney's Contemporary Resort and Bay Lake Tower most evenings.

Pirates and Pals Fireworks Voyage—after a dessert reception with Captain Hook and Mr. Smee sail out on the Seven Seas lagoon along with your pirate host for a viewing of the Wishes fireworks show with Peter Pan waiting for you on your return to shore. This non-private cruise is offered Friday, Saturday, Sunday, and Monday evenings for $54 per adult and $31 per child ages 3-9 (call 407-WDW-PLAY or 407-939-7529 for reservations).

Electrical Water Pageant. On the Seven Seas Lagoon nightly at 10:10 p.m., best viewed from Bay Lake view tower room balconies, pool, or the beach. Delightful 1,000-foot string of illuminated barges featuring King Neptune and his court of whales, sea serpents, and other deep-sea creatures. May be canceled due to inclement weather.

Fishing. Guided two-hour fishing excursion for as many as five people include boat, guide, and gear; catch-and-release only (call 407-WDW-BASS or 407-939-2277 for reservations).

Jogging. A jogging path loops around Bay Lake Tower and Contemporary Resort's South Garden Wing for just under one mile.

Swimming. Two heated pools with little theming. The Main Pool holds a waterslide, fountain jets, interactive water playground, and a whirlpool in the center of the pool. Smaller Bay Lake Pool protrudes out over the lake. Canvas cabanas available at the main pool for full- and half-day rentals with 32" flat-screen TV, lounge chairs, daybed, fan, safe, iPod docking station, mini refrigerator with bottled water and sodas, fruit platter, and a cabana attendant for $110 for half-day and $185 for full-day; in-cabana massages available.

Tennis. Two lighted courts located to the north of the adjoining Bay Lake Tower. Complimentary tennis racquets and balls are available at the Boat Nook Marina.

Volleyball. Sand volleyball court located on the beach; complimentary volleyballs at the Boat Nook Marina.

Waterskiing and parasailing. Disney's Contemporary Resort is the only Disney resort offering waterskiing, wakeboarding, jet skiing, and parasailing. (See Diversions Beyond the Walt Disney World Resort Theme Parks for full details.)

WORK, MOVE, SOOTHE

Business center. Located at Disney's Contemporary Resort Convention Center with fax, Internet, imaging services, shipping and receiving, notary public, and office supplies.

Fitness Center. Newly renovated, the Olympiad Fitness Center is located on 3rd floor of the Main Tower building with 24-hour access, Life Fitness treadmills, bicycles, ellipticals, Life Fitness strength training machines, free weights, coed dry sauna; personal training, massage, and facials available by appointment, including in-room. Fitness center is complimentary to resort guests.

GO

Board the monorail or walk the pathway to the Magic Kingdom. The monorail stops at the Transportation and Ticket Center where you can transfer to the Epcot Monorail. Buses run to Disney's Hollywood Studios, Animal Kingdom Theme Park, Blizzard Beach, Downtown Disney, and Typhoon Lagoon. The monorail takes you to Disney's Polynesian Resort and Disney's Grand Floridian Resort & Spa.

To reach other Disney resorts during park operating hours take the monorail or walk to the Magic Kingdom and from there pick up a bus to your resort destination. After park hours take the bus to Downtown Disney to transfer to your resort destination. Disney's Wilderness Lodge and Disney's Fort Wilderness Resort & Campground are reachable via the Blue Flag Launch.

Disney's Grand Floridian Resort & Spa

867 rooms. 4401 Floridian Way, Lake Buena Vista, FL 32830; phone (407) 824-3000, fax (407) 824-3186. Check-in 3:00 p.m., checkout 11:00 a.m. For reservations contact your travel advisor or call (407) 939-3476.

Claim To Fame. Disney's flagship resort.

Room To Book. A Main Building Theme Park View room with access to the Royal Palm Club concierge lounge and views of Cinderella Castle.

The Wow Factor! Dining at Victoria & Albert's, the only AAA Five-Diamond awarded restaurant in Central Florida.

Spreading along the shore of the Seven Seas Lagoon with views of the Magic Kingdom is Disney's flagship, the Grand Floridian Resort & Spa. Its red-gabled roofs and Victorian elegance transport you to the time of Florida's nineteenth-century grand seaside "palace hotels." Impeccably maintained and manicured grounds are strung with fragrant, blossom-filled lanes that meander among the gracious four- and five-story buildings fabricated with gleaming white clapboard siding, red shingled roofs, fairy-tale turrets, and intricate latticework.

Guests' preferred gathering spot is the soaring five-story Grand Lobby topped with stained-glass cupolas and massive filigreed chandeliers. Strewn with potted palms, cushy seating, and extravagant flower arrangements, it's at its liveliest in the late afternoon and evening hours when entertainment rotates between a relaxing piano player and a dynamic "big" band. Because the resort possesses a popular wedding chapel don't be surprised to see white-gowned brides frequently roaming the lobby. If you're in luck a Cinderella coach with footmen and white ponies will be on hand to whisk away the newly wedded couple.

Aquatic enticements include a sugar-soft sand beach dotted with canopied lounge chairs, a large pool in the central courtyard, a beachside Florida springs–style pool, and a marina sporting a wide assortment of watercraft including a 52-foot yacht. A full-service spa and health club, three lounges, and upscale shopping round out the list of exceptional offerings. The restaurants here are also quite a draw, notably Victoria & Albert's, central Florida's rightly famous, award-winning gem. And early rising guests on Monday and Friday can enjoy a parasol parade at 8:00 a.m. when over fifty members of the housekeeping staff, parasols in hand, stroll through the courtyard around the pool—a perfect start to the day!

REST

Guest rooms. Where I feel this resort falls flat are in guest rooms that do not live up to a flagship resort's reputation. My issue is that the furniture is way overdue for replacement, the wallpaper is almost silly looking, and the faded and dated bedspreads must go. A room refurbishment is scheduled to begin January 2014 with more sensible wallpaper and hopefully the elimination of spreads in place of white duvets. But the furnishings, to my knowledge, are being stripped and refinished, not replaced.

Nevertheless, guest rooms, at just over 440 square feet, are decorated in a period Victorian floral motif, each with either one king or two queen beds (only a few have kings), full-size sofa (those on the top dormer floors with only an easy chair and ottoman), and two chairs and a table. Large flat-screen TVs, under-counter refrigerators, and iHome clock radio with iPod docks are additional amenities along with a writing desk and bureau. DVD players can be added on request. Cream-colored marble baths have twin sinks, Spa H2O bath products, full-length and make-up mirrors, and hair dryer. The closet contains an electronic safe, iron and ironing board, and robes. All rooms have daily newspaper delivery, coffeemaker, and nightly turndown service.

Most accommodations come with generous balconies and vary only in view—*Garden View, Lagoon* View, or a *Theme Park View. Outer Building Theme Park View* rooms with vistas of the Theme Park do not always mean a view of the Castle (request the Sago Key or Conch Key building for a Castle view since the Boca Chica building looks mostly at Space Mountain). *Outer Building Lagoon View* rooms are also a nice choice facing the Seven Seas lagoon, The Villas at the Grand Floridian Resort, and Disney's Polynesian Resort. *Garden View* rooms overlook the flowering grounds, the sparkling courtyard pool, or the marina. *Top-floor* guest rooms have vaulted ceilings along with balconies that require standing for a view. Although their high ceilings give them a more open feel they are actually a bit smaller than a normal guest room and come with only a chair and ottoman in lieu of the standard daybed. *Outer Building Deluxe Garden View* rooms are located in the turreted corners of the buildings. Similar to a standard room with balcony, they offer the bonus of an additional sitting area and second TV for a total of 574 square feet.

> **CARA'S TIP:** Rooms in the Sago Cay building have maximum peacefulness in a setting far from the pool. However, they also require a longer walk to the main building. The Sugar Loaf (concierge) and Big Pine buildings are closest to the main building and the monorail.

Concierge rooms. Accommodations on the concierge level vary from standard guest rooms to larger Deluxe Rooms and suites. Beware requesting a Standard Concierge King Bed Room in the Main Building; two are corner rooms (one being Room 4329) that are smaller than normal with only enough room for the bed, one chair, and an armoire.

Concierge Theme Park View rooms in the Main Building all have a vista of the Castle.

Deluxe Rooms at 634 square feet, all located in the Main Building, offer a spacious sitting area within the guest room with a sofa, coffee table, entertainment center, wet bar, writing desk, two chairs and a table, and two queen-size beds (but never a Magic Kingdom view), three on the 4th floor and three more on the 3rd floor (if you want a quieter location request the 3rd floor since 4th floor rooms are found just off the lounge).

Deluxe King Rooms sleeping two are in the Main Building and are privy to the Royal Palm Club, but there are two variations: six turreted rooms with 648 square feet offering a 4-poster bed, bay window sitting area with sofa and easy chair, entertainment armoire, wet bar, small walk-in closet, and oversized tub, but no balcony and only a few offering a semi-view of the Castle; and 440 square feet standard-size guest rooms, all with a marina/Magic Kingdom view, balcony, and whirlpool tub located on the 2nd floor above Gasparilla Grill. Room type is on request only.

The *Royal Palm Club*, located on the 4th floor of the main building in a prime position overlooking the Grand Lobby, is the more upscale of the two concierge lounges with views of the Seven Seas Lagoon and the resort's lovely courtyard. Serving all rooms of the main building and all suites throughout the property regardless of location, you'll find a concierge staff on duty near the main elevator of the 3rd floor.

The *Sugar Loaf Club* in the Sugar Loaf outer building offers the services of a concierge desk and the same food and drink as the Royal Palm Club but in a less grand setting on the 1st floor of the building's atrium. Don't look for a lagoon view room in this building—you'll find only garden, marina, or pool views. Of course, the prices are lower than those in the Royal Palm Club.

At both lounges you'll find a continental breakfast of juice, fruit, yogurt, cereal, toast, bagels with salmon cream cheese, muffins, coffeecake, pastries, cinnamon rolls, croissants, hot oatmeal, cheese, and sandwich meats. Midday offerings are pretzels, chips, crudités with dip, hummus, cookies, lemonade, and iced tea. Late afternoon brings scones with Devonshire cream and marmalade, jam tarts, fruit, banana bread, coffee, and tea. Early evening features tasty hors d'oeuvres such as spanakopita, smoked pork loin with apple chutney, rosemary roasted vegetables, potato crepes with smoked salmon, duck pot stickers, beef and blue cheese bites, beef bruschetta with horseradish cream, Asian chicken with vermicelli noodles, spring rolls with sweet chili sauce, lamb meatballs, grilled vegetables, chicken fresh spring roll, chicken Wellington (yum!), Italian stuffed bread, sweet glazed salmon, sushi, crudités with dip and hummus, and cheese and crackers. Wines include Mirassou Pinot Noir, Beringer White Zinfandel, Penfolds Rawson's Retreat Merlot, Columbia Crest Chardonnay, and Mumm Napa Valley sparkling wine with a nice assortment of beer. Kids look forward to their own spread of turkey and cheese or PB&J sandwiches, mini corn dogs, cookies, and cupcakes with the occasional adult sneaking an irresistible taste of their own. A small spread of after-dinner desserts like mini-éclairs and cream puffs, fruit tarts, cheesecake tartlets, chocolate covered strawberries, cookies, cupcakes, brownies, and Rice Krispies treats are served with a selection of liqueurs. And everyone enjoys the self-service cappuccino machine and the refrigerator filled with beer and sodas.

Suites. Grand Floridian's suites can be had in all shapes and sizes. All come with more room than a standard guest room and a full living area or parlor as well as upgraded robes, DVD players, and fresh flowers.

In the main building are four *Signature Suites*: the Grand Suite, Walt Disney Suite, Roy O. Disney Suite, and Victorian Suite.

Grand Suite. From its fifth-floor perch, the Grand Suite at 2,220 square feet features five dormer-style balconies with sweeping views of the Seven Seas Lagoon, Cinderella Castle, Space Mountain, Disney's Contemporary Resort, Disney's Polynesian Resort, even Spaceship Earth in the far distance. A long entry hall with marble half bath leads to the sunny, turreted living room with hardwood flooring and massive chandelier lighting. Thankfully, an unattractive wall of mirrors has been removed and furnishings now include two fern-green and butter-cream sofas atop an area rug, two coffee tables, two peach-colored easy chairs, a dining table for four, desk, Bose stereo system, an oversized LCD TV with DVD player, an upright shiny white piano, and a corner marble wet bar with under-counter refrigerator, coffeemaker, and microwave. Off one side of the large foyer is the master bedroom with a four-poster king bed decorated in a soft green spread, desk and entertainment center with TV, and balcony views of Disney's Polynesian Resort and The Villas at Disney's Grand Floridian Resort, the wedding chapel, and the Beach Pool. The solid marble master bathroom has double sinks, mini-TV, two closets, large whirlpool tub, huge shower, and a separate toilet and bidet. On the other side of the entry foyer is a second bedroom with a queen bed and sleeper chair, entertainment center, a single-sink bath with mini-TV, and a balcony with the suite's best view of Cinderella Castle.

Walt Disney Suite. The 1,690-square-foot Walt Disney Suite is a favorite, filled with Walt's memorabilia including railroad models and family pictures. You can almost feel you're in Walt's apartment, expecting him to return any minute. Enter from the marble foyer into the cozy living room decorated in shades of rose, green, gold, and cream with rose-motif carpeting, wet bar, desk, entertainment center with flat-screen TV, chaise lounge, sofa, two easy chairs, coffee table, and four-person dining table. Off the foyer is a half bath. The master bedroom, painted in a pastel blue, has a king-size bed, desk, sofa, entertainment center with flat-screen TV, a large walk-in closet with a bureau, and a marble bathroom with two sinks, whirlpool tub, and separate, oversized shower. The second bedroom has twin sleigh beds, easy chair with ottoman, an entertainment center with flat-screen TV, and second double-sink bath. A balcony that is almost the length of the suite faces the courtyard pool, the beach, and the lagoon with views of Disney's Polynesian Resort and The Villas at Disney's Grand Floridian Resort.

Roy O. Disney Suite. Just below the Walt Disney Suite is the Roy O. Disney Suite, comparable in shape and size with a moss green and salmon color scheme and memorabilia representing Walt's brother Roy, including a wall of family photographs.

Victorian Suite. The intimate Victorian Suite at 1,083 square feet on the top floor of the main building is bedecked in soft green, peach, and rose hues. The living area holds a small sofa, coffee table, entertainment center, wet bar with refrigerator, four-person dining table, and even an old Victrola. Overlooking the courtyard pool are three balconies with views of the top of Cinderella Castle and Space Mountain, Disney's Polynesian Resort, and the Seven Seas Lagoon. Through French doors is the bedroom with a four-poster king-size bed, desk, oversize easy chair and ottoman, and bureau with flat-screen TV. The master bath has a large walk-in closet with dressing area, double-sinks, mini TV, and oversize tub. Off the small foyer is a half bath.

You'll also find *One- and Two-bedroom Suites,* all with a variety of views including marina, lagoon, theme park, and garden. Located in both the main building as well as all outlying lodge buildings, they all come with access to the concierge lounge and services regardless of location.

CARA'S TIP: If you're staying in a suite outside the main building you may choose to use either concierge lounge for convenience. Again, suites are in dire need of refurbishment, something due to begin January 2014.

Two-bedroom Outer Lodge Suites found throughout the resort are basically two standard-size guest rooms (one with a king and the other two queens), a living room with sleeper sofa, two occasional chairs, coffee table, desk, and four-person dining table. All sleep eight with an additional full bath off the living area. You can request a lagoon view, but be forewarned that these are smaller than those with a garden view. Two of these suites have a Magic Kingdom view but are a weird configuration—because they are corner suites you must go through a bedroom to access the rest of the suite.

A *One-bedroom Outer Lodge Suite* sleeping six comes with two queen beds in the standard bedroom and two full baths. In the smallish living area you'll find a sleeper sofa, entertainment center, two easy chairs, and a 4-person dining table. Those on the top floors come with only an easy chair in the bedroom instead of a daybed.

Two-bedroom Theme Park Suites each with 1,792 square feet offer the distinction of a straight on view of the lagoon and Cinderella Castle. Only two of these suites exist: the Everglades Suite in Conch Key and the Cape Coral Suite in Sago Cay, both located on the ground floor with a waterfront oversized patio. For more privacy and quiet request the Cape Coral Suite (the Everglades Suite is near the boat launch). The double-size living area is great for entertaining and features a full-size dining table and large wet bar. A standard-size bedroom is found (one with a king and the other two queens) on either side of the living area.

DINE

Citricos. Innovative, Mediterranean-inspired cuisine and a world-class wine list open for dinner only. (See full description in the Dining in Style at Walt Disney World Resort chapter.)

Garden View Tea Room. Serving English-style tea in high style with a wide assortment of teas, scones, tarts, trifles, pound cake, pâté, fruit and cheese, tea sandwiches, and champagne. Arrive after 3:00 p.m. when tea is accompanied by live entertainment from the Grand Lobby. Open 2:00 to 4:30 p.m.

Gasparilla Island Grill. Snack bar open 24/7 with both inside and outside dining overlooking the marina. *Breakfast:* scrambled egg platter, croissant breakfast sandwich, Mickey-shaped waffle, pancake platter, oatmeal, grits. *Lunch and dinner:* Grand Gatsby burger with the addition of Tillamook cheese, pulled pork, and onion frits, chicken cordon bleu sandwich, panini of the day, Angus bacon cheeseburger, chicken breast nuggets, flatbreads, create-your-own-salad with grilled chicken or flank steak (in the evenings it's create-your-own-pasta with grilled chicken or shrimp), ham and Swiss sandwich, turkey sandwich, roast beef sandwich. *Children's Menu:* Breakfast: Mickey-shaped waffles, pancakes, breakfast platter; Lunch and Dinner: mac 'n' cheese, chicken nuggets, hot dog, hamburger, and vegetable wrap.

Grand Floridian Café. Casual café serving breakfast, lunch, and dinner. *Breakfast:* frittata, ham and cheese omelet, lobster eggs benedict, steak and eggs, citrus pancakes. *Lunch:* tuna Nicoise salad prepared with fresh, seared rare tuna and a tart vinaigrette, cobb salad, Reuben sandwich, The Grand Sandwich (open-faced hot ham, turkey, bacon, and tomato with Boursin cheese sauce and fried onion straws), rustic chicken sandwich with balsamic onions, spinach, and fennel salad. *Dinner:* sustainable catch of the day, New York strip steak with brandy-green peppercorn sauce, shrimp and mascarpone cheese grits with chorizo and fennel, grilled pork chop with caramelized onions, wilted arugula, and balsamic demi.

Narcoossee's. Fresh seafood at a perfect waterside setting with views of the Magic Kingdom fireworks open for dinner only. (See full description in the Dining in Style at Walt Disney World Resort chapter.)

1900 Park Fare. Breakfast and dinner character buffet. Supercalifragilistic Breakfast with a bevy of characters; evenings it's the Cinderella's Happily-Ever-After Dinner.

Victoria & Albert's. Disney's grandest dining establishment and the only AAA Five-Diamond awarded restaurant in Central Florida open for dinner only. (See full description in the Dining in Style at Walt Disney World Resort chapter.)

Private dining. 24/7 In-Room Dining; also offered aboard the *Grand I* yacht.

SIP

Beaches Pool Bar and Grill. Located at the Beach Pool with cocktails, beer, frozen drinks, nonalcoholic beverages along with barbecue pork flatbread, *margherita* flatbread, Cuban sandwich, chicken breast nuggets, Angus bacon cheeseburger, Grand turkey sandwich, grilled chicken Caesar.

Courtyard Pool Bar. Located at the central Courtyard Pool with specialty drinks, beer, wine, nonalcoholic beverages; same food menu as Beaches Pool Bar and Grill above.

Mizner's Lounge. Second-story lobby lounge features picturesque views of the resort courtyard and pool. Fine wine and champagne by the glass, beers, single malt scotch, classic cocktails, martinis, port, cordials, and cigars; gourmet appetizer choices include hardwood grilled Berkshire pork belly with a tamarind glaze and spiced mascarpone, veal Bolognese, four-cheese flatbread, PEI mussels pan-seared with garlic and olive oil served with crusty bread and spiced tomato sauce, artisanal cheese selection, Ashley Farms chicken *b'steeya* with orange blossom honey, charcuterie, and sautéed shrimp with feta cheese and diced tomatoes. Desserts of lemon scented cheesecake with white chocolate ganache, warm chocolate banana tort, seasonal berry gratin with champagne Grand Marnier sabayon, and tropical fruit crème brûlée. Open 4:30 p.m. to midnight. Sit on the Magic Kingdom side of the lounge for a glimpse of the Wishes fireworks show. If you're not a fan of loud football games avoid this place during the season when the TV is blasting, and any chance of a quiet drink is nil.

Narcoossee's Lounge. Small counter bar inside Narcoossee's restaurant with specialty drinks, wine, and espresso along with a full dinner menu. Step outside to the boat dock for views of the Magic Kingdom fireworks and the Electrical Water Pageant.

PLAY

Arcade. Arcadia Games is located next to Gasparilla Island Grill.

Beach. Crescent of white-sand beach with canopy-covered lounge chairs can be found next to the Beach Pool; no swimming allowed in the lagoon.

Boating. Rentals at the Captain's Shipyard Marina with Sea Raycers, pontoon boats, Boston Whaler Montauks, and a 13-foot catamaran. Specialty cruises including a 52-foot Sea Ray Sedan Bridge yacht, a true indulgence and a perfect venue for viewing the Wishes fireworks show for up to 18 people (407) 824-2682.

Children's activities. Some of the very best children's activities are here at the Grand Floridian for ages four to twelve:

- *Disney's Pirate Adventure.* Two-hour supervised sail to "ports of call" with legends of pirates and a search for treasure. Offered every day except Sunday, 9:30 to 11:30 a.m. and includes lunch ($36; call (407) WDW-DINE or (407) 939-3463).

- *Wonderland Tea Party.* Monday through Friday at 1900 Park Fare from 2:00–3:00 p.m., hosted by characters from Alice in Wonderland ($43; call (407) WDW-DINE or (407) 939-3463).

- *My Disney Girl's Perfectly Princess Tea Party.* Receive the royal treatment in the Garden View Lounge including a meet and greet with Princess Aurora, a My Disney Girl Princess Aurora doll, a tiara and bracelet, and tea for two along with storytelling, sing-alongs, and a Grand Princess Parade through the resort's lobby ($250 for one adult and one child, $165 per additional child, and $85 per additional adult). Dressing in royal finery encouraged; royal princes may attend and receive a princely crown and a Disney plush bear. Offered Sunday, Monday, Wednesday, Thursday, and Friday, 10:30 a.m. to noon (call (407) WDW-DINE or (407) 939-3463).

Activities and a Pool Party Bash each afternoon at the Beach Pool including Disney trivia, Goofy bingo, crafts, sandcastle building, and chalk art. Movies Under the Stars most evenings by the courtyard pool.

Electrical Water Pageant. On the Seven Seas Lagoon nightly at 9:15 and best viewed from the beach or the boat dock near Narcoossee's; may be canceled due to inclement weather. Delightful 1,000-foot string of illuminated barges features King Neptune and his court of whales, sea serpents, and other deep-sea creatures.

Fishing. Two-hour guided bass fishing excursion includes guide, boat, and gear for as many as five guests; catch-and-release only (call 407-WDW-BASS or 407-939-2277 for reservations).

Jogging. Enjoy a one-mile trail along the beach and lagoon over to Disney's Polynesian Resort.

Swimming. Florida natural springs–style Beach Pool with a cooling waterfall, sunbathing deck, changing rooms, kiddie pool, waterslide, and pool bar. The freeform, zero-entry Courtyard Pool sits next to a kiddie pool, whirlpool, and pool bar. Alice in Wonderland-themed water play area located on the beach with a Mad Hatter's water dump, oversized teapot water spill, sprinklers, waterspouts, and two mini waterslides.

Beach Pool cabanas with TV, DVD/CD/MP3 player, satellite radio, wireless Internet, beverage-stocked refrigerator, ceiling fan, lounge furniture, and fruit basket can be rented for $110 half day and $185 full day (private in-cabana massage available for an additional fee).

WORK, MOVE, SOOTHE

Business center. Fax, Internet, imaging services, shipping and receiving, notary public, and office supplies at Disney's Grand Floridian Resort convention area.

Hair salon. Ivy Trellis Salon open daily 9:00 a.m. to 6:00 p.m.; full range of salon services including haircut, color, styling, and manicures.

Spa and fitness center. Senses–A Disney Spa at Disney's Grand Floridian Resort (see detailed review in the Beyond the Walt Disney World Resort Theme Parks chapter); an adjoining complimentary fitness center with Life Fitness treadmills, Precor elliptical cross trainers, upright and recumbent cycles, Smith machine, LifeFitness and Precor strength training equipment, and free weights; personal training available by appointment. Treatment hours 8:00 a.m. to 8:00 p.m.; fitness center open 24 hours.

GO

Transportation choices to the Magic Kingdom include both monorail and water launch. Take the monorail to the Transportation and Ticket Center (TTC) and transfer there to the Epcot Monorail. Take a bus to Disney's Hollywood Studios, Animal Kingdom Theme Park, Downtown Disney, Typhoon Lagoon, and Blizzard Beach. Use monorail service to reach Disney's Contemporary Resort. Walk (ten minutes) or take the water launch or monorail to Disney's Polynesian Resort.

To reach other Disney resorts during park operating hours, take the monorail to the Magic Kingdom and from there, pick up a bus to your resort destination. After park hours take a bus to Downtown Disney and then transfer to your resort destination.

The Villas at Disney's Grand Floridian Resort & Spa

> 4401 Floridian Way, Lake Buena Vista, FL 32830; phone (407) 824–3000, fax (407) 824-3186. Check-in 4:00 p.m., checkout 11:00 a.m.
> For reservations contact your travel advisor or call (407) 939-3476.

Claim To Fame. Victorian luxury at a Deluxe Villa Resort located on the monorail.

Room To Book. A Lagoon View villa overlooking the Seven Seas Lagoon that might even offer a peek at the Magic Kingdom from the balcony. The Grand Villas here are the only three-bedroom option at the Grand Floridian.

The Wow Factor! The newest Deluxe Villa Resort in Disney's repertoire.

This the newest of Disney's Deluxe Villa Resorts sits right next-door from the Grand Floridian just past the Beach Pool. With a perch on the shore of the Seven Seas Lagoon and the connection to Disney's flagship resort, it will surely prove to be one popular choice for families wanting luxury combined with the convenience of a living area and kitchen but at a lower price tag than the Grand Floridian's suites. And better yet,

DISNEY ALFRESCO

Who doesn't love a balcony? At Walt Disney World you'll find that most standard-type guest rooms at the Deluxe Resorts and Deluxe Villas come with at least one balcony, but the views they offer are not all created equal. Here are the best bets for balcony views:

- **Theme Park View Room at Disney's Contemporary Resort or Disney's Bay Lake Tower at the Contemporary Resort.** You won't find closer views of the Magic Kingdom, Cinderella Castle, and the Wishes fireworks show. Ask for a room on the North side of either resort and as high as possible. If you reserve a concierge room at Disney's Contemporary Resort then you are automatically on a higher floor; rooms and suites on the 14th floor's Tower Club have extra deep balconies.

- **Deluxe Club Room at Disney's Boardwalk Inn.** With 600 square feet and a full waterfront view overlooking Disney's BoardWalk Entertainment District and Crescent Lake, even a view of Spaceship Earth in the distance, these are what I consider Disney's best bargain.

- **Savanna View Room at Disney's Animal Kingdom Lodge or Disney's Animal Kingdom Villas–Kidani Village.** These are jackpot winners for their great views of the resort's savanna and exotic animals.

- **Main Building Theme Park View Room at Disney's Grand Floridian Resort.** Although not directly on the Seven Seas Lagoon these all have a guaranteed view of Cinderella Castle, unlike the Outer Building Theme Park View rooms that might only look at Space Mountain.

guests will enjoy all the recreation and services of the Grand Floridian Resort & Spa.

Built in the same casually elegant style as the next-door resort, inside the marble lobby is a soaring six-story atrium filled with Victorian grillwork and centered by a whimsical bronze fountain of frolicking penguins reminiscent of the Disney classic movie, *Mary Poppins,* while overhead are two massive antique brass chandeliers adorned with green crystals. In fact the entire lobby has a Mary Poppins theme found in the artwork, carousel horses, even an elevator hand in the form of Mary Poppins' umbrella. Scattered seating lends itself to relaxation. My biggest concern with the addition of the Villas with no pool of its own is that the Grand Floridian's existing pools will be overwhelmed now that both properties are utilizing them.

REST

Villas. Villas here are light and airy with white cabinetry and neutral décor accompanied by touches of soft blue, mint, and pistachio green wall color accents and furnishings. An iPod docking station, electronic safe, Blue-ray DVD players, iron and ironing board, Pack 'n' Play, coffeemaker, vacuum, hairdryer, robes, H2O Sea Salt bath products, and nightly turndown service are additional amenities included in each villa. Villa view choices: *Standard View* one with a look at the front or side of the resort; or a *Lagoon View* with views of the Seven Seas Lagoon (and if you are in luck a distant view of the Castle).

Studios are pleasant but they are a bit small at 374 square feet. Decorating the room is a queen bed topped with a soft white duvet and a pistachio green bed runner along with a cherry wood coffee table, two-person table with soft green upholstered chairs, a mirrored front bureau over which is a located a wall-mounted, flat-screen TV and inside of which is a fold-down single bed (with a Dumbo themed backdrop), and a taupe sofa sleeper. A mini kitchen has a sink, undercounter refrigerator, and microwave. The bath has two areas, both accessed from the entry hall: on one side is a white tiled tub/shower and commode; the other, separated by a pocket door, holds a single sink with a Magic TV built into the bath's mirror, and a shower with both hand held and rain showerheads. A balcony adjoins the studio (first-floor units come with a patio instead). Accommodates up to five guests plus an infant.

One-bedroom Villas are 844 square feet. Enter straight into the kitchen where an open floor plan and hardwood flooring adds to the feeling of a larger space. The full kitchen has white cabinets with glass upper doors and a panel-covered refrigerator and dishwasher. Featured are light gold granite countertops, white tile backsplash, and a farmhouse sink. A curved booth-style dining area upholstered in floral and leather fabric adjoins the kitchen. The living area, open to the kitchen, is furnished with a taupe sleeper sofa, mint green easy chair, coffee table, and an entertainment wall over which is mounted a flat-screen TV and where underneath can be found a foldout single bed with a Mary Poppins backdrop. The cream on white wallpaper is reminiscent of the Victorian age. A sliding door leads to a balcony or patio also accessed from the bedroom. Off the foyer is a full-size bonus bath with a smallish corner single sink. You'll also find a stacked washer/dryer in the hallway.

In the bedroom is a king-sized bed with pistachio green tufted headboard, white duvet, and a soft blue and green floral bed runner accented with a chocolate brown bolster pillow. Two round side tables flank the bed, a powder blue easy chair sits in the corner, and there is a nice-sized walk-in closet with electronic safe. Above the cherry wood bureau is a flat-screen TV beside which sits a desk and chair. The master bath's white and black marble flooring definitely harkens back to another era as does the freestanding tub. One area of the bath holds the tub and a single sink set in a marble vanity as well as a Magic TV built into the mirror; the other area holds the commode, an additional sink, and a sizeable white brick-style tile shower with rain showerhead (also accessible from the villa's entry hall). Accommodates up to five guests plus an infant.

A *Two-bedroom Villa* is simply a combination of the One-bedroom and a Studio at 1,232 square feet. Some are dedicated units with the second bedroom offering two queen beds and no mini-kitchen. Accommodates up to nine guests plus an infant.

With 2,800 square feet spread over one story the *Grand Villas* are the largest in Disney's villa repertoire and quite the luxury. In the oval entry hall is gold floral wallpaper, a definite Victorian touch. The large open living/dining area has parquet flooring with two cream-colored, cushy sofas and a large coffee table along with a giant flat-screen TV found above a yellow entertainment center. The dining table is massive seating twelve over which hangs a chandelier with crystal touches. Near the dining area is the full-size kitchen with white glass upper cabinet doors, oversized refrigerator, stove, dishwasher, microwave, and farmhouse-style sink, and at the kitchen bar are three stools for counter dining.

Off the entry hall to the master bedroom is a TV room with a long, cream-colored sectional sofa fronted with a row of small cocktail tables. An entertainment center with a large flat-screen TV and loads of cabinet space covers the opposite wall. Across the hall is a 4th full bath with single sink and shower. The master bedroom features a curtained king bed with bench seating at its foot, and the parquet flooring is covered with a soft floral area rug. A wood and mirrored armoire holds another flat-screen TV and beside it sits a desk and chair. The master bath has marble flooring and a marble vanity with two sinks over which you'll find a large glass framed mirror boasting a Magic TV. In an alcove is a sizeable whirlpool tub, and a large shower with rain showerhead is tiled in white. The commode is in a separate area.

On the opposite side of the villa are two bedrooms, each with two queen beds with soft blue tufted headboards, white duvets, and red bed runners. Each have a desk and entertainment armoire with flat-screen TV as well as a single-sink, tub/shower combination bath, one of which is located outside the guest room in the hallway. And each bath has a Magic TV built into the mirror.

DINE

In-Room Dining. Available 24/7 from the next-door Grand Floridian Resort.

PLAY

The Villas at Disney's Grand Floridian Resort shares all recreation with the adjacent Disney's Grand Floridian Resort & Spa. See previous entry for Disney's Grand Floridian Resort.

WORK, MOVE, SOOTHE

The Villas at Disney's Grand Floridian Resort shares all services with the adjacent Disney's Grand Floridian Resort & Spa. See previous entry for Disney's Grand Floridian Resort.

GO

The Villas at the Grand Floridian Resort shares all services with the adjacent Grand Floridian Resort. See also the GO section in the earlier entry for the Grand Floridian.

Disney's Polynesian Resort

847 rooms. 1600 Seven Seas Drive, Lake Buena Vista, FL 32830; phone (407) 824-2000, fax (407) 824-3174. Check-in 3:00 p.m., checkout 11:00 a.m. For reservations contact your travel advisor or call (407) 939-3476.

Claim To Fame. A prime location on the monorail with lush gardens, sandy beaches, and idyllic views of Cinderella Castle.

Room To Book. A Theme Park View concierge room facing the Seven Seas Lagoon and the Magic Kingdom with access to the Royal Polynesian Lounge.

The Wow Factor! A late night stroll on the tiki torch-lit beach with the sight of Cinderella Castle in the distance. Pick a hammock and stick around for a prime view of the Wishes fireworks show.

Along with a warm aloha and a lei greeting guests are invited to enter the South Seas environment of the Great Ceremonial House, a green oasis sheltering the front desk, shops, and restaurants. Vines encase the rugged lava rock cataracts that cool the two-story lobby resting below towering palm trees. The centerpiece garden has a profusion of flowering orchids, bromeliads, ginger, and anthurium scattered throughout banana trees, elephant's ear, and rubber plants. High-backed rattan and cane chairs and sofas with striking tangerine and moss green batik cushions and textiles sit on floors of polished flagstone and colorful rugs. Brilliantly colored macaws perch in the overarching branches of the surrounding foliage. Two-story picture windows draw the eye outdoors to the lush landscape surrounding the Volcano Pool and the Seven Seas Lagoon beyond.

Located on the monorail system and within walking distance of the Transportation and Ticket Center, the Polynesian is the most convenient of Disney's resorts with direct access to both the Magic Kingdom and Epcot. Lodging is in eleven tangerine and mahogany tinted longhouses scattered throughout the luxuriant grounds composed of more than seventy-five species of dense vegetation. Ducks and ibis roam the thick grassy lawns and rabbits hop along meandering pathways lined with volcanic rock. In the evenings the resort is torch-lit, and soft Hawaiian melodies set a romantic mood. Three white-sand beaches dotted with hammocks and lounge chairs are a spectacular place for sunning or a perfect perch for the Magic Kingdom fireworks.

> CARA'S TIP: Some find this resort a bit hokey and old-fashioned but it has a loyal following. Management here has certainly improved, almost a total turn-around from the last edition of this book. The pleasant, helpful staff now offers Ritz Carlton-style hospitality.

The Polynesian Resort will be undergoing an extensive construction project through 2015 with the addition of a new Disney Vacation Club property here. The extent to which this will affect guests is yet to be known, but check with your travel advisor for the latest updates before deciding on a stay here.

REST

Guest Rooms. Some of the largest standard rooms in Disney with around 400-440 square feet are here at the Polynesian. Everyone is buzzing about the major overhaul of the guest rooms, the result a much improved, lovely, fresh look. While there still remains a few longhouses yet to be completed, most guest rooms now have light celery-tinted walls and bamboo wainscoting, taupe carpeting, and furnishings that are a mixture of dark and blond wood. It's as if new life was breathed into what used to be dark and somewhat dreary accommodations. Two queen beds with bamboo bed frames are the norm along with fitted white comforters, "Sweet Dreams" bolsters, and orchid print bed runners. A few rooms come with king beds (on request only) making for a larger sitting area. Running the length of the wall opposite the bed is a bamboo bureau attached to a vanity/desk atop which sits a built-in 39-inch LCD flat-screen TV and a tiki god lamp. Many rooms also offer a carved, flip-over daybed, and all come with a rattan chair and ottoman. In the entry are built-in closets with reed motif etched glass paneling that feature a marble-topped bar with an undercounter refrigerator, coffeemaker, and electronic safe.

The biggest difference in the new look is the spiffy baths reconfigured with frosted glass doors, double sinks, and larger vanity counters in a man-made, granite-type material resembling lava rock. Although still without a separate commode area they are nice and bright with in-mirror lighting including a makeup mirror, chocolate and cream wallpaper in a Polynesian tiki print, and cream-colored porcelain tile surrounding the tub/tile area with a bamboo motif. Amenities include an iPod docking station clock radio, iron and ironing board, full-length mirror, and daily newspaper.

Your best chance of receiving the perfect room (of which there are many) is to educate yourself before check-in and request exactly what you would like, both at reservation time and again at the front desk. The following information may sound excessive, but it could make the difference between a perfect vacation and a disappointing one. The longhouses of Tokelau, Tahiti, and Rapa Nui feature the largest rooms, all of which come with patios or balconies and a convenient location near the Transportation and Ticket Center. Older longhouses, closer to the Great Ceremonial House, lack second-floor balconies although their large sliding door with a railing makes for an outdoor feel.

The two-story Niue and Tonga longhouses, with the Tonga an all-suite building, are small and intimate; the Tonga has second-floor balconies, the Niue does not. Water-view rooms in the Tahiti building front a lovely beach with great views across the lagoon but are also located very close to the Transportation and Ticket Center with noise from the ferryboat during park hours. One side of the Samoa and the Niue buildings faces the rambunctious Volcano Pool, a plus or minus depending on your personality. One side of the Fiji longhouse looks at the marina but is considered a garden view. One side of the Aotearoa, Tonga, and Rarotonga longhouses faces the monorail, and one side of the Rapa Nui faces the parking lot. A few Garden View rooms closest to the concierge lounge in the Hawaii building look at another building.

If staying in the Fiji, Tuvalu, Tonga, and Aotearoa you had better enjoy the beat of drums because the Spirit of Aloha dinner show is held nearby. The worst view is from the so-called Garden View side of the Tuvalu longhouse that stares at one end of the Fiji building only a few feet away. A Theme Park View category guarantees you a view of the Castle but at a higher price tag.

Concierge rooms. Nestled along the beach is the Hawaii concierge building offering the services of a concierge staff as well as private check-in and checkout. Newly renovated, the bi-level *King Kamehameha Club* is among the best in Disney's repertoire, affording a fantastic view of Cinderella Castle and the Magic Kingdom fireworks with quite delicious food to boot. But don't expect a relaxing atmosphere in the lounge where things are usually at a high frenzy during peak times. If you want peace and quiet consider the Royal Palm Club at the Grand Floridian next-door where a calming ambiance is much more likely. Accommodations come with: a *Lagoon View*, *Theme Park View* (a guaranteed view of the Castle without obstructions), or a *Garden View*, but second-floor rooms do not have balconies. Additional amenities include robes, DVD players, and nightly turndown service.

Open from 7:00 a.m. to 10:00 p.m., the concierge lounge has complimentary food and beverages beginning with a continental breakfast of juice, coffee, tea, fresh fruit, hot oatmeal, cinnamon rolls, croissants, pastries, bagels, and cereal. From noon to 4:00 p.m. juice, lemonade, coffee, and ice tea are served along with snacks such as cookies, gummy worms, and goldfish crackers. Evening choices include a variety of fresh fruit, pineapple with caramel dipping sauce, hummus, cheese and crackers, crudités and dip, and two more appetizers such as sushi rolls, vegetable spring rolls, BBQ pork satay, pulled pork, baked brie with raspberry en croute, mini beef Wellington with red wine demi glace, sweet and sour meatballs, crabmeat rangoon, pork dumplings, chilled banana and coconut soup, green bean tomato salad with rice vinegar dressing, smoked turkey mango salad, Asian slaw, and Kona sticky wings. Wine choices include Beringer White Zinfandel, Century Cellars Chardonnay, and Canyon Road Merlot; also Ku'u'lei, a specialty alcoholic concoction. Kids enjoy mini corn dogs and PB&J sandwiches. After dinner are cordials and desserts of chocolate chip and oatmeal-raisin cookies, strawberry mousse, cream puffs, and mini chocolate tarts. There's also a self-service espresso and cappuccino machine.

Suites. All suites are located in the intimate, two-story Tonga longhouse conveniently located adjacent to the Great Ceremonial House. Continental breakfast, afternoon snacks, and evening cold appetizers are also served in the Tonga building. However, if oatmeal in the mornings and hot appetizers in the evening appeal then it will require a trek over to the Hawaii concierge lounge. And expect a bit of activity from morning until night on marina-facing suites since they front a highly trafficked sidewalk.

Suites have a complete new look, one that is quite pleasing. Gone is the Tommy Bahama décor, replaced by a more contemporary, almost Asian influence. The living area rugs vary from suite to suite with a modern bamboo pattern in neutral colors in the Ambassador Suite to a bright ginger flower motif in the King Kamehameha Suite. Slatted barrel chairs flank sleeper sofas, and in the dining rooms the slatted look continues in the chairs with cozy wood tables topped with fun, textile lighting in a rectangular shape. Love, love, love the bedroom fabrics and furnishings—cane and/or bamboo four-poster beds in a dark wood complemented by gorgeous linens with white duvets, turquoise pillows and bolsters, touches of chocolate, and neutral bed runners. In fact, I was shocked to see that they were the same fabrics as in my newly re-decorated guest bedroom at home! Drapery is neutral with delightful leaf pattern in the white-on-white sheers.

Gone also is the dated frosted glass in baths, replaced by framed gold mirrors. Vanities are cream-hued granite, the modern Asian-style lighting is a nice touch, and my favorite addition is the sparkling glass tile fronts on the cabinets.

For the ultimate vacation, try the *King Kamehameha*, a two-story beauty with two bedrooms, two and a half baths, and living room. At 1,863 square feet the upstairs master offers a balcony with views of the Castle, lagoon, and marina, a dark wood and cane king bed, entertainment center, easy chair with ottoman, an enormous two-part bath with a sink, bidet, commode, whirlpool tub, TV, and walk-in closet on one side; tub, shower, sink, and commode on the other. The sizeable second bedroom has two queen bamboo beds, easy chair with ottoman, entertainment center, desk, bath with double sinks and separate shower and tub as well as a balcony with a view of the marina and Space Mountain. Downstairs is a comfortable living area with hardwood flooring with an oversized entertainment center, beige sleeper sofa, fern-green, rounded easy chairs, and coffee table along with a dining area with eight-person table. A bar opens to a small service kitchen with undercounter refrigerator, microwave, and dishwasher. Above are gently moving paddle fans, and off the entry is a half bath. A patio spanning the length of the suite overlooks the marina, the Seven Seas Lagoon, and Cinderella Castle in the distance.

> CARA'S TIP: If you can actually find availability for all at the same time the King Kamehameha opens downstairs on one side of the living area to the Honeymoon Room (actually underneath the suite's guest bedroom), and on the other side to the 2-bedroom Princess Suite making it a 5-bedroom suite.

The two-bedroom, three-bath *Ambassador Suites* at 1,513 square feet have a living room featuring hardwood flooring, a fern motif sleeper sofa, large TV, two rounded easy chairs in a chocolate and cream graphic print, dining table for eight, sleeper sofa, large garden-view balcony or patio, wet bar, full bath off the entry, and separate kitchen with a re-frigerator, microwave, and dishwasher. The oversized master features a cane king bed, entertainment armoire, easy chair and ottoman, desk, standard-size bath with two sinks, and balcony. The second bedroom is the same size as a standard guest room with two queen bamboo beds, easy chair, bureau with TV, and another balcony. There are two Ambas-sador Suites: one on the 1st floor and one on the second with preference on request only. The downstairs suite faces a small fenced garden; the upstairs Ambassador II suite, which is hearing accessible, looks at a slice of the parking lot but also a lovely garden. Both are close to and have a view of the monorail but come with much less traffic than those suites that face the marina.

The marina/Cinderella Castle-view, two-bedroom/two-bath *Prin-cess Suite* has 1,212 square feet and is located on the ground floor. It features a small, carpeted living area with beige sleeper sofa, rounded easy chair, and two occasional chairs in a creamy white fabric along with coffee table, oversized entertainment center, granite wet bar, and patio. Off to each side of the living area are two bedrooms, one slightly larger than the other, each with two queen beds, TV, bureau, desk, easy chair, and ottoman. Each bedroom has a bath: one is a standard-type bath with double sinks in the larger bedroom; the other is a two-part and larger accessible bath with double-sink vanity, bathtub, and roll-in shower.

The resort's *One-bedroom Suite* is located on the 2nd floor just above the Princess Suite with 760 square feet and is almost identical except for the elimination of one of the bedrooms. Views are of the marina, the Seven Seas Lagoon, and, in the far distance, the Castle.

The *Honeymoon Room* is a slightly oversized standard guest room offering a marina/Space Mountain view, king bed, easy chair and ottoman, table for two, and patio. The bath is found off the foyer with a whirlpool tub, double sinks, and separate shower.

DINE

Captain Cook's Snack Bar. Located in the Great Ceremonial House with indoor and outdoor seating; open 24/7 with grill closing at 11:00 p.m. *Breakfast:* Tonga Toast (battered and deep fried banana-stuffed sourdough bread), Mickey-shaped waffle, breakfast croissant sandwich, Bounty Platter with eggs, potatoes, bacon, sausage, and French toast. *Lunch and dinner:* fish of the day, chicken sandwich, Angus bacon cheeseburger, pork nachos, grilled cheese sandwich, Aloha pork sandwich, chicken Caesar salad, stir-fried noodles with chicken, Polynesian tossed salad, flatbreads; Dole whip (soft-serve pineapple ice cream), pastries. *Children's menu:* for breakfast Mickey waffles or an egg white scramble; lunch and dinner offers cheeseburgers, grilled cheese, chicken nuggets, turkey and cheese sandwich, sweet and sour chicken stir-fry, chicken and pineapple skewer, and seasonal fish.

Kona Café. Casual dining restaurant open for breakfast, lunch, and dinner. *Breakfast:* famous Tonga Toast (batter-fried, banana-stuffed sourdough bread rolled in cinnamon sugar), macadamia pineapple pancakes, steak and eggs, poached eggs with hollandaise over smoked pulled pork hash. *Lunch:* Asian noodle bowl, barbecued pork taco, Polynesian plate lunch, sustainable fish with Swiss chard, forbidden rice, and hibiscus *beurre rouge*. *Dinner:* teriyaki style New York strip, Pan-Asian noodles with wok-seared vegetables and chicken or tofu in ginger-garlic sauce, coconut-almond chicken, *togarashi* spiced ahi tuna, Kona coffee-rubbed pork chop.

Kona Island. Quick-service stand with limited seating near the monorail platform offering specialty coffee and pastry in the morning hours, reopening at 5 PM for sushi and menu items from the adjoining Kona Café along with wine, sake, beer, and island cocktails.

Ohana. Mickey Mouse hosts a family-style *breakfast* with scrambled eggs, island style potatoes, pork sausage links, bacon, Mickey-shaped waffles, breakfast breads, and seasonal fruit. At *dinner* is an all-you-care-to-eat Polynesian feast prepared on a fire pit with mixed greens and honey-lime dressing, pork fried dumplings, coriander wings, marinated sirloin steak, Asian barbecue pork loin, mesquite grilled turkey, spicy grilled shrimp, pad Thai noodles, stir-fried vegetables, and bread pudding á la mode with bananas foster sauce.

Spirit of Aloha Dinner Show. Luau dinner show with traditional song and dance featuring hula and fire dancing from the South Seas. *Menu items*: mango slaw, mixed greens with honey-lime vinaigrette, soba noodle salad, pineapple coconut bread, roasted chicken, pulled pork, barbecue pork ribs, jasmine rice with nori, vegetable medley, and warm pineapple bread pudding with caramel sauce. *Children's meal:* macaroni and cheese, hot dog, or PB& J sandwich. Unlimited drinks including beer and wine. Held at the Luau Cove Tuesday through Saturday with a three-category pricing according to seating at 5:15 and 8:00 p.m. Call (407) WDW-DINE or (407) 939-3463 for reservations.

In-Room Dining. Available 6:30 a.m. to midnight.

SIP

Barefoot Pool Bar. Volcano Pool thatch-roofed bar for beer, wine, sangria, and tropical alcoholic and nonalcoholic drinks, open noon until the Magic Kingdom fireworks.

Tambu Lounge. Located upstairs in the Great Ceremonial House overlooking the pool and the Seven Seas Lagoon in the distance. Tropical drinks, some served in hollowed-out pineapples and coconuts, wine, and beer. Appetizers of honey-coriander or spicy wings, pulled pork nachos, Kona coffee barbecued pork sliders, beef satay with *chimichurri* sauce, crisp breads with sun-dried tomato pesto, roasted red pepper hummus, and baba ghanoush dips. Open 1:00 p.m. to midnight with appetizers served 5:00 to 10:00 p.m.; best late at night after next-door Ohana closes.

PLAY

Arcade. Moana Mickey's Arcade is located next to Captain Cook's Snack Company with the latest in video equipment.

Beaches. Three idyllic beaches with perfect vistas of the Seven Seas Lagoon and Magic Kingdom; swimming is prohibited in the lagoon. All beaches have lounge chairs (some covered), beach hammocks, and swings with prime viewing for the Magic Kingdom fireworks. *Best view*: beach in front of the Tahiti longhouse. *Closest to Volcano Pool*: beach in front of Hawaii longhouse. *Most secluded*: beach on the Grand Floridian side of the property.

Bicycles. Two and four-seater surrey bicycles are for rent at the marina.

Boating. Boat rentals available at the Mikala Canoe Club Marina with Sea Raycers, 17' Boston Whaler Montauks, 21' Suntracker pontoons, and 14-foot Hobie catamaran. Also offered is a fireworks boating excursion with driver (call 407-WDW-PLAY or 407-939-7529 for reservations).

Children's activities and playground. Arts and crafts daily in the Great Ceremonial House, noon to 2:00 p.m.; beach and pool games, bingo, noodle races, hula hoop, Disney trivia, sandcastles on the beach. Hula dancing lessons in the lobby and a pool party each afternoon. Campfire followed by Movies Under the Stars nightly on the Volcano Pool beach.

Electrical Water Pageant. On the Seven Seas Lagoon nightly at 9:00 best viewed from the beach, Ohana restaurant, or a lagoon-view room; may be canceled due to inclement weather. Delightful 1,000-foot string of illuminated barges features King Neptune and his court of whales, sea serpents, and other deep-sea creatures.

Fishing. Guided two-hour fishing excursion for as many as five people include boat, guide, gear, and non-alcoholic beverages; catch-and-release only (call 407-WDW-BASS or 407-939-2277 for reservations).

Jogging. A one-mile scenic jogging path runs along the Seven Seas Lagoon between the Polynesian and Grand Floridian Resorts.

Swimming. Nanea Volcano Pool features a smoking volcano slide, underwater music, sparkling waterfall, and kiddie water play area, all with a superb view of the Seven Seas Lagoon. The Quieter East Pool is located in the gardens area.

Mauna Loa, a canvas-sided cabana, is located in a raised position next to the Volcano Pool and includes a cabana attendant, two padded lounge and four standard chairs, 32-inch LCD TV, DVD/CD/MP3 player, ceiling fan, mini-refrigerator stocked with sodas and water, and fruit basket for $185 full-day or $110 for half-day rentals. Nestled against the beach is the thatch-roofed and raised Kilauea premium cabana with cabana host, luxury furnishings and 55-inch TV inside, lounge chairs on the cabana deck, and a six-person dining table, two oversized chairs, and umbrellas next to the beach for a $300 full-day rental.

Volleyball. A sand court is located on the beach between the Hawaii and Tahiti buildings with complimentary equipment at Mikala Canoe Club Marina.

WORK, MOVE, SOOTHE

Childcare. The Never Land Club's Peter Pan–themed facility offers a replica of Wendy's bedroom, arcade games, arts and crafts, and Disney classic movies and cartoons on a giant screen. Open 4:00 p.m. to midnight only to registered guests of the Walt Disney World Resort for potty-trained children ages three to twelve. Cost includes dinner; call (407) 939-3463 for reservations. NOTE: The Never Land Club will be closed through the end of 2014.

Spa and fitness center. *Senses–A Disney Spa at Disney's Grand Floridian* Resort is located between the Grand Floridian and the Polynesian (see previous entry on the Grand Floridian Resort).

GO

Transportation choices to the Magic Kingdom include both monorail and water launch. To reach Epcot walk to the Transportation and Ticket Center (TTC)—you'll find signage throughout the resort—and hop on a direct monorail. Catch a direct bus to Disney's Hollywood Studios, Animal Kingdom, Downtown Disney, Typhoon Lagoon, and Blizzard Beach. Take the monorail or water launch or follow the walking path to the Grand Floridian Resort (about a ten-minute walk). To reach the Contemporary Resort utilize the Monorail.

To reach other Disney resorts during park operating hours, take the monorail to the Magic Kingdom and pick up a bus to your resort destination. After park hours take a bus to Downtown Disney and then transfer to your resort destination.

Disney's Wilderness Lodge

725 rooms. 901 Timberline Drive, Lake Buena Vista, FL 32830; phone (407) 824-3200, fax (407) 824-3232. Check-in 3:00 p.m., checkout 11:00 a.m. For reservations contact your travel advisor or call (407) 939-3476.

Claim To Fame. Surrounded by nature you'll feel as if you're ensconced in a lodge out West.

Room To Book. The Yosemite and the Yellowstone Suites, some of Disney's most reasonably priced top accommodations.

The Wow Factor! The resort's geyser show occurring every hour on the shore of Bay Lake.

Teddy Roosevelt would exclaim "bully" to Disney's dramatic depiction of an early 1900s national park lodge. I challenge you to keep your jaw from dropping open on your first encounter with its awesome eight-story lobby. A marvel of timber, sheer walls of lodgepole pine logs and rugged rock surround the huge, open expanse filled with oversize leather chairs and Native American crafts of beaded moccasins, feathered headdresses, textiles, and drums. Two authentic 55-foot Pacific Northwest totem poles overlook rustic stone and hardwood floors topped with Native American rugs, tepee-topped chandeliers, and a bevy of "park ranger" staff who roam the lodge attending to guests. A favorite pastime is relaxing in rocking chairs fronting the massive, 82-foot-tall fireplace composed of rockwork replicating the diverse strata of the Grand Canyon. Another is finding peace and quiet in the seductive nooks and crannies on the floors above the lobby or on the back porch rockers that overlook a serene scene of natural beauty.

Seven floors of guest rooms are to be found above the lobby level, and two six-story wings composed of quarry stone, chunky logs, and green tin rooftops are surrounded by an enchanting scene of roaring waterfalls, rushing creeks, and towering pines. What begins in the lobby as a bubbling hot spring turns into Silver Creek which in turn widens to become a sparkling waterfall emptying into the boulder-lined, hot springs–style swimming pool, one of Disney's best. Listen for crickets chirping beneath the bridges and along the meandering pathways lined with natural grasses, junipers, sotols, and wildflowers. On the shore of Bay Lake the resort's very own re-created geyser, surrounded by a steaming expanse of geothermal activity, erupts at the top of every hour from early morning to late night. Take an after-dark stroll when the waterfall is lit and the scenery is even more spectacular.

REST

Guest rooms. Those who have experienced other deluxe Disney resorts might be surprised by the smallish guest rooms here measuring only 340 square feet. Though pleasant, they are a tight squeeze lacking even the room for a sitting area. Bedding is either two queen-size beds or a king-size bed (wheelchair-accessible rooms). There's even an option of a queen-size bed with a set of bunk beds, an extremely popular choice with the kids (if you book guaranteed connecting rooms with a bunk bed your second guest room will have two queen beds). Inside you'll find a freshly renovated look. Gone is the hunter green color scheme and bedspreads, all replaced with crisp white duvets, striking royal blue runners in a Navaho design, and cranberry red throw pillows with a Thumper theme. Carpeting is a burnt orange, blue, and tan Native American print, walls are butter yellow, and a large flat-screen TV is built into a dark wood bureau accented in blue stripes. Headboards are padded red leather with a carved woodland scene, and linens are triple-sheeted with nice downy pillows. A second bureau is located in the foyer.

All rooms come with a table and two chairs, undercounter refrigerator, keyed safe, iPod clock radio, and coffeemaker. Bathrooms, a few feet smaller than other deluxe resorts, have attractive black/gold granite countertops in the separate vanity area holding two sinks; an adjoining bathtub/commode area is embellished with accent tiles featuring Meeko, Bambi, Chip 'n Dale. There's no makeup mirror, but the full-length mirror, curved shower curtain, and rain showerhead are a plus.

Other room amenities include a keyed safe, iron and ironing board, and daily newspaper.

Room view choices include: *Standard View* with a look at either the parking lot, service area, or rooftops; *Woods View* of either the forested area facing the Magic Kingdom and the Contemporary Resort (views of the park and the fireworks are mostly obscured by the trees) or the next-door Disney's Villas at Wilderness Lodge; picturesque *Courtyard View* of the pool and/or Bay Lake. Sixth-floor rooms in the outer wings closer to the lake come with dormer balconies that require standing for a view.

Concierge rooms. Concierge rooms on the 7th floor include standard rooms with a variety of views, four Honeymoon Rooms, and the Vice Presidential and Presidential Suites. All 7th-floor concierge rooms have dormer balconies that require standing for a view.

Although none are located on the club level's 7th floor, *Deluxe Rooms* do come with concierge privileges. At 500 square feet and sleeping six these rooms offer a comfortable but not huge balconied parlor area holding a queen-size sofa sleeper, two brown leather chairs, small table and two chairs, coffee table, flat-screen TV, wet bar, coffeemaker, and small refrigerator. The bedroom, separated by a frosted glass French door from the parlor, has two queen-size beds, TV, and a French-style, stand-up balcony. The double-sink bathroom with separate commode and shower area can be accessed from either the bedroom or the foyer. Most of these rooms come with some sort of water view some of which are nicely screened by trees.

Although they're the same size as a standard room the *Honeymoon Rooms* just feel larger because they come with only one king-size bed, leaving more room to walk around. Their claim to fame is a large whirlpool tub perfect for romance. They also have a table with two chairs and clothes bureau with built-in flat-screen TV. Two of the suites offer a not-so-great look at the rooftops and Disney's Villas at Wilderness Lodge in the distance, while the other two enjoy a view of the Seven Seas Lagoon, the Grand Floridian, the Contemporary, and just a small peek of the Magic Kingdom fireworks; preference is on request only.

Concierge guests receive the services of an accommodating private staff and access to the *Old Faithful Club*. Additional concierge amenities include DVD players, robes, and nightly turndown service. A scattering of tables set up around the balcony overlook the lobby, and a sizeable serving room adds to the appeal.

Breakfast consists of fresh fruit, juice, yogurt, pastries, cereal, oatmeal, mini bagels and muffins, cinnamon rolls, croissants, and afternoon snacks are potato chips and dip, goldfish crackers, nuts, fruit, gummy bears, sugar and chocolate chip cookies. Evenings bring hearty food catered from either Whispering Canyon Café or Artist Point where the spread includes cold items such as antipasti salad, cheese, smoked portobello mushroom salad, edamame with sea salt, turkey and cheese rollups, and arugula salad with black beans, feta, and oranges. Also served are two hot dishes such as chili, venison meatballs with curry sauce, BBQ chicken skewers, mini pulled pork sandwiches, ancho chili-rubbed scallops wrapped in bacon, spicy chicken skewers, duck pot stickers, cod chowder, and Black Angus tenderloin stew. Wine offerings are Two Vines Chardonnay and Merlot, and Columbia Crest Cabernet. There's also a self-service cappuccino machine. After dinner wine and cordials are served with scrumptious PB&J shooters, hot cobbler or crisps, chocolate chip cookies, brownies, and rightly famous Magic Bars.

Suites. The 885-square-foot *Vice Presidential Suite, also known as the Yosemite Suite,* is outfitted in upscale Western featuring rawhide curtains, branding-iron towel bars, wood-paneled walls, Native American artwork, and lodgepole trim. The living area offers a distressed leather sleeper sofa, two leather easy chairs, oversized desk, Remington-style lamp and framed prints, and an armoire with a flat-screen TV, DVD player, and stereo. A wooden walk-in bar is complete with swinging doors, microwave, undercounter refrigerator, sink, blender, Keurig coffeemaker, and two carved cowboy motif leather barstools. The small dining room has hardwood flooring with a circular, four-person table. Off the entry hall is a half bath with single sink. An amazing balcony, actually nicer than the resort's Presidential Suite because it's deeper, wraps around the living and dining area with marvelous views of the resort's pool and geyser as well as sparkling Bay Lake. In the bedroom is a king bed with western-style bedding, drum lamps, a carved wooden armoire with flat-screen TV, and leather easy chair and ottoman. The only disappointing aspect of the suite is the master bath's ultra-sensitive, automatic motion-detector vent fan that turns on upon entering the bath for irritating 30-second intervals. There's also the earth-toned mosaic tile that you either love or hate, and lack of good lighting and makeup mirror. Its pluses are the oversized, oval whirlpool tub, double sinks, and giant separate shower. The Yosemite Suite is one of the better-priced V.P. suites at the Disney Deluxe properties and certainly one to consider for a nice upgrade.

On the opposite side of the courtyard you'll find the 1,000-square-foot *Presidential Suite, also known as the Yellowstone Suite,* a true delight with shiny hardwood flooring, an elk-horn chandelier, and balconies running the length of this corner suite overlooking Bay Lake and the pool. The living area comes with a leather/chenille sleeper sofa, coffee table, three easy chairs (one leather), and wet bar with sink, under-counter refrigerator, microwave, coffeemaker, and dishes. A rustic dining table is separated from the living room by a granite buffet/bar. Off the foyer is a half bath as well as a cozy office with a balcony overlooking the courtyard. The bedroom has a king-sized bed, entertainment center, leather easy chair, and ottoman. An attractive chocolate and black marble bathroom has two sink areas, a commode and bidet in a separate room, vanity, a large stand-alone shower, and enormous tub.

DINE

Artist Point. Pacific Northwest cuisine and wine with views of Bay Lake and the courtyard waterfall, open for dinner only. (See full description in Dining in Style at Walt Disney World Resort.)

Roaring Forks Snacks. Quick-service dining either inside or out (a picturesque outdoor area is near the pool). *Breakfast:* waffles (banana foster, strawberry and cream, or chocolate), breakfast croissant sandwich, scrambled egg platter, pancakes with bacon, oatmeal, grits, create-your-own yogurt parfait. *Lunch and dinner:* Angus bacon cheeseburger, chicken breast nuggets, grilled chicken sandwich with Canadian bacon and cheddar, pasta of the day, turkey and dill Havarti sandwich, roast beef and blue cheese sandwich, barbecued pork and slaw sandwich, ham and cheddar panini, grilled chicken and apple salad, Caesar salad with chicken, chili, flatbreads. *Children's menu*: turkey sandwich, PB&J sandwich, hamburger, chicken nuggets, pizza.

Whispering Canyon Café. Kids adore this place where smoked meats are served along with plenty of hootin' and hollerin', open breakfast, lunch, and dinner for Western-style fun and hearty food. *Breakfast*: eggs benedict, slow smoked barbecue pulled pork and over-easy egg sandwich, chicken apple-raisin hash with eggs, banana bread French toast, chocolate chip buttermilk pancakes. *Lunch:* Angus bacon and egg burger with Tillamook cheese, fish and chips, tuna melt on sourdough, smoked chicken quesadilla, Kansas City-style smoked pork ribs, pulled pork sandwich. *Dinner:* build your own family platter with your choice of three meats plus sides of vegetables, potatoes, baked beans, corn on the cob and dessert sampler, sautéed red quinoa cakes with edamame salsa and greens, grilled buffalo meatloaf, citrus-glazed rainbow trout.

In-Room Dining. Available 7:00 a.m. to midnight.

SIP

Territory Lounge. Rustic atmosphere of lodge pole pine posts, old territorial maps, prints of the American West, vintage surveyor equipment, and carved wooden bears. Pacific Northwest wine, beer, martinis, specialty drinks and coffees along with appetizers of Asian fried boneless chicken with sweet Thai chili sauce, Northwest charcuterie and artisan cheese platter, sharp cheddar-beer fondue, wild mushroom flatbread, Northwest chips with a trio of dips, steamed edamame, onion soup, Artist Point cobbler, and drunken donuts with a maple-liquor glaze.

Trout Pass Pool Bar. Log cabin pool bar. Specialty drinks, beer, wine, sangria, frozen non-alcoholic beverages, full bar.

PLAY

Arcade. Buttons and Bells Game Arcade with state-of-the-art video games for all levels.

Beach. The smallish Bay Lake Beach is nestled against tall pine trees.

Bicycles. Bicycles and two- and four-seat surreys are rentable at the marina for exploration of wilderness trails connecting to Fort Wilderness.

Boating. Rentals available for the enjoyment of Bay Lake and the Seven Seas Lagoon at Teton Boat Rentals including Sea Raycers, 17' Boston Whaler Montauks, and 21' Sun Tracker pontoon boats. Wishes fireworks cruise. Call 407-WDW-PLAY or 407-939-7529 for reservations.

Children's activities and playground. A children's playground is located on the beach. Activities include chalk art, giant board games, temporary tattoos, sandcastle building, duck races, beach games, bingo, and pool volleyball. Campfire followed by Movies Under the Stars nightly on the beach. Magic Cookie Hour at Roaring Fork. Next door just a boat ride away, Fort Wilderness offers pony rides and nightly carriage and wagon rides (extra fee), and a complimentary sing-along campfire, marshmallow roast, and Disney movie program hosted by Chip 'n Dale.

Electrical Water Pageant. On the Seven Seas Lagoon nightly at 9:35 and best viewed from the beach, boat dock, or a Bay Lake–facing room; may be canceled due to inclement weather. Delightful 1,000-foot string of illuminated barges features King Neptune and his court of whales, sea serpents, and other deep-sea creatures.

Fishing. Two-hour fishing excursion for as many as five guests includes boat, fishing equipment, and guide; catch-and-release only. Call 407-WDW-BASS or 407-939-2277 for reservations.

Jogging. Jogging paths connect to Disney's Fort Wilderness where several trails through a forest of pines and along Bay Lake make for pleasant exercise routes.

Swimming. A top attraction at Wilderness Lodge is its boulder-lined, freeform Silver Springs Creek Pool featuring waterfalls, rocky overlooks, waterslide, nearby geyser, kiddie pool, and two whirlpools.

Volleyball. Sand volleyball court is located on Bay Lake Beach; pick up equipment at Teton Boat Rentals.

Wilderness Back Trail Adventure Segway Tour. Explore next-door Fort Wilderness on a two-hour Segway Tour. Offered Tuesday–Saturday for $90 per person, meet at the Bike Barn at Fort Wilderness. Call 407-WDW-TOUR for reservations.

Wonders of the Lodge Art and Architecture Tour. Complimentary ranger-led exploration of the art, artifacts, and craftsmanship of the resort. Check your resort guide for day and time, no reservation necessary.

WORK, MOVE, SOOTHE

Childcare. The Cub's Den features games and activities, Northwestern arts and crafts, and Disney movies. Open 4:30 p.m. to midnight for potty-trained cubs ages three to twelve for registered guests of any Disney-owned property. Cost includes dinner and late snack. Call (407) WDW-DINE or (407) 939-3463 for reservations.

Fitness Center. Sturdy Branches Health Club located at the adjoining Villas at Wilderness Lodge with 24-hour access offers Life Fitness treadmills, ellipticals, and bicycles, Cybex strength training equipment, and free weights. Complimentary to resort guests. Massage and facials available by appointment, including in-room.

GO

Since the monorail doesn't reach this neck of the woods, Wilderness Lodge is definitely less accessible than other Magic Kingdom resorts. Take the bus to the Magic Kingdom or, better yet, the Red Flag water launch departing from the Northwest Dock and Ferry (a separate area from the marina) to the Magic Kingdom. The Blue Flag water launch heads to the Contemporary Resort and Fort Wilderness. There is a direct bus to Epcot, Disney's Hollywood Studios, Animal Kingdom, Downtown Disney, Typhoon Lagoon, and Blizzard Beach.

To reach other Disney resorts during park operating hours take the boat to the Magic Kingdom and pick up a bus or monorail from there to your resort destination. After park hours take a bus to Downtown Disney and then transfer to the resort.

MUST-DO'S FOR A LUXURY WALT DISNEY WORLD VACATION

Would you like to create a perfect Walt Disney World vacation? Here are a few ideas to make that dream come true!

Charter the Grand I Yacht

For the ultimate in luxury, charter Disney's 52-foot Sea Ray yacht moored at Disney's Grand Floridian Resort, perfect for pampered VIP guests. It's available for a morning spin, a sunset cruise, or the ultimate viewing location for the Wishes fireworks show. Consider an elegant evening beginning with a sunset champagne cruise followed by viewing the Wishes fireworks extravaganza from the Seven Seas Lagoon. Or, spend an afternoon exploring the nearby resorts with a bevy of snacks to keep the appetite at bay as you sail past the beaches of the romantic Polynesian Resort and the Grand Floridian's Wedding Pavilion, check out the geyser on the shores of Wilderness Lodge, and watch the parasailing action around the Contemporary Resort.

Indulge at Victoria & Albert's

Fine dining in a stunning setting combined with virtually flawless service sets Victoria & Albert's apart. Overseen by the brilliant Chef de Cuisine Scott Hunnel and awarded the AAA Five Diamond and the Wine Spectator Best of Award of Excellence year after year, this is Disney's true gastronomic temple. And every year it keeps reinventing itself, raising the bar even higher. A seasonal prix fixe menu includes seven sumptuous courses served by an ultra-professional wait staff, accompanied by an expert harpist. Or for a truly special evening, reserve the Chef's Table in the kitchen or the Queen Victoria Room where ten to twelve innovative courses are served. Indulge in one exemplary dish after another, every morsel with its own distinctive flavor, no one ingredient overwhelming the other—the food is simply a work of art.

Pamper Yourself with a Spa Day

When your muscles are aching and your body is screaming for rest after days at the parks, soothe your jangled nerves at one of

Disney's spas. Immerse yourself in luxury with a feel-good treatment or two, guaranteed to rejuvenate and swiftly get you back on
your feet. Try nirvana for a day at the Walt Disney World Dolphin
Hotel's Mandara Spa where you'll begin with a Deep Tissue Massage made extra special with heated stones, followed by an Elemis
Facial. Enjoy a light lunch in the spa's Meru Temple, ending your
day with a Hand and Foot Ritual.

Reserve a VIP Tour

Make your visit to the theme parks as seamless and easy as possible
with Disney's personalized theme park tours. A Disney VIP guide
will maximize your time by assisting you and up to nine others with
a customized day at the parks and plenty of Disney trivia along the
way. Don't expect to move to the front of the line, but do expect
perks such as door-to-door transportation with back-door entrance
to the theme parks, expedited entry to FASTPASS attractions, and
special seating for parades, stage shows, and dining. It's a true indulgence but one that is well worth the steep price tag!

Reach for the Sky with Disney Signature Dreams

Would you like to create something truly magical for your family
and friends or live out a special story? Disney has a way to help you
make your dreams come true through the amazing and creative
team at Disney Signature Dreams. From immersive experiences
with you and your loved ones inside your favorite stories, to unexpected surprises and moments of true wonder, Disney can make it
happen for you. Just wish for your very own dream come true and
they'll create it!

Epcot Area Resorts

Those with older children who plan to spend plenty of time at Epcot
and Disney's Hollywood Studios should strongly consider selecting one
of the resorts in this terrific area of Walt Disney World. Disney's Beach
Club Resort, Disney's BoardWalk Inn, Disney's Yacht Club Resort, the
Walt Disney World Swan, and the Walt Disney World Dolphin all front

Crescent Lake, and all are within walking distance or a boat ride to Epcot, Disney's Hollywood Studios, and Disney's BoardWalk. With such easy access to so many resorts and Epcot just a few minutes away, you'll find more restaurant and entertainment choices than you can count.

Disney's Beach Club Resort

> 583 rooms. 1800 Epcot Resorts Boulevard, Lake Buena Vista, FL 32830; phone (407) 934-8000, fax (407) 934-3850. Check-in 3:00 p.m., checkout 11:00 a.m. For reservations contact your travel advisor or call (407) 939-3476.

Claim To Fame. Super easy access to Epcot just a 5-minute walk away.

Room To Book. A Lagoon View Concierge room with a panorama of Crescent Lake and access to the Stone Harbor Club.

The Wow Factor! Access to Stormalong Bay, Disney's best swimming pool complex.

Five-story, blue and white, "stick-style" buildings fronting a white-sand beach bordered with soft sea grass bring to mind late-nineteenth-century Cape May. In the airy, pastel lobby are high ceilings and limestone flooring centered by a seahorse chandelier. However, the chenille seating and curtained alcove sitting areas add little to create what should be a seaside ambience. Please don't expect a calm atmosphere anywhere near the lobby since there always seem to be crowds of diners waiting their turn at the popular Cape May Café, which may be the explanation (if there can be one) for the worn, tattered look of the seating here. For peace and quiet head outside where white rockers invite you to sit on the back porch, or to the sunny solarium with views of the resort's lovely gardens and the next-door Beach Club Villas where a variety of crape myrtles, gardenias, and roses reside.

The resort's highlight is the fantastic *Stormalong Bay*, a winding wonderland of a small-scale water park shared with the Yacht Club. Since this is the closest resort to Epcot it offers super easy access to the International Gateway entrance, a convenience that can't be beat. If room balconies are an important component to your vacation then choose a room over at the Yacht Club instead, where full-size balconies are found in every guest room (the majority of the Beach Club's room

balconies are standing-room-only). And if you prefer a quieter, less bustling environment, once again, I would choose the Yacht Club where a calmer setting is the norm.

REST

Guest rooms. Sporting 400 square feet and bedecked in a sea-blue and chocolate color scheme, guest rooms boast cheerful striped curtains, white duvets with soft, sea blue bed runners, and shutter-style distressed cherry wood headboards. Above a large cottage-white bureau is a wall-mounted flat-screen TV with an additional bureau in the foyer. In the room's corner sits a work desk with a Lifeguard Mickey lamp; some also come with a daybed sleeping one person. The lively decor continues in the bath where a sailing ship motif shower curtain and wallpaper adorn a separate tub and commode area of pale gold ceramic tile. Outside, there's a gray and white marble vanity, two sinks, non-lighted makeup mirror, and hair dryer. Amenities include a keyed safe, iron and ironing board, coffeemaker, refrigerator, iPod docking station clock radio, and daily newspaper.

> CARA'S TIP: Remember, standard-view rooms will have a view of the parking lot and the front of the resort, possibly even the valet area. If too much walking is not your idea of a vacation request a room close to the lobby since the resort is quite spread out, and long treks to your room are not uncommon.

Concierge rooms. Fifth-floor concierge-level rooms include the amenities of the *Stone Harbor Club*, a small but cozy lounge (one that tends to be a bit crowded and frenzied when the occupancy level is high) with complimentary food and beverages throughout the day. A balcony can be found off the lounge, but, unlike the one at the Yacht Club, this one, also overlooking the front of the resort, is stand-up only. Mornings bring coffee with a self-service cappuccino machine, juice, coffee cake, muffins, croissants, bagels, cinnamon rolls, banana bread, pastries, oatmeal, yogurt, hard-boiled eggs, fruit, and cereal. Midday Seaside Snacks consist of homemade potato chips with roasted red pepper ranch dip, Swedish fish, yogurt-covered pretzels, trail mix, fruit, cookies, lemonade, apple juice, and iced tea. Early evening wine choices are Penfolds Rawson's Retreat Merlot, Beringer White Zinfandel, Mirassou Pinot

Noir, and Columbia Crest Chardonnay along with an assortment of beer. Hors d'oeuvres include such items as hummus, crudités, artisan cheese and crackers, potato salad, orzo pasta salad, broccoli slaw, mozzarella and tomato salad, lobster salad, gravlax, mussels, seaweed and seared tuna, and Israeli couscous salad along with a hot item like potato and fennel fritters, ginger pork pot stickers, vegetable spring rolls with sweet chili sauce, conch fritters, red pepper and goat cheese in phyllo, crab rangoon, grilled chicken skewers with yogurt cucumber sauce, bacon-wrapped scallops with mustard dipping sauce, and spanakopita (kids feast on make-it-yourself peanut butter and jelly rolls and apple slices with caramel dipping sauce). After dinner is a selection of cordials and desserts such as raspberry or chocolate/peanut butter mousse, lemon cheesecake, chocolate cake, brownies, caramelized cheesecake, mini cupcakes, and Oreo bonbons.

Additional room amenities for concierge guests include the services of a friendly concierge staff, private check-in and checkout, DVD players, and nightly turndown service.

Suites. Located on the same floor as the 5th-floor concierge lounge the 2,200-square-foot *Presidential Newport Suite* has a large marble foyer leading to a living room with a somewhat small seating area sporting a sofa, two easy chairs, and seahorse motif fireplace on one side, wet bar and dining room with seating for eight on the other. Attractive drapery with a coral motif embellishes the wall of living room windows, but the overall look is overwhelmed by the sea blue carpeting, some of it studded with Ariel's sea friends, Flounder and Sebastian. In the colossal master bedroom the delicate furnishings almost look lost even though it's filled with a four-poster king bed with a linen floral spread, desk, settee, armoire, and loads of windows. The marble master bath holds a whirlpool tub, separate toilet area with bidet, shower, mini TV, double sinks, and small walk-in closet, but the sea blue coral-themed wallpaper clashes oddly with the terra cotta marble flooring making the bath somewhat disconcerting. What I do like is the second bedroom, actually the size of a one-bedroom suite with two queen beds in an upgraded sea-blue bedding, standard-size bath, walk-in closet, balcony, and separate sitting area with desk, daybed, and balcony. Three extended balconies almost

encircle the suite affording views of the gardens, Stormalong Bay, the garden pool, and lagoon. A half bath is found near the foyer.

Also located on the fifth-floor is the smallish *Vice Presidential Nantucket Suite*. With only 996 square feet this one-bedroom, one-and-a-half-bath suite offers the same unattractive pastel blue look as the Newport Suite. A diminutive parlor wallpapered in yellow stripes contains a coral sofa, coffee table, and easy chair. Behind closet doors is a wet bar with microwave and small refrigerator. There is a four-person dining table, desk, armoire strangely painted with a balloon scene, and a balcony overlooking a quiet garden courtyard. The bedroom has a four-poster king bed with floral linen spread, entertainment armoire, desk, and a small standing-room-only balcony facing Stormalong Bay. In the bath are a whirlpool tub, separate shower, double sinks, mini TV, and unfortunately the same clashing wallpaper and marble as the Newport Suite. Sleeps only two.

> CARA'S TIP: Both the Presidential Newport Suite and the V.P. Nantucket Suite are probably my least favorite of the Disney Deluxe Resorts top suites; I'm just not a fan of the pastel, old-fashioned décor. Although the TVs, soft goods, and sofas were upgraded in the last few years it's time to completely upgrade the furnishings with a much needed, new look more in line with the standard guest rooms.

Enter *Two-bedroom Suites* through a small marble foyer to a living area with a table and two chairs, sofa, easy chair, coffee table, bureau, wall-mounted flat-screen TV, and wet bar with coffeemaker and undercounter refrigerator. Off the living area is a long, narrow bathroom with a double-sink vanity and a separate shower/tub and toilet area. The smallish master bedroom is accessed through French doors with a standard guest room on the opposite side of the living area. These accommodate a maximum of seven people in 1,095 square feet and are all located on floors one through four.

One-bedroom Suites at 726 square feet offer a small parlor with a daybed, coffee table, and flat-screen TV. Through French doors enter the bedroom with its king bed, desk, daybed, second TV, and love seat. A standard-size bath and walk-in closet are located off the parlor with a

balcony running the length of the suite. Sleeps four and are all located on floors one through four.

Deluxe Concierge Rooms are corner rooms found on every floor except the 5th. At 533 square feet they afford extra room for a more comfortable stay although there really isn't a larger bath or more seating and bedding than that of a standard room, only a wider, longer room with more space for moving around. Just past a small marble foyer is a standard-size bath, then the sleeping area with two queen beds and a daybed set in a small alcove. The small balcony is a stand-up only although it comes with a nice view of Crescent Lake. Interestingly enough the Deluxe Concierge Rooms are less expensive than a Water/pool View Concierge Room with only 400 square feet, the difference being that the Water/pool Concierge Rooms have a more convenient location on the 5th floor with easier access to the concierge lounge.

DINE

Beach Club Marketplace. Located within the Atlantic Wear and Wardrobe store. *Breakfast:* scrambled egg platter, breakfast sandwich, oatmeal, fresh-baked pastries, muffins, bagels, and croissants. *Lunch and dinner:* individual flatbreads, roast beef sandwich with gravy, turkey sandwich with cranberry brie spread, ham and Swiss sandwich, quinoa vegetable wrap, New England clam chowder, soup of the day. *Children's menu:* scrambled eggs or French toast bread pudding for breakfast, and turkey sandwich or margarita pizza for lunch and dinner.

Beaches & Cream Soda Shop. Disney's best milk shake and ice cream stop, open for lunch and dinner. The menu includes a bacon Angus burger, turkey sub, grilled vegetable sandwich, chicken Caesar sandwich, pot roast sandwich, grilled cheese and tomato bisque, chopped Caesar salad with chicken, chili, Rachel sandwich with pastrami, and a hot dog with coleslaw and sautéed peppers. A huge array of ice cream desserts includes sundaes, shakes, malts, brownie a la mode, apple-cranberry pie, and ice cream sodas.

Cape May Café. *Breakfast buffet with Goofy and friends:* yogurt bar, fresh fruit, cereals, breakfast potatoes, bacon and sausage, smoked salmon with garnishes, cheeses and deli meats, hot quinoa cereal and oatmeal, cheddar grits, biscuits with gravy, healthy grains fruit salad, French toast with caramelized bananas, frittatas, scrambled eggs, Mickey waffles. *Evening New England–style clambake buffet:* New England seafood chowder, a variety of fresh salads, mashed potatoes, vegetable pasta, steamed red potatoes, corn on the cob, steamed mussels, paella, snow crab legs, steamed clams, baked seasonal fish, fried clams and shrimp, hand-carved strip loin, assorted desserts.

In-Room Dining. Available 24/7.

SIP

Hurricane Hanna's Grill. Poolside bar and grill with full bar, cocktails, beer, alcoholic and nonalcoholic frozen drinks. *Lunch and dinner:* light meals of sea salt fries, chilled shrimp with cocktail sauce, pulled pork sliders, bacon Angus cheeseburger, grilled chicken breast sandwich, grilled cheese and smoked bacon sandwich, chopped green salad with turkey and blue cheese, and vegetarian quinoa wrap. *Children's menu:* grilled cheese, grilled chicken sandwich, chicken nuggets, cheeseburger.

Martha's Vineyard. This cocktail lounge, almost devoid of atmosphere, adjoins Cape May Café offering a full bar, wine, beer, and specialty drinks. Appetizers of New England clam chowder, peel and eat shrimp cocktail, teriyaki BBQ ribs, and buffalo chicken breast nuggets.

PLAY

Arcade. Lafferty Place Arcade is located next to Beaches and Cream soda shop.

Beach. An enticing white-sand beach dotted with lounge chairs fronts Crescent Lake with views of the BoardWalk and the Epcot fireworks; swimming not allowed in Crescent Lake.

Bicycles. Rent bicycles from the Bayside Marina.

Children's playground and activities. A playground is located near Stormalong Bay. Poolside activities such as chalk art, beanbag toss, Hula Hoop, relay races, Frisbee and water balloon toss. A poolside party occurs each afternoon, and ceramics are offered each Wednesday at the Sandcastle Club for a fee. A campfire and marshmallow roast followed by Movies Under the Stars takes place each evening on the beach.

Children ages 4-12 set sail on the Albatross Treasure Cruise in search of pirate booty on Crescent Lake and the World Showcase Lagoon each Monday, Wednesday, and Friday at 9:30 a.m. ($34). Call 407-WDW-PLAY for reservations.

Fishing. See PLAY section for Disney's Yacht Club Resort.

Jogging. Either the circular 0.75-mile boardwalk or the path encircling the canal leading to Disney's Hollywood Studios can serve as a jogging track.

Swimming. Stormalong Bay, a freeform, miniature water park complex, meanders between the Beach and Yacht Club. The most divine pool at Disney, its three acres of winding, watery delight offer sandy-bottom pools, a 230-foot-long "shipwreck" waterslide, a snorkeling lagoon, tidal whirlpool, bubbling hot tubs, a kiddie pool with its own slide next to the beach, plenty of sand for castle building, and enough length to float lazily in inner tubes to your heart's content. The quiet Tidal Pool and whirlpool are located at the Epcot end of the resort; another at the Dolphin end of the Yacht Club. All pools are heated.

Tennis. See PLAY section in subsequent entry for Disney's Yacht Club Resort.

Volleyball. Sand court located at the Beach Club Resort near the quiet Tidal Pool; equipment can be checked out at Ship Shape Health Club.

WORK, MOVE, SOOTHE

Childcare. Sandcastle Club featuring video and board games, arts and crafts, Disney movies, and play kitchen. Open 4:30 p.m. to midnight for potty-trained children ages three to twelve; cost includes dinner and late night cookies and milk. Open only to registered guests of the Yacht Club, Beach Club, Beach Club Villas, and BoardWalk Inn and Villas. Call (407) WDW-DINE or (407) 939-3463 for reservations.

Fitness Center. The newly renovated Ship Shape Massage-Salon-Fitness is a combination fitness center/spa/salon with a Senses Spa feel. Cybex strength training machines, Life Fitness treadmills, bicycles, elliptical machines, and free weights are complimentary to resort guests with 24-hour access. Massage and facials available in one of four treatment rooms including a couple's room; 8:00 a.m. to 8:00 p.m. including in-room massage. Salon services including shampoo, cuts, blow-dry, foils, manicure, and pedicures available 9:00 a.m. to 6:00 p.m.

GO

Although boat transportation is available to Epcot, it's quicker to walk to the park than to walk to the marina to catch the boat. Take the watercraft launch to Disney's Hollywood Studios from the Bayside Marina at the Yacht Club. The BoardWalk is a stroll around the lagoon.

Bus service is available to the Magic Kingdom, Animal Kingdom, Typhoon Lagoon, Blizzard Beach, and Downtown Disney. To reach other Disney resorts outside of the Epcot area, you must first bus to Downtown Disney or an open theme park and then transfer to your resort destination.

Disney's BoardWalk Inn

372 rooms. 2101 Epcot Resorts Boulevard, Lake Buena Vista, FL 32830; phone (407) 939-5100, fax (407) 939-5150. Check-in 3:00 p.m., checkout 11:00 a.m. For reservations contact your travel advisor or call (407) 939-3476.

Claim To Fame. A charming ambience, easy access to Epcot, and some of the friendliest concierge cast members to be found.

Room To Book. A Deluxe Club Room, one of Disney's best bargains with over 600 square feet of space and prime views of Crescent Lake and the bustling BoardWalk.

The Wow Factor! Dinner at the Flying Fish whose creative seafood is something to write home about.

The BoardWalk Inn's intimate charm captures the feeling of a 1930s mid-Atlantic seacoast retreat. In the lobby is a nostalgic living room scene of chintz-covered, oversize chairs, invitingly plump sofas, and potted palms set atop gleaming hardwood floors and floral area rugs. Looming overhead is a barrel-shaped ceiling embellished with delicate latticework and a fanciful carousel chandelier consisting of half horse, half sea creatures finished in 22-karat gold leaf. Views from the lobby's lofty windows are of a courtyard green fronting a festive, old-fashioned boardwalk. Step outside and have a seat in one of the veranda's wicker rocking chairs, perfect for bathing in the pink glow of sunset as Disney's BoardWalk slowly comes alive.

The resort's gleaming white, four-story buildings, dotted with latticework and crowned with sea green roofs and striped awnings, surround interior courtyards fragrant with blooming roses and crepe myrtle. It may be just a short walk away from Epcot's International Gateway entrance, but a stay here has a somewhat different feel than other Disney Deluxe Resorts because shops and restaurants are located outside the Inn and lobby area on the BoardWalk instead of inside the resort.

REST

Guest rooms. Well-appointed Victorian-style accommodations average 434 square feet, all with French doors leading to full-size balconies or patios. Guest rooms are still looking fresh after a renovation a few years back with crisp white duvets and a buttercup yellow brocade bed runner topped with a cherry red accent pillow, but mattresses are in need of replacement. Most offer two queen-size beds (a few with a king bed), an overly bright yellow wood bureau topped with a built-in flat-screen TV, and a desk with a Mickey lamp. An apple green, single sofa sleeper and gold and white-striped wallpaper combined with soft yellow paint and fresh blue and cream carpeting completes the soothing look. A second clothes bureau is in the entry hall. In one area of the bath is a white vanity topped with dove gray marble, pewter-hued mirrors, double sinks, hair dryer, and makeup mirror. Next to it is a separate commode and a tub/shower surrounded by fresh white tile. Amenities include H2O Grapefruit Bergamot bath products, keyed wall safe, iron and ironing board, iPod docking station alarm clock, coffeemaker, small refrigerator, and daily newspaper.

> CARA'S TIP: Avoid if you can the five or so guest rooms that literally sit right above the Belle Vue Lounge's outdoor verandah (open until midnight), not exactly conducive to a quiet evening on your balcony. Many Standard View rooms come with a nice vista of the gardens or pool, but try and avoid those that overlook the front of the resort and the parking area.

Concierge rooms. Consider upgrading to one of the 65 concierge-level rooms. The *Innkeeper's Club* lounge on the 4th floor enjoys a super concierge staff and view of the Illuminations fireworks from its balcony. Breakfast is fruit, bagels, croissants, hot beignets, pastries, yogurt, cereal, oatmeal, hard-boiled eggs, juice, coffee, and tea. Midday refreshments are potato chips, gummy bears, banana chips, yogurt-covered pretzels, cookies, fruit, and beverages. Early evening comes with crudités, cheese and crackers, and tapenade along with two cold dishes such as chickpea salad, duck salad, orzo and feta salad, seared tuna, smoked salmon, coleslaw, and quinoa salad. Two hot appetizers might include raspberry and Brie puff pastries, beef empanadas, chicken Durban skewers, vegetable spring rolls, samosas, and potstickers. Wine (BV Century Cellar Chardonnay, Canyon Road Merlot, Beringer White Zinfandel), served in ridiculously small glasses, and beer is also included. PB&J sandwiches and apples with caramel dipping sauce are available for the children. After dinner are cordials and desserts of mini tarts, mini cheesecake, brownies, and cookies. There's also a self-service cappuccino machine. All this along with nightly turndown service, private check-in and checkout, and guest robes makes for one delightful vacation.

As well as standard-size rooms (six of which offer king beds), the concierge level has ten very spacious, 644-square-foot *Deluxe Rooms*, all with a spectacular view of the BoardWalk and Crescent Lake, and even a view of the Magic Kingdom's fireworks in the far distance. They come with two queen beds, bureau with flat-screen TV, desk, and an open seating area outfitted with a sleeper sofa, coffee table, easy chair, and extra bureau with an additional flat-screen TV and DVD player. Five Deluxe Rooms are on the 3rd floor and the other five on the 4th floor. Two actually adjoin, room numbers 3227 and 3229, perfect for families (on request only).

Suites. A gated, white picket fence encircles the serene, two-story *Garden Suites* (915 to 1,100 square feet), most with a private front yard complete with rose garden, arbor, mailbox, birdhouse, and porch. Downstairs is a homey living area with a flat-screen TV, malachite green, L-shaped sectional sleeper sofa, coffee table, desk, closet, half bath, and wet bar with microwave, coffeemaker, and small refrigerator. Upstairs is a loft bedroom with a king bed, bureau with built-in flat-screen TV, and a bathroom with double sink, whirlpool tub, separate shower, and mini-TV. Instead of a loft, three of the fourteen Garden Suites (rooms 1205, 1206, and 1207) have a large, upstairs bedroom with French doors leading out to a balcony that overlooks the quiet pool. Honeymooners should request the unit with the heart-shaped shrubbery. All require walking outside and over to the main building to access the concierge lounge.

Two-Bedroom Suites with 1,288 square feet offer a small parlor decorated in soft green and gold and furnished with a sleeper sofa, coffee table, easy chair, desk, bureau with built-in, flat-screen TV, and small dining table for four. There's also a wet bar with microwave and small refrigerator with a half bath off the foyer. French doors lead from the living room to the standard-size master with king bed and walk-in closet, and a cream-toned marble bath featuring a whirlpool tub, separate commode area, double sinks, shower, and mini-TV. Opposite the living area is a standard guest room with two queen beds. There are three balconies, and all have a view of the gardens. Suite number 4205 has a bonus of an Illuminations fireworks view but loses points with its view of two satellite dishes and a slice of the road; good nighttime view, but not so great during the day.

The *Vice Presidential Sonora Suite's* Victorian-style living room is perfect for entertaining with plush Victorian-style floral furnishings in a mellow mint and butterscotch palette with two easy chairs, sofa, coffee table, eight-person dining table, wet bar, buffet, flat-screen TV with stereo, service kitchen, marble half bath, and balcony the length of the suite. On one side of the living area is a standard guest room with two queen beds and upgraded spreads; on the other side, a somewhat feminine master bedroom featuring a four-poster king-size bed, armoire with TV, and easy chair. The marble master bathroom comes with double sink, separate shower, whirlpool tub, mini-TV, and separate commode area. 1,744 square feet. The outstanding view from the balcony is an all-encompassing panorama of Crescent Lake. I do like the story behind the suite's name: Sonora Carver was a woman who had a diving-horse act in the 1920s at the Atlantic City Boardwalk, plunging 40 feet on the back of a horse to land in a tank of water.

From deep balconies that run the length of the two-bedroom, two-and-a-half-bath *Presidential Steeplechase Suite* are sweeping views of the BoardWalk and Crescent Lake. This 2,170-square-foot beauty comes with a muraled domed ceiling in the massive living room done up in shades of soft blue, gold, and yellow. It features hardwood flooring topped with large area rugs, two seating areas, two sleeper chairs, a TV remotely controlled to ascend from the bureau, and an 8-person dining table. Off the dining room is a service kitchen with wet bar, under-counter refrigerator, and microwave, and features a pass-through counter to the dining room. The master bedroom boasts a curtained king four-poster bed and chandelier, and in the marble bath is a giant-size walk-in closet, vanity area, gargantuan whirlpool tub, shower, separate bidet and commode area, and double, hand-painted sinks. The second bedroom is standard in size with two queen beds and upgraded spreads and wallpaper. A marble half bath is off the hardwood floor entry.

DINE

See DINE section for Disney's BoardWalk in Diversions Beyond the Walt Disney World Resort Theme Parks.

In-Room Dining. Available 6:00 a.m. to midnight.

SIP

Belle Vue Lounge. Sentimental music by the likes of Benny Goodman plays from vintage radios in this comfy bar with additional balcony seating overlooking Disney's BoardWalk. Cocktails, specialty drinks, single-malt scotch, wine, and beer; continental breakfast available mornings from 6:30 a.m. until 11:00 a.m.

Leaping Horse Libations. Luna Park pool bar with specialty drinks, beer, and assorted cold sandwiches.

PLAY

Arcade. Side Show Games Arcade is just off the Village Green with the newest in video and computer games as well as the old reliable pinball machines.

Bicycle and surrey rentals. In front of the Village Green are two-, four-, and six-seater surreys available for rent 10:00 a.m. to 10:00 p.m., weather permitting. Single and tandem bicycles are available for rent at BoardWalk Villas Community Center next-door to the Inn.

Children's activities and playground. A playground is located next to Luna Park Pool. Arts and crafts are offered in the BoardWalk Villas Community Center for a small fee. Luna Park Pool activities include Name That Tune, dance party, chalk art, family Disney movie challenge, hula hoops, and rubber ducky scramble. Join in at the Yacht & Beach Club's Movie Under the Stars each evening weather permitting.

Jogging. Either the circular 0.75-mile BoardWalk or the path encircling the canal leading to Disney's Hollywood Studios can serve as a jogging track.

Swimming. Carnival-themed Luna Park Pool with 200-foot-long "Keister Coaster" waterslide as well as a kiddie pool and whirlpool. A smaller Inn Pool and whirlpool are located in the Rose Courtyard.

Tennis. Two hard-surface, lighted courts are found on the villa side of the property; complimentary to registered guests with rackets available at Community Hall.

WORK, MOVE, SOOTHE

Business center. Located at the BoardWalk Conference Center with fax, Internet, imaging services, shipping and receiving, notary public, and office supplies.

Muscles and Bustles Health Club. Offering Cybex strength training equipment, Life Fitness treadmills, elliptical trainers, bicycles, and free weights as well as a coed sauna and steam room (sauna and steam facilities also available to Yacht & Beach Club guests). Massage, including in-room, available. Club complimentary to resort guests with 24-hour access.

GO

Take a water launch or walk to Epcot and Disney's Hollywood Studios. It's a five to ten-minute walk to Epcot's International Gateway and about a twenty-minute walk to Disney's Hollywood Studios along the walkway found behind the villa side of the resort.

Bus service is available to the Magic Kingdom, Animal Kingdom, Typhoon Lagoon, Blizzard Beach, and Downtown Disney. To reach other Disney resorts outside of the Epcot area, you must first take a bus to Downtown Disney or an open theme park and then transfer to your resort destination.

WHAT'S YOUR DISNEY CONCIERGE PERSONALITY?

I've come to the conclusion that there's actually a Disney concierge personality. I just happened upon this phenomena on a Disney research trip when, in my usual fashion, I moved every two nights between resorts. I've stayed many times over at all the Deluxe Resorts, just about always in concierge. This go-round I happened to move immediately between the Grand Floridian and the Polynesian, following that with a move between the Yacht and the Beach Club. It struck me as never before how very different guest personalities are in each resort, particularly when it comes to concierge.

The Grand Floridian's Main Building's concierge lounge offers up a quiet and sedate atmosphere. Small plates of delicacies are nibbled in courtly fashion as music from the lobby floats upward to the Royal Palm Club. Well-behaved children patiently snack on crustless sandwiches while parents sip their pre-dinner wine and champagne. Next door at the Polynesian, however, parents chase down their children, guests pile their plates with hearty food, and a party-down vibe is in the air. What's more, the Polynesian's inevitable concierge campers who take over a table and never seem to leave are usually in residence, particularly on Asian chicken wing night when the beer flows.

It's a similar dichotomy at the Yacht and Beach Club. Peace prevails at the Yacht Club both in the lobby and in concierge. Fewer children are in residence (perhaps because it's a popular conventioneer choice), and uber polite guests make quiet trips between the buffet and a handful of tables located both inside and out on the lounge's small balcony. Moreover, the Yacht Club's concierge staff actually stand when you pass their desks (something that amazes me each and every time!). Over at the Beach Club you'll find a wilder setting that is if you can actually find the 1st floor elevator after maneuvering your way around the hoards of people in the lobby waiting to feast on the popular Cape May buffet. Here, concierge guests seem more animated and children are always underfoot in the tiny lounge. It's almost as if you've moved to a different area of the country instead of right next-door.

So when you're torn between which Disney resort is best for you and your family, consider your concierge personality. It will almost certainly make a big difference in your overall vacation enjoyment.

Disney's Yacht Club Resort

621 rooms. 1700 Epcot Resorts Boulevard, Lake Buena Vista, FL 32830; phone (407) 934-7000, fax (407) 934-3450. Check-in 3:00 p.m., checkout 11:00 a.m. For reservations contact your travel advisor or call (407) 939-3476.

Claim To Fame. Easy Epcot access and fun in the sun at Stormalong Bay, the resort's fantastic pool complex.

Room To Book. A Lagoon View Concierge room with vistas of Crescent Lake and easy access to the Regatta Club's lounge.

The Wow Factor! Take a private Illuminations cruise with nightly departures from the resort's marina.

The theme here is one of an old-style yacht club where a navy blue blazer should be in order for a stay. Four- and five-story oyster gray shingle-style buildings with balconies shaded by red and white striped awnings front Crescent Lake and a sliver of groomed beach that stretches over to the adjoining Beach Club Resort. This near perfect location is within walking distance of Epcot's International Gateway entrance as well as the BoardWalk and just a short boat ride away from Disney's Hollywood Studios.

The polished, sleek lobby of ship-shiny, dark oak hardwoods, potted palms, roped nautical railings, leather sofas, and overstuffed, striped easy chairs creates an environment reminiscent of an eastern seaboard hotel of the 1880's. The antique globe in the center of the room along with detailed ship models and oceans of gleaming brass complete the picture. The resort shares Stormalong Bay, Disney's fantasyland of a pool complex, and all recreational areas and facilities with its sister property, Disney's Beach Club.

REST

Guest rooms. You'll enter your casually elegant, fresh and tidy guest room through a yellow, yacht-style door. Two queen-size beds with gleaming white headboards in a ship's wheel motif are covered in white duvets with blue piping and topped with nautical bed runners and red velvet throw pillows. Brass sconce lighting, gold and blue striped drapery, and lots of maritime accents add to the charm. Rooms are fairly spacious at 400 square feet. Cheery white furnishings include a writing desk, a bureau with a wall-mounted flat-screen TV above, and an additional bureau near the bathroom. French doors lead to a private balcony or patio with a variety of views. Some rooms have a blue chenille daybed, others a deep red anchor motif easy chair and ottoman. The marble bath vanity holds double sinks (sinks are beginning to show their age and need replacing), hair dryer, non-lighted makeup mirror, full-length mirror, and porthole-style mirrors. There is a separate tub and commode area with a sailing ship motif shower curtain. Amenities include an iron and ironing board, coffeemaker, refrigerator, keyed safe, iPod docking station clock radio, and daily newspaper.

> CARA'S TIP: Standard View rooms come with a view of a slice of the parking lot or the rooftops so I would upgrade to at least a Garden View requesting one near the quiet pool that looks out on the grassy area with a fountain and duck pond. Lagoon/Pool View rooms face Crescent Lake, Stormalong Bay, or sometimes both; ask for one facing Epcot for a distant view of the Illuminations fireworks. If too much walking is not your idea of a vacation request a room close to the lobby since the resort is quite spread out, and long treks to your room are not uncommon.

Concierge rooms. Most are located on the 5th floor and privileged to the *Regatta Club*, one of only a few Disney concierge lounges with a full-size balcony but alas with a view of the front of the resort instead of Crescent Lake. A much calmer atmosphere prevails here as compared to the Beach Club's lounge next-door, so if it's peace and quite you are looking for choose this resort over its sister property. Most concierge rooms are standard size; for extra space choose *Deluxe Rooms* with 654 square feet although they are not located on the same floor as the concierge lounge.

In the lounge mornings begin with coffee from a self-service cappuccino machine, juice, coffeecake, muffins, croissants, bagels, cinnamon rolls, banana bread, pastries, oatmeal, yogurt, hard-boiled eggs, fruit, and cereal. Midday snacks consist of homemade potato chips with roasted red pepper ranch dip, gummy bears, fresh fruit, yogurt-covered pretzels, trail mix, cookies, lemonade, apple juice, and iced tea. Early evening brings wine (Penfolds Rawson's Retreat Merlot, Beringer White Zinfandel, Mirassou Pinot Noir, and Columbia Crest Chardonnay), beer, and hors d'oeuvres such as hummus, crudités, artisan cheeses and crackers, potato salad, orzo pasta salad, broccoli slaw, mozzarella and tomato salad, lobster salad, and Israeli couscous salad along with a hot item like potato and pea samosas with mango chutney, ginger pork potstickers, vegetable spring rolls with sweet chili sauce, conch fritters, red pepper and goat cheese in phyllo, crab rangoon, grilled chicken skewers with yogurt cucumber sauce, bacon-wrapped scallops with mustard dipping sauce, and spanakopita. Kids feast on peanut butter and jellyrolls and apple slices with caramel dipping sauce. After dinner is a selection of cordials and desserts such as raspberry or chocolate/peanut butter mousse, chocolate teacake, brownies, caramelized cheesecake, mini cupcakes, and Oreo bonbons.

Extra amenities include guest robes, turndown service, private check-in and checkout, DVD players, and the services of a pleasant and service-oriented concierge staff.

Suites. A variety of suites are available, all with concierge lounge access.

Turret Two-Bedroom Suites offer 1,160 square feet. You'll first encounter a long and narrow standard guest room off the entry hall with two queen-size beds and bath. An equally narrow hallway leads to the second bedroom also with two queens and a slightly larger-than-standard bath; next to it is a six-sided turreted living area with sofa, two easy chairs with ottoman, TV, and four-person dining room. The suite's only balcony is in the standard guest room; not the most ideal setting but saved by views of Crescent Lake and Stormalong Bay.

Almost identical at 2,017 square feet but with different décor are the two-bedroom, two-and-a-half-bath *Presidential (4th floor) and Admiral (5th floor) Suites.* The Presidential Suite overlooks the BoardWalk and Crescent Lake and is decorated in shades of rose and navy blue.

There's a hardwood foyer with a marble half bath sporting a somewhat gaudy wallpaper, as well as two living areas—one a bright and airy turreted room with loads of windows and hardwood flooring overlooking Crescent Lake, the BoardWalk, and the pool with a sofa, three occasional chairs, and entertainment center; the other carpeted with a sofa, two easy chairs, coffee table, game table, desk, and gas fireplace over which is mounted a flat-screen TV. A separate six-person dining room adjoins a wet bar.

The fairly small master bedroom offers a four-poster king bed, easy chair and ottoman, entertainment center, and settee. In its charcoal and white marble bathroom is an oversized whirlpool tub, shower, separate toilet area with bidet, and dual sinks. Off the dining area a standard size second bedroom comes with two queen beds with upgraded bedding. Balconies are found in each bedroom and off the living area. Although I was told that these suites had been upgraded in the last few years the only changes I could see were the addition of larger flat-screen TVs.

The two-bedroom *Vice Presidential Commodore Suite* is not a favorite of mine. Just outside the entry is a housekeeping pantry whose door is open much of the day giving the small hallway a commercial feel. A marble entry hall has a half bath opening into the suite's small parlor. Decorated with pale, yellow-striped wallpaper and nautical carpeting there is a cherry wood entertainment armoire, "understuffed" navy blue sofa, easy chair, diminutive coffee table, and stand-up balcony. The master bedroom's sleigh-style king bed is in need of a good refinishing to cover the scratches, and the room seems a bit empty although it also contains an armoire, desk, easy chair, and full-size balcony. I do like the chocolate and cream-colored marble master bath with its whirlpool tub, shower, TV, separate toilet area, and double sink vanity. On the other side of the parlor is a slightly larger-than-standard guest room with two queen beds, sailing ship spreads, and full-size balcony. All views are of Crescent Lake and Stormalong Bay.

The largest suite at 2,374 square feet is the 1st floor, two-bedroom, two-and-a-half-bath *Captain's Deck Suite*. A marble octagonal foyer leads to a nautically decorated suite decked out in a rich sea blue and rose palette. The parlor features an open sitting area, living area, large business desk in its own alcove, dining room with seating for ten, full kitchen (minus a stove), and oversized brick garden patio (shrubbery blocks the view of the adjoining parking area). Each of the bedrooms has its own private patio, with the master bedroom offering a king-size bed, bureau, entertainment center, easy chair and ottoman, walk-in closet, and luxuriously large marble bathroom with vanity area, TV, immense shower, whirlpool tub, separate commode area, and double sinks. The second bedroom is similar to a regular guest room with slightly upgraded decor. Here also the only upgrades in quite a few years are flat-screen TVs and a new lighting and sound system.

DINE

Captain's Grille. Casual all-day eatery open for breakfast, lunch, and dinner. *Breakfast:* lobster omelet, citrus French toast, dark chocolate waffles, petite sirloin and quiche, steel-cut oatmeal brûlée, lemon-ricotta hotcakes, tailored omelet. *Lunch:* lobster sliders, fish and chips, seared tuna salad, tomato and mozzarella on focaccia, clam linguini. *Dinner:* Cabernet-braised short rib, rosemary-brined pork tenderloin, lump crab cakes, pan-seared chicken with truffle brown butter vinaigrette, snow crab legs with new potatoes and corn on the cob.

Yachtsman Steakhouse. Oak grilled steaks and seafood open for dinner only. (See full description in the Dining in Style at Walt Disney World chapter.)

In-Room Dining. Served 24/7.

SIP

Ale and Compass Lounge. Lobby bar serving specialty drinks, wine, and beer; continental breakfast served in the morning hours.

Crew's Cup Lounge. Cozy seaport-style lounge adjoining Yachtsman Steakhouse, open from noon to midnight, offering a nice beer selection along with Disney's standard drink menu. Appetizers from Captain's Grille include New England clam chowder, buffalo chicken nuggets, crab cakes, house-cut truffle fries, buttermilk-fried rock shrimp, and pot-braised mussels and clams.

Hurricane Hanna's Grill. Poolside bar and grill; full bar, cocktails, sangria, beer, alcoholic and nonalcoholic frozen drinks. *Food choices:*

lobster and shrimp roll, grilled chicken breast sandwich, chopped salad with turkey and blue cheese, vegetarian quinoa wrap, bacon Angus
cheeseburger, grilled cheese and smoked bacon sandwich. *Children's
menu:* grilled cheese, grilled chicken sandwich, chicken nuggets, and a
cheeseburger.

PLAY

The Yacht Club shares all recreational activities with the adjacent Disney's Beach Club Resort. See also the PLAY section in the earlier entry
for the Beach Club.

Beach. Small beach with lounge chairs; no swimming allowed in the
lake.

ORLANDO HOT SPOTS

Not everyone comes to Walt Disney World thinking of spending
his or her time in the theme parks. Some crave not only a freshly
shaken martini but also a chic crowd. Here are options that will
satisfy their needs:

- *Il Mulino Bar at the Walt Disney World Swan.* This swank spot
  adorned in shades of tangerine and chocolate and a cool illuminated bar is the place to be. Savory antipasti selections and
  a spiffy crowd may be complemented by fine Italian wines, even
  cigars on the terrace.

- *Bluezoo Lounge at the Walt Disney World Dolphin.* Classy lounge
  with chocolate brown leather booths, mango orange accents,
  and copper lighting. Sip on a martini while savoring the action
  and a selection from the restaurant's raw bar.

- *Sir Harry's Lounge at the Waldorf Astoria Orlando.* Jewel box
  of a bar with a laid-back vibe of leather club chairs, single malt
  scotch, and live piano music on weekend evenings.

- *Peacock Alley.* Yet another great choice at the Waldorf Astoria
  where you'll find "delish" cocktails and small plates along with
  live piano music and great people watching nightly.

Bicycles. Bicycles available for rent at Bayside Marina.

Boating. Rentals at Bayside Marina for touring Crescent Lake and the adjacent waterways include Sea Raycers, Boston Whaler Montauks, and pontoon boats.

An Illumination cruise on a pontoon boat for up to 10 guests is available—the viewing point under Epcot's International Bridge is unrivaled; call (407) WDW-PLAY or (407) 939-7529 for reservations.

Children's activities. Children ages 4-12 set sail on the Albatross Treasure Cruise in search of pirate booty on Crescent Lake and the World Showcase Lagoon each Monday, Wednesday, and Friday at 9:30 a.m. ($34). Call 407-WDW-PLAY for reservations

Fishing. Two and four-hour guided fishing excursions on Crescent Lake depart from the Yacht Club's Bayside Marina for a maximum of five guests, including gear and beverages; strictly catch-and-release (call 407-WDW-BASS or 407-939-2277 for reservations; 24-hour notice required).

Tennis. One lighted, hard-surface court is available for complimentary use. Located near the quiet Admiral Pool with complimentary equipment available at Ship Shape Health Club.

WORK, MOVE, SOOTHE

The Yacht Club shares all services with the adjacent Disney's Beach Club Resort. See also the WORK, MOVE, SOOTHE section in the earlier entry for the Beach Club.

Business center. Located at the Yacht Club Convention Center; fax, Internet, imaging services, shipping and receiving, notary public, office supplies.

GO

Take a water launch or walk to Epcot and Disney's Hollywood Studios. It's a ten-minute walk to Epcot's International Gateway entrance and five minutes to Disney's BoardWalk with bus service to the Magic Kingdom, Animal Kingdom, Typhoon Lagoon, Blizzard Beach, and Downtown Disney.

To reach other Disney resorts outside the Epcot Resorts area you must first take a bus to Downtown Disney or an open theme park and then transfer to your resort destination.

Walt Disney World Dolphin

> 1,509 rooms. 1500 Epcot Resorts Boulevard, Lake Buena Vista, FL 32830; phone (407) 934-4000, fax (407) 934-4099. Check-in 3:00 p.m., checkout 11:00 a.m. For reservations contact your travel advisor or call (407) 939-3476. Reservations and information also available online at SwanDolphin.com.

Claim To Fame. Great access to Epcot and Disney's Hollywood Studios at a good price.

Room To Book. Sweeping views and lovely furnishings make the top suites here some of Disney's best. Consider one of the Dolphin's Presidential Suites for a taste of sheer luxury.

The Wow Factor! Dinner at Todd English's Bluezoo, the most stylish restaurant around.

What can I say about the Swan and Dolphin? It's a tough call. The reason I include both in the book is for their lovely suites, super dining options, gracious spa, and location in the midst of Epcot, the Board-Walk, and Disney's Hollywood Studios areas. But you must be willing to contend with claustrophobic, low-ceiling hallways, and smallish and outdated standard baths left over from the 80s. At least the hallways have been renovated with a modern, linen-look wallpaper in soft green and beige and the elimination of the formerly jarring carpeting. Either be content with a bargain priced guest room or pony up for one of the stunning Presidential or Governor's Suites and be done with it.

Operated by Sheraton Hotels but situated within the grounds of Walt Disney World, the Dolphin's pyramid shape and Michael Graves-designed look can certainly be described as whimsical. Atop the twenty-seven-story complex are five-story dolphins accompanied by giant clamshells cascading down nine stories. An outdated look of sea blue and terra cotta colors are featured throughout the resort and into a lobby draped with billowing fabric floating above a fanciful fountain of dolphins.

Extensive meeting facilities, ballrooms, and exhibit halls make this property a popular choice for conventioneers, so come prepared for large groups roaming the public areas both here and at the neighboring Swan which shares all recreational and service facilities with the Dolphin.

Although this is not a Disney-owned resort, guests receive some of the same amenities as at other Disney properties including Extra Magic Hours, Disney transportation to all attractions, and package delivery. However, charging privileges to your resort account do not extend outside of the Dolphin or Swan, and Disney's Magical Express is not offered when staying here.

REST

Guest rooms. Guest rooms have a soft, contemporary style with maple wood furnishings and frosted blue accents. Heavenly Beds feature pillow-top mattresses, triple-sheeted linens, down blankets and pillows, and snow-white duvets. Earth tone accents include chocolate and taupe tinted carpeting, pumpkin-colored bolsters, and taupe and sea blue drapery as well as 32-flat-screen TVs. While comfortable, these 360-square-foot rooms are a bit too cozy. They have either two double beds with easy chair and ottoman or a king-size bed with sofa. A single sink in a super-cramped corner marble vanity sits just outside the small tub/shower and toilet area with outdated, old-fashioned tile. The slate-floored foyer has a vanity with hair dryer and coffeemaker. Amenities include iron and ironing board, two dual-line telephones, makeup mirror, undercounter refrigerator, electronic safe, and cable TV with on-demand movies. A nice option is a room with a balcony (for which an extra charge is assessed). The best views are on the higher floors facing Epcot with a panoramic vista of Spaceship Earth, World Showcase, Crescent Lake, Illuminations, and the entire BoardWalk area; the hotel's Traditional Rooms have a very unattractive view of the rooftop.

A mandatory $20 per night resort fee includes two bottles of water, unlimited domestic and long-distance phone calls, fitness center access, and in-room Internet access.

Suites. *Executive Suites* offer a 600 square foot parlor (sofa, easy chairs, coffee table, bureau with TV, full bath with two sinks, and wet bar) to which one or two standard guest rooms (one with a king-size bed and the other with two doubles) can be added on either side of the living area.

Premium Suites offer quite a bit more room than a regular guest room along with upgraded furnishings. In one large room is a king bed, sleeper sofa, desk, bureau with 42" flat-screen TV, 4-person dining table, wet bar, and two easy chairs totaling 650 square feet.

Grand Suites are very much like Executive Suites but with a larger living area. A combination living/dining room with a six-person dining table and desk is on one side; a tangerine-tinted sofa, two contemporary easy chairs, and flat-screen TV is in another. A service kitchen sits to one side of the dining area, and a second full bath is found off the entry hall. The bedroom is the same as a standard guest room with a king bed. Another bedroom can be connected to it with two double beds to make a two-bedroom suite.

The Dolphin boasts several *Presidential Suites* each with a lovely, contemporary look. But on the 20th floor sits the loftiest suites on property, both two-story, three-bedroom/four bath units, both 2,589 square feet, and both with a breathtaking panorama of all four parks seen not only through massive windows but also from the splendid downstairs balcony running the length of the living area. The look and feel of opulence begins when you walk across the hardwood floor of the entry hall onto soothing taupe-colored carpet. Enter a capacious vaulted living room with two deluxe, tastefully contemporary sitting areas: one has a cherry red, chenille sectional sofa; the other a wasabi green sofa, tangerine easy chairs, and large square coffee table underneath which sit four white leather ottomans for additional seating. In the center of it all sits a shiny black baby grand piano. Proceed through rooms filled with live greenery and flowering orchids, multiple oversized flat-screen TVs, leather headboards, and other spiffy furnishings. The dining table with eight white leather chairs allows guests to enjoy meals *en suite*. A service kitchen sits off the dining area with sink, full size refrigerator, and dishwasher. Work, if you must, on a trendy desk in the spacious office. All four full baths and the living room's half bath have been fitted with contemporary fixtures, cream marble countertops, cutting-edge square sinks, and chocolate marble flooring. Both the downstairs and upstairs guest rooms are fit for royalty with two queen beds upstairs and a king downstairs adorned in white silk spreads. Upstairs the enormous master is striking with its red and chocolate décor; the bath is outfitted with a walk-in closet, double sinks, whirlpool tub, stand-alone shower, and a separate commode and bidet room. In short, this suite is modern renovation at its best.

DINE

The Fountain. Retro 1950s soda fountain open for lunch and dinner; buffalo chicken salad, seared salmon salad, classic BLT, seared chicken sandwich with scallion aioli, build-your-favorite-hot dog or hamburger, Rueben sandwich, lamb gyro; fountain treats such as hand-scooped and soft-serve ice cream, banana split, floats, shakes, malts, create-your-own sundae.

Fresh Mediterranean Market. Open for breakfast and lunch. *Breakfast buffet or a la carte:* pastries, fruit, breakfast and rotisserie meats, hot and cold cereals, omelets, pancakes, waffles. *Lunch buffet:* soups, grilled and rotisserie meats, salads, hot sandwiches, desserts.

Shula's Steak House. Steakhouse open for dinner only. (See full description in the Dining in Style at Walt Disney World Resort chapter.)

Todd English's Bluezoo. Fresh seafood in a stunning setting open for dinner only. (See full description in the Dining in Style at Walt Disney World Resort chapter.)

Picabu Buffeteria. Twenty-four-hour cafeteria. Grill usually open until 11:00 p.m., but hours are seasonal. *Breakfast:* fresh fruit, omelets, cinnamon buns, funnel cake, oatmeal, grits, cereal, biscuits and gravy, corned beef hash, eggs-your-way, ciabatta breakfast sandwich, fruit turnovers. *Lunch and dinner:* chicken sandwich, loaded nachos, burgers and hot dogs your way, oriental glazed salmon, chicken pot pie, potato bar, strip steak and caramelized onions, pizza, beef lasagna, cold sandwiches, salads. *Children's menu:* hamburgers, hot dogs, mac 'n' cheese, and chicken fingers.

In-Room Dining. Available 24/7.

SIP

Cabana Bar and Beach Club. Contemporary pool grill with full bar, alcoholic and nonalcoholic frozen tropical drinks. *Light Meals:* fish tacos, tuna *tataki* salad, tomato mozzarella salad, Korean BBQ beef sliders, grilled chicken BLT, Cuban cheese steak, build-your-own flatbread.

Lobby Lounge. In the morning are specialty coffees and pastries with seasonal cocktail service late afternoon and evening.

Shula's Lounge. Sports bar adjoining Shula's Steakhouse serving cocktails, wine, champagne, port, single-malt scotches; full restaurant menu available.

Todd English's Bluezoo Lounge. Chic lounge adjoining Todd English's Bluezoo restaurant open 3:30 to 11:00 p.m. daily. Full bar, specialty cocktails and martinis; raw bar, flatbreads, crab nachos, and lamb mezze as well as the full restaurant menu.

PLAY

Arcade. A small Game Room is located downstairs near the fitness center.

Boating. Swan paddleboats are available for rent.

Children's playground. Located on the beach area.

Jogging. Three miles of jogging trails surround the resort and extend to the BoardWalk and Disney's Hollywood Studios; pick up a map at the fitness center.

Swimming. Rambling, three-acre Grotto Pool with waterfall and waterslide located between the Dolphin and the Swan. Children's pool, four whirlpools, Spring Pool, two lap pools, and sand beach. Nightly Dive-in Movies at the Grotto Pool.

Tennis. Four lighted tennis courts located just across Epcot Resorts Boulevard on the Swan side of the resort with private lessons available. Check out equipment at the Dolphin Health Club.

Volleyball. A sand court is located on the Swan's beach.

WORK, MOVE, SOOTHE

Business center. 11th Hour Business Centers manages parcel handling, printing, computer workstations, fax, scanning, office equipment rental, custom signage and banners. Open Monday through Friday and 7:30 a.m. to 5:00 p.m. on Saturday.

Car rental. An Alamo/National Car Rental desk is located just off the lobby.

Childcare. Camp Dolphin offering arts and crafts, a trip to the game room, and movie time. Open 5:30 p.m. to midnight for potty-trained children ages four to twelve; cost includes dinner at Picabu. Open to all Walt Disney World guests with complimentary two hours for children of Il Mulino, Bluezoo, and Shula diners (one child complimentary for each adult entrée purchased) as well as spa-goers at Mandara Spa who purchase a treatment of 75 minutes or more; reservations required, call (407) 934-4241.

Hair salon. Located at the Mandara Spa; cut and color, shampoo and blow dry, hair and scalp conditioning, manicures, pedicures, acrylics, waxing, and makeup.

Health studio. Free weights, Life Fitness strength training machines, cycles, treadmills, and elliptical trainers. Open 6:00 a.m. to 9:00 p.m. with personalized training available by appointment.

Jogging. Jog around the one-mile BoardWalk and over to Disney's Hollywood Studios; jogging strollers and pedometers are available at the health studio.

Spa. Mandara Spa featuring Balinese treatments, a retail store, and hair salon. Open from 8:00 a.m. until 9:00 p.m. (See full description in the Diversions Beyond the Walt Disney World Resort Theme Parks chapter.)

GO

Take a water launch to Epcot's International Gateway and Disney's Hollywood Studio with bus service to the Magic Kingdom, Animal Kingdom, Downtown Disney, Typhoon Lagoon, and Blizzard Beach. If you prefer to walk it's a pleasant ten- to fifteen-minute walk to Epcot's International Gateway entrance (one that is sometimes quicker than the boat service) or a fifteen- to twenty-minute walk to Disney's Hollywood Studios.

To reach other Disney resorts during park operating hours take a bus to an open theme park and pick up a bus or monorail from there to your resort destination. After park hours take a bus to Downtown Disney and then transfer to the resort.

Walt Disney World Swan

758 rooms. 1200 Epcot Resorts Boulevard, Lake Buena Vista, FL 32830; phone (407) 934-3000, fax (407) 934-4099. Check-in 3:00 p.m., checkout 11:00 a.m. For reservations contact your travel advisor or call (407) 939-3476. Reservations and information also available online at SwanDolphin.com.

Claim To Fame. Convenient Epcot and Disney Studios access by boat and a great price point for guest rooms.

Room To Book. The Governors Suite with plenty of room to spread out in gracious surroundings.

The Wow Factor! Dinner at Il Mulino where savory Italian food and a sophisticated ambience make for a memorable meal.

Designed by Michael Graves and operated by the Westin, the Swan, composed of a twelve-story main building and two seven-story wings, is a bit more subdued than the Dolphin but with the same issues as the Dolphin including a dated 80's-style look and small, outmoded standard baths. Linked by an awning-covered walkway (the place to catch the boat launch to Epcot and Disney's Hollywood Studios) it shares the same three-acre grotto pool. The lobby is small with contemporary cylindrical glass lighting, potted palms, and a sparkling swan fountain. If the colossal style of the Dolphin is simply not your scene the smaller-scale Swan is the place for you.

Although not a Disney-owned resort, guests receive some of the same amenities as at other Disney properties including Extra Magic Hours, Disney transportation to all attractions, complimentary parking at Disney's theme parks, and package delivery. However, charging privileges to your resort account do not extend outside of the Swan or Dolphin, and Disney's Magical Express is not offered.

REST

Guest rooms. Guest rooms embody a contemporary style with room size, furnishings, and decor the same as at the Dolphin (see REST section of previous entry for the Walt Disney World Dolphin). At the Swan there are two queen beds instead of two doubles, carpeting in the entries instead of slate, and a different bathroom configuration. As at the Dolphin baths have not been upgraded. Here there are two sinks—one outside the bath area with a hair dryer, non-lighted makeup mirror, and coffeemaker; and one inside with the tub-shower and toilet. Amenities include an iron and ironing board, minibar, a pair of two-line telephones, and cable TV with on-demand movies. Views from the upper floors can be impressive with panoramas of either Disney Studios or Epcot and the Grotto Pool. The hotel's Traditional Rooms have a not-so-great look at the resort's rooftops. A nice option is a room with a balcony for which an extra charge is assessed. Corner balcony rooms come with an extra wall of windows that make for a bright, airy space; Room 626 offers a view of both the Magic Kingdom and Epcot fireworks.

A mandatory $20 per night resort fee includes two bottles of water, unlimited domestic and long-distance phone calls, fitness center access, and in-room internet access.

> **CARA'S TIP:** A small percentage of guest rooms offer a view of the Epcot fireworks in the distance. Request one at the time of booking and again at check-in.

Suites. Decorated in attractive pumpkin and gold hues the *Executive Suites* feature a standard guest room connected to a 600 square foot parlor in which you'll find a wet bar, desk, four-person dining table, buffet, sofa, two easy chairs, sofa table, oversized flat-screen TV, an extra full bath, and a balcony. This type of suite also can be reserved as a two-bedroom with another standard guest room opening from the other side of the parlor.

Grand Suites feature charcoal carpeting and upgraded contemporary living room furnishings. Two standard rooms with standard decor, one with a king bed and the other with two queens, flank a 680 square foot parlor with sleeper sofa, two easy chairs, TV, eight-person dining table, desk, service kitchen, and a single-sink full bath. There are a total of four balconies. This suite can also be booked as a one-bedroom.

The one-bedroom *Governors Suite* is exceptional with upgraded décor even in the guest rooms. Ice blue and chocolate tones accent the modern furniture surrounded by sleek accessories and lighting, but it's the bedroom that adds the extra flair. A king bed is sectioned off from the bedroom's sitting area with its sofa and three easy chairs, and the double-sink bath features marble flooring and a separate shower and tub. You'll find two balconies in the living area and two more in the bedroom. A dining table seats six and there is an additional full-size bath in the entry hall as well as a service kitchen.

There are four *Presidential Suites*, each one story, each with one or an optional second bedroom (the master with a king-size bed and the second bedroom with two queen-size beds), three full baths, large parlor with a grand piano, dining room with seating for eight, and full kitchen. All have a similar décor as the Presidential Suites at the Dolphin.

DINE

Garden Grove. Serving breakfast, lunch, and dinner; nightly character meals with Goofy and Pluto as well as Saturday and Sunday for breakfast. *Breakfast:* buffet and a la carte items such as an egg sandwich, lobster omelet, corned beef hash with poached eggs, raisin bread French toast, Belgium waffle, apple crepes. *Lunch:* cobb salad, chicken BLT, fish tacos, fish 'n' chips, vegetable wrap, prime rib melt. *Dinner:* prime rib, thyme roasted organic chicken, cedar plank blackened salmon, chef's vegetarian creation; Seafood Sensation buffet is offered on Friday night.

Il Mulino New York Trattoria. One of Disney's best Italian restaurants, open for dinner only. (See full description in the Dining in Style at Walt Disney World Resort chapter.)

Splash Terrace. Lap pool grill with full-service bar; open seasonally for lunch serving tuna salad, vegetarian salad, specialty subs, and New York style pizza.

In-Room Dining. Available 24/7.

SIP

Il Mulino Lounge. Super-slick bar with specialty drinks, Italian wines, antipasti of zucchini and calamari *fritti*, Italian rice balls, carpaccio, and mini pizzas; cigar terrace.

Java Bar. Lobby bar for specialty coffees, pastries, fruit, and berry parfaits in the morning hours, and seasonal cocktail service late afternoon into the evening hours.

Kimonos Lounge. Sushi and sake bar with super-fun karaoke nightly beginning at 9:30 p.m. Wine, single-malt scotch, port, small batch bourbons as well as hot appetizers, sushi, and sashimi; open 5:30 to midnight.

PLAY

The Swan shares all recreational activities with the Dolphin. See the PLAY section in the previous entry for additional information.

Arcade. A small Game Room is located near Splash Terrace.

WORK, MOVE, SOOTHE

Business center. 11th Hour Business Centers manages parcel handling, printing, computer workstations, fax, scanning, office equipment rental, custom signage and banners.

Childcare. Available at the Dolphin (see WORK, MOVE, SOOTHE section of the previous entry for Walt Disney World Dolphin).

Fitness Center. Swan Health Studio, a small workout room with Life Fitness strength training machines, elliptical trainers, bicycles, treadmills, and free weights. Open daily 6:00 a.m. to 9:00 p.m.

GO

See GO section of previous entry for Walt Disney World Dolphin.

Animal Kingdom Area Resorts

Walt Disney World's only deluxe resort in the Animal Kingdom area is the extraordinary Animal Kingdom Lodge. At Jambo House are standard hotel rooms and suites as well as Disney Deluxe Villas offering studio, one-, two-, and three-bedroom units found on the 5th and 6th floors of the resort. Next door is the peaceful Disney's Animal Kingdom Villas–Kidani Village. Although the solitude in this area of Walt Disney World adds to the allure, the isolation also makes for a less convenient choice than resorts in the Magic Kingdom or Epcot area. Consider renting a car to take full advantage of all that Walt Disney World has to offer in the way of resort restaurants and entertainment. Nearby you'll find the Animal Kingdom theme park as well as Blizzard Beach, Winter Summerland miniature golf, and *ESPN Wide World of Sports* Complex.

SHOP THE RESORTS!

A treasure trove of shopping awaits you at the many boutiques and shops found throughout the Walt Disney World resorts. Here are some of best items offered:

- *Boutiki, Polynesian Resort.* Hawaiian Kahala aloha shirts and swim trunks for men.

- *Johari Treasures, Animal Kingdom Villas–Kidani Village.* Hand-carved, brightly painted giraffes from Zimbabwe.

- *Lamont's, Walt Disney World Dolphin.* In need of resort wear? This is where you'll find your best choice.

- *Summer Lace, Grand Floridian Resort.* Disney-themed Dooney & Bourke bags with iconic Disney characters and Lily Pulitzer resort wear.

- *Zawahiri Market, Animal Kingdom Lodge Jambo House.* Original African artwork, African caftans, and hand-painted ostrich eggs from South Africa.

- *Wilderness Lodge Mercantile.* Coonskin hats a la Davy Crockett

Disney's Animal Kingdom Lodge

1,186 rooms including villas. 2901 Osceola Parkway, Bay Lake, FL 32830; phone (407) 938-3000, fax (407) 938-7102. Check-in 3:00 p.m., checkout 11:00 a.m. For reservations contact your travel advisor or call (407) 939-3476.

Claim To Fame. Magical views of the resort's savanna teaming with exotic wildlife.

Room To Book. The Royal Assante Presidential Suite, Disney's best accommodation.

The Wow Factor! The Wanyama Sunset Safari, an evening game drive on the savanna followed by a multicourse dinner at the resort's premier restaurant, Jiko (available only for guests of the Animal Kingdom Lodge and Animal Kingdom Villas–Kidani Village).

Disney's version of a safari lodge is certainly thrilling and respectfully faithful to African wildlife, culture, and cuisine. Its authentic architecture combined with grasslands filled with hundreds of roaming exotic animals makes for one of Disney's best resorts. This six-story, horseshoe-shaped structure is topped with extravagant thatch rooftops and rustically surrounded by eucalyptus fencing and three glorious savannas.

In the imposing, five-story thatch-roofed lobby, just as at Disney's Wilderness Lodge, the first impression is nothing but *wow*! Resplendent overhead chandeliers formed by Masai shields and spears tower over the boulder-lined lobby. Safari-chic seating areas offer hand-carved coffee tables, handsome hand-woven rugs, richly tinted rattan and cane chairs, and relaxing leather sofas adorned with African textile throw pillows. A rope suspension bridge spans the lobby and draws the eye to balconies carved with graceful antelopes and a 46-foot picture window framed by branches of an intricate ironwork tree. The centerpiece of the lobby is the one-of-a-kind sacred *Ijele*, a 16-foot, dazzling mask created by the Igbo people of Nigeria.

Out back sits a massive yellow flame tree poised atop Arusha Rock, an outcropping with panoramic views of the savanna where a nearby fire pit surrounded by rocking chairs is the site of nightly storytelling by the largely African staff. Many of the lobby and restaurant greeters together with the savanna guides are all cultural representatives from Africa, more than delighted to answer questions or share information and tales of their homeland. "Safari guides" who help in identifying wildlife and communicating interesting information about the animals staff several viewing platforms.

Located within a five-minute drive to the Animal Kingdom Theme Park (but with no walking path to the park), the animals you'll see here are exclusively those of the lodge and not part of the theme park's menagerie. The design is one that encourages observation of the animals from both common lookouts as well as from 75 percent of the rooms. Each savanna holds different species, and patience is sometimes required to spot them. But more times than not you'll find the savanna brimming with an abundance of prime viewing opportunities, including zebras, giraffes, gazelles, ankole (African cattle), wildebeests, exotic birds, and more.

If you can somehow find the time take a tour of the resort's outstanding collection of more than 500 pieces of museum quality African art, including intricate masks, amazing beadwork, artifacts dating as far back as 8,500 B.C., and much, much more.

REST

Guest rooms. Don't even consider booking a room without a savanna view, well worth every penny for a front row seat from which to view the animals. And don't forget to bring your binoculars! Through a shield-covered door is an attractively designed, honey-colored room outfitted with handcrafted and carved furnishings, torch-shaped lamps, tribal baskets, and ethnic prints. Intricately engraved headboards are draped in a gauzy fabric reminiscent of mosquito netting and beds are covered in vibrant African print spreads. Flat-screen TVs are built into a bureau (one that really takes up too much room space) flanked by a table and two chairs. Baths have a separate granite-topped vanity area with double sinks, hair dryer, full-length mirror, and too-dim lighting. The bathroom walls are papered with maps of Africa, and the vanity holds a wonderful hand-carved mirror.

Amenities include an iron and ironing board, keyed safe, refrigerator, coffeemaker, and daily newspaper. Room bedding includes one king or two queens, or a queen-size bed and bunk bed. All rooms have balconies, 75 percent of them offering savanna views. However, guest rooms at 344 square feet are a bit cramped.

Views are: *Standard*, overlooking the front of the resort and the parking area; *Pool*, overlooking the pool area; and *Savanna*, overlooking one of three savannas with an additional charge for the central Arusha savanna.

CARA'S TIP: At the Animal Kingdom Lodge there are three savannas, each with their own charm. The Kudu Trail savanna facing the Animal Kingdom Villas–Kidani Village is probably my least favorite. Beware the Standard View rooms that look at the parking area and could possibly be in the valet parking drop-off area with a constant stream of buses and cars passing by your room balcony at all hours of the day and night.

Concierge rooms. Concierge guest rooms all come with a view of the savanna and are located mostly on the 4th and 5th floors. The thatch-roofed, sixth-floor *Kilimanjaro Club* overlooking the lobby offers delicious and unusual food and a pleasant ambience. Extra amenities include the services of a concierge staff, DVD players, and nightly turndown service.

Morning brings a continental breakfast of juice, bagels, croissants, muffins, cinnamon rolls, fresh fruit, oatmeal, yogurt, and cereal. Later you'll find afternoon beverages and snacks of trail mix, yogurt covered pretzels, cookies, granola bars, fruit, goldfish crackers, nuts, and gummy bears, with the addition of scones at teatime. Evenings enjoy South African Indaba Chardonnay, Shiraz, and Merlot in addition to a selection of beer (Sam Adams, Heineken, Bud Light, Tusker, and Yuengling). Appetizers include cold items such as chilled mango-ginger soup, goat cheese Peppadew crème brûlée, tabouleh salad with shaved beef, roasted eggplant with goat cheese in phyllo cups, artichoke and curry shrimp, and falafel and cucumber with *harissa* yogurt; warm items might be mushroom *duxelle* with goat cheese and toasted flat bread, seafood beignets with *sambal* dip, lamb patties with tomato jam, African-spiced salmon cake with roasted sweet pepper glaze, vegetable samosas, warm African shrimp, pearl couscous, chicken bastille, and turkey *bobotie*—all from the on-site restaurants, Boma and Jiko. After-dinner treats include cookies, pineapple cheesecake, mini-tarts, Rice Krispies treats, mango-filled phyllo dough, cordials, and sometimes zebra domes (ganache-covered chocolate-coffee mousse). Soda, lemonade, iced tea, and Jungle Juice are available throughout the day. You'll even find a self-service espresso and cappuccino machine.

A special early morning excursion, the Sunrise Safari Breakfast Adventure, is available to Animal Kingdom Lodge concierge guests only on Thursday and Sunday at 7:00 a.m. It includes a 45-minute before-park-hours ride through the Animal Kingdom's *Kilimanjaro Safaris®*

Expedition followed by a buffet breakfast at Pizzafari. Advance reservations can be made 180 days prior through the concierge itinerary planning office by calling (407) 938-4755.

Suites. *One-bedroom Suites* at 777 square feet feature a separate parlor with a queen-size sofa bed, easy chair, coffee table, entertainment center, four-person dining table, wet bar with small refrigerator and microwave, writing desk, half bath, and balcony with savanna view. In the bedroom are two queen-size beds, entertainment center, vanity desk, and balcony. The bath has a double sink, tub and large shower, plus a separate room for the commode. Sleeps six.

Two-bedroom Suites have the same living room layout, but the master bedroom has a king-size bed, easy chair and ottoman, and a separate vanity area. A standard-size second bedroom with two queen-size beds, or a queen and a bunk with a standard bath sits off the foyer. Sleeps eight with a savanna view.

For truly grand surroundings book Disney's best suite, the two-bedroom, two-and-a-half-bath *Royal Assante Presidential Suite* with more than 2,115 square feet of exotic luxury. Located on the 5th floor and reminiscent of famous African lodges, it offers panoramic views of the main savanna teeming with exotic wildlife. Just off the entry is the dining room boasting a massive table made from a single tree trunk and seating eight in faux zebra-upholstered chairs. The suite's highlight is its circular living room with a fascinating thatch ceiling completely surrounded by a stand-up balcony, hardwood and stone flooring, rich African textiles and artwork, rock fireplace, and hand-carved furnishings including an assortment of easy chairs and a curved sofa. The master bedroom comes with a mosquito net-draped king bed composed of tree trunks, a wall of reed built-ins filled with drawers and a flat-screen TV, and a sitting area with sleeper sofa, another TV, and drum-style table. The adjoining bath is one of Disney's most interesting with its freestanding soaking tub, double sinks, vanity, shower, mini TV, and separate commode and bidet area. The second bedroom is standard size with two queen beds. A deep balcony with lounge chairs and outdoor dining table runs the length of both bedrooms and over to the suite's dining room, perfect for dinner *alfresco* overlooking the savanna. You'll also find a half bath with a river rock vanity and raised basin, an office featuring a grass cloth and copper clad desk, and a service kitchen with a full-size refrigerator, wet bar, microwave, and separate entry.

The two-bedroom, two-and-a-half-bath *Royal Kuba Vice Presidential Suite* at 1,619 square feet, also located on the 5th floor, is another gem. Similar to the Royal Assante it comes with rooms that are a bit smaller in size and without an office, but with the same amazing décor, thatch ceiling, master bedroom, bath, and balcony. Both the Presidential and VP Suites welcome you with exotic fresh floral arrangements.

Animal Kingdom Villas–Jambo House. Within the Animal Kingdom Lodge on the 5th or 6th floors are the Jambo House Villas, available in studio, one-, two-, and three-bedroom units. Similar to the lodge's guest rooms with rich, warm fabrics, lovely carved wood furnishings, and earthy colors, they offer, except for the studios, a small kitchen area and quite a bit more room to spread out than the standard rooms here.

Studios are 316-365 square feet and come with a queen bed, double-size sleeper sofa, table and two chairs, flat-screen TV in a bureau, freestanding armoire closet, and balcony. There's also a wet bar mini-kitchen with microwave, sink, and refrigerator. In the bathroom is a tub/shower and double sink with the commode separate.

One-Bedroom Villas have 629-710 square feet. You'll find a small kitchen with a full-size stove and refrigerator, sink, dishwasher, and kitchen island. The parlor has a chocolate brown queen-size sleeper sofa, oversized, pumpkin-colored sleeper easy chair (except in the Value Villas which are smaller), table with a two-person bench and two chairs, coffee table, flat-screen TV, and balcony. Most sleep five. The master comes with a king bed, leopard motif carpeting, bureau with TV, desk, and a second balcony. In the bath are double sinks in a granite vanity, whirlpool bathtub decorated with a setting sun Lion King mural, and separate commode area. There's also a washer, dryer, and two balconies. A *Two-Bedroom Villa* is simply a One-Bedroom Villa plus a connecting Studio with 945-1075 square feet.

There are six *Grand Villas,* each with three bedrooms, four baths in 2,349 square feet. A totally different layout than the next-door Kidani's Grand Villas, these are on one level and located at the end of the resort's wings. A combination living and dining room has tile floors topped with colorful rugs, sleeper sofa with two easy chairs and entertainment armoire, and a dining table seating ten. A nice-size granite-top kitchen has a full-size refrigerator, stove, microwave, dishwasher, and sink. There are three balconies—one off the living/dining room, one off the master bedroom, and a shared balcony off the two guest rooms. In the master is a king bed, entertainment center, and desk; its bath comes with a whirlpool tub, shower, double sinks, oversized TV, and separate toilet area. Each of the standard-size guest rooms has two queen beds and a bath, and there is a half bath off the entry hall area. A playroom with pool table is exclusive to these villas.

> **CARA'S TIP:** What the Animal Kingdom Villas—Jambo House call Value Villas are smaller villas minus the sleeper chair in the living area.

DINE

An interesting array of dining choices with an African flair should please even the most timid eaters. Wine connoisseurs will love the fact that the Animal Kingdom Lodge has one of the largest offerings of South African wines in the United States.

Boma. Lively African and American buffet open for breakfast and dinner. *Breakfast buffet:* fruit, cereal, pancakes, omelets, sausage and biscuits, breakfast meats and potatoes, scrambled eggs, brioche, quinoa porridge, *bobotie* (traditional African dish of ground meat and egg custard), breakfast pizza, cured pork loin, carved ham. *Dinner buffet:* hummus, large variety of interesting salads, fresh fruit, *matar paneer*, roasted root vegetables, salmon with orange-almond rice, Durban spiced chicken, ancho barbecue pork ribs, carved strip loin, and a bevy of desserts including famous zebra domes.

Jiko. One of Disney's loveliest restaurants open for dinner only; international food with an African flair and an extensive South African wine list. (See full description in the Dining in Style at Walt Disney World Resort chapter.)

The Mara. Self-service restaurant. *Breakfast:* African-inspired breakfast platter with scrambled eggs, Merguez sausage, pap, *chakalaka* and grilled tomatoes, egg and bacon croissant sandwich, *bobotie* platter, Mickey shaped waffle, quinoa cereal. *Lunch and dinner:* Angus bacon cheeseburger, flatbreads, African stew, falafel pita, chicken pita with hummus, oak-smoked rotisserie chicken, Mara salad with chicken, chicken breast nuggets, hand carved sandwich, South African wine and beer. *Children's menu:* for breakfast Mickey-shaped waffle or a breakfast platter; for lunch hamburger, chicken nuggets, chicken leg, rotisserie chicken, mac 'n' cheese, cheese pizza.

In-Room Dining. Available 6:00 a.m. to midnight.

SIP

Capetown Lounge and Wine Bar. Jiko's small bar offering an extensive South African wine list along with hand-crafted cocktails, beer, after-dinner drinks, single malt scotch, and port.

Uzima Springs Watering Hole. Thatch-roofed pool bar for specialty drinks, sangria, African beer, wine, and nonalcoholic smoothies. Food can be ordered here from *Private Dining:* a selection of hot and cold sandwiches served in a bento box with watermelon, tomato and blue cheese salad, sun-dried tomato hummus with *lavosh* crackers, and white chocolate mousse; Angus cheeseburger, grilled chicken sandwich, South African-style Cuban sandwich, club turkey ciabatta, vegetarian falafel, and mixed green salad; *children:* grilled cheese, grilled chicken breast, macaroni and cheese, and a cheeseburger.

Victoria Falls Lounge. African bush lodge-style bar overlooking Boma (Sigh! Too bad it doesn't overlook the savanna.) open 4:00 p.m. to midnight offering African-inspired cocktails, sangria, beer, and South African wine. *Appetizers:* cheese platter with spiced fruit jam and crostini, nut mix with African spices, crisp breads and dip.

PLAY

Arcade. Pumbaa's Fun and Games arcade located near the pool.

Children's playground and activities. Hakuna Matata playground is located near the pool with a nice view of the flamingo area and the savanna. Pool activities include wildlife games and parties, Name That Tune, chalk art, hula hoop contest, critter round-up, and water relays. A nightly campfire can be found at Arusha Savanna Overlook.

Swimming. Uzima Pool, the lodge's 11,000 square-foot version of a watering hole is surrounded by towering bamboo and palm trees and highlighted by a 67-foot waterslide; cement is darkened to create the effect of swimming out in the bush, minus the crocodiles. Two secluded whirlpools and a kiddie pool.

Tennis. Two lighted hard courts are located next-door at Animal Kingdom Villas–Kidani Village; check out equipment at Community Hall.

Tours and Activities. Offered are Animal Programs such as Meet a Savanna Guide, Flamingo Feeding, Animal Tracking and Enrichment, and African Face Painting; Cultural Immersion such as Medallion Rubbing, Music of the Savanna, African Folktales, Cultural Safaris, and Primal Parade. A half-hour daily culinary tour of the resort's restaurants is available every day.

Wine Tasting. Each Wednesday from 3:00–4:00 p.m. explore the wine regions of South Africa and sample three delicious vintages paired with South African food. Cost is $25 plus tax and gratuity; reservations can be made at 407-938-7149.

THREE EXCITING ADVENTURES EXCLUSIVE TO DISNEY'S ANIMAL KINGDOM LODGE

- *Sunrise Safari Breakfast Adventure.* Begin your day at Disney's Animal Kingdom theme park, entering through a backstage area before boarding a jeep onto the savanna at Kilimanjaro Safaris Expedition. Enjoy a one-hour ride with frequent stops for photos and plenty of time for questions. Afterwards there is a breakfast buffet at an Animal Kingdom restaurant. Offered on Thursdays and Sundays between 6:30 and 7:30 a.m. depending on the Animal Kingdom park opening time. $65.00 for adults and $32.50 for children ages 3 to 9 plus tax. Exclusive to Disney's Animal Kingdom Lodge concierge guests only.

- *Wanyama Safari.* One of Disney's best resort tours begins late afternoon with tea in Jiko followed by an up-close-and-personal, one and a half-hour game drive around the resort's savannas.

As it is led by one of the Lodge's Animal Programs team in an open-air safari van there are incredible photo opportunities. A sumptuous preset family-style meal with several courses and wine pairings at Jiko ends your experience. Open only to guests of the Animal Kingdom Lodge and Animal Kingdom Villas–Kidani Village. Offered daily for $179 per person including gratuity plus tax; minimum age is eight.

- *Night Vision Safari.* Join an Animal Programs Cast Member on an hour-long safari at the Animal Kingdom Lodge. This experience takes place after dark and is reminiscent of nighttime African game drives through the savanna. Guests use night vision goggles to make the most of their viewing experience, perfect for seeing the animals and the resort like never before. $70 plus tax; participants must be at least 8 years of age. Offered on Wednesday, Friday, Saturday, and Sunday; limited to ten guests so book early. Open only for guests of the Animal Kingdom Lodge and Disney's Animal Kingdom Villas–Kidani Village.

Make reservations for all three experiences through the Animal Kingdom Lodge Concierge Itinerary Planning Office or your travel advisor beginning 180 days in advance.

WORK, MOVE, SOOTHE

Childcare. Simba's Cubhouse with classic Disney movies, play kitchen, viewing window to the savanna, arts and crafts, arcade and computer games. Open 4:30 p.m. to midnight for potty-trained children ages three to twelve; cost includes dinner and snacks. Available to all registered guests of Walt Disney World resorts; call (407) WDW-DINE or (407) 939-3463 for reservations.

Fitness Center. Zahanati Massage and Fitness Center offers 24-hour access with free weights, Life Fitness strength training equipment, Life Fitness treadmills, exercise bicycles, and ellipticals. A steam room and sauna is found in each locker room. Fitness center is complimentary to resort guests; personal training for a fee. Facials and massage with in-room service available.

GO

Bus transportation is available to all four Disney theme parks, Downtown Disney, Typhoon Lagoon, and Blizzard Beach.

To reach other Disney resorts, you must first take a bus to Downtown Disney or an open theme park and then transfer to your resort destination.

THE HOLIDAYS AT WALT DISNEY WORLD

The holidays are a special time at Walt Disney World when it's adorned with more than 1,300 Christmas trees, 15 miles of garland, 8.5 million lights, 1,314 wreaths, and 300,000 yards of ribbon. If you'd like to raise your holiday spirit a few notches just head to one of the following locations:

The Magic Kingdom features a 65-foot high Christmas tree in Town Square with a 3-foot star on top, Main Street shop windows adorned with animated characters, garland, and lights draping Main Street, as well as a special Christmas parade. Mickey's Very Merry Christmas Party, an after-park-hours ticketed event, is one of the most popular holiday happenings, so book early. And the Castle Dream Lights is a holiday favorite experience when Cinderella Castle transforms into a shimmering "ice palace" with 200,000 white lights from early November just through the New Year.

At Epcot, World Showcase features Christmas storytelling from around the world, and a meet and greet with Santa and Mrs. Claus in the American Adventure pavilion. There's even a special Illuminations seasonal finale. Best of all is the Candlelight Processional staged three times each evening from late November through December 30 with a massed choir, fifty-piece orchestra, and celebrity narrators who tell the story of Christmas.

Disney's Hollywood Studios is one of the most popular places around with its fantastic Osborne Family Spectacle of Lights

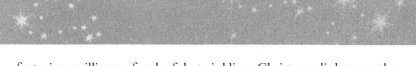

featuring millions of colorful, twinkling Christmas lights on the Streets of America along with Santa Goofy to greet the crowds. A 65-foot tree sits outside the park with film reel decorations and a Disney character train that travels around its base.

The Animal Kingdom hosts *Mickey's Jingle Jungle* Parade complete with Santa, Goofy, and falling snow.

At Disney's Contemporary Resort is Walt Disney World's largest wreath at 25 feet in diameter and a 70-foot tree out front decorated in over 35,000 LED lights. In the Grand Canyon Concourse is a gigantic gingerbread holiday tree.

The Grand Floridian lobby's life-size, 300-square-foot gingerbread house is a holiday wonder. It doubles as a real bakeshop from which you can purchase all sorts of delicious goodies.

Animal Kingdom Lodge features an entirely edible miniature African village of sugar, chocolate, and gingerbread, and a tree decorated with handmade ornaments from African villages.

The Beach Club's display is a life-size gingerbread and chocolate carousel featuring ponies made of chocolate and fondant, giant candy cane poles, handcrafted poinsettias, and hand-painted portraits of famous Disney characters.

The Yacht Club presents a miniature working train running through a sugary village and a mountain made of sweets.

The BoardWalk Inn sells gingerbread treats next to the beautifully lit tree.

The Animal Kingdom Villas–Kidani Village

492 units. 3701 Osceola Parkway, Bay Lake, FL 32830; phone (407) 938–3000, fax (407) 938–4799. Check-in 4:00 p.m., checkout 11:00 a.m. For reservations contact your travel advisor or call (407) 939-3476.

Claim To Fame. Great savanna views in roomy villas and a remote resort far from the madness of the theme parks.

Room To Book. Definitely one with savanna views, but the three-bedroom, two-story Grand Villas, if the pocketbook allows, are the best treat of all.

The Wow Factor! Time spent at the fire pit, the perfect place to enjoy the wildlife on a starry night.

As at the next-door Animal Kingdom Lodge, this Disney Vacation Club property has the advantage of a savanna teeming with wildlife along with roomy and distinctive villas. The sound of the jungle greets you at every turn as you walk the pathways amidst lush, exotic greenery. An attractive two-story lobby area with African rustic chic seating, hardwood flooring, and tribal rugs sports a delightful thatched ceiling. Scattered here and there throughout the resort are superb viewing areas with rockers, perfect for those guests without a savanna view. Off the lobby The Library offers a restful sitting room with a fireplace as well as a balcony with savanna views. Although the villas offer a table-service restaurant, feature pool, fitness center, and water play area, guests are also entitled to all privileges of the Animal Kingdom Lodge next-door including the pool, playground, and childcare with a 10-minute walk between the two.

REST

Villas. Villas here are atmospheric and very similar to the Jambo House next-door where you'll discover hand carved furnishings, tile entries, ostrich egg lamps, mural-decorated tub surrounds, chocolate brown granite countertops, animal print carpeting, khaki curtains with leather strapping, a Lion King theme, and a chocolate and persimmon-colored décor with African textile touches. Headboards are made of carved, dark wood, bedspreads are the same as at the next-door Jambo house, and each bed is topped with a mosquito netting decoration. Every bedroom has its own TV, DVD player, and iPod docking station clock radio. And each unit has a laptop-size electronic safe, vacuum, iron and ironing board, and Pack 'n' Play.

Studios, sleeping up to four in 316 square feet, offer a queen-size bed accompanied by a sleeper sofa, table and two chairs, and bureau with built-in flat-screen TV. There are two closets, one of which is a carved wood armoire. You'll also find a mini-kitchen with sink, undercounter refrigerator, microwave, toaster, and coffeemaker. Baths have a single sink granite vanity (no makeup mirror), a tub/shower combination, and separate commode area. All have a balcony with varying views.

One-Bedroom Villas sleep five in 710 square feet. The living room has a chocolate brown sleeper sofa as well as a persimmon-colored sleeper chair and a flat-screen TV. A dining booth seating five sits off the small granite kitchen with a two-seat dining bar as well as a coffeemaker, dinnerware, glassware, flatware, pots and pans, microwave, toaster, stove, refrigerator, and dishwasher. A laundry closet contains a stacked washer and dryer, and in the entry is an additional full bath. The master bedroom suite is comfortable with a king-size bed, ostrich egg lamps, desk, and bureau with flat-screen TV. In the adjoining terra cotta bath is a whirlpool tub, large shower, single sink, and separate commode area. A balcony is accessed from both the living area and master bedroom.

The *Two-Bedroom Villa* is a One-Bedroom Villa plus a Studio and sleeps up to nine people in 1,173 square feet. Some villas are dedicated Two-Bedrooms with the second bedroom offering two queen-size beds and no mini-kitchen.

Sixteen *Grand Villas* sleep up to twelve people in 2,201 square feet with most offering spectacular views (try and avoid those located at the very end of the property where views are not quite up to par with those located in the central resort). Three bedrooms and four baths are on two levels with the kitchen, dining area, living room, master bedroom, and extra bath on the 1st floor, and two bedrooms, two baths, and a TV room on the 2nd floor (entry doors are found on both floors). The kitchen is open to the adjoining six-person dining table and buffet. The soaring two-story living area has tile flooring, colorful rug, sleeper sofa, sleeper chair, easy chair, and entertainment center with TV and stereo system. A balcony extends the length of the bottom floor. A master with king bed, similar to the one found in the standard villas, is just off the living area; single sink, whirlpool tub, and extra TV in the bath. Climb the kraal fence stairwell to the 2nd floor where two identical bedrooms, each with two queen beds and a balcony, flank the loft with its sleeper sofa. A full-size laundry room is found downstairs.

CARA'S TIP: Standard View Villas offer a view of the front of the resort or the pool, but might also face the valet area with a constant stream of buses and cars passing by your room balcony at all hours of the day and night. From the Savanna View Villas you will also have a view of the next-door Animal Kingdom Lodge. A lobby level villa (floor two) comes with up-close-and-personal savanna views so think about requesting one.

DINE

Sanaa. Kidani's only full-service restaurant offers African cooking with Indian flavors, open for lunch and dinner. Huge picture windows overlook the resort's savanna. (See full description in the Dining in Style at Walt Disney World Resort chapter.)

SIP

Maji Pool Bar. Great pool bar with interesting views of a bird sanctuary offering frozen drinks, specialty drinks, beer, wine, and sangria; turkey panini, hot dog, vegetarian falafel, South-African-style Cuban sandwich, Caesar salad with tandoori chicken; or you can order food from Private Dining served in a bento box with choices of grilled lamb *kefta*, tandoori Angus chuck burger, and tandoori chicken or shrimp.

Sanaa Lounge. Small but unique thatch roof bar located within Sanaa restaurant with specialty drinks such as African mojitos, Malawi mango margaritas, and Kande coconut coolers along with beer and South African wines. *Appetizers:* Indian-style bread service with your choice of three breads and three accompaniments, salad sampler, potato and pea samosas, lamb *kefta* kabobs with mint chutney.

PLAY

Arcade. Safari So Good Arcade is located near the lobby area.

Barbeque Pavilion. Fire up the grill and picnic alfresco in this atmospheric natural setting with views of a wildlife pond; located near the sports court.

Basketball and Shuffleboard. Courts are located across the street in a nature setting; complimentary equipment available at Community Hall.

Children's playground and activities. Arts and crafts in Community

Hall from 2:00 to 5:00 p.m. Pool parties and activities such as bingo, chalk art, Disney trivia, Hula Hoop contest, bean bag toss, and Name That Tune.

Community Hall. Located on the 2nd floor just off the lobby area, this is where you head for arts and crafts, board games, table tennis, foosball, game stations, and TV viewing.

Fire pit. An atmospheric fire is lit nightly at Pembe Savanna Overlook, perfect for stargazing.

Swimming. Samawati Springs Pool has a prime setting overlooking a nature area of pines and grasses with a 128-foot water slide and two whirlpools, one that is nicely hidden. Uwanja Camp, a super-fun interactive water play area for children, has water cannons, an overflowing tower of water buckets, rope bridges, geyser jets, and a waterfall lagoon (watch out for the spitting African masks!).

Tennis. Two lighted hard courts are located across the street in a nature setting; complimentary equipment available at Community Hall.

Tours and Activities. Animal Programs such as Meet a Savanna Guide, Animal Enrichment, Bio Blocks, Have Your Heard?, and Night Vision Animal Viewing are on the resort's agenda. Also Cultural Immersion such as African Inspired–Disney Designed, Drum Café, African Journey, and African Wonders.

WORK, MOVE, SOOTHE

The Animal Kingdom Villas–Kidani Village shares all services with the adjacent Animal Kingdom Lodge. (See the earlier entry for the Animal Kingdom Lodge).

Fitness Center. Survival of the Fittest Fitness Center located in the Kidani pool area with free weights, Life Fitness treadmills, elliptical cross trainers, and weight machines; complimentary to resort guests with 24-hour access.

GO

Bus transportation is available to all four Disney theme parks, Downtown Disney, Typhoon Lagoon, and Blizzard Beach.

To reach other Disney resorts you must first take a bus to Downtown Disney or an open theme park and then transfer to your resort destination.

WHAT I'M CRAZY ABOUT AT WALT DISNEY WORLD!

- Dinner with a view at California Grill

- A drink on the Belle Vue Lounge's balcony overlooking Disney's BoardWalk

- Disney's best suite, the Royal Assante at the Animal Kingdom Lodge

- Strolling World Showcase after dark with a glass of wine in hand

- The Magic Kingdom's fireworks show, Wishes

- The magical feeling of any of the monorail resorts

- Nibbling on appetizers while listening to the music from the Grand Floridian lobby from the Royal Palm Club concierge lounge

- Tiki torch-lit pathway at the Polynesian Resort after dark

- The nighttime view of Cinderella Castle from a theme park view room at a monorail resort

- A window table and fresh seafood at Narcoossee's

- Any table at California Grill followed by a fireworks viewing from the restaurant's catwalk

- An after-dinner drink late at night at California Grill Lounge with a prime window seat

- The sense of excitement I feel each and every time I drive under the Walt Disney World welcome sign—Whee!!

Other Notable Resorts

If it's 5-star luxury you're seeking then consider either the Waldorf Astoria Orlando or the soon-to-open Four Seasons Resort Orlando at the Walt Disney World Resort.

Waldorf Astoria Orlando

> 497 rooms. 14200 Bonnet Creek Resort Lane, Orlando, Florida 32821; (407) 597-5500; Fax (407) 597-5501. Check-in 3:00 p.m., checkout 11:00 a.m. For reservations call your travel advisor or (407) 597-5500, or online at WaldorfAstoriaOrlando.com.

Claim To Fame. Simply put, it's one of the most luxurious resorts in Orlando.

Room To Book. A lavish Luxury Suite with views of the golf course and nature sanctuary; or the Waldorf Suite with sweeping Disney views.

The Wow Factor! A visit to the resort's spa followed by cabana time at the pool, or better yet, a massage in your cabana.

The first Waldorf-Astoria to be built from the ground up since its New York flagship property opened seventy-eight years ago, this luxury resort sits right in the middle of Walt Disney World Resort. Swank and sophisticated it redefined local luxury in Orlando. Although not technically on Disney property it's almost next-door to Disney's Hollywood Studios and just a 5-minute drive to Downtown Disney. The reasons to love the resort are many: a sophisticated spa, the Rees Jones-designed golf course, two divine pools, seventy-five acres of wetlands . . . the list goes on. It's certainly my pick, for now at least, as the most splendid resort around.

Stunningly impressive is the circular, high gloss marble lobby studded with glittering mosaic tile and an aquamarine blue glass reception desk. Its centerpiece is a round velvet settee topped with a handcrafted replica of the New York Waldorf's signature clock. Old World with a touch of the contemporary, there are dark, rich woods and miles of marble as far as the eye can see. Though refined, expect a more casual atmosphere than the New York counterpart. This is Orlando after all.

SLEEP

Guest rooms. As you would expect elegant guest rooms are stylishly appointed. They offer crown molding, maple wood furnishings, 42-inch HD LCD televisions with Blu-ray DVD players and surround sound, two-line phones, iPod docking station clock radio, oversized work desk, glass lamps, heavy silk curtains with shimmery shears, plush muted gold carpeting, and Italian marble entry halls and baths. Luxuriate in the very best beds in Orlando made with triple sheeted Egyptian cotton linens, fluffy white down duvets and pillows, feather mattresses, and a black and white houndstooth throw. Dual sink vanities can only be found in the top suites, but Deluxe Suites and Rooms do offer an enormous shower, amber glass tile-fronted soaking tub, Salvatore Ferragamo bath products, and a lighted makeup mirror. A daily $25 resort fee is assessed and includes unlimited internet access, two welcome drinks in Peacock Alley, access to the Golf Club's golf driving facility including equipment rental, access to the fitness facility, and discounts on golf merchandise, spa, and pool cabanas.

Amenities include twice-daily housekeeping, evening turndown service, luxurious robes and slippers, daily coffee and tea service, weekday newspaper delivery, laptop-fit safe, iron and ironing board . . . in short, a tastefully designed and supremely comfortable room. The hotel does offer balconies but unfortunately only in suites.

Deluxe Rooms have 448 square feet and offer a king bed or two queen beds. There's a desk/bureau combination with flat-screen TV. A seating area within the bedroom holds a small sofa and chair in the king rooms and a chair only in the two-bed rooms. Baths feature black granite vanities with a single sink, a large frameless shower as well as a separate soaking tub but not a separate room for the commode. Views are of either the golf course or Disney, and none have balconies.

Suites. The 945 square feet *Deluxe Suites* have a separate living area with a four-person dining table, a gold sleeper sofa and sky blue easy chair, a bureau with a large flat-screen TV, and a balcony. Within the living area is a buffet with wine refrigerator and wet bar. A king bed is found in the master along with a work desk, easy chair, and bureau with flat-screen TV. Baths are slightly larger but similar to those in a Deluxe Room. This becomes a 2-bedroom Chairman's Suite with the addition of a Deluxe Room with two queen beds on the other side of the living area. Views are of the resort, golf course, or a distant view of the theme parks.

If you're lucky enough to be ensconced in one of the *Luxury Suites* you'll enjoy a 1,460 square foot corner beauty with a large living area, separate bedroom, and master bath. Within the living room are a chenille sleeper sofa, sea blue easy chair and ottoman, amber glass lamps, oversized flat-screen TV, and balcony. There's also a black granite kitchen of sorts with a counter and three bar stools. While nice it doesn't seem to serve much of a function since there's only an undercounter wine refrigerator and sink with loads of unnecessary drawer space. These suites come in one- and two-bedroom options, the second bedroom being a Deluxe Room with two queen beds. Views are always of the front of the resort facing the nature sanctuary, some with additional golf course views.

The one-bedroom *Waldorf Astoria Suites* are corner suites with 1,780 square feet of space. There's an oversized bar as in the Luxury Suite, but here the living area is longer and narrower with two easy chairs, sleeper sofa, coffee table and TV. Ask for one on a higher floor and enjoy gorgeous Disney views and spectacular sunsets (oh, yes!). Another plus is a half-bath strangely located off the bedroom entry instead of in the main entry hall, but perfectly okay if only two are using the suite. The bedroom is a standard size and has a king bed, easy chair, desk, bureau, and TV with a full-size bath. The addition of a connecting Deluxe Room off the entry hall makes this a two-bedroom option.

And then there are the grand dames, the resort's two *Presidential Suites* (one on the 14th floor, the other on the 15th), both with golf course corner views, both with the same décor, and both with 3,330 square feet. The oversized living area has a game table with oversized high back chairs, a ten-person formal dining table graced with double chandeliers, a full kitchen minus a stove, an elegant sitting area with a soft gold velvet sofa, an alcove office, and two terraces. A half-bath with a Venetian mirror is off the living area. From the dining room French doors open into the massive master bedroom with a king bed and its lovely white linen headboard, red and platinum accents, the luxurious gold velvet settee, beige chenille sofa, easy chair, a TV that raises and lowers from a bureau, and another balcony. Baths have two vanities, separate shower, and whirlpool tub with a huge picture window. A second bedroom can be connected.

> CARA'S TIP: Rooms on floor eight or above enjoy an all-encompassing view of the entire area and are on request only. If you are wondering where the listing is for the Waldorf concierge room options, unfortunately there is not a concierge lounge at this resort. Strange but true.

DINE

Bull & Bear. Overlooking the first hole of the golf course, offerings include inspired steakhouse fare and a club-like atmosphere. (See full description in the Dining in Style at Walt Disney World Resort chapter.)

The Clubhouse Grille. The Waldorf Astoria's Golf Club restaurant, open for lunch only with Cobb salad, Nicoise salad, Rueben or Rachel sandwich, club sandwiches, Angus burger, Chicago-style hot dog, and hot turkey sandwich.

Oscar's. Informal dining in a casual setting, open for breakfast only. *Breakfast buffet:* brioche, muffins, donuts, croissants, scones, smoked salmon, breakfast risotto, steel cut oatmeal and toppings, yellow hominy grits, Greek yogurt, crepes, Madagascar vanilla filled waffles, fresh fruit pop tarts, scrambled eggs, smoked bacon, fingerling potatoes, charcuterie board, made-to-order omelets, and a cereal and parfait bar. *A la carte items:* lump crab gratin, omelets, huevos rancheros, eggs benedict, French toast, buttermilk pancakes, smoked salmon and bagels, charcuterie and artisan cheeses.

AquaMarine. Poolside restaurant open for lunch and early dinner with flatbreads (*margherita*, chicken feta, or portobello mushroom), Greek salad, Asian chop salad, Maine lobster and shrimp wrap, local catch sandwich, burger, fish tacos, fire roasted chicken and prosciutto focaccia sandwich along with specialty drinks, wine, and beer.

In-Room Dining. New York's Waldorf Astoria was the world's first hotel to offer in-room dining and the tradition continues here with round-the-clock service.

SIP

Bull & Bear Lounge. Classy bar adjoining the restaurant with fine wines, single malt scotch, and specialty cocktails; appetizers from the restaurant are also available.

Peacock Alley. Found just off the lobby area with prime people watching. You'll fall hard for the peacock feather carpeting and the delish cocktails, "mocktails", and small plates of nibbles like a charcuterie board, Caesar salad (add chicken, shrimp, or scallops), Waldorf salad, artisan cheese board, avocado and crab summer roll, lobster BLT popovers, four-cheese fondue and braised artichoke, preserved tomato soup, club sandwich, ham and cheese waffle, filet mignon sliders, natural chicken sandwich on challah bread, and a grilled portobello sandwich. Desserts of apple cranberry tart, red velvet cake, and crème brûlée are also served. Live piano music nightly as well as Royal Tea on Sunday afternoon.

Sir Harry's Lounge. At the end of the day unwind in this gem of a lounge with its private club atmosphere. Cocktails, port, single-malt scotch, beer, and wines from around the world with live piano music on Friday and Saturday evening; closed in the summer season.

PLAY

Bicycles. Complimentary bicycles for resort guests are found just outside the fitness room, perfect for a spin around the property.

Children's Programs and Activities. *WA Kids* offers both day and evening programs with a variety of creative and educational activities for children ages 5-12 including arts and crafts, movies, themed evening events, scavenger hunts, and gaming equipment. *Day Escape* is $75 for one child and $25 for each additional child. *Astoria After Dark* Friday and Saturday evenings for the same price including dinner and activities.

Golf. Rees Jones-designed, 18-hole championship course surrounded by a natural setting of palms, pines, and wetlands. (See full description in the Beyond the Walt Disney World Resort Theme Parks chapter, Golf section.)

Jogging. A brick path between the Waldorf and its sister property, Hilton Bonnet Creek, overlooks the golf course.

Swimming. Put on your Gucci sunglasses and head out to the your choice of swimming pools. The formal signature pool is lined with private cabanas available for full-day rentals offering chaise lounges or a sofa and table, Wi-Fi access, 42" HD flat-screen TVs, refrigerator, soft drinks and bottled water, fruit, and bathrobes. A second zero-entry pool adjoins with one whirlpool.

WORK, MOVE, SOOTHE

Business Center. 24-hour business center for printing, copying, binding, shipping, signs, and graphics.

Car Rental. A Hertz Car Rental is found in the lobby.

Fitness Center. Impressively outfitted workout room with an amazing array of equipment—Precor ellipticals as well as recumbent and upright bicycles, Cybex ellipticals, Life Fitness treadmills with flat-screen TVs, Precor weight machines, free weights, and cable and pulley machine. Morning yoga class and personal instruction are available for a fee.

Spa. The Waldorf Astoria Spa offers 22 treatment suites. (See full description in the Diversions Beyond Walt Disney World Resort Theme Parks chapter, Spa section.)

GO

Regularly scheduled transfers to all four Disney theme parks departing as often as every half hour. Private transportation can be arranged through concierge.

THE VERY BEST OF
WALT DISNEY WORLD
THEME PARKS

Newcomers often think Walt Disney World is comparable in size to California's Disneyland, the Magic Kingdom being first and foremost in their minds. Most never envision a complex twice the size of Manhattan with four theme parks spread out over nearly 40 square miles along with 35 resort hotels, 66,000 cast members, 81 holes of golf . . . the list goes on!

The Magic Kingdom, opened in 1971, was the first theme park at Walt Disney World with three more parks following in succession, beginning with Epcot a little over a decade later. Twice the size of the Magic Kingdom, Epcot was a totally different concept—an education in technology and innovation, other lands and cultures. Disney's Hollywood Studios opened in 1988, and with it came the glamour and glitz of show business. Then came the Animal Kingdom in 1998, conveying the theme of unity and harmony among all living creatures. Each park is unique and offers its own brand of enjoyment with new additions and attractions constantly in the works.

General Information

First I'll go over what you need to know about getting into and around the parks, then I'll examine the best of each park. Walt Disney World features such a wealth of attractions that most people don't have enough time on a single vacation to experience it all. That's why I've narrowed down the field for you and have chosen to feature the attractions that are, in my expert opinion, the very best each park has to offer. You'll find important information on only the best attractions and dining, the most anticipated special events, the most memorable entertainment, plus loads of tips for making your vacation an exceptional one.

WHO WANTS TO BE A VIP?

Those wishing to make their visit to the theme parks as seamless and easy as possible should consider Disney's personalized tours. For $315-355 per hour ($340-380 for non-Disney resort guests) with a minimum of six consecutive hours, a Disney VIP tour guide will completely customize your experience and maximize your time by assisting you and up to nine others with a day at the parks and plenty of Disney trivia along the way. You'll have flexibility of start time, the option of visiting multiple theme parks, private transportation to and from the parks with back-door entrance, expedited entry to FASTPASS attractions, and VIP seating for parades, select shows, and nighttime spectaculars. Reservations must be made at least forty-eight hours in advance by calling (407) 560–4033 or your travel advisor. I've never heard of anyone who afterwards doesn't say it was worth every penny.

Walt Disney World Theme Park Admission

Many options are available for Disney theme park passes, beginning with a *Magic Your Way* base ticket. Choose the number of days you wish to purchase and then consider the additional choices available to you. To purchase tickets: consult a travel advisor specializing in Disney; call (407) WDW-MAGIC or (407) 939-6244; go online at Disneyworld. disney.go.com/tickets-passes/; or purchase at either a Disney retail store or at the theme parks on arrival. Regardless of your ticket plan children ages two or younger will receive free admission.

Magic Your Way Park Tickets

Magic Your Way **Base Ticket.** Choose the number of days you'll need, allowing entrance to one theme park each day. Those purchasing only a 1-day ticket must choose between a 1-day ticket to the Magic Kingdom or a 1-day ticket that provides admission to any one of Disney's other three theme parks. Multi-day base tickets are offered for as many as ten days and tickets expire fourteen days after first use. You'll save with each additional day added.

Magic Your Way **Ticket with** *Park Hopper*® **Option.** Allows park-hopping privileges for a flat rate of $34-39 for one day and $59 for two days or more.

Magic Your Way **Ticket with** *Water Park Fun & More* **Option**. Includes one admission per day depending on the length of your ticket (you may use more than one option per day) to your choice of Typhoon Lagoon, Blizzard Beach, DisneyQuest, Disney's Oak Trail Golf Course (advance reservations required), a round of mini golf at *Disney's Fantasia Gardens* Miniature Golf Course or *Disney's Winter Summerland* Miniature Golf Course, or ESPN Wide World of Sports, all for a flat rate of $54 if purchasing only a 1-day ticket and $59 for multi-day tickets. Add park hopping and Water Parks Fun for a total of $79 if purchasing only a 1-day ticket, and $84 for multi-day tickets.

No Expiration **Option**. Allows the freedom to return to Walt Disney World anytime in the future and take advantage of unused days on your *Magic Your Way* tickets that normally expire fourteen days after first use. Price varies according to how many days of tickets are purchased.

Theme Park Annual Pass. Entitles you to unlimited access to all four Disney theme parks as well as complimentary parking and an array of discounts for 365 days. If you plan to return within a year this is the way to go. You may even consider this type of pass for shorter stays simply to receive the great savings available to Annual Passholders; only one person in your party must have an annual pass to obtain the discount. If you make an annual trip to Disney you should plan your return trip a few weeks shy of the expiration date of your pass since your park admission will already be paid. At press time Annual Pass rates were $609 for all ages.

Theme Park Premium Annual Pass. Same as the Annual Pass but also includes Blizzard Beach, Typhoon Lagoon, and DisneyQuest. At press time Premium Annual Pass rates were $729 for all ages.

Premier Passport. Allows unlimited access to all four Disney theme parks as well as the two theme parks at the Disneyland Resort and includes complimentary parking and an array of discounts. At press time Premier Passport rates were $979 for all ages.

MyMagic+

Disney's personalized vacation planner for Walt Disney World Resort, MyMagic+ features online and mobile tools like My Disney Experience, Family & Friends, FastPass+ and more. Definitely an enhancement to your guest experience, it makes it easier than ever to make the most of your Walt Disney World vacation.

Included in MyMagic+ are three components:

- *My Disney Experience*, a new area within Disneyworld.com that includes a free mobile app that will help in personalizing your vacation experience. Go to MyDisneyExperience.com to get started.

    Use My Disney Experience to link your Walt Disney World resort reservation and theme park tickets, customize your MagicBand, make FastPass+ selections, make dining reservations, look up attraction wait times and more.

- *Disney FastPass+ Service* allows you to reserve access to favorite attractions and experiences in advance. With FastPass+ you can skip the standby line at the attractions you reserve in advance, and now with more than double the previous number of experiences to choose from it's also possible to select character greetings, entertainment, parades, and firework shows as your FastPass+ selections. Only three FastPass+ selections can be chosen per day and they must all be within one theme park. But if your plans change, update your FastPass+ selections on the My Disney Experience mobile app, at your Disney resort's Lobby Concierge, or at the FastPass+ kiosks located throughout all four theme parks.

- *MagicBand* is your key to unlocking all of the magic. Available in seven colors, use it to unlock your resort guest room door, for park entry, connect to your credit card for cashless sales transactions where touch-to-pay functionality is available, and FastPass+ redemption.

  For now guests staying at Walt Disney World Resort hotels and Annual Passholders will receive a MagicBand. Guests who stay at non-Disney hotels will receive an RFID enabled ticket with features of touch to enter the park, touch to redeem FastPass+, and touch to pay. These guests can participate in My Disney Experience and purchase a MagicBand if they wish.

Touring Advice

Much ado is made of exactly how to approach each park and in what direction and order to tour. I do think a plan of action is necessary. However, it does take the fun out of your vacation time if you're tied down to a crazy, high-speed timetable. A good strategy is to make FastPass+ reservations in advance and then be in place at rope-drop and head immediately to the most popular rides in the park, avoiding those that are already planned with FastPass+ (unless, that is, you would like to ride an attraction more than once). In the Magic Kingdom this means *Splash Mountain*® Attraction or *Space Mountain*® Attraction as well as *New Fantasyland* attractions, *Under the Sea ~ Journey of the Little Mermaid* and *Enchanted Tales with Belle*. In Epcot it's the *Soarin*™ Attraction and *Test Track*® Presented by Chevrolet. At Disney's Hollywood Studios the biggies are *Toy Story Mania!*® Attraction, The Twilight Zone Tower of Terror, and *Rock 'n' Roller Coaster*® Starring Aerosmith. At the Animal Kingdom move quickly to the *Expedition Everest*® Attraction then *Kilimanjaro Safaris*® Expedition. When you're finished with these big name attractions, pick one or two of the more popular rides and knock them off. After that you'll have lost your edge on the latecomers, so simply explore each attraction as you come to it, utilizing FastPass+ when your time is scheduled.

At the very least plan a loose itinerary for each day, or have your travel advisor who specializes in Disney do that for you, and make Advance Dining Reservations for any table-service restaurants. Find out before leaving home the park hours for the days of your vacation and what special events might be happening during your stay by going online at Disneyworld.disney.go.com/calendars/ or calling (407) 824-4321. What you want to avoid is waking up each morning and deciding then what you want to do on that day; that's best left for free days when you plan to just relax by the pool (speaking of free days, try to schedule one at some point in the middle of your trip to ease sore feet, unwind, and just enjoy). Failure to plan at least a bit could mean perhaps losing out on that great restaurant your friends told you about or missing a special show like Cirque du Soleil because it's totally booked. Of course, don't plan so stringently that there's no spontaneity in your day, no time to smell the roses. This is Disney after all.

The best advice I can give is to come during the slower times of the year (see Planning Your Trip, for details) by avoiding holiday weekends (except for maybe Labor Day and Veterans Day), spring break, and the height of summer. Of course, this may not be possible for those tied down to school schedules, but if you can make it work you'll find it well worth the effort!

Rider Switch Service

Disney extends this option to parents with small children at all attractions with a height restriction. Just advise the cast member on duty upon entering the line. Your entire party will wait in line as usual until you reach the loading area. Then one adult rides while the other stays behind with the children. When the first adult returns from the ride, the second adult boards without delay.

The Magic Kingdom

Most people's image of Disney is encompassed in a mere 142 acres of pure enchantment. Walt Disney World's first theme park is a kid's fantasy of marvelous themed lands created to charge the imagination of young and old alike. Around every corner is a vision bound to take the breath away, one that's guaranteed to draw you back time and time again. Cinderella Castle, the park's visual magnet, hits you square in the face as you walk under the train station and into a world of make-believe with all the glory of Main Street spread out before you and that fairytale Castle at the end. Get ready for the time of your life!

An expanded New Fantasyland area opened in 2013 with a very popular Be Our Guest Restaurant located in the Beast's enchanted castle as well as quick-service fare at Gaston's Tavern. Here in this area of the park you'll be able to meet and greet Disney princesses in Princess Fairytale Hall and become part of a Beauty and the Beast storytelling experience at Enchanted Tales with Belle. Not to mention Under the Sea ~ Journey of the Little Mermaid as well as an expanded *Dumbo the Flying Elephant*® attraction offering double the capacity. And super exciting is the Seven Dwarfs Mine Train's scheduled to open in spring of 2014!

Park Basics

GETTING THERE

Those driving to Walt Disney World should take Interstate 4 to exit 64 and then follow the signs to the Magic Kingdom.

USING WALT DISNEY WORLD TRANSPORTATION

From Disney's Bay Lake Tower, Disney's Grand Floridian Resort, The Villas at Disney's Grand Floridian, Disney's Polynesian Resort, and Disney's Contemporary Resort: Board the monorail and disembark at the park's entrance. Take the water launch from the Grand Floridian, Villas at Disney's Grand Floridian, and Polynesian to the Magic Kingdom's dock. You can also walk from the Contemporary and Bay Lake Tower.

From Disney's Wilderness Lodge: Take the Red Flag water launch to the Magic Kingdom dock or use bus service.

From other Disney Resorts, Disney's Hollywood Studios, and the Animal Kingdom: Board the bus marked Magic Kingdom.

From Epcot: Take the monorail to the Transportation and Ticket Center (TTC), and then transfer to the Magic Kingdom either by ferry or Express Monorail.

From Downtown Disney: Take a bus to a Disney resort, transferring there to a Magic Kingdom bus. Or take a bus to the Contemporary Resort and walk to the Magic Kingdom.

PARKING

Cost is $15 per day for automobiles, free to registered guests of the Walt Disney Resort Hotels and Annual Passholders. Keep your receipt, also good for parking at the Animal Kingdom, Epcot, and Disney's Hollywood Studios for that day only.

Because of the beautiful obstacle of the Seven Seas Lagoon, parking at the Magic Kingdom is a bit different than the other three Disney theme parks. Park in the lot, make a note of the section and aisle, and board the tram to the Transportation and Ticket Center. From there take the ferry or monorail to the park entrance. When riding the monorail make sure you board the one departing for the Magic Kingdom, not Epcot.

OPERATING HOURS

Open 9:00 a.m. to 8:00 p.m. with extended hours during holidays and busy seasons. Call (407) 824-4321 or log on to Disneyworld.disney.go.com for updated park hours along with parade and fireworks information.

Get a jump on the crowds by arriving about 45 minutes early, allowing plenty of time to park, ride the monorail or ferry, purchase park tickets if necessary, and be one of the first to hit the big attractions. I recommend heading straight to Splash or Space Mountain, or if traveling with little ones to *Peter Pan's Flight*® Attraction or Enchanted Tales with Belle.

PARK SERVICES

ATMs. Six cash-dispensing ATMs are located in the park: just outside the park entrance on the right; next to the locker rentals; next to City Hall; in the *Fantasyland*® Area near the Pinocchio Village Haus restrooms; near the Frontier Shootin' Arcade; and in Tomorrowland Arcade. An additional machine is located at the TTC.

Baby Care Center. An infant facility found next to the Crystal Palace at the Castle end of Main Street is outfitted with private nursing rooms with rocking chairs, changing rooms with tables, feeding area with highchairs, and kitchen with microwave, oven, and sink. Formula, baby food, juice, diapers, wipes, sunscreen, over-the-counter medications and clothing may be purchased. Most restrooms throughout the park have baby changing stations.

First aid. The First Aid Center is located at the end of Main Street next to Crystal Palace. Nurses are available during normal park operating hours to offer over-the-counter medications, bandages, and other quick remedies.

Guest Services. City Hall, just inside the park entrance on the left, houses Guest Services where a knowledgeable staff is ready to assist with dining, ticket upgrades, accessibility, complimentary attraction translation devices, foreign guide maps for international guests, foreign currency exchange, lost guest retrieval, and general assistance. An additional Guest Services is located just outside the park entrance to the right of the park.

Guests with disabilities. A guide for guests with disabilities is available at Guest Services. Guests with mobility disabilities should park adjacent to the Entrance Complex (ask at the Auto Plaza for directions). Wheelchairs and ECVs are available for rent.

Most restaurants and shops are accessible to guests with disabilities, although some quick-service locations have narrow queues with railings (ask a host or hostess for assistance). Companion-assisted restrooms are located at the lower level of Cinderella's Royal Table, *Pirates of the Caribbean*® Attraction, Splash Mountain, near the Pinocchio Village Haus, near Casey Jr. Splash 'N' Soak Station, next to Gaston's Tavern in Fantasyland, to the right of Space Mountain, and at the TTC East Gate.

Most attractions provide access through the main queue while others have auxiliary entrances for wheelchairs and service animals along with as many as five members of your party. Certain attractions require guests to transfer from their wheelchair to a ride system. Parade routes and some shows have designated viewing areas on a first-come, first-served basis.

Braille guidebooks, assistive listening devices, video and handheld captioning devices, and audiotape guides are available at City Hall for a $25 refundable deposit. Reflective captioning is provided at select theater-type attractions and video captioning at some attractions (see a Cast Member at the attraction for assistance). With a seven-day notice a sign language interpreter will be provided at live shows on Monday and Thursday. For more information call (407) 824-4321 or (407) 827-5141 (TTY).

Lockers. Lockers are located at the TTC as well as on the right as you enter the Magic Kingdom. The cost per day is $7 for a small locker and $9 for a large locker plus a $5 refundable key deposit. If you're park hopping keep your receipt for a replacement locker at the other three Disney theme parks for no additional charge.

Lost and Found. Located at City Hall or call (407) 824-4245.

Lost children. Locate lost children at the Baby Care Center next to the Crystal Palace at the Castle end of Main Street. Go to City Hall after operating hours.

Package pickup. Located at Main Street Chamber of Commerce on your immediate right before exiting the park. Allow three hours for delivery. Registered guests of a Disney Resort may send packages directly to their hotel for next-day arrival.

Strollers and wheelchairs. Stroller rentals are located under the Main Street Railroad Station. Single strollers are $15 per day ($13 per day for a multi-day length of stay rental), double strollers $31 ($27 per day for a multi-day length of stay rental).

Wheelchair rentals are just inside the park entrance on the right for $12; $10 per day for a multi-day length of stay rental. Electric convenience vehicles are $50.00 plus a $20.00 refundable deposit. Rental units must be returned to the original rental location to receive a security deposit refund. If you're park hopping keep your receipt for a same-day replacement at the other three Disney theme parks and Downtown Disney.

The Lay of the Land

The compact Magic Kingdom consists of six bewitching lands accessed by five bridges leading from a central hub in front of Cinderella Castle. Travel down Main Street to reach the hub from the front entrance.

Moving counterclockwise around the hub you first encounter the bridge to the *Tomorrowland*® Area. The second and third bridges take you to Fantasyland, the fourth to the *Liberty Square* Area and the *Frontierland*® Area, and the fifth brings you to the *Adventureland*® Area.

The Very Best Attractions in the Magic Kingdom

BIG THUNDER MOUNTAIN RAILROAD® ATTRACTION

Inside Frontierland's 200-foot rocky outcropping resembling the scenery in Monument Valley is a zippy coaster ride offering visitors a peek at the mining country of the Old West. Disney rounded up an amazing assortment of old mining equipment to give a taste of the gold rush to this blast of an attraction. A new interactive queue passes through the mining company's offices, into the explosives room packed with sticks of dynamite, through the foreman's office for a look down into the mine, and then a test of the ventilation system with an "auto canary" for safety purposes.

Finally you'll board a fifteen-car "runaway" mining train led by a puffing and chugging engine for a wild journey through creepy bat caves, steaming geysers, bubbling mud pots, hazardous rockslides, rumbling earthquakes, and collapsing mine shafts. The details whip by so quickly you'll have difficulty absorbing them all. For those who like speed but not big drops this is your coaster; there are plenty of curves and small dips, but all in all you'll find it fairly tame and loads of rip roarin' fun. **Not recommended for expectant mothers or those with back or neck problems. Minimum height 40 inches (3 feet, 4 inches). Children age six or younger must be accompanied by an adult. 4-minute ride.**

MAGIC KINGDOM BEHIND-THE-SCENES TOURS

Call (407) WDW-TOUR or (407) 939-8687 for reservations.

- **Backstage Magic.** This seven-hour tour encompasses all four parks. Check out the Utilidors (subterranean tunnels) at the Magic Kingdom and learn about the inner workings at Epcot's American Adventure attraction. At Disney's Hollywood Studios learn how Disney Imagineers deliver hair-raising thrills on The

Twilight Zone Tower of Terror and visit the Creative Costuming department. At the Animal Kingdom take a backstage look at the Jammin' Jungle Parade. The cost is $229 including lunch at Wilderness Lodge's Whispering Canyon Café. Park admission not required. Begins at 8:45 a.m. Monday through Friday. Guests must be age sixteen or older and have a valid photo ID.

- **The Magic Behind Our Steam Trains Tour.** Join the Disney crew early in the morning for three hours as they prepare the trains for operation. Ride the rails in a fully restored antique freight train, learn what it takes to keep the Magic Kingdom's trains in working order, see the roundhouse where the trains are stored overnight, and learn about Walt Disney's fascination with steam trains. $49 plus park admission; guests must be age ten or older.

- **Disney's Family Magic Tour.** Solve riddles along with a guide and map as you tour the Magic Kingdom. Come prepared to meet some surprising characters along the way. The cost is $34 plus park admission.

- **Keys to the Kingdom**. One of the best behind-the-scenes tours offered in all of Disney. Meet at City Hall for a five-hour trip around the park to learn the hidden secrets and history of the Magic Kingdom. Visit at least two attractions as well as the Production Center where floats line up for the daily parade and the Utilidors, the tunnels below the park. The cost of $74 plus park admission also includes lunch at Columbia Harbour House. Several morning departures offered. Guests must be age sixteen or older.

- **Walt Disney: Marceline to Walt Disney World Tour.** Follow in Walt's footsteps as your tour guide shares little-known facts about Walt, the man behind the magic. Learn about the design and operation of several classic Fantasyland attractions and Walt's participation in the 1964 World's Fair. $30 plus park admission; guests must be 12 years of age or older.

ENCHANTED TALES WITH BELLE

If you've ever wondered what it is like to step into a Disney film then here is the perfect chance. Follow the winding stone pathway in Belle's village to Maurice's Cottage above which looms the Beast's Castle, then inside the cottage where an Enchanted Mirror comes to life transforming into the castle's entry. A talking wardrobe and a three-dimensional Lumiere encourages young guests to gather in a surprise for Belle herself. Everyone becomes involved in role-playing, culminating with a fun parade and intimate meet 'n' greet with Belle in all her ballroom finery.

> CARA'S TIP: This attraction only holds 45 people per show so what looks like a fairly short line might possibly translate into a lengthier wait time than anticipated.

HAUNTED MANSION® ATTRACTION

Eerie sounds, toppled fountains, unkempt grounds, and not even a hint of a smile on the faces of the creepy cast member "servants" cause a definite sense of foreboding on approach to this Tudor-style, redbrick mansion in Liberty Square. While in line choose from one of two queues: the left side offers an interactive graveyard overlooking the Rivers of America where there's plenty of spooky fun; or go the shorter right hand route where you'll head directly into the gargoyle-guarded Stretch Room. Here your "ghost host" asks all to gather tightly in the "dead" center of the room and warns that "there is no turning back." Then board a "doom buggy," your conveyance through this dusty, ghostly retreat where many terrific special effects and hair-raising sounds up the ante. And beware hitchhiking ghosts who always pull a prank or two for a hilarious ending. Even though it may sound frightening it's really nothing but fun and only the smallest and most timid of children might become alarmed. **9-minute ride.**

> CARA'S TIP: If you're prone to allergies don't worry, the "dust" used here is an artificial, non-allergenic material.

MICKEY'S PHILHARMAGIC® ATTRACTION

This 3-D attraction located in Fantasyland is one of Disney's best! Even though Mickey's name is featured in the title the mischievous Donald Duck steals the show as he takes visitors along on a wild ride through

Disney animated movies, interacting with the largest cast of Disney characters ever in a single 3-D movie. You'll see Ariel, Aladdin, Jasmine, Lumiere, Simba, Peter Pan, Tinker Bell, and more, all accompanied by popular Disney music and fun effects of squirting water and delicious aromas. Shown on one of the largest seamless projections screen in the world (150 feet long and 28 feet high), it's an attraction kids as well as kids-at-heart will absolutely adore. **Ten-minute show.**

PETER PAN'S FLIGHT

This is one of the most endearing attractions in Fantasyland, sure to steal your heart. Though old-fashioned and certainly not a thrill a minute you'll find it hard to resist "flying" with Peter Pan, Wendy, and the boys on gently soaring pirate ships. Your adventure begins in the Darling nursery "and off we go," flying over the twinkling lights of London with Big Ben and the London Bridge standing out against a starry, moonlit night (definitely the best part of the ride). Next stop, Never Never Land where far below are glistening waterfalls, glowing volcanoes, sunning mermaids, an Indian Village, the Lost Boys, and Captain Hook's ship. All the while the movie's theme song tells us "you can fly." The sight of Wendy walking the plank is hair-raising, but of course Peter Pan saves the day. This ride is a real charmer, perfect for all ages. **3-minute ride.**

PIRATES OF THE CARIBBEAN

The tune "Yo Ho, Yo Ho, a Pirate's Life for Me" will ring in your ears for hours after leaving this likable ride. Float through dripping caves and into a darkened bombardment of a Caribbean town at the merciless hands of scruffy pirates. Hundreds of shouting, singing, and grunting *Audio-Animatronics*® buccaneers chase women (with some women chasing the men), pillage and burn the town, and party through the night. It may sound a bit rough, but it's quite a charmer and executed in nothing but good humor. Captain Jack Sparrow is prominently part of the theme, and you'll find music from the Pirates of the Caribbean movie and Jack's lifelike image throughout. **10-minute ride.**

CHARACTER GREETING SPOTS IN THE MAGIC KINGDOM

The Mickey head on your guide map will help you find the following locations:

- An assortment of Disney characters in Town Square from opening until mid-afternoon
- Buzz Lightyear near the Carousel of Progress
- Gaston in New Fantasyland's Gaston's Tavern Courtyard
- Ariel in her Grotto in New Fantasyland
- Classic Disney characters in Pete's Silly Sideshow in Storybook Circus
- Aladdin and Jasmine in Adventureland's Agrabah Bazaar
- Tinker Bell and her fairy friends in their Magical Nook in Adventureland
- Princess Merida at Fantasyland's Fairytale Garden
- An assortment of Disney princesses in Fantasyland's Princess Fairytale Hall
- Mickey Mouse in Town Square Theater
- Princess Tiana and characters from The Princess and the Frog at Liberty Square Bridge
- Woody and Jessie at the exit of Splash Mountain in Frontierland
- Winnie the Pooh and Tigger at Fantasyland's A Place For Friends To Meet, located next-door to The Many Adventures of Winnie the Pooh attraction

SPACE MOUNTAIN

Tomorrowland's180-foot, conical-shaped "mountain" is one of the most popular attractions in the park, a cosmic roller coaster shooting through the darkest depths of the solar system. Load into six-passenger, single-file rockets before blasting into orbit and plunging through an almost pitch-black interior filled with sparkling comets, shooting stars, and glowing planets. Look closely to spot the other coaster ripping around on the second track. An interactive queue area helps pass the time during your wait, and a super audio system only serves to enhance this blast (pun intended) of a ride. Moving along at only 28 miles per hour there are only small drops and no loops or twists; it's just the darkness that makes it such a thrill. **Minimum height 44 inches (3 feet, 8 inches). Not recommended for expectant mothers, those with back or neck problems, or those prone to motion sickness. 2-1/2-minute ride.**

> CARA'S TIP: Lines can sometimes be extremely long. Come first thing in the morning or before park closing and plan this as a FastPass+ choice. And hang onto your valuables or risk losing them in the deep, dark vastness of space.

SPLASH MOUNTAIN

This is one ride guaranteed to put a smile on your face. Who can resist the charms of Brer Rabbit, Brer Fox, Brer Bear, and the rest of the gang, even if it culminates in one heck of a plunge? Float in a hollowed-out log through Audio-Animatronics scenes from Disney's classic film *Song of the South,* splashing and dropping through Brer Rabbit's Laughin' Place. Drift 'round the briar patch while toe-tapping music plays among the cabbages and carrots, jugs of moonshine, chirpin' birds, and croakin' frogs as you relax and bob your head to the beat. Inside the mountain Brer Fox and Brer Bear cause plenty of commotion along the way as Brer Rabbit outwits them at every turn. As you float through bayous, marshes, and caverns, all a delight to the eye with loads of colorful detail and too-cute cavorting characters, the addictive theme song "Time to Be Moving Along" plays. When the ride creeps upward, heed the doomsday warnings of a gloomy pair of buzzards ("It's turning back time" and "We'll show you a laughing place") just before the final doozy of a splashdown over a five-story waterfall and into an oversize briar patch. It's pretty tough to keep your eyes open (at least for first-timers), but try to grab a peek of the park from the top. And don't think you missed the cherished "Zip-A-Dee-Doo-Da" tune; you'll hear it on the way out. **Minimum height 40 inches (3 feet, 4 inches). Not** recommended for expectant mothers or those with back or neck problems. 11-minute ride.

CARA'S TIP: The drop's really not as bad as it looks, so don't let it keep you from experiencing one of the best rides Disney has to offer. Parents who want to stay behind with the little ones will want to utilize the playground area just to the right of the attraction.

UNDER THE SEA ~ JOURNEY OF THE LITTLE MERMAID

In this attraction, located in New Fantasyland, the interactive, seaside-themed queue is really part of the fun with many things to explore in and around Prince Eric's castle including shipwrecks, lapping tides, and rushing waterfalls, grottos and caverns, and an abundance of sea life. It's

WHO DOESN'T LOVE A MAKEOVER?

Aspiring pirates will want to reserve a place at the *Magic Kingdom's Pirates League* for a true buccaneer makeover. The multi-eyed Jack is a kick; watch the surprise when you flash your painted eyelids. Even girls get into the act with the Empress Package including vibrant makeup and bandana, a face gem, and nail polish. Other options include a Jake and the Never Land Pirates package or a lovely Mermaid choice. Once your transformation is complete take your photo in the "secret room", and, now that you're in character, it's time to hop onboard the Pirates of the Caribbean attraction or take part in Adventureland's Captain Jack Sparrow's Pirate Tutorial. Call (407) WDW-CREW (939-2739) for reservations.

Young girls love the Magic Kingdom's *Bibbidi Bobbidi Boutique*, a beauty salon that transforms them into little princesses. Offering multiple hairstyles, nail color, make-up, and extra enchantments including Disney Princess costumes, accessories, and photographs, it's simply irresistible. There's even a Knight's Package transformation for young boys with colored gel hairstyling and shield and sword accessories. Call (407) WDW-STYLE or (407) 939-7895 for reservations.

as if you're truly heading "under the sea." Then board your clam vehicle and move through scene after scene through Ariel's grotto where
famous songs combined with Audio-Animatronics tell the story of everyone's favorite mermaid.

> CARA'S TIP: After departing the ride line up next-door to meet
> Ariel in her colorful Grotto.

The Very Best Dining in the Magic Kingdom

The Magic Kingdom is certainly not known for fine dining, but sometimes it's easiest to plan on having dinner at the park while waiting for
the nighttime festivities to begin. Just don't expect fantastic cuisine.

Be Our Guest. Lines for the quick-service lunch here are long and
table-service dinner reservations almost impossible, but this is probably
the best food in the park (See full description in the Dining In Style
at Walt Disney World Resort chapter in the Magic Kingdom Dining
section.)

Cinderella's Royal Table. The second toughest ticket in town and perhaps the most expensive entitles you to dine high above Fantasyland in
the towers of Cinderella Castle; character breakfast, lunch, and dinner.
(See full description in the Dining In Style at Walt Disney World Resort
chapter in the Magic Kingdom Dining section.)

The Crystal Palace. Breakfast, lunch, and dinner buffet with Winnie the Pooh characters. (See full description in the Dining In Style
at Walt Disney World Resort chapter in the Magic Kingdom Dining
section.).

Pecos Bill Tall Tale Inn & Café. Good char-grilled burgers and such in
an Old West atmosphere; 1/3 lb. deluxe Angus cheeseburger with bacon, onion rings, and barbecue sauce, barbecued pork sandwich, Southwest chicken salad, taco salad, vegetable burger, chicken sandwich with
arugula, bacon, and chipotle ranch, and chili cheese fries, great toppings
bar with hot skillets of onions and mushrooms; strawberry yogurt, carrot cake, chocolate cake. *Children's menu:* burger, turkey sandwich, and
PB&J.

Special Entertainment

Dream-Along with Mickey. Gather 'round Cinderella Castle stage for this live show about a Mickey Mouse dream-inspired party in which the whole cast of characters are invited. There's music, dancing, and adventurous exploits, with Maleficent stirring up trouble. However, the party guests prove that believing in your dreams is strongest of all. Check your guide map for times. **20-minute show.**

Celebrate a Dream Come True Parade. This outstanding afternoon parade is a huge hit with guests of all ages. Giant floats topped with scores of Disney characters such as Mickey Mouse, Pinocchio, Aladdin, and more, accompanied by dancers, dancers, and more dancers. Don't miss it! **15-minute parade.**

> CARA'S TIP: Those not interested in the parade will find this to be a great time to ride the big-name attractions when the crowds are elsewhere. Celebrate a Dream Come True will be replaced with Festival of Fantasy in spring of 2014.

If you can score a FastPass+ here go for it. It is in a perfect location right in front of the Castle.

Main Street Electrical Parade. Nighttime parade of glowing, twinkling, spinning, and sparkling floats with half a million shimmering lights all synchronized to the parade's distinctive soundtrack. Watch for your favorite Disney characters including the Little Mermaid, Snow White and the Seven Dwarfs, Pinocchio, Alice in Wonderland, even Pete's Dragon. **20-minute parade.**

> CARA'S TIP: The FastPass+ area for this parade is the same as the afternoon parade so another great FastPass+ to score.

Wishes. What a way to end your day at this magical park! Jiminy Cricket narrates the story of how wishes come true, accompanied by Disney songs, character voices, and unbelievable pyrotechnics. While the Castle constantly changes color be wowed by 557 firing cues and 683 individual pieces of fireworks launched from 11 locations. Everyone's favorite part of the show is the flight of Tinker Bell from the tip-top of the Castle down past Tomorrowland. **12-minute show.**

CARA'S TIP: Here are some of the best place from which to view Wishes: in the FastPass+ Rose Garden lawn area with perfect views of the Castle; on the bridge to Tomorrowland for a prime view of Tinker Bell on her flight from the top of the Castle; in the hub directly in front of the castle near Walt and Mickey's statue; in front of The Crystal Palace restaurant with picture perfect views of the Castle; the California Grill's fifteenth-floor observation deck at the Contemporary Resort (dining reservations required); one of the Polynesian Resort's romantic beaches; the boat dock or Narcoossee's restaurant at the Grand Floridian Resort; the balcony of a tower guest room on the Magic Kingdom side of the Contemporary and Bay Lake Tower Resorts; a theme park view room at the Polynesian Resort; at the Tomorrowland Terrace's Fireworks Dessert Party at the Magic Kingdom where you'll enjoy Wishes from an exclusive viewing area along with a cornucopia of desserts. Call 407-WDW-DINE for reservations.

Special Events

Mickey's Not-So-Scary Halloween Party. On selected nights in September and October Halloween is celebrated at a kid-friendly, after-hours party. The park's most popular attractions are open plus other merriment, such as character dance parties, costumed Disney characters, trick-or-treating, street entertainment, Mickey's "Boo to You" Parade, and a special Happy HalloWishes fireworks display. Call (407) W-DISNEY, or (407) 924-7639 for ticketing information or visit Disneyworld.disney.go.com.

Mickey's Very Merry Christmas Party. "Snow" falls on the decorated streets of the Magic Kingdom on select nights in November and December. The park's most popular attractions are open along with special Castle Dream Lights, the Once Upon a Christmas Time Parade (worth the cost of admission alone), special shows, character greetings, cocoa and cookies, and a presentation of the Wishes fireworks with a holiday twist. Call (407) W-DISNEY, or (407) 924-7639 for ticketing information and pricing or visit Disneyworld.disney.go.com.

Epcot

Although its founder died in 1966 the Walt Disney Company brought Walt Disney's dream of an experimental prototype community of tomorrow to reality in 1982, only in a much broader fashion: an atypical theme park dedicated to the resourcefulness and imagination of the American free enterprise system—a continual showcase of imagination, instruction, research, and invention It's an education in technology and innovation and in other lands and cultures.

Comprising 260 acres (more than twice the size of the Magic Kingdom) and divided into two parts, Future World and World Showcase, it takes almost two full days and a good pair of walking shoes to truly explore the park's full scope.

At Future World visitors encounter shining glass pyramids, choreographed fountains, shimmering steel, unconventional landscaping, and towering above it all Epcot's symbol, Spaceship Earth. Here visitors learn about communications, energy, innovation and technology, agriculture, transportation, the oceans, space, even their imagination. If it sounds a bit like school don't worry. Disney always manages to add its special style to the learning process, transforming it into sheer fun for all ages.

At World Showcase you'll see authentic-looking replicas of famous landmarks and buildings, typical streets overflowing with marvelous architectural detail, shops presenting the world's merchandise, exotic food and wine, and captivating entertainment. Without leaving the country, or the park for that matter, behold the Eiffel Tower, stroll a Japanese garden, witness Venice's St. Mark's Square, or visit a Mexican market. Definitely plan to spend an evening here when all the countries are lit with shimmering lights and the true romance of this wonderful area of the park shines through.

Strolling in a counterclockwise direction around the 1.3-mile World Showcase walkway you'll encounter each country in this order: Canada, United Kingdom, France, Morocco, Japan, America, Italy, Germany, China, Norway, and finally Mexico. Those weary of walking can utilize the very slow Friendship water taxis that ply the World Showcase Lagoon.

While there are plenty of attractions and activities for the little ones,

Epcot's appeal is mainly to older children and adults. The draw: a huge variety of dining choices, loads of exciting entertainment, magnificent gardens, around-the-world shopping, and attractions that simultaneously entertain and educate. The grounds alone are worth the price of admission, a fact well known to horticulturists worldwide.

Park Basics

GETTING THERE

Those driving to Walt Disney World should take exit 67 off I-4 and follow the signs to Epcot's main entrance.

USING WALT DISNEY WORLD TRANSPORTATION

From the Grand Floridian Resort, The Villas at Disney's Grand Floridian, Polynesian Resort, Contemporary Resort, Bay Lake Tower at the Contemporary Resort, and the Magic Kingdom: Board the monorail, disembark at the Transportation and Ticket Center (TTC), and then transfer to the Epcot Monorail.

From the Yacht & Beach Club, BoardWalk Inn, and Walt Disney World Swan & Dolphin: Walk or take a water launch to Epcot's International Gateway entrance leading into World Showcase. Although World Showcase isn't open until 11:00 a.m., entrance is allowed anytime after Future World opens. Park tickets may also be purchased here.

From all other Disney resorts, Disney's Hollywood Studios, and Animal Kingdom: Board the bus marked Epcot. Water launch transportation is also provided between Disney's Hollywood Studios and Epcot's International Gateway.

PARKING

Cost is $15 per day for automobiles; free to registered guests of the Walt Disney Resort Hotels and Annual Passholders. Keep your receipt—good for parking at the Magic Kingdom, Disney's Hollywood Studios, and Animal Kingdom on that day only.

Parking is conveniently located in front of the park. Trams circulate throughout the parking area for easy transportation to the entry gate. Be sure to make a note of your aisle and section.

OPERATING HOURS

Future World is open 9:00 a.m. to 9:00 p.m. with Ellen's Energy Adventure, Innoventions, Journey Into Imagination With Figment, Living With the Land, and Circle of Life closing at 7:00 p.m. World Showcase is open from 11:00 a.m. to 9:00 p.m. Call (407) 824-4321 or log on to Disneyworld.disney.go.com for updated park hours.

To get a jump on the crowds arrive at least thirty minutes early to allow time to park, purchase park tickets if necessary, pick up a snack or cup of coffee, and be one of the first to hit the big attractions. I recommend heading straight to Soarin' or Test Track.

ENTRY GATES

Epcot has two entrances: the main gate in front of Spaceship Earth, and the International Gateway Entrance in World Showcase located between the United Kingdom and France. Visitors staying at the Epcot Resorts should use the International Gateway entrance that opens at the same time as Future World. Park passes may be purchased at both entrances.

PARK SERVICES

ATMs. There are four locations: next to the stroller rentals at Entrance Plaza; on the center walkway between Future World and World Showcase; the International Gateway entrance; and the America pavilion in World Showcase.

Baby Care Center. An infant facility located in the Odyssey Center between Test Track and the Mexico Pavilion on the east side of the park is outfitted with private nursing rooms and rocking chairs, changing rooms with tables, feeding area with highchairs, and kitchen with microwave, oven, and sink. Formula, baby food, juice, diapers, wipes, sunscreen, over-the-counter medications, and clothing may be purchased. Most restrooms throughout the park have baby changing stations.

First aid. For minor medical problems head to the First Aid Center in the Odyssey Center located between Test Track and the Mexico Pavilion on the east side of the park. Nurses are available during normal park operating hours to offer over-the-counter medications, bandages, and other quick remedies.

Guest Services. On the east side of Spaceship Earth is Guest Services where a knowledgeable staff is ready to assist with dining, ticket upgrades, accessibility, complimentary attraction translation devices, foreign guide maps for international guests, foreign currency exchange, lost guest retrieval, and general assistance. Additional Guest Services windows are located just outside the Future World entrance on the right and just outside the International Gateway on the right.

Guests with Disabilities. A guide for guests with disabilities is available at Guest Services. Guests with mobility disabilities can park adjacent to the Entrance Complex (ask at the Auto Plaza for directions). Wheelchairs and ECVs are available for rent. Most restaurants and shops are accessible to guests with disabilities, although some quick-service locations have narrow queues with railings (ask a host or hostess for assistance). Companion-assisted restrooms are located at First Aid, near Spaceship Earth, in Future World East opposite Test Track, in Future World West opposite The Land, near Showcase Plaza Refreshment Port, and in World Showcase near the pavilions for Norway, Germany, and Morocco.

Most attractions in Future World and the ride at Norway in World Showcase provide access through the main queue, while others have auxiliary entrances for wheelchairs and service animals (service animals are not permitted on Soarin', Mission: SPACE® Attraction, and Test Track) along with as many as five members of your party. Certain attractions require guests to transfer from their wheelchair to a ride system.

Braille guides, audio guides, audio description handheld devices, assistive listening handheld devices, and video and handheld captioning devices are available at Guest Services with a $25 refundable deposit. Many theater-type attractions have reflective captioning, and stationary braille maps are located in several areas within the park. With a seven-day notice a sign language interpreter will be provided at live shows on Fridays. Call (407) 824-4321 with any questions.

Information Central. Check the up-to-the-minute tip board between Innovations East and West near the Fountain of Nations for wait times and special event information.

Lockers. Locker rentals, available next-door to the Camera Center in

Entrance Plaza and at the International Gateway entrance, are $7 per day plus a $5 refundable key deposit for a small locker and $9 plus a $5 key deposit for large lockers. If you're park hopping keep your receipt for a replacement locker at the three other Disney theme parks for no extra charge.

Lost and found. Located at Guest Services or call (407) 824-4245.

Lost children. Locate lost children at the Baby Care Center or Guest Services.

Package pickup. Purchases may be sent to The Gift Stop located just outside the main entrance as well as to World Traveler at the International Gateway for pickup at the end of the day; allow three hours for delivery. Registered guests of a Disney Resort may send packages directly to their hotel for next-day arrival.

Stroller and wheelchairs. Rentals are located on the left as you enter the park's main entrance as well as at the International Gateway. Single strollers are $15 per day ($13 per day for a multi-day length of stay rental), double strollers $31 ($27 per day for a multi-day length of stay rental). If you're park hopping keep your receipt for a same-day replacement at the three other Disney theme parks and Downtown Disney.

Wheelchairs are $12.00 for a single day; Length of Stay $10 per day when rented for multiple days. Electrical convenience vehicles are $50.00 plus a $20.00 refundable deposit. Rented units must be returned to the original rental location to receive a security deposit refund.

The Lay of the Land

Epcot looks a bit like a figure eight, with Future World the northern region (shown on the guide map at the bottom—think "upside down") and World Showcase the southern region. Future World is composed of two concentric rings with Spaceship Earth forming the inner circle and six pavilions the outer. The Universe of Energy, *Mission: SPACE®* Attraction, and Test Track are located on the east side of Spaceship Earth; and Imagination!, The Land, and *The Seas with Nemo & Friends®* Attraction on the west side. Walkways connect Future World to World Showcase composed of eleven pavilions fronted by a 1.3-mile promenade surrounding the forty-acre World Showcase Lagoon.

The Very Best Attractions in Epcot

SPACESHIP EARTH

Visible for miles this symbol of Epcot comprises more than 2 million cubic feet of expanse: a silver geosphere 180 feet tall and 164 feet in diameter composed of 954 glowing panels of various shapes and sizes. Inside, the attraction chronicles the story of human communications beginning with the dawn of recorded time. The slow journey to the top takes visitors through marvelous Audio-Animatronics scenes representing humankind's quest for more efficient means of communication. Narrated by Judi Dench you'll see Cro-Magnon storytellers, Egyptian papyrus scroll readers, ancient Greek actors, Roman couriers, Islamic scholars, even Michelangelo painting the Sistine Chapel.

Following in swift succession are the new tools and technologies of the Teletype, Telephone, Radio, Moving Pictures, and Television, then giant-size versions of the first computers, the birth of the first personal computer, and a tech tunnel. The most captivating scene is found at the top of the sphere where, in the middle of a sky thick with stars, the earth sits suspended in space. The finale utilizes touch-screens that enable guests to create their own funny vision of the future. **15-minute ride**.

> CARA'S TIP: Lines move quickly and efficiently on this continu-
> ally loading ride. Because this is the first attraction you encounter
> when entering from the front of the park, lines can get lengthy
> in the morning. If the wait looks reasonable go for it; if not,
> come back in the afternoon when most people are touring World
> Showcase.

MISSION: SPACE

The year is 2036. You're off to Mars in an X-2 Deep Space Shuttle with a team of four—Commander, Pilot, Navigator, and Engineer. As the engines rumble seats tilt back in preparation for countdown and then a WOW of a liftoff! Experience the heart-palpitating, G-force thrill of rocketing into outer space through clouds of exhaust. As you peer out the window into a computer-generated imagery of space panic sets in. But after the first thirty seconds or so you'll settle down for the ride of your life with a brief sense of weightlessness, a slingshot maneuver around the moon, and one heck of a landing on Mars. What a rush!

Afterward, head to the Advanced Training Lab where you can further your space training in a rocket race from Mars to Earth. **Minimum height 44 inches (3 feet, 8 inches). An adult must accompany children age six or younger. This is a highly turbulent motion simulator ride and not recommended for expectant mothers or those with high blood pressure; back, heart, or neck problems; motion sickness; or other medical conditions. 4-minute ride with a short preshow.**

> CARA'S TIP: Those who want a milder alternative to this somewhat disconcerting ride may choose a less intense version by entering the "green" line, one that eliminates the spinning centrifuge.

TEST TRACK

In a six-passenger vehicle riders move through a series of rigorous tests normally used on prototype cars. Completely redesigned, the attraction has a much more high-tech feel than its previous incarnation with all-new exhibits, videos, and interaction areas in the queue, each pertaining to the design process. Begin your journey at the Chevrolet Design Studios where you'll have the chance to design and customize your very own concept car on a touch pad kiosk, something you will use in various capacities throughout the rest of the attraction. Then board your six-passenger Sim car and proceed through a futuristic darkness with high-tech lighting for a series of tests and scans including the rigors of off-road driving and extreme weather challenges, responsiveness, and automated crashes, ending in a long-awaited power test where you will barrel outside onto a high-speed banking loop at more than 60 mph. It's quite a ride, not really scary but fast and absolutely loads of fun! Minimum height 40 inches (3 feet, 4 inches). An adult must accompany children age six or younger. **Not recommended for expectant mothers or those with back, heart, or neck problems. Closed in inclement weather. Singles Line. 5-minute ride with a short preshow.**

> CARA'S TIP: If you're willing to ride without other members of your party the single-riders' line is a quicker alternative.

LIVING WITH THE LAND

Explore the past, present, and future of farming on a boat tour through three diverse ecosystems: a stormy rain forest; a harsh, arid desert land-scape; and the rolling American prairie complete with an early twenti-eth-century family farm. Then proceed to immense greenhouses where more efficient and environmentally friendly ways of producing food are researched and developed. You'll see exotic to everyday plants grown hydroponically (without soil), even trees with 9-pound lemons! Much of the attraction's produce and fish is used in the The Land's restaurants and even at the Flying Fish Café at Disney's BoardWalk. Work is also done here in conjunction with the US Department of Agriculture. This is a remarkably absorbing attraction for all ages. **13-minute ride.**

> CARA'S TIP: At lunchtime the overflow from the food court pro-duces long waits so pick another time to visit.

SOARIN'™ ATTRACTION

Hang glide over California in an attraction guaranteed to leave you speechless. After rising 40 feet inside a giant 80-foot projection screen dome, you're completely surrounded with phenomenal bird's-eye views of the Golden State. Soar over the Golden Gate Bridge, towering red-wood forests, hot air balloons drifting over the Napa Valley wine coun-try, a golf course in Palm Springs, the majesty of Yosemite, and more, ending high above Disneyland just in time for a fireworks display. Smell the aroma of the orange groves and feel the wind in your face, all the while listening to a stirring musical score. This is one fantastic ride! **Minimum height 40 inches (3 feet, 4 inches). Not recommend-ed for expectant mothers or those with motion sickness, or heart, back, or neck problems. 10-minute ride.**

> CARA'S TIP: Ask for the first row; if not you'll be a bit distracted with dangling feet above you.

THE SEAS WITH NEMO & FRIENDS

This attraction is a winner, combining a kid-friendly ride with Epcot's 5.7-million-gallon aquarium filled with more than 2,000 sea creatures. The queue winds through a seashore setting that gradually transitions to a dark underwater theme before boarding your "clamobile" that slowly moves through animated projection scenes under the ocean. Nemo has wandered off again from his teacher, Mr. Ray, and everyone is in search of him in the "Big Blue World." Meet up with Nemo's dad and his friend Dory, check out the larger-than-life ultraviolet jellyfish, and travel through a fast-moving-current tunnel with sea turtle, Crush, finally ending up in front of the pavilion's massive aquarium.

In Sea Base don't skip *Turtle Talk with Crush*, a fun show starring the surfer dude turtle interacting in a full-blown conversation with the audience. Then play in Bruce's Sub House's hands-on area featuring the Nemo characters. Other attractions include fish feeds, dolphin presentations, educational talks by the research team on the Observation Deck, and, my favorite, the fascinating Marine Mammal Research Center where manatees reside.

THE AMERICAN ADVENTURE

Momentous film, inspiring music, and lifelike, talking, gesturing, and walking Audio-Animatronics characters weave the impressive tale of the United States of America with Ben Franklin and Mark Twain serving as hosts. The grand finale film montage is a real tearjerker. Some adore this show while others sleep right through it; personally, I'm one of its greatest fans. **Shows every 35 minutes**.

> CARA'S TIP: It's fairly easy to get a seat in this huge theater. Try to catch the Voices of Liberty performance in the rotunda waiting area and just feel your patriotism shoot up a few notches.

MAELSTROM

A favorite of World Showcase visitors is this watery boat ride through both real and mythical scenes of Norway's history. In your dragon-headed longboat drift past a tenth-century Viking village and then on to a dark, mysterious forest where a hairy, three-headed troll casts a spell on your vessel, causing it to drop backward down a soggy cataract. Sail past glacier-bound polar bears, narrowly miss a plunge off the edge of a waterfall, and finally drop into a stormy North Sea. Your voyage ends with a pleasant, short film on Norway. **10-minute ride and show, including the film**.

> CARA'S TIP: Drops are very small and of no consequence on this tame ride. If you would rather not see the film walk into the theater and then immediately out the doors on the opposite side.

SALUTE! SALUD!

Two intimate lounges that should not be missed during your trip around World Showcase are to be found in the Italy and Mexico pavilions:

- Italy's **Tutto Gusto** is composed of stone walls and floors, exposed brick arches, wine barrels, even a discreet fireplace area. Dim lighting, comfy sofas, and small tavern-type tables feels so inviting that you'll be tempted to hang out here for a good part of the day. Believe me when I say this is an excellent way to sip Italian wines and nosh on small plates of cured meats, cheeses, authentic panini, antipasti, even pasta and dessert. Just in case you're enjoying yourself too much to leave and dinnertime happens to roll around, no worries. You can order anything you wish to be brought over from the next-door's Tutto Italia menu.

- At **La Cava del Tequila in Mexico** choose from an amazing variety (over 100 choices) of tequila and margaritas. Purists should steer away from the ultra-sweet margaritas, in particular the Midnight Blue, and go for what Mexico is truly known for, the Classic (see if they won't use real limes instead of a mix for the true taste). If you just can't decide, margarita flights offer a tasting of several delightful selections with a variety of interesting salt rims. To go along with your drinks are traditional chips, salsa, and guacamole.

In early 2014 look for Morocco's Spice Road to join the list of exciting eateries offering small plates in a great atmosphere to join this roster.

REFLECTIONS OF CHINA

Behold the wonders of China in this remarkable 360-degree film narrated by Tang Dynasty poet Li Bai. In Circle-Vision walk atop the Great Wall, enter the Forbidden City, stand in the middle of Tiananmen Square, and cruise down the mighty Yangtze River. The modern world of Hong Kong, Macau, and Shanghai along with stunning vistas of rice terraces,

Inner Mongolia's nomadic people, the misty mountains of Huangshan, the Gobi desert, extraordinary Terra Cotta Warriors, and the haunting landscape of Guey Ling only serve to make you want more. Come prepared to stand throughout the presentation. **12-minute show**.

CHARACTER GREETING SPOTS AT EPCOT

The Mickey head on your guide map will help you find the following locations:

- Snow White in Germany
- An assortment of characters at Entrance Plaza in front of Spaceship Earth
- Aladdin and Jasmine in Morocco near Restaurant Marrakesh
- Princess Aurora and Belle in France
- Epcot Character Spot for Mickey, Minnie, and Pluto
- Winnie the Pooh and Friends, Mary Poppins, and Alice in Wonderland in the UK
- Mulan in China
- Donald Duck in Mexico
- Anna and Elsa from *Frozen* in Norway

The Very Best Dining in Epcot

Coral Reef Restaurant. Your table has a front-row seat of The Seas with Nemo & Friends' massive aquarium for lunch and dinner. (See full description in the Dining In Style at Walt Disney World Resort chapter in the Epcot section.)

Monsieur Paul. French food in an upscale atmosphere, open for dinner only. (See full description in the Dining In Style at Walt Disney World Resort chapter in the Epcot section.)

Tangierine Café. Excellent quick-service café with shawarma sandwiches and platters (marinated, rotisserie-roasted sliced chicken and lamb), meatball platter, lamb or tabouleh wraps, vegetarian platter (couscous, hummus, and tabouleh). Moroccan wine, Casablanca beer, and specialty coffees. *Children's menu:* hamburgers and chicken tenders.

San Angel Inn. This is unquestionably Epcot's most romantic restaurant, open for lunch and dinner, with traditional Mexican dishes in a candlelit riverside setting. (See full description in the Dining In Style at Walt Disney World Resort chapter in the Epcot section.)

Sunshine Seasons. Here you'll find prepared-to-order, quick-service options at several different counters.

The Grill: Oak-grilled rotisserie chicken with black beans and yellow rice, oak-grilled fish with vegetables, slow roasted pork chop with cheddar mashed potatoes and barbecue sauce. *Children's menu:* chicken leg with mashed potatoes.

Asian: Breakfast: Breakfast croissant sandwich, oatmeal, breakfast platter with bacon, sausage, biscuit, and scrambled eggs. *Lunch and dinner:* Mongolian beef, spicy cashew chicken, orange sesame glazed vegan chick'n chunks with stir fry noodles, sweet and sour chicken. *Children's menu:* sweet and sour chicken.

Sandwiches: Roasted pork banh mi style panini, turkey and Monterey jack on ciabatta with chipotle mayonnaise, oak-grilled vegetable flatbread. *Children's menu:* mini-sub sandwich.

Soup and Salad: Caesar salad with oak-fired chicken, *togarashi* seared tuna noodle salad, roasted beet and goat cheese salad with honey sherry dressing, freshly made soups including potato and bacon, vegetable barley, chicken corn chowder, New England clam chowder, and pumpkin squash. *Children's menu:* macaroni and cheese.

The Bakery: Rice Krispies treats, cheesecake with berries, strawberry shortcake, apple caramel crunch, key lime tartlets, s'mores brownie, hand-dipped Edy's ice cream, cookies, crème brûlée, and carrot cake cupcakes.

SHOP YOUR WAY AROUND THE "WORLD"

If shopping is your thing then Epcot is the place for you offering a world of international goodies. Here is the best selection of merchandise to be found:

- **Canada.** Cute, stuffed animal moose and bear heads perfect for hanging

- **United Kingdom.** Proper English tea sets, Beatles and Rolling Stone Merchandise, and family crests

- **France**. Table linens from Provence

- **Morocco.** Caftans, Moroccan rugs, and *thuya* wood boxes

- **Japan.** Silk kimonos

- **Italy**. Venetian masks

- **Germany.** Christmas ornaments (especially the pickle ornament), nutcracker dolls, Steiff bears and lambs

- **China.** Silk Cheongsam dresses

- **Norway.** Trolls, Viking horned hats, and everyone's favorite— Laila body lotion

- **Mexico.** Giant-size sombreros, colorful piñatas, and cotton dresses and blouses

Special Entertainment

Illuminations: Reflections of Earth. Each evening at closing time, crowds gather around the World Showcase Lagoon to witness Walt Disney World's most spectacular nighttime extravaganza. The story of planet Earth is told in a combination of unbelievable pyrotechnic displays, amazing lasers, stirring music, and fanciful water movement. **13-minute show.**

CARA'S TIP: To avoid smoke from the fireworks check which direction the flames in the torches are blowing and avoid that side of the lagoon. Illuminations will not cancel during inclement weather.

Special Events

Epcot International Flower & Garden Festival. For seventy-five days each spring Epcot is covered in more than thirty million blooms with seventy-five extravagant topiaries, a children's play area, a floating wonderland in East Lake, a Pixie Hollow Fairy butterfly house, and an array of amazing gardens throughout World Showcase. There are special appearances by nationally recognized gardening experts, HGTV stars, how-to presentations by Disney horticulturists, and food kiosks offering garden-fresh goodies. A nightly Flower Power concert series add to the festivities with such acts as Micky Dolenz, Chubby Checker & the Wildcats, The Guess Who, Paul Revere & The Raiders, Village People, and Herman's Hermits. Entrance is included in the price of park admission.

Epcot International Food & Wine Festival. This six-week fall extravaganza is the most heavily visited food festival in the world attracting more than one million visitors. Booths representing the cuisine of more than thirty countries line the World Showcase walkway, each one selling small plates of food along with wine and beer. Included in the price of admission are daily cooking demonstrations by some of the country's top chefs, book signings and meet & greets with celebrity authors, wine-tasting seminars, and Eat to the Beat nightly concerts with such past performers as Billy Ocean, Smash Mouth, Boyz II Men, Hanson, The Pointer Sisters, and Air Supply. Avoid the weekends if you can, when the locals come out in full force.

Special themed dinners and wine seminars sold out months in advance include:

Sweet Sundays. Some of the country's top pastry chefs demonstrate the preparation of three sweet delights with tastings; includes a buffet breakfast and sparkling wine ($95).

Kitchen Memories. A three-course lunch demonstration prepared by a celebrated chef with a notable winery pairing each course with a wine selection ($110-160).

Epcot Wine Schools. Sunday afternoon seminar hosted by a prestigious wine authority that concludes with a celebratory reception and a certificate of completion ($135).

Party for the Senses. Saturday evening extravaganza with tasting stations in World Showcase prepared by more than two dozen eminent chefs along with seventy wines and beers at this party of all parties. Entertainment is courtesy of Cirque du Soleil and included is reserved seating for the Eat to the Beat Concert ($145-270).

Cheese Seminars. Learn about cheese paired with wine and beer from an expert "fromager" ($80).

Culinary Adventures in Signature Dining. Walt Disney World signature chefs prepare dinner along with a hosting winery with accompanying wines ($125-495).

Holidays Around the World. Christmas is a special time at Epcot, with loads of decorations, a nightly tree-lighting ceremony with Mickey and friends, storytelling around World Showcase, and a special Illuminations holiday finale.

The Candlelight Processional, a thrice-nightly event staged from late November until the end of December at the America Gardens Theater, features a celebrity narrator, a mass choir, and a fifty-piece orchestra who together retell the story of Christmas. Entrance is included in the price of park admission. To guarantee seats for this performance book a Candlelight Processional Lunch or Dinner Package that includes a meal at a select World Showcase restaurant and reserved general seating for the show followed by a reserved Illuminations viewing area (call 407-WDW-DINE or 407-939-3463 for reservations).

EPCOT'S BEHIND-THE-SCENES TOURS

Call (407) WDW-TOUR or (407) 939-8687 for reservations.

- **Behind the Seeds Tour**. See the Living with the Land greenhouses and fish farm on this one-hour journey. $18 per adult and $14 per child ages three to nine. Offered four to five times daily. Book ahead or simply sign up the same day at the desk next to the Soarin' attraction in The Land pavilion.

- **Disney's Dolphins in Depth**. Meet the dolphins at The Seas With Nemo & Friends. Learn about their care, behavior, and training with a chance to enter the water and get up close to these astonishing creatures. The three-hour program includes a souvenir photo and T-shirt. 9:45 a.m. Tuesday through Saturday for $194. Be sure to bring a bathing suit. No swimming required. Theme park admission is neither required nor included, and guests must be age thirteen or older to participate; those ages thirteen through seventeen must have a parent or guardian participating in the tour.

- Epcot DiveQuest. This three-hour program includes a pre-dive briefing, a talk on oceanography, and a forty-minute dive in the 5.7-million-gallon aquarium at The Seas With Nemo & Friends. Non-diving family and friends can watch through the aquarium windows! $175 with theme park admission neither required nor included. Offered daily at 4:30 and 5:30 p.m. to all certified divers; guests ages ten and up welcome, but those ages ten through twelve must dive with a paying adult. Dive equipment provided.

- Seas Aqua Tour. This two-and-a-half-hour program takes place in the backstage area of The Seas With Nemo & Friends where you'll also explore the aquarium for thirty minutes using a supplied air snorkel system. Includes gear, T-shirt, and group photo. Daily at 12:30 p.m. for $140; theme park admission is neither required nor included. Bring a bathing suit. Available to guests ages eight and older; those ages eight through twelve must be accompanied by a paying adult.

- The Undiscovered Future World. See how Walt's vision of a future Utopia became the Epcot of today on this four-and-a-half-hour tour. Learn in-depth information on each pavilion (even a few peeks backstage) and take a look at the Epcot marina where the Illuminations fireworks show is prepared. 9:00 a.m. Monday, Wednesday, and Friday for $55 plus park admission. Guests must be age sixteen or older.

Disney's Hollywood Studios

Welcome to the glamour and glitz of show business. Although Disney's version of the heyday of Hollywood is certainly a rose-colored one, its entertainment value can't be beat. On the boulevards of Hollywood and Sunset legendary Los Angeles buildings re-created in romanticized and appealing art deco forms literally scream excitement. It's as if the whole place is on the brink of breaking into a zany show at any minute. Here you are part of the action with attractions and exciting entertainment based on movies and TV shows. Here, Hollywood-style action with live shows, backstage tours, and exhilarating attractions is Disney's version of movie magic!

This is a small park, one that can be seen in a full day. Because many of the shows are scheduled check your park guide on arrival for show times and plan your day accordingly.

Park Basics

GETTING THERE

Those driving to Walt Disney World should take exit 64 off I-4 and follow the signs to Disney's Hollywood Studios.

USING WALT DISNEY WORLD TRANSPORTATION

From the Yacht & Beach Club, the BoardWalk Inn, and the Walt Disney World Swan and Dolphin: Take the water launch, or walk the path located behind the BoardWalk Inn.

From all other Disney resorts, the Magic Kingdom, Epcot, and Animal Kingdom: Board the bus marked Disney's Hollywood Studios. A water launch is also provided from Epcot's International Gateway.

PARKING

Cost is $15 per day for automobiles; free to registered guests of the Walt Disney Resort Hotels and Annual Passholders. Keep your receipt, good for parking at Epcot, Magic Kingdom, and Animal Kingdom on that day only.

Parking is conveniently located in front of the park. Trams circulate throughout the parking area for easy transportation to the entry gate. Make a note of what aisle and section you've parked in.

OPERATING HOURS

Open from 9:00 a.m. until an hour or so after dark. Call (407) 824-4321 or log on to Disneyworld.disney.go.com for updated park hours.

Arrive at least thirty minutes early, allowing time to park, purchase park tickets if necessary, and be one of the first to hit the big attractions. I recommend heading straight to Toy Story Midway Mania! followed by Tower of Terror and Rock 'n' Roller Coaster.

PARK SERVICES

ATMs. For quick cash three ATMs are located at the park: just outside the park entrance; in the Echo Lake area; and inside the Pizza Planet Arcade.

Baby Care Center. At the Guest Services center is an infant facility outfitted with private nursing rooms complete with rocking chairs, changing rooms with tables, feeding area with highchairs, and kitchen with microwave, oven, and sink. Formula, baby food, juice, diapers, wipes, sunscreen, over-the-counter medications and clothing may be purchased. Most restrooms throughout the park have baby changing stations.

First aid. For minor medical problems head to the First Aid Center located next to Guest Services. Nurses are available during normal park operating hours to offer over-the-counter medications, bandages, and other quick remedies.

Guest Services. Located just inside the park on the left is Guest Services where a knowledgeable staff is ready to assist with dining, ticket upgrades, accessibility, complimentary attraction translation devices, foreign guide maps for international guests, foreign currency exchange, lost guest retrieval, and general assistance. An additional Guest Services window is just outside the park entrance on the left.

Guests with disabilities. A guide for guests with disabilities is available at Guest Services. Guests with mobility disabilities should park adjacent to the Entrance Complex (ask at the Auto Plaza for directions). Wheelchairs and ECVs are available for rent. Most restaurants and shops are accessible to guests with disabilities, although some quick-service locations have narrow queues with railings (ask a host or hostess for assistance). Companion-assisted restrooms are located at First Aid, opposite The Twilight Zone Tower of Terror, at the Fantasmic! theater, *Star Tours®*—The Adventures Continue Attraction area in Echo Lake, the *Lights, Motors, Action!® Extreme Stunt Show* theater, next to Toy Story Midway Mania!, and at Rock 'n' Roller Coaster.

Most attractions provide access through the main queue, while others have auxiliary entrances for wheelchairs and service animals along with as many as five members of your party. Certain attractions require guests to transfer from their wheelchair to a ride system. Braille guidebooks, assistive listening devices, video captioning, handheld captioning, and audiotape guides are available at Guest Services for a $25 refundable deposit. Many theater-type attractions have reflective or video captioning. With a seven-day notice, a sign language interpreter will be provided at live shows on Sunday and Wednesday. Call (407) 824-4321 with any questions.

Lockers. Lockers are located at Oscar's Super Service on the right as you enter the park, available for $7 per day plus a $5 refundable key deposit for a small locker and $9 plus a $5 key deposit for large lockers. If you're park hopping keep your receipt for a replacement locker at no additional charge at the three other Disney theme parks.

Lost and found. Located next to Oscar's Super Service or call (407) 824-4245.

Lost children. Locate lost children at Guest Services.

Package pickup. Purchases may be sent to the package pickup window located next to Oscar's Super Service near the Main Entrance for pickup at the end of the day. Allow three hours for delivery. Registered guests of a Disney Resort may send packages directly to their hotel for next-day arrival.

Strollers and wheelchairs. Rentals are located at Oscar's Super Service on the right as you enter the park. Single strollers are $15 per day ($13 per day for a multi-day length of stay rental), double strollers $31 ($27 per day for a multi-day length of stay rental).

Wheelchairs are $12.00; $10 for a multi-day length of stay rental. Electric convenience vehicles are $50.00 plus a $20.00 refundable deposit.

Rented units must be returned to the original rental location to receive a security deposit refund. If you're park hopping keep your receipt for a same-day replacement at the three other Disney theme parks and Downtown Disney.

The Lay of the Land

Disney's Hollywood Studios' main street is Hollywood Boulevard with two walkways branching off to the right heading to Sunset Boulevard and Animation Courtyard. On the left is the Echo Lake area of the park that leads to the Streets of America section. Mickey Avenue and Pixar Place sit behind the Chinese theater and may be accessed via Animation Courtyard. It's a bit more confusing than the Magic Kingdom but fairly easy to maneuver.

The Very Best Attractions in Disney's Hollywood Studios

LIGHTS, MOTORS, ACTION® EXTREME STUNT SHOW

Movie stunts are the highlight of this thrill-a-minute show of superfast, high-flying stunt cars, screaming motorcycles, and crazy jet-skis. The 5,000-seat theater's 6.5-acre stage is set in a quiet French village, one that suddenly comes alive with action. The premise is the filming of a European spy thriller complete with production crew, director, and stunt coordinator who show the audience the making of complex vehicle stunts including creation, design, and filming. Extra highlights include pyrotechnic effects, ramp jumps, and high falls. Even Lightning McQueen, star of *Cars*, makes a cameo appearance. After completion each scene is edited with the addition of "real" actors then played with close-up detail on a giant video screen. The final explosion will blow you away! **38-minute show**.

> CARA'S TIP: Guests who wish to meet Lightning McQueen and Tow Mater before or after the show can do so at the Winner's Circle located nearby on the Streets of America.

ROCK 'N' ROLLER COASTER® STARRING AEROSMITH

You've nabbed a special invitation to an Aerosmith concert, but it's clear across town and you're late! Disney's wildest coaster ride takes place inside a twenty-four passenger "stretch limo" speeding down a Los Angeles freeway amid blasting Aerosmith music. Zooming past, through, and around neon Hollywood landmarks you'll loop and corkscrew in the night. And that's after you've accelerated to a speed of 60 mph in just under three seconds. Hold onto your hat (or anything else you might treasure) because this is pure Disney fun. **Minimum height 48 inches (4 feet). Not recommended for expectant mothers; those with back, heart, or neck problems; or those prone to motion sickness. Single Rider Line. 10-minute ride.**

> **CARA'S TIP:** If you'd like to sit in the front seat just ask, but be prepared for a wait because every other daredevil around has the same idea. The chicken-hearted can take comfort in knowing that although there are three inversions on the ride there are no steep drops.

STAR TOURS®—THE ADVENTURES CONTINUE ATTRACTION

Just when you think that a Disney attraction is so outdated that it's too far gone, they up and make it more fun than ever. Pick up a pair of 3-D glasses before boarding your interstellar space vehicle flight simulator from the Star Tours spaceport. Unfortunately, your launch isn't going to be a standard one; this go-round C-3PO inadvertently is your pilot on a wild voyage through the depths of the galaxy. Hang tight as he navigates you through jagged rocks on Tatooine, maneuvers around AT-ATs in a crazy battle on the icy planet of Hoth, hyperspaces to Naboo, and flees inside the Death Star in an attempt to escape Darth Vader . . . all this before nearly crash landing back in the hanger bay! And believe it or not this is only one of over fifty scenarios, each with different storylines, so ride again and again if you would like to attempt to experience them all. This is certainly one instance that you had better hope the "Force" is with you. **Minimum height 40 inches (3 feet, 4 inches). Not recommended for expectant mothers; those with back, heart, or neck problems; or those prone to motion sickness. 5-minute ride.**

TOY STORY MANIA!® ATTRACTION

Walk through "Andy's bedroom" past oversized Crayolas, checkers, Tinkertoys, and an interactive, Audio-Animatronics Mr. Potato Head boardwalk barker. Then don your 3-D glasses before boarding a carnival tram to embark on a 4-D virtual version of midway-style game play. Use your spring-action shooter to plug away at a series of giant-size video screens, each hosted by a member of the *Toy Story* gang featuring virtual spinning plates, tossing cream pies, bursting balloons, and funny little green aliens as you zip through game after game, each lasting 30 seconds, each more fun than the last. Adding to the entertainment is a 4th dimension of air shots and water spritzers while Toy Story characters yell hints and cheer you along. Watch out for bonus targets and simply have a blast (pun intended)! Don't think this is just another version of the Magic Kingdom's *Buzz Lightyear's Space Ranger Spin*® attraction; you'll find Toy Story Midway Mania! way more fun. **5-minute ride.**

CARA'S TIP: This is the Studios' most popular attraction. Head here first to avoid an hour and a half wait in line or pre-reserve it with FastPass+.

TWILIGHT ZONE TOWER OF TERROR

On this free-falling adventure you'll certainly feel you've entered the twilight zone or at the very least a brand-new dimension of fright. The waiting line snakes through the crumbling grounds of the deserted, thirteen-story Hollywood Tower Hotel with its rusty grillwork, cracking fountains, and overgrown, unkempt foliage, before proceeding through the spooky, abandoned lobby, dusty with forgotten luggage and dead flower arrangements. Step into the gloomy hotel library for a message from *Twilight Zone* TV show host Rod Serling (on a black-and-white television, of course) who relays the tale of a stormy night in 1939 when an elevator full of guests was struck by lightning and then disappeared. A bellhop invites you into a seemingly old, rusty service elevator that ascends and moves horizontally through several remarkable special effects in pitch-black space and, without warning, plummets thirteen stories to the bottom. Up you go again, then down, and up, and down, during which you'll be treated to dazzling views of the park. If you can stand the thrill don't miss this one; just be sure to ride it on an empty stomach. **Minimum height 40 inches (3 feet, 4 inches). Not recommended for expectant mothers; those with back, heart, or neck problems; or those prone to motion sickness. 10-minute ride.**

CARA'S TIP: If you chicken out there's an escape route immediately before entering the elevator; just ask a bellhop for directions.

VOYAGE OF THE LITTLE MERMAID

Journey under the sea at one of Disney's Hollywood Studios' most beloved attractions. This tribute to the auburn-haired mermaid Ariel combines puppetry, live actors, animated film, and delightful music with the adorable sidekicks Flounder and Sebastian and the not-so-adorable sea witch Ursula. Favorite songs from the movie, such as "Under the Sea," "Part of Your World," and "Poor Unfortunate Souls," along with fun special effects including black lights, lasers, rain showers, bubbles, and lightning make this show quite a hit with children. Besides, how often do you have the opportunity to behold a seemingly live mermaid with a flopping tail? **17-minute show.**

CHARACTER GREETING SPOTS AT DISNEY'S HOLLYWOOD STUDIOS

The Mickey head on your guide map will help you find the following locations:

- Pixar Place across from Toy Story Midway Mania! for an assortment of *Toy Story* friends throughout the day

- *Monsters Inc.* characters near Studio Backlot Tour

- Meet the stars of *Cars 2* at Team McQueen Headquarters near Streets of America

- Phineas and Ferb can be found near Mama Melrose's Ristorante

- Wreck-It Ralph and Vanellope Von Schweetz, The Incredibles, and Mickey Mouse at The Magic of Disney Animation

- Sophia the First outside of Disney Junior—Live on Stage! Attraction

CARA'S TIP: Don't skip this wonderful attraction simply because you don't have small children in tow. If you would like a center seat stand back a bit when the doors open into the theater from the preshow holding room and allow about half the crowd to enter before you.

The Very Best Dining in Disney's Hollywood Studios

Hollywood Brown Derby. Re-creation of the famous Hollywood dining spot offering the best food and most sophisticated atmosphere in the park; open for lunch and dinner. (See full description in the Dining In Style at Walt Disney World Resort chapter in the Disney's Hollywood Studios section.)

'50s Prime Time Café. Dine in a 1950s sitcom where Mom is your waitress and all vegetables must be consumed; open for lunch and dinner. (See full description in the Dining In Style at Walt Disney World Resort chapter in the Disney's Hollywood Studios section.)

Sci-Fi Dine-In Theater Restaurant. Relive the drive-in of your youth at this most unusual restaurant; open for lunch and dinner. (See full description in the Dining In Style at Walt Disney World Resort chapter in the Disney's Hollywood Studios section.)

Special Entertainment

FANTASMIC! **Show.** Sorcerer Mickey's fantasies soar to new heights in the 8,000-seat Hollywood Hills Amphitheater (with standing room for another 3,000). The Mouse himself orchestrates this extravaganza atop a 40-foot mountain on his lagoon-bound island. While Mickey struggles with the forces of good and evil in a series of lavish dreams and wild nightmares, guests thrill to the sight of walls of dancing water and wild, windy storms accompanied by stirring music, choreographed laser effects, and projecting flames. A favorite segment is the procession of floats representing the best of Disney happy endings, quickly followed by a bevy of Disney villains. Of course, Mickey wins out and, to the delight of the audience, a steamboat, captained by Steamboat Willie and stuffed with Disney characters, sails past in anticipation of the grand finale of water, lasers, and fireworks. Nightly performance.

For guaranteed seating with less waiting book a FANTASMIC! Dining Package for lunch or dinner at Hollywood Brown Derby, Mama Melrose's, and Hollywood and Vine (dinner only). Reservations can be made as early as 180 days in advance by calling (407) WDW-DINE, or (407) 939-3463, or online at Disneyworld.disney.go.com. After your meal you'll receive a seat ticket in a special reserved area making it possible to arrive only thirty minutes prior to show time. Reservations fill up quickly, so book as early as possible. **25-minute show.**

CARA'S TIP: Another option is to pre-reserve this show as Fast-Pass+ if possible. If not it's necessary to arrive about 45 minutes to one hour prior to snare a seat. Once the theater is full you're out of luck. If you wait until fifteen minutes prior you have a good chance of the leftover seats in the reserved FANTASMIC! Dining Package area or a standing-room-only spot whose only advantage is a quick dash out once the show is over. If you'd like to be among the first out of the theater take a seat in one of the back rows (really some of the better seats; the front rows can be a bit soggy). On windy or rainy nights the show is sometimes canceled.

Special Events

Star Wars Weekends. During four weekends in May and June Disney's Hollywood Studios is filled with dozens of Star Wars characters, heroes, and villains. Hyperspace Hoopla! Show, Padawan Mind Challenge, celebrity talk shows, character encounters, special parades, and autographs sessions are on the schedule throughout each day of the event. For updated information visit Disneyworld.disney.go.com/parks/hollywood-studios/special-events/star-wars-weekend. Included in regular park admission.

Night of Joy. On two consecutive nights in early September some of the biggest names in contemporary Christian music perform on several stages at Disney's Hollywood Studios for this ticketed event. 2013 acts include such names as Steven Curtis Chapman, Michael W. Smith, Skillet, MercyMe, Audio Adrenaline, Mandisa, Newsboys, TobyMac, Francesca Battistelli, and more. Call (877) NITE-JOY or (877) 648-3569 for ticketing information and pricing. Additional information is available at NightOfJoy.com.

The Osborne Family Spectacle of Dancing Lights. From mid-November until early January the park's Streets of America are dusted with "snow" and lit by five million colorful, "dancing" lights from dusk until park closing. It's a don't-miss, walk-through attraction. Included in regular park admission.

Disney's Animal Kingdom

"We inherited this earth from our parents and are borrowing it from our children." This is the important message Disney strives to convey in its environmentally conscious theme park, the Animal Kingdom. It's quite a beauty with more than four million lush, towering plants, trees, and grasses. Although the Animal Kingdom is five times the size of the Magic Kingdom, don't panic; it won't take two days to see everything. Remember much of the land is an enclave for the animals; the rest is easily conquered in a day.

The beauty of the Oasis hits you square in the face as you enter the park, a tropical jungle of flowering plants, cooling waterfalls, and overgrown plant life thriving with a menagerie of fascinating creatures. A cool mist pervades the air amid a cacophony of chattering birds and the aroma of fragrant trees and flowers on a variety of pathways leading to hidden grottoes, rushing streams, and towering vegetation. Critters housed in replicas of their natural habitats include barking deer (yes, they actually emit a barking sound when alarmed), exotic boar, macaws, iguana, wallabies, a giant anteater, Indonesian babirusa, and African spoonbills, all surrounded by colossal banana trees, swaying palms, massive bamboos, and flowering orchids.

After making your way through the Oasis, cross the bridge over the Discovery River into the park's central hub, *Discovery Island*® Land. Here visitors congregate to wander streets filled with lampposts, benches, and storefront facades carved with folk art animals. And here all eyes are immediately drawn to the focal point of the park, the awesome *Tree of Life*® Attraction.

Along with the main attractions are great hidden nooks and mysterious trails just waiting to be discovered. If you see a path leading off the

WANT TO ADD SOME CREATIVE ROLE-PLAY TO YOUR WALT DISNEY WORLD VACATION?

The interactive gaming craze has taken hold at Walt Disney World with plenty of opportunity for kids of all ages to participate at three of the four theme parks. And better yet it is included in park admission; simply sign up on arrival.

- **Magic Kingdom**. Apprentice sorcerers eliminate evil villains in the interactive *Sorcerers of the Magic Kingdom*. Pick up your play card at the Fire Station on Main Street to cast magic spells as you search for a bevy of villains in hiding places throughout the park. Also at the Magic Kingdom is *A Pirate's Adventure: Treasures of the Seven Seas*. Obtain your mission, map, and "magic talisman" from the Enlistment Center, a small building just outside the Adventureland arch on the Frontierland side, then embark on one of five different pirate raids throughout Adventureland fending off some of Captain Jack's enemies, including the Royal Navy and Captain Barbossa.

- **Epcot**. Kids will love becoming a secret agent and going undercover at *Disney Phineas and Ferb: Agent P's World Showcase Adventure*. Scour World Showcase and help solve clues to thwart some of Dr. Doofenshmirtz's most daringly evil plots. Visit a recruitment center at Odyssey Bridge, Norway pavilion, Italy pavilion, or near the International Gateway where you'll receive your assignment and begin your detective work with an interactive handheld device that will guide you on your mission.

- **Animal Kingdom**. Inspired by young Russell from the Pixar movie *Up*, *Wilderness Explorers at Disney's Animal Kingdom* experience the park using Wilderness Explorer Handbooks, earning badge stickers as they complete 30 different challenges throughout the park. It's a great way to encourage your children to take a more "up close and personal" look at the world around them.

main walkway, by all means follow; it may just take you to a place of sheer enchantment. Find time to explore and discover the many marvelous natural settings throughout or risk leaving a bit disappointed when you haven't grasped the true significance of this magnificent theme park.

Park Basics

GETTING THERE

Those driving to Walt Disney World should take exit 65 off I-4 and follow the signs to the Animal Kingdom.

USING WALT DISNEY WORLD TRANSPORTATION

From all Disney Resorts and theme parks: Board the bus marked Animal Kingdom.

PARKING

Cost is $15 per day for automobiles; free to registered guests of the Walt Disney Resort Hotels and Annual Passholders. Keep your receipt, good for parking at the Magic Kingdom, Epcot, and Disney's Hollywood Studios on that day only. Parking is conveniently located in front of the park. Trams circulate throughout the parking area for easy transportation to the entry gate. Make a note of what aisle and section you have parked in.

OPERATING HOURS

Open from 9:00 a.m. until around dark. Call (407) 824-4321 or log on to Disneyworld.disney.go.com for updated park hours.

Arrive thirty minutes early, allowing time to park, buy tickets, and be one of the first to hit the big attractions. I recommend heading straight to Expedition Everest followed by Kilimanjaro Safaris.

PARK SERVICES

ATMs. A cash-dispensing bank machine is located just outside the park entrance and another in *Dinoland U.S.A.®* Area outside of Chester and Hester's Dinosaur Treasures gift shop.

Baby Care Center. An infant facility located behind the Creature Comforts shop on Discovery Island is outfitted with private nursing rooms with rocking chairs, changing rooms with tables, feeding area with highchairs, and kitchen with microwave, oven, and sink. Formula, baby food, juice, diapers, wipes, sunscreen, over-the-counter medications, and clothing may be purchased. Most restrooms throughout the park have baby changing stations.

First aid. For minor medical problems head to the First Aid Center located behind the Creature Comforts shop on Discovery Island. Nurses are available during normal park operating hours to offer over-the-counter medications, bandages, and other quick remedies.

Guest Services. Located just inside the park on the left is Guest Services, where a knowledgeable staff is ready to assist with dining, ticket upgrades, accessibility, complimentary attraction translation devices, foreign guide maps for international guests, foreign currency exchange, lost guest retrieval, and general assistance. An additional Guest Services window is just outside the park entrance on the left.

Guests with disabilities. A guide for guests with disabilities is available at Guest Services. Guests with mobility disabilities should park adjacent to the Entrance Complex (ask at the Auto Plaza for directions). Wheelchairs and ECVs are available for rent. Most restaurants and shops are accessible to guests with disabilities, although some quick-service locations have narrow queues with railings (ask a host or hostess for assistance). Companion-assisted restrooms are located at Discovery Island opposite Flame Tree Barbecue, at First Aid, in Africa next to the Mombasa Marketplace, at Chester and Hester's Dinosaur Treasures in DinoLand, in *Asia*® Land inside *Maharajah Jungle Trek*® Attraction to the right as you exit the Bat House, near Expedition Everest, and at *Conservation Station*® Attraction at *Rafiki's Planet Watch*® Land.

Most attractions provide access through the main queue while others have auxiliary entrances for wheelchairs and service animals along with as many as five members of your party. Certain attractions require guests to transfer from their wheelchair to a ride system. Service animals are welcome in most locations of the park but are restricted in Affection Section at Rafiki's Planet Watch, *Kali River Rapids Attraction*® Attraction, Expedition Everest, and *Primeval Whirl*® Attraction. Braille guidebooks, assistive listening devices, video captioning, and audiotape guides are available at Guest Services for a $25 refundable deposit. With a seven-day notice a sign language interpreter will be provided at live shows on Tuesdays and Saturdays. Call (407) 824-4321 for more information.

Lockers. Lockers are located just outside the park entrance and just inside on the left for $7 per day plus a $5 refundable key deposit for a small locker, and $9 plus a $5 key deposit for large lockers. If you're park hopping keep your receipt for a replacement locker at the three other Disney theme parks for no extra charge.

Lost and found. Located at Guest Services or call (407) 824-4245.

Lost children. Locate lost children at the Baby Care Center or Guest Services.

Package pickup. Purchases may be sent to Garden Gate Gifts for pick-up at the end of the day. Allow three hours for delivery. Registered guests of a Disney Resort may send packages directly to their hotel for next-day arrival.

Strollers and wheelchairs. Rentals are located next to Garden Gate Gifts on the right as you enter the park. Single strollers are $15 per day ($13 per day for a multi-day length of stay rental), double strollers $31 ($27 per day for a multi-day length of stay rental).

Wheelchairs are $12.00; $10 for a multi-day length of stay rental. Electric convenience vehicles are $50.00 plus a $20.00 refundable deposit. Rented units must be returned to the original rental location to receive a security deposit refund. If you're park hopping keep your receipt for a same-day replacement at the three other Disney theme parks and Downtown Disney.

The Lay of the Land

The Animal Kingdom's Main Street of sorts is the Oasis, a winding series of pathways leading to the hub, Discovery Island, whose focal point is the Tree of Life. Three of the Animal Kingdom's four lands—Africa, Asia, and DinoLand U.S.A.—are accessible by crossing one of the bridges spanning the Discovery River that encircles Discovery Island. Africa, Asia, and DinoLand U.S.A. are interconnected by back pathways with Africa and Rafiki's Planet Watch connected to one another by train.

CHARACTER GREETING SPOTS AT THE ANIMAL KINGDOM

The Mickey head on your guide map will help you find the following locations:

- Donald and Daisy on Discovery Island across from Flame Tree Barbecue

- Mickey and Minnie at Adventurers Outpost on Discovery Island

- Lilo and Stitch at Island Mercantile

- Goofy and Pluto across from TriceraTop Spin in DinoLand U.S.A

- Terk, Flik and Baloo at the Africa Greeting Trails just off the pathway leading from Africa to Asia

- Wilderness Explorer Friends (characters from *Up*) near the entrance to the *It's Tough to Be a Bug!*® Attraction

- Chip and Dale at Rafiki's Planet Watch

- Pocahontas on Discover Island Trail

The Very Best Attractions in Disney's Animal Kingdom

DINOSAUR

Face fiery meteors and voracious predators on a trip back 65 million years to retrieve a 16-foot tall, plant-eating dinosaur and return with it before the big asteroid hits the earth. Load into twelve-passenger, all-terrain Dino Institute Time Rovers that rock, tilt, twist, and turn as they move through a dense, dark, prehistoric forest teeming with shrieking dinosaurs, giant lizards, and massive insects. When a hail of meteors strikes off you go on a wild ride dodging shrieking, nostril-flaring Audio-Animatronics dinosaurs until the big scream encounter with a huge carnotaurus (the only meat-eating dinosaur) who'd like you for his dinner. **Minimum height 40 inches (3 feet, 4 inches). Not recommended for expectant mothers or those with heart, back, or neck problems. 4-minute ride.**

> CARA'S TIP: This ride is pretty intense for children not only because of massive, screaming dinosaurs but also because of the scary anticipation in an extremely dark attraction.

EXPEDITION EVEREST® ATTRACTION

Disney's best coaster is combined with an innovative story line and a queue so interesting you tend to forget the long wait. The premise is a trekking company base camp, the Himalayan Escapes Tours and Expeditions, overflowing with bunks and supplies as well as a Yeti Museum filled with fascinating artifacts. Board the Anandapur Rail Service, your transportation for an expedition to the summit of a 199-foot mountain, ascending through bamboo forests, over teetering bridges, past waterfalls and glacier fields, then up to the snow-capped peak. The excitement truly begins when the train races forward then careens wildly backward through icy caves and dark canyons until the crazy encounter with the hulking Yeti himself! A twisting, turning escape ending in an 80-foot plunge down the mountain is the exciting conclusion. **Minimum height requirement 44 inches (3 feet, 8 inches). Not recommended for expectant mothers or those with heart, back, or neck problems. Single Riders Line. 4-minute ride.**

FESTIVAL OF THE LION KING

The all-important message of the continuing "circle of life" is wonderfully portrayed in this sensational stage extravaganza of Broadway-caliber song and dance. The story of the Lion King is told through a combination of elaborate costumes, wild acrobatic tumble monkeys, daring fire-twirlers, and massive Audio-Animatronics animal floats accompanied by the beat of tribal drums and jungle noise. Don't worry, if you're not acquainted with the music; you'll be an expert by the time you leave. Plan your day around this don't-you-dare-miss extravaganza. Check your guide map for showtimes. **30-minute show.**

> CARA'S TIP: The show will soon be moving to an all-new theater, in the Africa section of the park. Children who would like to be

chosen to participate in the closing parade should try to sit in the bottom section of the bleachers.

FINDING NEMO—THE MUSICAL

A Broadway-caliber, original stage show brings the *Finding Nemo* characters to life in a combination of puppetry, live performance, and original music and lyrics. Inside an enclosed theater is a magical undersea environment with dazzling oversize puppetry (designed by Michael Curry, creator of Broadway's *The Lion King*), charming songs, and a way-fun animated backdrop with special effects. The puppeteers are not hidden; you see the actor and the puppet together, making for one unusual performance. This is Disney at its best. **40-minute show.**

> CARA'S TIP: Check your guide map for show times. The first show of the day is usually the least crowded and does not require much of an early arrival.

IT'S TOUGH TO BE A BUG!® ATTRACTION

On the winding walkway leading to this attraction is a menagerie of wildlife, lush foliage, waterfalls, caves, and, most importantly, an up-close view of the marvelous animal carvings that make up the Tree of Life. It's always twilight in the low-ceilinged waiting area underneath the Tree, where chirping crickets sing Broadway tunes from such insect shows as The Dung and I (featuring the hit song "Hello Dung Lovers"), Beauty and the Bees, and A Cockroach Line. Flik (the star of *A Bug's Life*) is the host of this creepy-crawly 3-D movie of assorted bugs who only want humans to understand them. But much to the glee of the audience, they just can't help misbehaving.

A favorite opening act is the stinkbug accidentally letting his smelly, gaseous fumes rip into the crowd. As the show progresses you'll be doused with bug spray, stung sharply in the back, and showered with termite acid, all innocently achieved through special effects. Receive one final surprise as the beetles, maggots, and cockroaches exit safely ahead of you. This is one super show, a highlight of the park! **8-minute show.**

> CARA'S TIP: Definitely one attraction too intense for young children, particularly when Hopper, the despicable grasshopper from A Bug's Life, scares the dickens out of every child under age five.

If you'd like to sit in the center of the auditorium, hang back a little in the waiting area and allow some of the audience to enter ahead of you. And try not to sit on the far sides of the theater where the 3-D effects are slightly minimized.

KILIMANJARO SAFARIS® EXPEDITON

Load into safari vehicles for your trip around Disney's 110-acre African savanna brimming with baobab trees, waterfalls, rivers, watering holes, and rickety bridges. Each excursion is different and depends entirely upon which animals decide to make an appearance. As you rumble across the authentic-looking landscape, your driver will assist in locating the wide assortment of wildlife including lions, cheetahs, warthogs, elephants, gazelles, crocodiles, wildebeests, exotic birds, giraffes, even white rhinos. Those with luck might encounter a male lion, rare because they sleep about eighteen hours a day. Some animals may come close to your vehicle, while predators and more perilous species only look as if they could leap from behind their seemingly invisible barriers. **Not recommended for expectant mothers or people with heart, back, or neck problems. 20-minute ride.**

> CARA'S TIP: Don't run for cover during an afternoon thundershower; it's the animals' favorite time to come out for a rain bath.

MAHARAJA JUNGLE TREK® ATTRACTION

Wander the grounds of the Anandapur Royal Forest through the ruins of a crumbling palace where you'll encounter spectacular wildlife beginning with a Komodo dragon (look hard; it's in there somewhere). Next are vampire-like flying foxes and Rodrigues fruit bats with 6-foot wingspans. Then the walk's highlight—Bengal tigers roaming the grasslands surrounded by gentle deer and blackbuck antelope. This remarkable journey ends in the Asian bird sanctuary filled with the most exotic varieties imaginable.

> CARA'S TIP: Take time to gaze at the marvelous details along the trail such as walls of fading murals, flapping Tibetan prayer flags, abandoned rickshaws, and authentic-looking pagodas.

PANGANI FOREST EXPLORATION TRAIL WALKING TOUR

Many people walk right past this self-guided trail and only when it's too late find out what they've missed. Your first encounter is with colobus monkeys at the Endangered Animal Rehabilitation Center and naked mole rats at the Research Center. Then on to an aviary teeming with birds native to Africa in the midst of a cooling waterfall and an aquarium overflowing with kaleidoscopic fish. Soon all visitors are drawn to a terrific underwater observation tank of swimming hippos before hitting the real highlight—lowland gorillas. You'll find a family of gorillas on the right side of the pathway and a group of bachelors on the other side. Take time to search for them; it can sometimes be difficult to spot them in the profuse vegetation. Experts are scattered throughout to answer questions and give short, informative talks about each exhibit.

> CARA'S TIP: Go early after the safari or late in the afternoon when crowds are low. It can be difficult to spot wildlife from behind rows of human heads.

The Very Best Dining in Disney's Animal Kingdom

The Animal Kingdom offers some of the most visually delightful quick-service dining in all of Walt Disney World. While the food is just so-so, you'll love the dining terrace at Flame Tree Barbecue with views of Asia and the hulking Expedition Everest. Even Pizzafari offers a great screened eating porch with a tropical view.

Rainforest Café. Enter through a thundering waterfall to dine among screeching and roaring jungle animals. Open for breakfast, lunch, and dinner. *Breakfast:* Tonga toast, cranberry waffle, egg white omelet, eggs benedict, breakfast sliders. *Lunch and dinner:* BBQ bacon cheeseburger, portobello mushroom sandwich, Caribbean coconut shrimp, turkey wrap, chicken fried chicken, pot roast, Italian sausage and penne pasta with shrimp, slow-roasted St. Louis-style pork spareribs.

Tusker House. Character buffet breakfast and lunch with Donald and Daisy Duck, Mickey, and Goofy offering African-inspired fare. Dinner is a non-character meal. (See full description in the Dining In Style at Walt Disney World Resort chapter in the Animal Kingdom section.)

Special Entertainment

Mickey's Jammin' Jungle Parade. Carousing around the Tree of Life each afternoon is an island street party procession featuring Mickey and his gang joined by a bevy of giant, rolling animal sculpture drums sounding out an energetic beat. Mickey, Minnie, Goofy, and Donald overload zany safari vehicles with their idea of exactly what should be taken on an extended vacation. They're accompanied by lofty animal puppets on stilts and rickshaws filled with lucky visitors chosen from the crowd, all adding up to one wacky parade. **15 minutes.**

> CARA'S TIP: A great place to watch the parade is from the bridge between Africa and Discovery Island, quite often almost empty of people unless it is reserved for VIP Tour guests.

ANIMAL KINGDOM'S BEHIND-THE-SCENES TOURS

Call (407) WDW-TOUR or (407) 939-7687 for reservations.

- **Backstage Safari.** On this three-hour tour guests explore the animal housing areas, meet the keepers, and learn how the animals are cared for. Visit the nutrition center where animal food is prepared and see the backstage area of the Veterinary Care Hospital at Conservation Station, finishing with a special tour through Kilimanjaro Safaris. $72 plus park admission. Two tours, one at 8:30 a.m. and another at 1:00 p.m., are offered on Monday, Wednesday, Thursday, and Friday. Guests must be age sixteen or older to participate.

- **Wild By Design.** On this three-hour tour discover how the park's designers combined ethnic art and artifacts, authentic architecture, and story lines to create the Animal Kingdom. Meet the animal keepers who will clue you in on the training, feeding and care of their charges. $60 plus park admission and includes a continental breakfast at Pizzafari. 8:30 a.m. Monday, Wednesday, Thursday, and Friday. Guests must be age fourteen or older to participate; those ages fourteen or fifteen must be accompanied by a participating adult.

- **Wild Africa Trek.** Guests wanting to venture off the beaten path at Disney's Animal Kingdom, here's your chance! A small group of adventurers are led on a 3-hour personalized, guided excursion that includes a bushwalk through unexplored areas of the forest and an exciting ride in customized vehicles across an animal-filled savanna. You'll even clip into a safety-line harness and cross over a rickety bridge underneath which is the home of crocodiles. On these expert-led treks time is spent observing and learning about the wildlife with extended photo opportunities. Offered several times per day the cost is $189-249 depending on the season and includes a light snack and a photo CD. Guests must be age eight or older to participate; guests under age 18 and younger must be accompanied by a participating adult. Minimum of 45 pounds, maximum of 300 pounds.

5

DIVERSIONS BEYOND THE WALT DISNEY WORLD THEME PARKS

Disney's BoardWalk

Inspired by the turn-of-the-century, Mid-Atlantic seaboard promenades found in such places as Atlantic City and Coney Island, Disney's BoardWalk offers dining, shopping, and entertainment on the shore of Crescent Lake. Situated out back of the BoardWalk Inn and just outside of Epcot's International Gateway, it's the perfect destination for a before- or after-Illuminations dinner at the Flying Fish, or just a place to party down at Jellyrolls and Atlantic Dance, two very different nightclubs. The BoardWalk is at its best in the evening hours when restaurants are open and entertainment in the form of arcades, midway games, musical performers, magicians, jugglers, sword swallowers, caricature artists, and more is in high gear; don't bother during the daytime when many of the restaurants are closed and entertainment is nil. Although Jellyrolls charges a cover, there's no admission fee to stroll the BoardWalk. For up-to-date information call (407) 939-3492.

Getting There

Disney's BoardWalk Entertainment District sits in back of the Board-Walk Inn about a ten-minute walk from Epcot's International Gateway, a short stroll from Disney's Yacht and Beach Club and the Walt Disney World Swan and Dolphin, and a water launch or twenty-minute walk from Disney's Hollywood Studios. If traveling from a Disney resort during park hours take bus transportation to the closest theme park and then another bus to the BoardWalk Inn. After park hours it requires a trip to Downtown Disney and then a transfer to the BoardWalk Inn; a much less frustrating choice is to either drive a car or simply cab it.

Parking

Park in the complimentary self-park lot in front of the BoardWalk Inn, a feat that is sometimes difficult during events such as the Epcot International Food and Wine Festival. Valet parking is available for $15 at BoardWalk Inn.

Hours

Dining hours vary, with some spots open as early as 7:00 a.m. for breakfast and others not closing until after midnight. Shop from 10:00 a.m. to 11:00 p.m. with the exception of the Screen Door General Store, open from 8:00 a.m. to midnight.

The Very Best Dining at Disney's BoardWalk

Flying Fish Café. Excellent seafood in whimsical surroundings, open for dinner only. (See full description in the Dining In Style at Walt Disney World Resort chapter in the Resort Dining section.)

Kouzzina by Cat Cora. Dine on Iron Chef Cat Cora's Greek and Mediterranean family recipes and favorites, open for breakfast and dinner. *Breakfast:* steel cut cinnamon oatmeal with bananas and walnuts, turkey-sweet potato hash, country French toast with grilled fig and anise country bread, blueberry granola pancakes, spinach, tomato, and feta scrambled eggs. *Dinner:* cinnamon stewed chicken topped with Greek cheese, pastitsio (Greek lasagna), slow cooked lamb shank with *gigantes* beans and lamb jus, whole pan-roasted fish with braised greens, Greek olives, fennel, and smoked chili.

Disney's BoardWalk Nightclubs

Atlantic Dance. Enjoy video DJ music of the 80s, 90s, and today in an Art Deco ballroom setting. Arrive at opening time and make a quick dash upstairs to the outdoor terrace for an excellent view of the Illuminations fireworks. Open 9:00 p.m. to 1:45 a.m.; guests must be at least twenty-one years old for admittance; closed Sunday and Monday. No cover charge.

Jellyrolls. For great fun, head to this popular dueling pianos and sing-along bar. Open 7:00 p.m. to 2:00 a.m.; guests must be twenty-one or older for admittance; $12 cover charge.

Downtown Disney

Many changes and additions over the years have created what is now known as the very successful Downtown Disney, a combination of over 70 restaurants and shops. During the day it's a perfect getaway from the parks, but at night after the parks close, Downtown Disney truly comes alive.

At *Downtown Disney*® Marketplace you'll find the largest World of Disney Store in the world, a boat marina, plenty of shopping, a rip-roaring T-Rex Cafe, and the volcano-smoking Rainforest Cafe. And then there's *Downtown Disney*® West Side loaded with dining and entertainment venues including Splitsville Luxury Lanes, Wolfgang Puck Café, Crossroads at House of Blues, Bongos Cuban Cafe, Cirque du Soleil, a 24-complex movie theater, and DisneyQuest. It's always hopping, but those preferring a bit of peace and quiet can opt for a quiet stroll along the pleasant promenade running beside Village Lake.

Downtown Disney® Pleasure Island, where only a few shops and restaurants are to be found, as well as the entire Downtown Disney complex is undergoing a dramatic and ongoing change with double the number of shops, restaurants and other venues as well as open-air promenades along the waterfront. The new complex, to be named Disney Springs, will have a Town Center area, elevated spaces at West Side, an expanded *World of Disney* Store, The Landing waterfront, and more, all to be completed in 2016.

Getting There

Direct buses operate from all Disney resort hotels. Buses stop first at the Marketplace near Once Upon a Toy and then at Pleasure Island between Pleasure Island and West Side. Those driving from outside the Walt Disney World area should take Interstate 4 to exit 67 and follow the signs to Downtown Disney.

Parking

Parking here can prove difficult, particularly during busy season and weekend evenings. If you're a guest of a Disney resort consider using Disney transportation to avoid the hassle of parking. Self-parking is free. Valet parking is $15 and available from 4:00 p.m. to 2:00 a.m. daily; use Entrance 4 at Downtown Disney West Side.

Hours

Shops at Downtown Disney Marketplace are open Sunday through Thursday from 9:30 a.m. to 11:00 p.m. and Friday and Saturday from 9:30 a.m. to 11:30 p.m. Pleasure Island shops are open Sunday through Thursday from 10:30 a.m. to 11:00 p.m., and Friday and Saturday from 10:30 a.m. until midnight. Downtown Disney West Side shops are open Sunday through Thursday from 10:30 a.m. to 11:00 p.m. and Friday and Saturday from 10:30 a.m. to midnight. Restaurant hours vary; see specific restaurants for exact times.

Basic Information

ATMs. Withdraw cash at ATMs located at House of Blues and Wetzel's Pretzels on the West Side; and across from Ghirardelli Ice Cream Shop, the World of Disney Store, and by the restrooms near Once Upon a Toy at the Marketplace.

Guest Relations. Stop here for Advance Dining Reservations, lost and found, ticketing needs, and services for Guests with Disabilities and international guests along with general information. Facilities are located at both the West Side outside of DisneyQuest, and the Marketplace next to Marketplace CoOp.

Stroller and Wheelchairs. Rentals are located near Once Upon a Toy at

Downtown Disney Marketplace, and DisneyQuest Emporium at Downtown Disney on the West Side. Single strollers are $15.00 per day with a $100 credit card deposit required; double strollers are not available. Wheelchairs are $12.00 and electric convenience vehicles are $50.00 plus a $100.00 refundable deposit. Rented units must be returned to the original rental location to receive a security deposit refund. If you're park hopping keep your receipt for a same-day replacement at the four Disney theme parks.

Downtown Disney Diversions

AMC Downtown Disney 24 and AMC Downtown Disney 24 Dine-In Theatres. Watch newly released flicks in stadium seating with THX Surround Sound and Sony Dynamic Digital Sound in this state-of-the-art, twenty-four-screen theater. There are now two areas: 18 standard movie theaters and six Dine-in Theaters with Fork & Screen dining offering a full menu of appetizers, entrées, desserts, and drinks, as well as cushier seating fronted by a dining table. For movie listings and show times, call 1-888-262-4926 or (407) 827-1308 or go online at https://www.amctheatres.com/movie-theatres/amc-downtown-disney-24-with-dine-in-theatres.

Characters in Flight. A tethered, helium-filled balloon takes guests 400 feet above Disney World for a breathtaking, 360-degree view of the surrounding area. Holding up to 30 people at a time, prices are $18 for adults and $12 for children ages 3-9 (guests under age 12 must be accompanied by an adult). Open 8:30 a.m. to midnight.

La Nouba by Cirque du Soleil. The tent-shaped building overpowering the West Side of Downtown Disney is none other than Cirque du Soleil. Although it's sometimes described as a type of circus, it's actually a mixture of circus, dance, drama, and street entertainment, more than worth the price of admission.

It's hard to describe this extraordinary event. The show has more than sixty mesmerizing human performers (no animals) in outrageous costumes entertaining in the midst of exciting live music (not one syllable is uttered throughout the show) and surrealistic choreography. Witness daring, gravity-defying acts, each one more outlandish and bizarre than the next. Two showstoppers are the young Chinese girls who perform a routine with a *diabolo*, a Chinese yo-yo (you won't believe it!), and a trampoline finale with powerful performers literally running up the sides of a wall. The sheer physical strength is absolutely astonishing and quite a sight to see. Tickets can be purchased up to 180 days in advance by calling (407) 939-7600 or online at cirquedusoleil.com/en/shows/lanouba/tickets/florida.aspx. Two ninety-minute performances Tuesday through Saturday at 6:00 and 9:00 p.m. with six levels of ticket prices according to seat location.

> CARA'S TIP: Although some seats are better than others there really isn't a bad seat in the house. You may want to avoid the first row of the highest tier; the wheelchair-accessible seats in front block your view a bit.

DisneyQuest Indoor Interactive Theme Park. With five floors of virtual games and interactive adventures diverse enough to entertain the entire family, this indoor theme park offers a multitude of attractions (including more than 180 video games) that can be played over and over for the single cost of admission. Become a swashbuckling pirate in a fierce battle for treasure at the virtual 3-D *Pirates of the Caribbean: Battle for Buccaneer Gold*; watch a large projection screen while paddling with motion-sensor oars on a prehistoric, white-water adventure on the *Virtual Jungle Cruise*; fly through the ancient city of Agrabah on your magic carpet in search of precious jewels in a virtual reality setting on *Aladdin's Magic Carpet Ride*; design your own thrilling roller coaster ride with *Cyberspace Mountain*; play space-age bumper cars with *Buzz Lightyear's AstroBlaster*; or wield a light saber to fight supervillains sword-to-sword in virtual reality with *Ride the Comix*.

Upstairs, FoodQuest offers a quick bite with bacon cheeseburgers, chicken BLT sandwiches, meatball subs, hot dogs, wraps, pizza, pasta, salads and more.

Open Sunday through Thursday from 11:30 a.m. to 10:00 p.m. and Friday and Saturday from 11:30 a.m. to 11:00 p.m. Admission prices are $37 for adults and $31 for children ages three through nine; same-day reentry allowed with ticket and hand stamp. Guests age nine or younger must be accompanied by someone age sixteen or older, all of whom must pay admission. For information and tickets call 407-824-4321.

CARA'S TIP: Come during the daytime on weekdays and avoid rainy days. Although DisneyQuest is mainly geared to kids and adolescents, it's a great place for quality family time. Adults traveling alone may want to pass unless you really enjoy this type of entertainment.

Splitsville Luxury Lanes. Downtown Disney's latest addition has definitely livened up the atmosphere at the West Side. With an upscale spin on America's classic pastime, here bowling comes along with dining; and when I say dining, I mean tables edging the perimeter of 30 lanes on two floors, all with lane concierges! Finally you don't have to decide between a night of bowling or going out to dinner

Don't expect gourmet food, but in such a fun atmosphere you can just about forgive anything. There's also patio and indoor dining areas on both floors, a sushi bar, four drink bars, TV monitors everywhere you look, live music, billiards and more. Some of the menu items include hand-tossed pizza, fresh-rolled sushi, burgers, entrée salads, hand-cut filet sliders, steak *chimichurri*, etc., served right at the lane if you prefer. And with over a dozen gluten-free dishes on the menu there's something for everyone.

Open Sunday 10:00 a.m. to 1:00 a.m., Monday through Wednesday 10:30 a.m. to 1:00 a.m., Thursday and Friday 10:30 a.m. to 2:00 a.m., and Saturday 10:00 a.m. to 2:00 a.m. Bowling lane reservations can be made online at Splitsvillelanes.com/#/locations/disney/reservations; walk-ups also welcome. For more information about Splitsville visit their website at SplitsvilleLanes.com.

The Very Best Shopping at Downtown Disney

The Art of Disney. Shop for Disney animation cells, paintings, and sketches; visiting Disney animation artists.

Curl by Sammy Duvall. Trendy surf shop for the younger generation now located at the West Side with Hurley, Quiksilver, Billabong, and Roxy clothing and accessories for men and women. An entire wall of flip-flops including Reef and TOMS shoes, and loads of sunglasses including Oakley and Ray Ban.

Disney's Days of Christmas. Visit this whopper of a Disney Christmas store with Disney character ornaments and stockings, Victorian Disney character plush toys, tree skirts, and toppers. Have your purchases personalized or engraved on the spot. You'll also find an entire room of *The Nightmare Before Christmas* merchandise.

Fit2Run. Find the perfect athletic footwear with a complimentary video-taped gait analysis and iStep barometric scanning at this West Side store. Then test your new shoes on the indoor track to make sure they fit perfectly.

Goofy's Candy Co. Cookies, fudge, a wall of bulk candy and jellybeans, boxed and individual chocolates, candy apples, pastries, cupcakes, and Goofy's Glaciers frozen drinks. Create-Your-Own-Treat with gingerbread cookies, caramel apples, Krispy Rice Treats, marshmallows, etc. with your choice of a dipping flavor, toppings, and drizzle. Reserve a Birthday Bash party here with either a Goofy Scien-Terrific or Perfectly Princess theme (no characters)–call (407) WDW-BDAY or (407) 939-2329 for reservations.

Hoypoloi. Shop for glassware and art, sculpture, Zen-inspired gifts and books, wind chimes, jewelry, and porcelain nightlights.

LEGO Imagination Center. Marvel at giant LEGO models both inside and outside the store with an interactive outdoor play area and every LEGO set imaginable.

Once Upon a Toy. 16,000 square feet of Disney and Hasbro toys, many of them exclusive. "Build-Your-Own Mr. Potato Head" and "Star Wars Droid Factory" stations, exclusive Indiana Jones, Pirates of the Caribbean, and Star Wars merchandise, monorail playsets, Animator Collection Disney princess dolls, and a huge assortment of Disney CDs, DVDs, and games.

Pop Gallery. Art gallery featuring original contemporary art. Artists featured are Todd White, Todd Warner, Michelle Mardis, Markus Pierson, and more. Also limited edition Dr. Seuss lithographs.

Sosa Family Cigars. Cigar aficionados will love the hand-rolled cigars, smoking accessories, and a master cigar roller in action Thursday through Saturday evenings.

World of Disney Store. Largest Disney merchandise store in the world with a giant-size, spitting Stitch hanging over the entrance and 50,000 square feet crammed with just about every Disney item imaginable. "Create Your Own Pirate Hat," "Build a Magic Wand," and "Fill Your Own Treasure Chest" stations.

Bibbidi Bobbidi Boutique, located inside World of Disney, where little princesses are made up with royal hair topped with crowns, sparkling jewels, shimmering nail paints and makeup, a complete costume, and other magical accessories followed by a photo shoot. Reservations are taken 180 days prior at (407) WDW-STYLE or (407) 939-7895.

The Very Best Dining at Downtown Disney

Bongos. Cuban-themed restaurant and entertainment spot open for lunch and dinner. Mojo marinated fried shredded flank steak with grilled onions, mojo marinated fried pork bites topped with grilled onions, *criolla* minced beef, seasoned roasted half chicken marinated in lemon juice and garlic in a tomato *criolla* sauce, chicken with yellow rice, *parrillada de mariscos*, a skillet of seafood, fish, clams, mussels, jumbo shrimp and a lobster tail with garlic lime butter.

Fulton's Crab House. Fresh seafood served in a moored riverboat open for lunch and dinner. (See full description in the Dining In Style at Walt Disney World Resort in the Downtown Disney section.)

Portobello. Italian food in a countryside trattoria atmosphere, open for lunch and dinner. (See full description in the Dining In Style at Walt Disney World Resort in the Downtown Disney section.)

Raglan Road Irish Pub and Restaurant. Irish cooking served up with authentic music open for lunch and dinner as well as Sunday brunch. Citrus salmon, shepherd's pie, fish and chips, lemon parsley crusted cod with a citrus white wine sauce, beef curry pie, grilled lollipop pork chop with colcannon potatoes and port cider jus, Guinness and onion bangers on mash, beef stew.

T-Rex Cafe. Downtown Disney's most entertaining dining spot with life-size Audio-Animatronics dinosaurs and wild meteor showers open for lunch and dinner. Gigantosaurus burger, Triassic tortellini with grilled chicken, mammoth mushroom ravioli, stegosaurus steak & cheese sandwich, tar pit fried shrimp, tribal fish tacos, fire-roasted rotisserie chicken, Neanderthal New York strip.

Wolfgang Puck Grand Café. Four separate dining concepts in one facility: café for lunch and dinner; upscale dining room on 2nd floor (dinner only); The Sushi Bar; and Express with patio dining. (See the Dining Room full description in the Dining In Style at Walt Disney World Resort chapter in the Downtown Disney section.)

Walt Disney World Water Parks

Walt Disney World offers two world-class water parks, each with its own brand of entertainment. Blizzard Beach's highlight is the exhilarating 120-foot Summit Plummet slide, and at tropical Typhoon Lagoon is a whopper of a surf pool as well as Crush'n'Gusher, a water coaster thrill ride. Both parks are beautifully themed and landscaped, and each offers something for just about everyone. And because pools are heated in the cooler months, it's a year-round playground (both parks are on a rotating schedule of refurbishment in the winter months so it's best to check ahead).

During the sizzling summer months it's important to arrive early in the morning if you want to avoid long lines that begin forming at almost every attraction by midday. In fact, parks are sometimes filled to capacity by late morning, and new guests are kept from entering until late in the afternoon. Weekends are the worst when the locals add to the swell. Be sure to bring along water footwear to protect tender feet from the scorching hot pavements.

Locker and towel rentals are available at both parks, and life jackets are complimentary. Ice chests are allowed as long as they don't contain alcoholic beverages or glass containers (alcoholic drinks may be purchased at both water parks). An adult must accompany children ages nine or younger, and all swim attire must be free of rivets, buckles, or exposed metal. Parking is complimentary.

CARA'S TIP: In the busy summer months when the water parks are open until 8:00 p.m., think about arriving mid- to late afternoon when the morning guests are beginning to depart. It's the best time to enjoy the attractions minus the crowds.

Disney's Blizzard Beach

Disney's largest water park features the strange theme of a melting alpine ski resort in the middle of the hot Florida sunshine. The thaw has created a watery "winter" wonderland where chairlifts carry swimmers instead of skiers up a 90-foot-high mountain to slalom bobsled runs that are now thrilling waterslides. Although you'll find plenty of tame attractions, this is Disney's water park for daredevils with wild, rushing water and thrill slides. Upon arrival, head straight for Summit Plummet in order to avoid huge lines later in the day.

Hours vary according to the season but are usually 10:00 a.m. to 5:00 p.m., with extended hours until 8:00 p.m. in summer. In cooler months the two water parks are open on a rotating basis, with one open and the other closed for refurbishment. Call (407) 560-3400 or go online at Disneyworld.disney.go.com/calendars/ for up-to-date information.

GETTING THERE

Blizzard Beach is located in the Animal Kingdom area on West Buena Vista Drive. If using Disney transportation, direct buses depart from all resorts. Those driving from outside the Walt Disney World area should take exit 65 off I-4.

THE VERY BEST ATTRACTIONS AT BLIZZARD BEACH

Runoff Rapids. Those in search of a thrill but not a scare will love this attraction. Tube down your choice of three runs (one is enclosed, the others open) for a blast of a ride. To reach this attraction, go behind Mt. Gushmore to pick up a tube at the bottom of a tall flight of stairs and start climbing.

Summit Plummet. The king of water park attractions! From the top a 120-foot plunge reaches speeds of up to 55 mph. The slide itself is a 350-foot speed trap where daredevils body slide so fast they don't know what hit them as they plummet to the bottom.

Ski Patrol Training Camp. For the preteen set under age thirteen. Not-so-scary slides, an inner tube ride, floating icebergs, even a t-bar where riders can drop into the water below.

Slusher Gusher. A bit less crazy than Summit Plummet it hurtles straight to the bottom of a snow-banked slide, double dipping over two wild, rolling hills.

Teamboat Springs Water Ride. One of the most popular rides in the park, this 1,200-foot attraction accommodates anywhere from three to five people per raft as it twists and turns through a fun-filled succession of rushing waterfalls.

Tike's Peak. Perfect for the toddler set, here are miniature versions of some of the water park's best attractions with gentle slides, an inner tube ride, and water splash and sand areas.

WATER PARK VIPs

If the thought of fighting for a lounge chair sounds just too exhausting consider premium space rentals. Available at both water parks are the personalized services of an attendant, private lockers, all-day drink mugs, a cooler with ice and bottled water, Adirondack lounge furniture, and towels.

Blizzard Beach's Polar Patios are deck retreats with a big umbrella for shade. *Beach Shacks at Typhoon Lagoon* are a bit more civilized in that they offer a roof for shading, but you must like the sand since you sit directly on it. Both run from $213 to $319, depending on the season, for six guests with up to four additional guests possible for $25 per person.

If you want something a bit less pricey then opt for *Premium Beach Chair Space* at either park with two lounge chairs, a cocktail table, and two towels; $40 available for up to four people. Call 407-WDW-PLAY or 407-939-7529 for reservations up to 180 days in advance.

Disney's Typhoon Lagoon

At this beauty of a water park you'll find a sixty-one-acre tropical fantasyland. The premise is that a great storm swept everything in its path to a once sleepy resort town that became Typhoon Lagoon. The unfortunate shipwrecked shrimp boat, Miss Tilly, perched atop the 95-foot-high summit of Mount Mayday, creates a ruckus every half hour when it tries in vain to dislodge itself by spewing a geyser of water high above the park. Geared toward a bit tamer crowd than Blizzard Beach, only one waterslide here is a daredevil's delight.

The park's main draw is the 2.75-million-gallon wave pool that boasts some of the tallest simulated waves in the world (some as high as 6 feet!). Here you have a chance to take "Learn to Surf" lessons before park opening on Monday, Tuesday, Thursday, and Friday, with surfboards provided. Participants must be at least eight years old and strong swimmers. Cost is $150 per person. Call (407) WDW-PLAY or (407) 939-7529 for reservations.

Hours vary according to the season but are usually 10:00 a.m. to 5:00 p.m. with extended hours until 8:00 p.m. in summer. During the cooler months the two parks open on a rotating basis with one always closed for refurbishment. Call (407) 560-4120 or go online at disney-world.disney.go.com/calendars/ for up-to-date information.

GETTING THERE

Typhoon Lagoon is located across Buena Vista Drive from Downtown Disney West Side. If using Disney transportation, direct buses depart from all resorts marked Downtown Disney/Typhoon Lagoon. Those driving from outside the Walt Disney World area should take exit 67 off I-4.

THE VERY BEST ATTRACTIONS AT TYPHOON LAGOON

Crush 'n' Gusher **Water Thrill Ride.** This exciting attraction, billed as a water coaster thrill ride, is the only one of its kind in Central Florida. Whisk along a series of flumes and spillways, experiencing torrents of water while weaving in and out of a rusty old tropical fruit factory. Choose from three different spillways ranging between 410 and 420 feet long with a variation of slopes and turns.

Humunga Kowabunga. This trio of 214-foot speed slides is only for the most daring of thrill-seekers. Fly along at speeds of around 30 mph, a feat only for those with strong hearts. Lines can be excruciatingly long so head for this attraction first thing in the morning.

Ketchakiddee Creek. For those 48 inches tall or less, kids can man the deck and fire off water cannons, hop on an inner tube ride, enjoy slides especially for them, and participate in sand play.

Shark Reef. Pick up your snorkeling gear and prepare yourself for the bracingly cold saltwater of Shark Reef. Instructors are on hand to help guide inexperienced snorkelers as they swim through a short-but-sweet pool of tropical fish, stingrays, and harmless sharks.

Storm Slides. Corkscrew through 300 feet of caves and waterfalls at speeds of 20 mph. Try all three slides—each offer a different experience.

Typhoon Lagoon Surf Pool. This is the park's main attraction. What sounds like a typhoon warning is a foghorn announcing the impending wave soon to follow, some as high as six feet. Separate but nearby you'll find a lagoon made for children too small to handle the big waves.

The Very Best Walt Disney World Area Spas

When your muscles are aching and your body is screaming for rest after days at the parks, soothe your jangled nerves at one of the Walt Disney World area spas. Immerse yourself in luxury with a feel-good treatment or two, guaranteed to rejuvenate and swiftly get you back on your feet and ready for another long day of walking the parks.

Look for the new Spa at the Four Seasons to open summer of 2014 with extensive spa options, even a private patio with plunge pool. It's sure to be a favorite!

Senses–A Disney Spa at Disney's Grand Floridian Resort

Newly remodeled and now managed by Disney, here exists a spa with a sense of sophistication and luxury missing in its previous incarnation. On arrival you'll choose from three different experiences—Relax, Re-new, or Imagine—with the theme carried throughout in the treatments, lighting, even juice and snacks.

Separate women's and men's locker rooms are equipped with luxury robes in addition to a sparkling glass mosaic tile "fantasy wet room" with whirlpool and heated tile loungers and an adjoining steam room. Within each waiting lounge are comfortable, draped lounging chairs with neck warmers along with organic teas, cucumber and basil water, and healthy cupcake bites.

Fifteen treatment rooms are equipped with heated tables, silky-to-the-touch microfiber sheets, and soft, "chakra" lighting whose color can be chosen to match your Relax, Renew, or Imagine theme. Each guest is enveloped in a warmed robe at the end of their massage in order to extend the sense of wellbeing and relaxation. Two tub rooms enable a massage accompanied by either a custom or bubble bath treatment, and a couples room offers a romantic option for those so inclined.

A large hand and foot treatment area is perfect for a customized bridal party or family get-togethers. There's even a children's pedicure station inspired by the Mad Hatter, allowing for mother/daughter time together. The retail store offers robes for sale along with products from Archipelago Botanical's Milk Line, Vera Bradley, Love This Life t-shirts, and Sonoma Lavender products.

Open from 8:00 a.m. to 8:00 p.m. daily. An adult must accompany anyone under age eighteen receiving services, with specific treatments for guests age 4-12 ending in a sprinkling of pixie dust! Call (407) WDW-SPAS or (407) 939-7727 for information and reservations.

SAMPLE SERVICES

Warm Stone Massage. Combining Swedish techniques with stone therapy, smooth basalt rocks are warmed and used to gently glide along key points on the body.

Grand Romantic Couples Massage. In a candlelit couples room each person receives an aromatherapy massage.

Skin Brightening Facial. Perfect for those with hyperpigmentation, bring new life to a dull complexion with this rejuvenating facial experience. Incorporates active ingredients to improve skin tone and texture for a bright, even complexion.

Bubbly Bath Body Treatment. A champagne grape and sugar scrub followed by a Mimosa Champagne bubbly bath. Finish with a hydrating Mimosa body lotion application.

Sweet Red Rose Body Treatment. Unwind with a hydrating sugar scrub enhanced with cranberry and pomegranate, followed by a wrap of sweet red rose petals.

Mandara Spa at the Walt Disney World Dolphin

Offering creative treatments based on both East and West traditions and one of the prettiest tea lounges in all of Orlando, this spa is a great choice for a day of tranquility. You'll feel worlds away from the bustling parks as you wait in a replica of a centralized "Asian Bale"—beautiful but a bit uncomfortable—around which are situated the treatment rooms. Try one of the ultra interesting Eastern-style treatments such as the Four Hands Balinese massage, almost too exotic to pass up, where two therapists work simultaneously and in total synchronicity and silence. Relax afterwards in the spa's hand-carved Meru Temple sanctuary, where hot tea and light snacks are served overlooking a garden courtyard. Consider timing your treatment to coincide with lunch since a cold spa menu is available in the temple. The only thing lacking is a sauna and whirlpool in the locker rooms; only a small steam room is to be found. A small salon and separate pedicure and manicure rooms complete the list of services.

Open from 8:00 a.m. until 9:00 p.m.; call (407) 934-4772 for reservations. For more information go online at SwanDolphin.com/ mandaraspa.

CARA'S TIP: Children ages 4-12 may enjoy two complimentary hours of fun at Camp Dolphin while their parent is enjoying a spa service lasting 75 minutes or more.

SAMPLE SERVICES

Elemis Exotic Frangipani Body Nourish Wrap. A Tahitian blend of coconut and frangipani flowers is massaged into the body, then a wrap to let the ingredients absorb while enjoying a scalp massage.

Ionithermie Cellulite Reduction Program. A noninvasive technique to detoxify, reduce fluid retention, and tone muscles. Lose up to eight inches after a single treatment.

Elemis Pro-Collagen Quartz Lift Facial. Anti-wrinkle facial proven to reduce wrinkles and improve firmness with Padina Pavonica, accelerated by the electrical energy of precious minerals to re-energize cell communication.

Nurturing Massage for Mother-to-Be. A safe pregnancy massage with special positioning adapted to each stage of pregnancy for the ultimate in comfort and relaxation.

TIPS FOR MAKING THE MOST OF YOUR SPA TIME

- Arrive on a semi-empty stomach. Drink plenty of water afterward which will help in the removal of toxins released during your treatment.

- Show up 15 to 20 minutes early. This will allow time to check in, don your robe, sip a cup of tea, and have quiet time before your treatment. Better yet, arrive one hour early and enjoy a pre-treatment whirlpool.

- Be comfortable. It's not necessary to remove underclothing if it truly makes you uneasy; your masseuse is able to do their job either way. But you'll certainly receive a more thorough treatment with clothing removed. Remember that therapists go to great length to maintain guest modesty and only small parts of the body are exposed at one time with the rest of you well covered with a sheet or towel.

- Communicate any trouble spots before your treatment begins. Let you therapist know if you have any sensitive areas or whether you like soft or firm pressure. During your treatment let he/she know if they're talking more than you care for (a good therapist will take their talking cue from their client), or if the temperature or lighting in the room is to your liking. After all, it is your treatment, and it's essential that you receive what you are looking for.

- Feel absolutely no pressure to buy spa products that your therapist will more than likely try and sell. On the other hand, some of the best products I've found have been from my spa experiences.

- Relax and be open. After just one treatment you'll more than likely be hooked on this pleasurable experience.

Couples Retreat Ritual. Indulge together with an aromatic massage side-by-side in a beautiful Balinese-style treatment room followed by a river-rock rimmed hydrotherapy Jacuzzi tub. Enhance your experience with lunch or even strawberries and champagne.

Waldorf Astoria Spa

This exceptional spa comes with the luxury of being at the Waldorf Astoria Orlando, an oasis of true style. 24,000 square feet in two stories includes twenty-two treatment rooms with services also available outdoors in one of the resort's pool cabanas. Locker rooms offer an experiential, full-body shower, eucalyptus-scented steam shower, whirlpool, and separate men and women's tearoom.

Therapists here take a holistic approach and customize each treatment specifically with your emotional and physical revitalization in mind. For the ultimate in decadence go for the Diamond Body with precious stones and gold-enriched creams massaged into the skin along with hot stones. End with a soothing milky footbath.

If relaxing in the spa's tea lounge, steam room, and Jacuzzi *sans* treatment is your preference, a fee of $20 is applied. Open daily 9:00 a.m. until 8:00 p.m. Call 407-597-5360 for reservations.

SAMPLE SERVICES

The Perfect Body. Begin with a total body exfoliation, then a firming and sculpting massage with anti-aging ingredients leaving your skin silky and smooth with a youthful appearance.

Couples Massage. A personalized couples massage in a spacious shared room allowing you and your partner a custom, side-by-side experience.

Beauty Diamond Facial. Treat your skin to the purity of diamond and other precious stones ingredients combined with massage techniques to restore natural suppleness.

Contouring Body Treatment. A slimming treatment that targets critical areas for a toned body. Begin with a full body exfoliation to help refine your skin's texture, then a refining body masque with stimulating massage, reducing the look of cellulite. End with a refining serum and moisturizer.

Hydrafacial. Machine assisted facial using breakthrough aesthetic technology to remove dead skin cells and impurities while at the same time cleansing, hydrating, and moisturizing new skin.

WALT DISNEY WORLD WOW EXPERIENCES!

So many things at Walt Disney World seem special, but a handful of experiences really take the cake. Plan on at least one or two of the following excursions to make your stay extra-unique, a memory to last a lifetime.

Swim with the Sharks

Take the ultimate dive in Epcot's 5.7-million-gallon aquarium at The Seas with Nemo & Friends with more than 65 species of marine life, including sharks, turtles, eagle rays, and diverse tropical fish. With DiveQuest you become part of the show and enjoy guaranteed calm seas, no current, and unlimited visibility. Even more fun, your family and friends can view your dive through the aquarium's giant acrylic windows. Guests must be at least 10 years of age and provide proof of SCUBA certification to participate. $175. Call 407/WDW-TOUR for information.

Catch a Wave

If the ocean is a bit too intimidating, learn to "Hang 10" from the experts in a safe and controlled environment at Typhoon Lagoon with waves up to six feet and up to four rounds of surfing. Lessons begin before park opening hours so guests must furnish their own transportation to the park since buses are not up and running quite so early in the morning. Offered Monday, Tuesday, Thursday, and Friday for $150. Participants must be at least eight years old and strong swimmers. Maximum of thirteen people per class with surfboards provided. Call (407) WDW-PLAY or (407) 939-7529 for reservations.

Celebrate Your Special Day

Step aboard a pontoon boat for an especially memorable birthday cruise around Disney's waterways complete with driver, bag snacks, and beverages. Offered at any of the Walt Disney World marinas or

around Disney's waterways. Boats carry a maximum of eight for $275 or ten for $325 with balloons, ice cream, cake, and a banner offered for an additional charge. Call (407) WDW-BDAY or (407) 939-2329 for reservations.

Get the Royal Treatment

Talk about luxury for kids! Little princesses and princes dressed in all their finery enjoy tea in the Garden View Lounge at the Grand Floridian with Princess Aurora along with sing-alongs, storytelling, and a parade, all for the princely sum of $250 (price for one child and one adult). Each little princess receives a tiara and a My Disney Girl Princess Aurora doll; little princes get a princely crown and a bear. Children must be accompanied by an adult who receives only tea. Reservations can be made 180 days prior by calling (407) WDW-DINE or (407) 939-3463.

Adults can participate in their own high tea here *sans* tiara and all the hoopla from 2:00 to 4:30 p.m. with a wide assortment of teas, scones, tarts, trifle, pound cake, pâté, tea sandwiches and, of course, champagne. Come after 3:00 p.m. when tea is accompanied by live entertainment in the Grand Lobby.

Hit the Water

For true action head to the Contemporary Resort where water-skiing, kneeboarding, wakeboarding, and tubing are on offer for $165 per hour including boat, driver, and instruction (boats carry up to five guests). Morning guided Personal Watercraft excursions on Bay Lake and the Seven Seas Lagoon or afternoon free-styling Personal Watercraft fun in a roped-off area the size of three football fields are $135 per hour per watercraft holding up to three people with a combined weight under 400 pounds (only four personal watercraft are allowed on the water at any one time). Regular para-sailing packages begin at $95 per flight for a single and $170 for a tandem, including eight to ten minutes in the air and 450 feet of line. Premium packages begin at $130 for a single and $195 for a

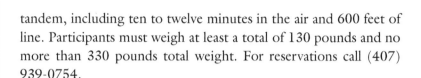

tandem, including ten to twelve minutes in the air and 600 feet of line. Participants must weigh at least a total of 130 pounds and no more than 330 pounds total weight. For reservations call (407) 939-0754.

Hunt for Treasure

Children ages four through ten board their own pint-sized ship, don their mouse-ear pirate caps, and depart the Grand Floridian's marina to sail the Seven Seas Lagoon. At each "port of call" a.k.a. the surrounding Magic Kingdom resorts, a new treasure hunt awaits with all booty divided between the adventurers. A similar Albatross Treasure Cruise can be found at the Yacht and Beach Club. $36 per child, grub included. Call (407) WDW-DINE or (407) 939-3463, for reservations.

Indulge in Your Very Own Yacht

For the ultimate in luxury, charter Disney's 52-foot Sea Ray Sedan Bridge yacht, the *Grand I*, moored at the Grand Floridian's marina, perfect for pampered VIP guests. Available for a morning spin, a sunset cruise, or the ultimate viewing location for the Wishes fireworks show, *Grand I* includes your own captain and deckhand with room enough for up to eighteen people. Perhaps the perfect elegant evening would include a sunset gourmet dinner onboard complete with private butler service followed by champagne while viewing the fireworks extravaganza. If your party is a large one you'll have to be content with appetizers and drinks since a plated dinner is available only for three people or less.

Or consider an afternoon excursion exploring the nearby resorts on the Seven Seas Lagoon and Bay Lake with a bevy of snacks to keep the appetite at bay: sail past the beaches of the romantic Polynesian and the Grand Floridian's Wedding Pavilion, check out the geyser on the shore of Wilderness Lodge, and watch the parasailing action around the Contemporary Resort. Basic cost is $520 per hour. Call (407) 824-2682 for reservations and information.

Experience a Culinary Feast

At Victoria & Albert's Chef's Table at Disney's Grand Floridian Resort chef Scott Hunnell prepares a feast just for you. Your table, seating from one to ten, is located in the restaurant's kitchen, but it's exclusively yours without the need to share once reserved. Up to thirteen courses are served over four hours, each tailored to your tastes. If you're smart you'll choose the wine pairings with each course coupled by a specially chosen vintage.

Spin Through the Wilderness

On Disney's Wilderness Back Trail Adventure enjoy Florida's natural beauty on a Segway X2, a treaded model with all-terrain tires, on a two-hour trip around Ft. Wilderness and Wilderness Lodge. Begin with a short training session, followed by a ride along numerous nature trails, a visit to the stables, and a quick trip around Wilderness Lodge with descriptions of foliage and wildlife along the way. The cost is $90 per person; call 407-WDW-TOUR or (407) 939-8687 for reservations.

Take Tea with Alice

Children simply love the Wonderland Tea Party held at the Grand Floridian Resort hosted by Alice in Wonderland characters. The one-hour event includes games, storytelling, sandwiches, and apple juice "tea" along with their very own photo with their special hosts. Strictly for children ages four to twelve. Held Monday through Friday at 2:00 p.m. for $43. Call (407) WDW-DINE, or (407) 939-3463, for reservations.

Sail Away on a Fireworks Cruise

Depart from the docks of the Yacht Club and Magic Kingdom Resorts for a private viewing of either the Wishes fireworks display at the Magic Kingdom or Illuminations at Epcot. Anchor at the perfect viewing spot facing the Magic Kingdom or under the International Gateway Bridge at Epcot just minutes before the nighttime spectacular begins and you'll be set. There's nothing quite as magical as the scene over the glistening water along with Disney's best fireworks presentations. A driver, beverages, and bag snacks are included, but wine, champagne, hors d'oeuvres, cheese and fruit platters, dessert, even chocolate covered strawberries can be ordered ahead from Private Dining, perfect for a special floating party. Boats carry a maximum of eight for $292 or ten for $346. Call (407) WDW-PLAY or (407) 939-7529.

Those who love the story of Peter Pan should reserve space on the Pirates and Pals Fireworks Voyage departing from the marina at the Contemporary Resort. Upon arrival snacks and beverages are served with Captain Hook and Mr. Smee who join the fun for a meet-and-greet. Then march off to board your vessel with a mischievous pirate named Patch, your guide through the unpredictable waters of the Seven Seas Lagoon, who leads the sing-alongs and Disney trivia games. Back on land after viewing the Wishes fireworks show there's a surprise visit by none other than Peter Pan, ready to pose for photos and sign autographs. Non-private cruise offered Friday through Monday for $54 per adult and $34 per child ages 3-9. Call (407) WDW-PLAY or (407) 939-7529.

Wet a Line

Drop a line on one of Disney's private guided bass fishing excursions. Angle for a trophy-size catch on Walt Disney World's lakes and canals onboard a 21-foot Tracker pontoon boat that fits five people or a tournament style Nitro Bass boat for one or two people. It's the perfect opportunity to return home with a good fish tale about the one that got away. $235 (afternoon) and $270 (morning) on two-hour trips; $455 for morning four-hour trips. Call (407) WDW-PLAY or (407) 939-7529.

The Very Best of Walt Disney World Area Golf

There's certainly no lack of choice when it comes to playing a round of golf while visiting Mickey Mouse. In fact, some people have been known to never quite make it to the parks, so intent are they on playing all of Disney's courses. Each is designated as an Audubon Cooperative

Sanctuary System and offers full-service clubhouse facilities including pro shops, driving ranges, locker rooms, course beverage service, snack bars, and equipment rentals. Golf carts at all Disney courses are equipped with a Global Positioning System (GPS) featuring "smart" full-color monitors providing detailed 3-D renderings of golf holes and course features, exact distances from the golf ball to the flagstick, and tips from professionals with helpful strategies for each hole.

Instruction is available from Arnold Palmer Golf Management staff at any Disney course where you can check your swing with video analysis. 45-minute private lessons are $75 per adult and $50 for youth age seventeen and under. Reservations are essential; call (407) 939-4653.

Tee time reservations for Disney courses may be made by calling (407) WDW-GOLF or (407) 939-4653 or online at Golfwdw.com. Be sure to ask for any special rates at time of booking such as two-round discounts, military rates, twilight specials, and last-minute specials. And remember that registered guests of Disney resorts receive complimentary taxi transportation vouchers and special rates at Disney courses.

Disney's Palm and Magnolia Golf Courses

Located near the Magic Kingdom within the grounds of the Shades of Green Resort (an armed forces resort on Disney property) are the first courses ever opened at Walt Disney World, both designed by Joe Lee. Part of the PGA Tour is held here each October, and the eighteenth hole of the Palm is rated as one of the toughest on the tour.

The heavily wooded Palm is one of Disney's most difficult courses, with fairways cinched by tall trees and elevated tees and greens, nine water holes, and ninety-four bunkers. 6,957 yards. Slope: 133.

At Magnolia, the longest of all Disney's courses, more than 1,500 magnolia trees magnificently frame wide fairways. It too doesn't lack for challenge with its eleven holes of water and ninety-eight bunkers in the midst of large, undulating greens. Check out the sixth-hole hazard in the shape of Mickey Mouse! 7,190 yards. Slope: 133.

Disney's Lake Buena Vista Golf Course

Located in the Downtown Disney area within the grounds of *Disney's Saratoga Springs* Resort & Spa is this Joe Lee-designed course in a country club setting. Meandering through pine forests and tall cypress this shortest of Disney's 18-hole courses sports small, elevated greens with plenty of bunkers, narrow fairways, and an island green on the seventh hole. This is a great place for beginners but challenging enough for the more experienced. 6,749 yards. Slope: 133.

Enjoy dinner beginning at 5:00 p.m. at The Turf Club Bar and Grill at Disney's Saratoga Springs Resort. A quick-service breakfast and lunch options are available at the adjoining Artist Palette.

Waldorf Astoria Golf Course

This Rees Jones-designed course has the added luxury of its location at the Waldorf Astoria Orlando sitting in the middle of Walt Disney World property. Using the land's natural contours and elements as it winds through a wetlands preserve, this environmentally responsible course is designed with a 5-tee system, bunkers reminiscent of the hazards from those a century ago, towering pine and cypress lining the fairways, and lakes dotting a course that evokes an old world, classic look.

The Clubhouse Grille features sandwiches and salads, and you'll find a Pro Shop on site with the latest apparel and equipment. A practice facility and private lessons are available. Call 407-597-3782 or go to WaldorfAstoriaOrlando.com/golf/ for information and to reserve tee times. 7,108 yards. Slope: 139.

Miniature Golf

Miniature golf fans have four courses to play at Disney, each sporting 18 fun-filled holes. Fees are $12 for adults and $10 for children ages three through nine; receive a 50 percent discount on a second round played the same day. Open from 10:00 a.m. to 11:00 p.m. daily, subject to weather and seasonal changes, reservations for tee times are only available in person. For more information call (407) WDW-PLAY or (407) 939-7529.

Fantasia Gardens

Two 18-hole miniature golf courses, Fantasia Gardens and Fantasia Fairways, are located across Buena Vista Drive from the Swan Hotel near Epcot, Disney's Hollywood Studios, and the BoardWalk. Play amid tutu-clothed hippos, silly alligators, and cavorting fountains ending with Sorcerer Mickey splashing guests with his mop and buckets at the

Fantasia-inspired *Fantasia Garden* course. The more challenging *Fantasia Fairways*, designed as a pint-size golf course, is great for those who like a more traditional round amid sand traps, water hazards, doglegs, roughs, and putting greens. A limited snack bar with a small arcade, the Starter Shack, is on-site.

Winter Summerland

Designed for Santa and his elves as an off-season vacation spot, this hot-and-cold, sand-and-snow miniature golf course is a kick. Sitting adjacent to Blizzard Beach, guests play either the *Snow Course*—amid Christmas music, ice hockey rings, snowmen, ice castles, and igloos—or the *Sand Course*, where Caribbean music plays while Santa grills turkey outside his mobile home surrounded by sand castles and surfboards. A limited snack bar is on the premises.

Tennis

Tennis courts can be found at Bay Lake Tower at the Contemporary Resort (two hard surface), Yacht and Beach Club (one hard), BoardWalk Inn (two hard), the Swan and Dolphin Hotels (four hard), and Animal Kingdom Villas–Kidani Village (two hard). Courts are available on a first-come, first-served basis and generally accessible from 8:00 a.m. to 10:00 p.m. Private lessons can be arranged by calling Orlando Tennis at (321) 228-1146. At the Swan and Dolphin Resorts lessons can be arranged at the Health Club.

Bicycle Rentals

Bicycles for all ages are available for rent at the BoardWalk Inn, Wilderness Lodge, the Polynesian, and the Yacht and Beach Club. At the BoardWalk Inn and the Yacht and Beach Club, bikers on both standard and surrey bicycles can pedal their way around the walkway surrounding the 0.75-mile Crescent Lake or the pathway that circles to Disney's Hollywood Studios. Wilderness Lodge guests can explore on both standard and surrey bicycles at the adjoining Fort Wilderness and its miles of pine forests. At the Polynesian Resort take a spin around the property on a surrey. Helmets are provided free of charge. Young people under the age of eighteen must have a signed waiver from a parent or legal guardian.

Jogging and Walt Disney World

Those amazing folks with enough energy to jog after traipsing through the parks day after day will be glad to know that a nice variety of pathways are to be found throughout Walt Disney World property. Information and jogging maps are available at the front desk of each resort. At the Polynesian a path is laid out through the tropical grounds; the Grand Floridian and Villas at the Grand Floridian have a pathway along the Seven Seas Lagoon; and the Wilderness Lodge offers miles of trails winding through the adjoining Fort Wilderness among pines and cypress trees. Epcot Resort guests should take advantage of the boardwalk-style walkway surrounding the twenty-five-acre Crescent Lake or the path encircling the canal leading to Disney's Hollywood Studios.

For those who wish to add an active challenge to their Walt Disney World vacation, be sure to try a runDisney event! With five race weekends dispersed throughout the year at the Walt Disney World Resort, runners are sure to find an event that will fit into their schedule. Race distances include 5K (3.1 miles), 10K (6.2 miles), half marathon (13.1 miles) and marathon (26.2) as well as extreme challenges combining multiple races over multiple days. Even the smallest runner can join in on the fun as Kids Races are available, from infants who can participate in the Diaper Dash to a 1-mile fun run for children up to 13 years old. With events in mid-January, late February, early May, early October, and early November, guests can easily incorporate a vacation into a race or a race into a vacation.

If you are one of those individuals that enjoys running then you can rest assured that a race through Walt Disney World theme parks is not the only way to enjoy a unique Disney race experience. Each race includes a special Disney theme along with extra opportunities to join in the on the fun! These additions include pre-race meals, post-race breakfasts, spectator packages, and post-race parties. A can't-miss addition to your race weekend is Race Retreat offering admission to a private pre- and post-race tent that includes food, beverages, a temperature-controlled lounge area, character interactions, massage tables, and other special experiences.

For those wanting even more of a VIP experience be sure to take advantage of the Runner's World Challenge during the Walt Disney

World Marathon weekend. This experience offers individual training, interaction with the Runner's World magazine editors, access to a private area within Race Retreat with private bag check, a short-cut to the race starting line, preferred corral placement, and much more. Sign up early for runDisney events; many race events sell out within the first few days of registration opening and sometimes within the first hours! For registration, go to runDisney.com.

For more information about preparing and planning for your runDisney vacation, visit RunnersGuideToWDW.com or purchase Magical Miles: The Runner's Guide to Walt Disney World at Amazon.com.

Boating and Waterways

With 850 acres of lakes, 130,000 feet of shoreline, 3.122 billion gallons of water, 66 miles of canals, and more than 500 watercraft, boating is a major pastime at Walt Disney World. And with some of the most incredible weather in the nation, water sports are an important draw. Most resorts as well as Downtown Disney have marinas with a variety of boats available for hire (see individual resort listings for specific details). Call 407-939-7529 for reservations. Boating takes place on the following waterways:

- *Seven Seas Lagoon* is accessed from the Grand Floridian, The Villas at the Grand Floridian, and Polynesian Resorts and connected to Bay Lake.

- *Bay Lake* is accessed from the Contemporary Resort, Bay Lake Tower, and the Wilderness Lodge. Bay Lake is also connected to the Seven Seas Lagoon.

- *Crescent Lake* shores hold the Epcot resorts of the Yacht and Beach Club, the BoardWalk Inn, and the Walt Disney World Swan and Dolphin.

- *Village Lake* fronts Downtown Disney.

Boating choices include Boston Whalers, a luxury yacht, pontoon boats, sailboats, and Sea Raycers.

Boston Whaler Montauks. These 17-foot, canopy-covered, motorized boats accommodate as many as six adults and are available at the marinas of the Grand Floridian Resort, Contemporary Resort, Yacht Club Resort, Wilderness Lodge, and Downtown Disney. Approximately $45 per half hour.

Luxury Yacht. For the ultimate in indulgence charter the 52-foot Sea Ray Sedan Bridge yacht, the *Grand I*, docked at the Grand Floridian Resort. Accommodating up to eighteen people it includes a captain and deckhand. Food and cocktails are available at an additional charge. Basic cost is $520 per hour.

Pontoon Boat. Sun Tracker 21-foot canopied pontoon boats holding as many as ten people are perfect for those who want a soothing ride around Disney's waterways. Available at the marinas of the Grand Floridian Resort, Contemporary Resort, Polynesian Resort, Yacht Club Resort, Wilderness Lodge, and Downtown Disney. Approximately $45 per half hour.

Sea Raycer by Sea Ray. What could be more fun than a Sea Raycer, a two-seater mini-powerboat perfect for zipping around Disney's waterways and lakes? You'll get the most bang for your buck at one of the resorts in the Magic Kingdom area where there are miles of recreation on the Seven Seas Lagoon and Bay Lake. Guests at least twelve years old and 5 feet tall can operate the boat as long as one person in the boat has a valid driver's license (those under eighteen must bring along a parent to sign a waiver). Sea Raycers are available at the marinas of the Grand Floridian Resort, Contemporary Resort, Polynesian Resort, Yacht Club Resort, Wilderness Lodge, and Downtown Disney. Approximately $32 per half hour.

Waterskiing and Parasailing

Head to the Contemporary Resort for waterskiing and parasailing action. Sammy Duvall Water Sports offers waterskiing, wakeboarding, kneeboarding, and tubing for $165 per hour including boat, driver, and instruction. Guided personal watercraft excursions on Bay Lake and the Seven Seas Lagoon are offered in the morning, or in the afternoon there is freestyling personal watercraft fun in a roped-off area; $135 per hour per watercraft holding up to three people with a combined weight under 400 pounds. Parasailing packages begin at $95 per flight for a single and $170 for a tandem, including eight to ten minutes in the air and 450 feet of line. Premium parasailing packages begin at $130 for a single and $195 for a tandem, including ten to twelve minutes in the air and 600 feet of line. Participants must weigh at least a total of 130 pounds and no more than 330 pounds. For reservations call (407) 939-0754 up to ninety days in advance.

Fishing

Walt Disney World's stocked fishing lakes are filled with an abundance of largemouth bass, perfect for the amateur as well as the seasoned angler. In fact, the largest bass caught at Walt Disney World weighed in at 14.25 pounds! Boats departing from the marinas of the Contemporary Resort, Polynesian Resort, Grand Floridian Resort, and the Wilderness Lodge fish the waters of Bay Lake and the Seven Seas Lagoon with an experienced guide. The waterways surrounding Epcot and Disney's Hollywood Studios are your fishing holes for boats departing the Yacht Club marina. From Downtown Disney Marketplace's Marina angle for bass on Village Lake. No fishing license is required, and it's strictly catch-and-release.

Fish from either a pontoon boat accommodating five guests, or a high-speed, tournament-style Nitro bass boat for one or two people. Two-hour trips (maximum of five people) are $235 (afternoon) and $270 (mornings); four-hour trips are $455. All include a boat with driver and experienced guide, rod and reel, tackle, artificial and live bait, and non-alcoholic beverages as well as a one-year BASS membership including 11 issues of Bassmaster Magazine. Excursions may be prearranged by calling (407) WDW-BASS or (407) 939-2277 and must be made at least twenty-four hours in advance.

Richard Petty Driving Experience

Those who dream of sitting behind the wheel of a racecar have a chance right here at Walt Disney World. White-knuckle rides in a 600 HP NASCAR racecar are offered for those that dare on a 1-mile tri-oval track. All driving participants must have a valid driver's license and know how to operate a stick shift with each experience beginning with a one-hour training session. Spectators are welcome for no charge. Since the track sometimes closes due to inclement weather, it's always best to call ahead. Call (800) BE-PETTY, or (800) 237-3889, for information. DrivePetty.com

Getting There

With its location virtually in the parking lot of the Magic Kingdom, it's necessary to either make your way to the Transportation and Ticket Center (TTC) and take the shuttle from there, or enter the Magic Kingdom parking lot (parking is free) and follow the signs driving through the tunnel to the infield.

Programs

Ride-Along Program. For $99 ride shotgun at speeds of up to 120 mph for three laps around the track with an experienced driving instructor. Also available are Junior Ride-Along Experiences for children between the ages of six to thirteen who are at least 48 inches in height for $59. Sessions are generally offered between 9:00 a.m. and 4:00 p.m. This is the only program not requiring reservations operating on a first-come, first-served basis.

Rookie Experience. Those age eighteen or older can drive the car themselves for eight laps around the course. The three-hour program costs $449.

King's Experience. You'll feel like a king after five hours of driving eighteen laps (one eight-lap and one ten-lap session) around the speedway for the princely sum of $849. Only those age eighteen or older may participate.

Experience of a Lifetime. For $1,299, drive three ten-lap sessions, improve your skills, and maybe change careers in this half-day driving experience. Only for those age eighteen or older.

Speedway Challenge. Experience a one-of-a-kind program with 50 laps behind the wheel over five sessions for $2,099. Half-day experience only for those age eighteen or older.

Exotic Experience. Featuring "supercars" by Ferrari, Lamborghini, Aston Martin, Audi, and Porsche on a separate track specifically designed for this experience. Starting at $189 for six laps around the circuit. Thrill rides with a professional driver are available for $99.

Walt Disney World Area Shopping

For many people shopping is the best part of a vacation. The parks are loaded with Disney merchandise with something for everyone in just about every price range. But those who would like to bring home something minus a Mickey Mouse or Cinderella motif will want to check out Orlando's best shopping options away from the parks.

The Florida Mall

While less upscale than the Mall at Millenia, this 260-store mall does have anchors—Saks Fifth Avenue, Nordstrom (shoe heaven), Macy's, JC Penny, Dillard's, and Sears. Other stores include Apple Store, Brookstone, COACH, Abercrombie & Fitch, Guess, H&M, Bebe, MAC Cosmetics, Michael Kors, Microsoft Store, Rolex, Zara, and Sephora. Located at the corner of South Orange Blossom Trail and Sand Lake Road, from Disney take Interstate 4 east to Sand Lake Road and go east for 4 miles. Open Monday through Saturday from 10:00 a.m. to 9:00 p.m. and Sunday 11:00 a.m. to 6:00 p.m.; (407) 851-6255. Simon.com/mall/the-florida-mall.

The Mall at Millenia

If you have time for only one mall make it this one. Only a twenty-minute drive from Disney, this high-end shopping experience is Orlando's best. Anchored by Bloomingdale's, Macy's, and Neiman Marcus, other shopping choices here include Chanel, Tiffany & Co., Gucci, Louis Vuitton, Boss Store, Burberry, Cartier, Jimmy Choo, Kate Spade, Tory Burch, Prada, and Brooks Brothers. When the shopping gets too much for you, rest your feet at one of the mall's restaurants including P.F. Chang's China Bistro, Brio Tuscan Grill, The Capital Grille, California Pizza Kitchen, Panera Bread, and The Cheesecake Factory, or stop in for a drink at Blue Martini. From Walt Disney World take I-4 east to exit 78 (right on Conroy Road). Open Monday through Saturday from 10:00 a.m. to 9:00 p.m. and Sunday 11:00 a.m. to 7:00 p.m.; (407) 363-3555. Valet parking available outside the Main Entrance. MallAt-Millenia.com.

Orlando Premium Outlets, Vineland Ave.

As it is the closest shopping mall to Walt Disney World, you'll be tempted to run over and shop several times during your stay. With 110 stores you'll find the likes of Burberry, Ermenegildo Zegna Outlet Store, Fendi, Hugo Boss Factory Store, Salvatore Ferragamo, Michael Kors, CH Carolina Herrera, Polo Ralph Lauren Factory Store, Tory Burch, Lacoste, and Lululemon Athletica. Located at 8200 Vineland Avenue just off I-4 (exit 68 or SR535) close to Downtown Disney. Open Monday through Saturday from 10:00 a.m. to 11:00 p.m. and Sunday 10:00 a.m. to 9:00 p.m.; (407) 238-7787. PremiumOutlets.com/outlets/outlet.asp?id=17.

Orlando Premium Outlets, International Drive

Orlando's best outlet stop offers stores such as Last Call by Neiman Marcus, Baccarat/Lalique, Vince, Cole Haan, Saks Fifth Avenue OFF 5TH, St. John Outlet, Bose, Dooney & Bourke, Calvin Klein, Ann Taylor Factory Store, COACH, Tumi, Nautica, Kate Spade New York, and Robert Graham. Located at 4951 International Drive 12 miles from Disney World; take I-4 East to Exit 75A, follow it to International Drive and turn left. Open Monday through Saturday 10:00 a.m. to 11:00 p.m. and Sunday10:00 a.m. to 9:00 p.m.; (407) 352-9600. PremiumOutlets.com/outlets/outlet.asp?id=96.

> CARA'S TIP: If you've made it this far from Walt Disney World keep going another mile or so down I-4 to the Mall at Millenia after you've finished your shopping here.

Winter Park

This quaint village of beautiful gardens and three notable art museums is only a twenty-five-minute drive from Walt Disney World. Shop along Park Avenue or in and around Hannibal Square in the historical district where blocks of small boutiques, jewelry stores, and art galleries are scattered among well-known names like Eileen Fisher, Lily Pulitzer, and Williams-Sonoma. Relax along the way at any number of sidewalk cafes and restaurants, the best being Café de France or Paris Bistro for French fare, Bosphorus for Turkish delights, Hannibal's on the Square for fish and meat in a hip atmosphere, Luma on Park for an upscale dinner, or Armando's Cucina Italiana & Pizzaria. Or just stop in for a glass of wine at one of the many wine bars in the area such as Eola Wine Company,

Vino!, and The Wine Room. For more information go to Experien-ceParkAvenue.com

Also in Winter Park The Charles Hosmer Morse Museum of Ameri-can Art has the world's most comprehensive collection of Tiffany glass, including an exquisite Tiffany chapel interior built for the 1892 Chicago World Columbian Exposition. Or enjoy a 12-mile scenic boat tour on the town's chain of lakes. To reach downtown Winter Park take I-4 east to exit 87 and go east on Fairbanks Avenue for two miles.

DINING IN STYLE AT WALT DISNEY WORLD

Slow-roasted buffalo strip steak with truffle macaroni & cheese, rainbow chard, and blackberry Pinot Noir reduction. Pan-seared yellowtail snapper, tea-smoked lentils, South African lobster, and citrus-curry beurre blanc. Poulet rouge "Oscar" with Alaskan king crab and jumbo aspa*ragu*s. Madeira-braised short ribs, trofie pasta, wild mushroom ragoût, and truffle crème fraîche. Just a sampling of some of the incredible cuisine found at Walt Disney World restaurants where a remarkable culinary transformation has taken place since the mid-1990s. Extraordinary choices are especially evident in such renowned dining establishments as the California Grill at the Contemporary Resort, Jiko at Animal Kingdom Lodge, Flying Fish Café at Disney's BoardWalk, and Citricos, Narcoossee's, and Victoria & Albert's (many time winner of the AAA Five-Diamond Award) at the Grand Floridian. Top-notch chefs are the norm, creating exciting menus at some of the highest-rated restaurants in the country, and first-rate sommeliers (almost 300 on Disney property, more than any other company in the world) have fashioned outstanding wine lists, particularly at Victoria & Albert's, California Grill, Citricos, Jiko, and Flying Fish Café. In fact, Disney sells more than a million bottles of wine every year if you count the Disney Cruise Line.

Even Disney's reputation for dreadful theme park food has changed. Once just a hot dog and hamburger haven, at Disney it's now quite possible to find pleasurable choices ranging from fine dining to more-than-palatable and sometimes healthy quick-service food. Though you'll always find burgers and chicken tenders, you'll also discover restaurants with outstanding cuisine and unique ambience. My only complaint is the non-atmospherically lit dining rooms that are sometimes so bright you'll feel as if you're in the operating room.

Children are always treated as special guests with almost every restaurant, along with all quick-service spots, offering a menu just for kids. They even feature the Mickey Check, part of Disney Magic of Healthy Living, which helps identify nutritious food choices for children. Meals are delivered quickly, so if a speedy dinner is not your cup of tea stretch it out a bit by ordering an appetizer only and then your entrée when you are finished with your first course.

Disney certainly gets a gold star in my book for its efforts to add whole grains and healthy choices to dining menus, and, in particular, the elimination of trans fats and the addition of healthy alternatives. Those in need of vegetarian meals will easily find at least one option in both table-service restaurants and most quick-service spots; vegetarian choices are included in the sample entrées in this chapter. Those with special needs—such as low-fat, no sugar added, and low-sodium, as well as special dietary requests regarding allergies to gluten or wheat, shellfish, soy, lactose, peanuts, tree nuts, fish, egg, and corn—will be accommodated at most table-service restaurants and select quick-service restaurants. When making Advance Dining Reservations specify your particular need either online or with a Disney Dining reservationist, and address any questions to the Allergy Hotline at (407) 824-2634.

Kosher meals are offered at most full-service restaurants; however, they do require a 24-hour notice by calling (407) 939-3463. Kosher meals are always available without advance notice at the following quick-service locations: Cosmic Ray's Starlight Café in the Magic Kingdom, ABC Commissary at Disney's Hollywood Studios, Liberty Inn and Electric Umbrella at Epcot, and Pizzafari at Disney's Animal Kingdom.

Guests who plan on eating all their meals exclusively on Disney property should consider the Magic Your Way Plus Dining Plan at a cost of approximately $59 per adult per night and $20 per child per night for ages three through nine. Included is one table-service meal of an entrée, nonalcoholic beverage, and dessert; one quick-service meal including entrée, dessert, and nonalcoholic beverage; and one snack such as fruit, popcorn, sodas, or ice cream per person per night. Character meals count as one table-service meal. Those who plan on dining much of the time at Disney's signature restaurants such as California Grill, Flying Fish, Jiko, etc., Disney dinner shows, or using in-room dining should probably opt out of this particular plan since it is necessary to exchange two table-service meals to dine once at this type of luxury restaurant.

The Deluxe Dining Plan for approximately $104 per adult per night and $30 per child per night comes with three table-service meals per night thus allowing you to pay for a quick-service breakfast or lunch on your own leaving enough credits for a signature meal each evening. Also consider that these dining plans add up to a lot of food so if your family likes to share entrées or dessert you might be better off simply purchasing meals as you go.

As for dress code, casual is the word. Theme park restaurants are extremely informal; however, you'll find that in many resort Signature Restaurants dress is a bit more sophisticated. Smart-casual clothing is usually fine, but, to be certain, see my notes for the dress at each restaurant outside the theme parks. The only exception to the super casual dress code in the theme parks is at Epcot's Monsieur Paul where resort casual dress is requested although not always adhered to.

If you wish to preview the menus of many of these restaurants, go online to WDWLuxuryGuide.com.

Advance Dining Reservations

Advance Dining Reservations is Disney's dining reservation system whereby on arrival at the designated time you'll receive the next table available for your party size. In other words, they won't save a table for you but will seat you as soon as possible, certainly before any walk-ups. This sometimes translates into a bit of a wait, but it's undoubtedly better than simply taking your chances and walking in without any sort of reservation.

Advance Dining Reservations are available at Disney's full-service restaurants at the theme parks, resorts, and most Downtown Disney table-service restaurants beginning 180 days in advance by calling (407) WDW-DINE or (407) 939-3463 unless otherwise noted. Reservations can also be made online at Disneyworld.disney.go.com/dining. Those staying in a Disney concierge room or suite may also make dining reservations with the concierge staff. Those not on a concierge floor can utilize the Lobby Concierge at each Disney resort. Non-Disney dining reservation phone numbers are listed with their full descriptions.

Honestly, dining reservations at Walt Disney World is almost a blood sport. I cannot emphasize enough how important it is to secure advance reservations; without them, you'll be spending way too much time cooling your heels waiting for a table, particularly at character meals and better resort restaurants where demand is high. In fact, if you try and dine at some of the most popular restaurants you'll more than likely be advised that no walk-ins at all are taken. This is especially true in the busier times of the year and for spots like Be Our Guest, Le Cellier, California Grill, Citricos, Narcoossee's, and Flying Fish Café, along with all character meals.

Dining With Disney Characters

For those traveling with children at least one or two character meals are a must. These extremely popular dining spots, offered both at the theme parks and at several of the Disney resorts, are a perfect way for children to spend extra time with their favorite characters. Meals are all-you-care-to-eat, offered in one of three ways: buffet-style, family-style, or pre-plated. Characters work the room, stopping at each table to interact with guests, pose for photos, and sign autographs (it's a good idea to pick up an autograph book for your child right away at one of Disney's gift shops). Book advance reservations early (180 days out), particularly for Cinderella's Royal Table and Chef Mickey's by calling (407) WDW-DINE or (407) 939-3463. Characters may vary somewhat from day to day.

Magic Kingdom

Cinderella's Royal Table. Breakfast, lunch, and dinner. Breakfast is an assortment of pastries with your choice of a plated entrée; lunch and dinner with a family-style salad at lunch and your choice of appetizers at dinner, and both meals with your choice of entrées, then dessert. This is Disney's most popular character meal served high atop Cinderella Castle with Disney princesses such as Belle, Aurora, Jasmine, Snow White, and Ariel; all meals include a photo package with Cinderella.

Crystal Palace. Breakfast, lunch, and dinner buffet with Winnie the Pooh, Eeyore, Piglet, and Tigger.

Epcot

Garden Grill. Dinner served family-style with a harvest salad starter, your choice of entrées, and fruit cobbler dessert with characters Farmer Mickey, Chip 'n' Dale, and Pluto.

Akershus Royal Banquet Hall. Buffet/family-style breakfast; lunch and dinner includes a cold-table appetizer buffet of salad, meats, seafood, and cheese followed by your choice of entrées and a family-style dessert platter. On a rotating schedule are Disney princesses Belle, Cinderella, Jasmine, Snow White, Aurora, Mary Poppins, Mulan, and Ariel; also includes a photo package with Belle.

Disney's Hollywood Studios

Disney Junior Play 'n Dine. Buffet breakfast and lunch with Playhouse Disney characters Sofia the First, Doc McStuffins, Handy Manny, and Jake from The Neverland Pirates.

Animal Kingdom

Donald's Dining Safari at Tusker House. Breakfast and lunch buffet with Donald Duck, Goofy, Mickey, and Daisy Duck.

Walt Disney World Resorts

Chef Mickey's. Breakfast and dinner buffet at the Contemporary Resort with Mickey, Goofy, Pluto, Donald Duck, and Minnie.

Cape May Café. Breakfast buffet at the Beach Club Resort with Goofy, Minnie, and Donald Duck.

1900 Park Fare. Breakfast and dinner buffet at the Grand Floridian

Resort. Supercalifragilistic Breakfast with Mary Poppins, Pooh, Tigger, Alice in Wonderland, and Mad Hatter; Cinderella's Happily Ever After Dinner with Cinderella, Prince Charming, Anastasia, Drizella, and Lady Tremaine.

Ohana. Breakfast family-style at the Polynesian Resort with Mickey, Pluto, Lilo, and Stitch.

THE BEST OF THE BEST
WALT DISNEY WORLD DINING

- **Best Italian:** La Luce at the Hilton Bonnet Creek (sister property to the Waldorf Astoria Orlando) where incredible handmade pasta such as fettuccine *alla lina* with a rich porcini and sausage *ragù*, and perfect pizzas are the order of the day.

- **Best seafood:** Flying Fish Café at Disney's BoardWalk for their ever-changing Chef's Thunder fish choice.

- **Best steak:** Bull & Bear at the Waldorf Astoria Orlando whose 38 oz., aged 32 days Tomahawk for Two is de rigueur; or Yachtsman Steakhouse at Disney's Yacht Club Resort for the must-order New York strip steak with peppercorn brandy sauce, aged in-house and cooked to perfection.

- **Best for romance:** Victoria & Albert's at Disney's Grand Floridian Resort where you'll savor a sumptuous seven-course meal in an intimate atmosphere.

- **Best for kids:** Children love T-Rex Café at Downtown Disney with giant Audio-Animatronics dinosaurs, an ice cave, and a paleontology dig. A close runner up is Whispering Canyon Café at Disney's Wilderness Lodge, but come prepared for plenty of whoopin' and hollerin', and please, whatever you do, don't ask for the ketchup—unless, that is, you like a lot of attention.

- **Best character meal:** Cinderella's Royal Table at the Magic Kingdom, a chance to dine in a fairy-tale castle with Disney princesses.

- **Best Disney view:** California Grill at Disney's Contemporary Resort with its picture-perfect views of the Magic Kingdom, the Seven Seas Lagoon, and the Wishes fireworks.

- **Best Disney resort restaurant:** Tough call. My favorites are California Grill at the Contemporary Resort (just about anything on their exceptional menu is fantastic), or Victoria & Albert's at the Grand Floridian Resort (particularly the Chef's Table where Chef Scott Hunnel oversees a 10- to 12-course meal designed especially for you).

- **Best Epcot Illuminations view:** Rose and Crown in World Showcase's United Kingdom. Set your priority seating for about one hour prior to showtime and pray for a lagoonside table with a great view. Second runner up is La Hacienda de San Angel in Mexico, but you won't receive an alfresco view here.

- **Best food at the Magic Kingdom:** Restaurant: Be Our Guest in New Fantasyland; fast food: Pecos Bill Café in Frontierland.

- **Best food at Disney's Hollywood Studios:** Restaurant: Hollywood Brown Derby.

- **Best food at Epcot:** Restaurant: Monsieur Paul in France; fast food: Tangierine Café in Morocco.

- **Best food at the Animal Kingdom:** Restaurant: Tusker House in Africa.

Best Magic Kingdom Dining

Be Our Guest

French-inspired cuisine. Quick-service lunch open 10:30 a.m. to
2:30 p.m.; table-service dinner begins at 4:00 p.m. with closing
times varying according to park hours.

A pair of minotaurs are your greeters as you cross a stone bridge and
into the Beast's castle and this fantasy of a restaurant. While lunch is a
quick-service option with food delivered to your table on rolling carts,
dinner here is a festive table-service event with, believe it or not, French
and California wine along with Belgium beer, the first time ever that alcohol has been offered at the Magic Kingdom. Inside, the Beast's castle
has been recreated from the terrazzo floors to the massive chandeliers
and cherubs frolicking on a frescoed, domed ceiling, even talking suits
of armor lining the entry hall with royal purple and gold décor.

At dinner dine inside one of two dining rooms: the Ballroom where
music from "Beauty and the Beast" plays and your view outside the
tall, arched windows is one of a softly falling snow in a moonlit sky; or
a darker, more sinister West Wing dining area where intermittent thunder and lightning set the scene as a portrait hanging over the fireplace
changes from the prince to the Beast as an enchanted rose slowly loses
its petals.

Sorry . . . I almost forgot about the food which is actually quite
good, particularly when the Magic Kingdom and good food is rarely
used in the same sentence. Tasty starters are the French onion soup,
nice and bubbly with crusty cheese and a simpler broth than most, and
equally delicious is the potato leek soup, a thick and savory concoction.
And you can't forget the mussels served a la Provencal with white wine,
lots of chopped tomatoes and onions, a touch of basil, and plenty of
butter and garlic . . . ooh la la!

A thyme-seasoned pork chop rack arrived overcooked and dry in one
instance and almost rare in another, but you can't fault the sinful side of
au gratin macaroni. Nice and flaky pan-seared salmon with a perfectly
pink center sits atop saffron flavored smashed potatoes and layered in
between with a creamy leek "fondue" sauce (my only wish is that the
salmon be wild and not farm-raised). Even those who are not vegetarian

will appreciate the flavorful ratatouille overflowing with rich roasted vegetable and caramelized onions served on slightly crunchy quinoa with bell pepper sauce. At lunch there's no question that the best entrée is the braised pork, cooked for eight hours, fork tender and super savory.

For dessert go ahead and order at least one of each of the three cupcake choices and share with the table. All are quite delicious, light and not too sweet with perhaps the lemon meringue (or maybe the triple chocolate . . . tough call) the best of all.

> CARA'S TIP: After hearing many reports of rude and grumpy staff here I witnessed it myself on my last visit. Obviously there needs to be a management change in the works. Nevertheless, at least for now this is the most difficult ticket in town; it is essential to call (407) WDW-DINE, or (407) 939-3463, at 7:00 a.m. Eastern Time Zone exactly 180 days prior, and even then be prepared to find nothing available except for maybe on one of the last days of your vacation.

While this is not a character meal, you can get your photo taken with Beast on departure.

SAMPLE MENU ITEMS

Dinner entrées: Grilled strip steak with pommes frites; sautéed shrimp and scallops with veggies in puff pastry; oven-baked ratatouille; chicken breast Provencal with tomatoes, olives, and white wine.

Cinderella's Royal Table

American cuisine. Breakfast, lunch, and dinner.

Those who want to feel like a six-year-old again should definitely plan to dine in Cinderella's fairy-tale castle, a medieval dream with thick stone floors, shining shields, dazzling suits of armor, and resplendent banners. Up a spiral staircase is the grand dining room where through glittering leaded-glass windows is a bird's-eye view of Fantasyland and, if you time it correctly, Wishes fireworks. It's a great respite from the throngs below with satisfying food and where everyone is a prince or princess waited on by "royal attendants" clad in Renaissance clothing.

All meals are hosted by Cinderella who you'll take your photo with on arrival downstairs, while upstairs is Disney's best princess meal with such characters as Ariel, Snow White, Jasmine, Belle, and Aurora. Each little princess receives a sparkling wand, each prince a knight's sword, and all leave with a nice photo package of your visit with Cinderella.

CARA'S TIP: While it's an uber-popular place to dine, it's only worth the high price tag if little ones, particularly little princesses, are part of your vacation party. To ensure a seat here it's almost essential to call (407) WDW-DINE or (407) 939-3463 at 7:00 a.m. Eastern Time Zone exactly 180 days prior. Food arrives very quickly so if possible drag out each course so you'll be able to see each and every princess before the end of the meal. Full payment is taken at time of booking with a one-day cancellation policy.

SAMPLE MENU ITEMS

Breakfast: Begin with a pastry basket, followed by your choices: platter of scrambled eggs, bacon, sausage, and potato casserole; caramel apple-stuffed French toast; baked goat cheese, spinach, and mushroom quiche; a healthy choice of scrambled egg whites, hot ten-grain cereal, and Greek yogurt topped with granola; steak and eggs; or lobster and crab crepes. Cheese frittata or breakfast platter is available for children.

Lunch entrées: Begin with a Chef's Tasting Platter of salads, followed by your choice of entrées: chef's fish of the day, gnocchi with roasted vegetables; farro with roasted vegetables; Major Domo's short rib on potato and parsnip puree; *panzanella* salad with shrimp; pork sandwich with apricot barbecue sauce and broccoli slaw; oven roasted chicken breast with farro wheat risotto; or pan-seared cod with Meyer lemon butter.

Dinner entrées: Your choice of five appetizers with these entrée selections: braised pork shank with slow-roasted root vegetables; beef tenderloin in a tarragon demi-glace with roasted fingerling potatoes and asparagus; pan-seared cod with Meyer lemon-butter sauce and quinoa salad; oven-roasted chicken breast with farro wheat risotto, wild mushroom and leek ragout; or gnocchi with roasted vegetables. End your meal with your choice of four desserts, one of them a dessert trio.

Crystal Palace

American buffet. Breakfast, lunch, and dinner.

Winnie the Pooh and his friends Eeyore, Piglet, and Tigger are your hosts in this sunlight-drenched, conservatory-style restaurant found at the Castle end of Main Street. Patio-style wrought-iron furnishings, lofty windows, tall palms, and ceilings hung with baskets of greenery create an alfresco, greenhouse atmosphere. A surprisingly good and bountiful buffet is the fare, definitely one of the better spreads in the park. This is a popular dining choice so make advance reservations, and on arrival ask for the dining room closest to Main Street with its charming view of Cinderella Castle. Kids will love the Friendship Day Celebration parade led by Winnie and Friends, but those dining without children should avoid dinnertime when the place is at a high frenzied fever pitch.

SAMPLE MENU ITEMS

Breakfast buffet: Juice, fresh fruit, pastries, muffins, croissants, cereal, oatmeal, sweet breakfast lasagna, French toast, Mickey waffles, pancakes, breakfast meats, made-to-order omelets, scrambled eggs, frittata, roasted potatoes, puff French toast, pancakes.

Lunch buffet: Mixed baby greens with various dressings, Hawaiian coleslaw, antipasto salad, fresh fruit salad, Mediterranean pasta salad, apple slices and carrots, romaine and bleu cheese salad, cucumber salad, Southwest chicken salad, potato salad, Moroccan couscous salad, edamame salad, assorted breads, soup; wild mushroom and chicken pasta with basil Asiago cream sauce, green Thai curry chicken, fruit and vegetable tofu curry, citrus-marinated flank steak, barbecue pork tenderloin, mashed potatoes, chili-garlic broccoli, stir-fried curry noodles, braised kale, fire-roasted corn spoon bread; banana chocolate tart, chocolate hazelnut cannoli, raspberry cake, peach and honey cheesecake, German chocolate cake, applesauce cake, coffee-amaretto mouse tart, assorted cookies, key lime pie, coconut flan, make-your-own sundae bar with soft-serve ice cream, hot apple crisp, banana bread pudding with hazelnut cream sauce. *Children's buffet:* mac 'n' cheese, multi grain pasta with meatballs, corn and green peas, roasted sweet potato wedges.

Dinner buffet: Peel-and-eat shrimp, salads the same as lunch, New England clam chowder, mussels Provencal, Mediterranean chicken with feta and tomatoes, baked salmon with basil aioli, cod and spinach pie, pork masala, chicken nuggets, vegetarian orecchiette pasta, rotisserie chicken, beef tip loin, roasted turkey breast, mashed potatoes, sautéed root vegetables, ratatouille, fire-roasted corn spoon bread, chili-garlic broccoli with key lime ponzu, basmati rice. Desserts and children's buffet same as lunch.

Best Epcot Dining

Akershus Royal Banquet Hall

Scandinavian cuisine at the Norway pavilion in World Showcase.
Breakfast, lunch, and dinner.

Those traveling with their own little princess should definitely book a meal at this fairy-tale dining spot. Housed in a replica of Oslo's Akershus Castle, the dining room sparkles with massive iron chandeliers, high-beamed ceilings, cut glass windows, and a friendly wait staff clothed in traditional Norwegian dress. Disney princesses are in attendance for all meals and may include Aurora, Snow White, Ariel, and Cinderella with all meals beginning at a photo shoot with Belle (a photo package is included in the price of the meal). Breakfast is a combination buffet/family-style meal of both American and Norwegian fare, but where Akershus really shines is at lunch and dinner. Begin with *koldtbord*, a cold buffet of Scandinavian-style salads, seafood, meats, cheese, and bread. Then choose one of the delicious entrées followed by a family-style trio of desserts. Usually whatever form of seared salmon they are offering is tough to beat, but the traditional *kjottkaker*, a plate of luscious Norwegian meatballs, might be a good choice for those who enjoy adventuresome eating. It's an excellent way to sample a bit of unfamiliar fare.

CARA'S TIP: This is a great alternative for those that didn't make the cut on Cinderella's Royal Table reservations where you'll basically find the exact same princesses and a reservation quite a bit easier to obtain.

SAMPLE MENU ITEMS

Buffet/family-style breakfast: Buffet of lingonberry muffins, pastries, croissants, cinnamon rolls, apple turnovers, granola, fruit, yogurt, cheeses, and smoked fish with a family-style platter of scrambled eggs, sausage, bacon, and potato casserole delivered to the table.

Lunch entrées: Seared salmon cakes with remoulade; grilled beef sandwich with roasted shallot mayo, caramelized onions, and crumbled blue cheese; open-faced chicken sandwich with arugula, bacon, mushrooms, Jarlsburg cheese and lingonberry mayo; mushroom stuffed pasta with Swiss chard and parmesan cheese; oven-roasted chicken breast with vegetable barley risotto and champagne mushroom sauce.

Dinner entrées: Pan-seared salmon with sweet corn, applewood smoked bacon, and lemon-herb butter; braised beef short ribs with potato casserole and blueberry *gastrique*; grilled pork chop with lingonberry barbecue sauce; pan seared beef tips with cremini mushrooms, shallots, and maple peppercorn sauce.

Coral Reef Restaurant

Seafood at The Seas With Nemo & Friends pavilion in Future World. Lunch and dinner.

Feel like the Little Mermaid in this one-of-a-kind, softly lit dining room of tiered leather banquettes lined with shimmering blue mosaic tiles. Dominating the restaurant and just a trident's throw away from all seats is the six-million-gallon aquarium rife with coral reef and sea creatures, about as close as you get to an interactive restaurant at Disney without a character meal. Children (as well as adults) are jumping with excitement and squealing in delight when a particularly interesting species swims by.

Fittingly, the menu is strong on seafood and fish. A garlicky Caesar is a nice starter with whole romaine leaves and crispy sourdough croutons, but most can't resist the creamy, but very rich lobster soup, one of the restaurant's longtime signature offerings. An entrée salad of super fresh sautéed trout served atop arugula, cannellini beans, and delicate cherry tomatoes with tart vinaigrette is astonishingly tasty, in fact it's one of the best dishes I've had at Disney. To satisfy the environmentalist in you, choose the sustainable fish which, on my last visit, was seared golden brown and paired with basil risotto studded with bay scallops atop a pool of white wine butter sauce, all sprinkled with lightly sautéed yellow and red baby tomatoes. Regardless of what you eat here, I think the view of the aquarium alone is worth the price of your meal.

SAMPLE MENU ITEMS

Lunch and dinner entrées: Orange and ginger-glazed Scottish salmon with vegetable stir-fry; grilled New York strip with cheddar mashed potatoes and peppercorn sauce; lobster orecchiette pasta with white cheddar cheese and basil oil; red curry vegetable and noodle bowl with Gardein chick'n breast; grilled mahi mahi with laughing bird shrimp and a coconut lime sauce; soy and ginger braised beef short rib with Asian vegetable slaw.

La Hacienda de San Angel

Authentic Mexican food at the Mexico pavilion in World Showcase. Dinner only.

One of two full-service restaurants in Mexico, the other San Angel Inn, La Hacienda has the advantage of a location outside the main pavilion with a prime location on the World Showcase Lagoon. It's not as romantic as the candlelit San Angel Inn, but you'll find excellent, traditionally-made Mexican food and, if luck has it, a prime view of Epcot's nighttime spectacular, Illuminations.

A basket of homemade tostadas, as good as any you'll find in Mexico, arrives promptly with tasty, but gringo-style (minus the normal tongue-numbing chilis) salsas in chipotle and tomatillo flavors. If you're smart you will charm your waiter into bringing the spicy concoction that the kitchen staff privately enjoys which comes with a dynamite kick!

Don't hesitate to order the grilled *arrachera*, a New York strip steak served with grilled spring onions, a *tamal* with *rajas* (peppers in a cream sauce), and refried black beans sprinkled with *cojita* cheese made extra good with the addition of the table salsa. The *pollo al pastor*, a chicken breast grilled and lightly charred is acceptably authentic if not a touch dry, made spicy with achiote and sweet with a fresh pineapple relish accompanied by sides of beautifully roasted fresh vegetables, so-so Mexican-style rice, and refried black beans. But the baby handmade corn tortillas are the icing on the cake, and you'll have to stop yourself from downing a dozen of them.

The impressive margarita list is a big draw here; however, if you go for the classic margarita then ask for it to be served with extra lime to cut the sweetness. While I'm normally a classic kind of gal when it comes to my margaritas, I am somewhat drawn to the Rosita made with silver tequila, a rose infused syrup, slivered rose petals, even a pink hibiscus and Himalayan salted rim.

CARA'S TIP: While most of the tables have a fairly good view of Illuminations along with the accompanying musical score, ask on your arrival for a prime window seat. There's no outdoor seating so if you want to see Illuminations al fresco then grab a bite at La Cantina de San Angel next-door where you'll find quick-service food.

SAMPLE MENU ITEMS

Dinner entrées: *Parillada*, a mixed grill of New York strip, chicken al pastor, chorizo and vegetables; *ostillas en salsa de chile*, braised short ribs with potato puree and *chili de arbol*; *puerco en salsa de ciruela*, grilled pork rib eye served with carrot puree, caramelized onions, and plum sauce; *pescado a la talla*, grilled tilapia served with roasted corn, nopales (cactus), and mango chutney; *parillada del mar*, mixed grill of fish, shrimp, scallops, and vegetables.

Monsieur Paul

French cuisine at the France pavilion in World Showcase. Dinner only.

Upstairs from Chefs de France is Monsieur Paul, a tribute to Chef Paul Bocuse who achieved three Michelin stars at his famous Lyon restaurant for 48 straight years. With a menu created by Chef Francesco Santin who worked with Chef Paul, the restaurant has been updated and modernized since its last incarnation as Bistro de Paris. Serving classic French dishes, or at least modern interpretations of them, gone are the old traditional red banquettes and white tablecloths. What's in now is a more casual, updated Art Nouveau space with grape purple and asparagus green décor (more tasteful than it sounds), fun bubble lighting, and a lovely, understated look. But never fear, the same classic French service is still in place.

Make your first bite an updated twist on typical escargot encased in ravioli with a sublime cream of parsley sauce. Follow that with a phenomenal layered salad of shaved white asparagus tossed in a remoulade dressing topped with Serrano ham, then a layer of frisée and baby greens, all sprinkled with dill and curls of salted red beets. Very different is the gorgeous truffle soup with its dome of puff pastry that is almost too pretty to eat . . . I said almost. Oh, and can we talk about the bread here . . . five types, all so perfect, the best being the mushroom and bacon roll, or perhaps the braided sundried tomato and basil bread.

Only five main courses are available, several offering their own dramatic presentation: grilled beef tenderloin with a thick mushroom crust surrounded by rich, dark bordelaise sauce; or an even lovelier red snapper topped with golden brown potato "fish scales," served with braised, tender fennel and a somewhat overwhelming yet delicious rosemary sauce. If it's seafood you're craving a better choice might be the delectable scallops, seared and served in a pool of ginger lobster consommé surrounded by crunchy vegetables and cream of cauliflower puree. And for dessert a sable Breton pastry cream topped with citrus segments and a side of citrus sorbet is the choice—all else pales in comparison.

CARA'S TIP: Those dining a deux should request a window table (most are only for two) to receive a nice view of the lagoon.

SAMPLE MENU ITEMS

Dinner entrées: Free-range chicken *ballotine*, carrot and sunchoke puree, creamy spinach; roasted duck breast *a l'orange*, grated potatoes and baby carrots; grilled beef tenderloin with mushroom crust, mashed potato, Bordelaise sauce.

Le Cellier Steakhouse

Steaks and such at the Canada pavilion in World Showcase. Lunch and dinner.

I'm never quite sure what to think about this restaurant. It is one of the most popular restaurants (if not THE most popular) in all of Epcot, and, for the life of me, I can't see what the draw is. Yes, the cellar-like, dimly lit atmosphere is a bit cozier than some of the other restaurants although the décor is nothing to write home about. The porcini-crusted filet mignon is one of Disney's best as is the top-notch mushroom risotto that comes with it, and the fact that it is all soaked in truffle butter certainly adds to the allure. And the famous Canadian cheese soup here is incredible (am I talking myself into actually liking this place?).

Other steaks on the menu are good, but not particularly great. Then again menu items such as *poutine*—french fries smothered in red wine reduction gravy, cheddar, and truffle salt—seems like something you might find at the county fair. So if it's a great filet you want go for it; if not, save yourself the frustration of finding a reservation here and head over to Yachtstman Steakhouse at the nearby Yacht Club Resort instead where just about anything on the menu is outstanding.

SAMPLE MENU ITEMS

Lunch and dinner entrées: Dry-aged bone-in rib-eye with roasted garlic butter; pepper-crusted sirloin with *au poivre* sauce; lamb rack with truffle-celeriac purée and lamb jus; Kurobuta pork tenderloin wrapped in prosciutto, braised pork belly, soft corn grits, ramps, and natural jus; ricotta *cavatelli* pasta with asparagus, morels, English peas, tomato pesto, and parmesan.

San Angel Inn Restaurante

South-of-the-border cuisine at the Mexico pavilion in World Showcase. Lunch and dinner.

A romantic ambience where it is perpetual nighttime alongside the inky *Rio del Tiempo* (River of Time) combined with a much improved menu is a great recipe for one of Epcot's better dining choices. The somewhat new addition of white tablecloths and the historic ambience of the original San Angel in Mexico City scores bonus points for a more refined feel than the restaurant's previous atmosphere.

Start with a specialty margarita like blood orange or passion fruit, or one of the more classic varieties, but beware that all are quite sweet; if a tart margarita is more to your liking ask for extra lime to be added. Good first course options are *tlacoyos de chilorio*, corn cakes topped with refried beans, savory pork, *queso fresco*, a touch of sour cream, and tart green tomatillo sauce; or *tostadas de tinga*, crispy tortillas topped with grilled chicken, black beans, and tasty *queso fresco*.

Entrées such as *pollo a las rajas*, grilled chicken breast served over red peppers, an overload of onions, chile poblano, chorizo, and melted cheese fits the bill for those who crave rich flavors, but meat lovers might consider the *tacos de* carne with tender strip steak, avocados, whole grilled green onions, and chipotle sauce in soft flour tortillas. Seafood seekers will enjoy the Veracruzana fish, a savory combination of fresh fish topped with capers, olives, bell peppers, onions, and tomato sauce. Or, if it's a kick you're wanting then the piquant shrimp *a la diabla* with *cascabel* chili sauce served over a creamy *yuca* puree is the way to go. An authentic dessert choice is the *helado del dulce de leche*, a vanilla ice cream mixed with delicious Mexican caramel sauce. If you're in luck the fabulous Mariachi Cobre will be performing during your meal.

SAMPLE MENU ITEMS

Lunch entrées: *Huarache de res*, thin sliced New York strip steak served over a corn and bean flatbread, topped with arugula, avocado, roasted chipotle sauce, and *queso fresco*; *enchiladas verdes con pollo*, corn tortillas filled with pulled chicken covered with green tomatillo sauce, topped with sour cream, *queso fresco*, and onions; *arrachera con chilaquiles*, New York strip with *chilaquiles* (layers of fried corn tortilla, green tomatillo sauce, topped with fresh cheese, sour cream, and onions).

Dinner entrées: *Peto in salsa* poblano, grilled wahoo fish served over roasted potatoes, vegetables, and poblano sauce; *carne asada*, New York strip steak served with cheese enchilada, black refried beans, bell pepper, and onions; chili *relleno*, a poblano pepper stuffed with pork, pine nuts, and almonds topped with a roasted tomato sauce; *lomo del puerco in pipian*, pork tenderloin served over roasted vegetables and pumpkin seeds, chiles, and almond sauce.

Tutto Italia Ristorante

Italian cuisine at the Italy pavilion in World Showcase. Lunch and dinner.

With an obligatory charming *maitre d'* and no less than three flirty waiters to serve you, this is one of the better restaurants in World Showcase.

The décor is one of glittering chandeliers and walls of murals depicting ancient Rome; definitely a slightly formal, Old World ambience. And from my place at a window table overlooking the piazza and its fountain, with Italian arias playing in the background, I could almost swear I was smack dab in the center of my much-loved Rome.

On the menu is a mound of mozzarella *di bufala* paired with sweet red peppers then drizzled with olive oil, and sprinkled with fresh basil and sea salt. Or a Grand Antipasto platter served family style with an assortment of meats, cheeses, and peppers is a definite winner. Pasta is Tutto Italia's best asset, and a stellar *tonnarelli*, perfectly al dente handmade egg pasta similar to spaghetti, *burrata*-studded, tossed with cubed zucchini, and plenty of fresh mint and basil, was one of the best pastas I've had in years. And I know that every Italian restaurant west of the Tiber claims their lasagna is fabulous, but here it's the truth—superb with a meaty *ragù* and a creamy béchamel.

Filet of sole is an another excellent option at dinner, lightly dusted with flour then sautéed and presented in a lemon and caper sauce, swirled with butter, and served with a surprise of tender white asparagus; this same dish can be had at lunchtime only made with chicken breast. But a must-have is the Polenta Valsugana, creamy and delicious, smothered in Fontina cheese and enlivened with meatballs and short ribs in a robust tomato sauce. A side of whatever vegetable is being served is always a good bet, my last taste that of crisp-tender green beans glistening with fruity olive oil and sprinkled with ripe cherry tomatoes and fresh tarragon.

Dessert might be best spent on the *torta di nocciole cortemilia*, a heavy hazelnut polenta cake adorned with dabs of Nutella and whipped Piemonte cream. Simply dreamy!

SAMPLE MENU ITEMS

Lunch entrées: Fettuccine Vecchia Roma, with prosciutto and parmesan cream; *porchetta* panini, roasted pork, Fontina, pickled peppers, arugula, and garlic mayonnaise; *risotto ai fruitti di mare*, Carnaroli rice, shrimp, squid, clams, mussels, and a light tomato sauce; baked salmon filet with artichokes, potato, and olives.

Dinner entrées: *Pollo al forno*, roasted chicken, rosemary, lemon, farro risotto, and pancetta; spaghetti with beef and veal meatballs, *pomodoro* sauce; *bistecca del Macellaio*, grilled butcher's steak, rosemary potatoes, *cipolline* onions.

Via Napoli

Italian cuisine at the Italy pavilion in World Showcase. Lunch and dinner.

You must plan a meal here if only to try the best pizza I've had in ages. More like a neighborhood trattoria, I almost prefer it to its next-door neighbor, Tutto Italia, although both have their assets. On beautiful days you might want to choose the outdoor patio, but it would be a shame to miss the entertaining hustle and bustle of the main dining room with its open kitchen, frescoed walls, and the massive faces of the three pizza ovens appropriately named Stromboli, Vesuvius, and Etna after Italy's active volcanoes. There's even a huge communal dining table perfect for those eating solo.

To start, the *Fritto Misto* platter gives you a sampling of the fried appetizers on the menu including the calamari, zucchini, mozzarella, asparagus, artichoke hearts, even the *arancini*, all served with a zingy *pomodoro* sauce. And speaking of arancini, these fried risotto balls are quite the delicacy with a touch of meat *ragù* filling on a bed of light tomato-basil sauce. But don't neglect to think about ordering the *gamberretti fagioli*, a cold antipasto with plump shrimp and cannellini beans tossed in olive oil, red onions, chopped fresh tomatoes, a plethora of rosemary, and a good squeeze of lemon. In fact, you really could make a fine meal just from the starter list.

Your best pasta choice is probably the *candele*, a baked dish of pasta tubes, sausage, tiny meatballs, ricotta, mozzarella, and a delicious, fresh *ragù*. When it comes to pizza it's a tough decision, but I would go with the *Carciofi Bianca*, a white pizza (sans the tomato sauce) topped with freshly grilled chopped artichokes and sprinkled with heady truffle oil. Wood-fired, thin yet chewy, and cooked to smoky excellence with a perfectly blistered crust, it's topped with a tasty blend of Fontina and mozzarella cheese and just a touch of garlic. This is the stuff dreams are made of! And no question about it, order the *zeppole* for dessert, crispy ricotta cheese fritters served with whipped cream and oh-so-good chocolate sauce!

SAMPLE MENU ITEMS

Lunch and dinner entrées: Lasagne *verde,* spinach, parmesan, and béchamel; *mezzi rigatoni alla crema con pollo,* pasta with cream, chicken and peas; *spaghetti con polpettine,* hand-crafted veal meatballs & tomato sauce; *linguine frutti di mare,* shrimp, clams, mussels & squid tossed in marinara picante; *piatti alla parmigiana pollo,* traditional preparation of chicken breast with tomato sauce, parmesan & mozzarella, served with roasted potatoes; *capricciosa* pizza, eggplant, artichokes, *cotto* ham, mushrooms; *prosciutto e melone* pizza, white pizza, Fontina, mozzarella, prosciutto, cantaloupe, arugula.

Best Disney's Hollywood Studios Dining

'50s Prime Time Café

American cuisine. Lunch and dinner.

Loosen your belt for lip-smacking comfort food as you pass through a time warp into a 1950s family kitchen. Here, guests dine while watching *The Dick Van Dyke Show* and *Dennis the Menace* on black-and-white TVs sitting on the counter between the toaster and the blender. Linoleum floors, Formica tables, pull-down lamps, plenty of knickknacks, and windows covered in venetian blinds and tacky drapes are accompanied by a menu of savory renditions of good old-fashioned American cuisine. The only thing missing is the sliced white bread. "Mom" herself is oftentimes your server, making sure everyone in the "family" observes good manners. No fighting at the table! No throwing spitballs! Mustn't forget to eat your vegetables! Our "cousin" told us to "put away your walkie talkies" (meaning cell phones) and that he had no intention of doing chores, delegating us to set the table.

Stick with the basics here for the best results. My favorite is the sampler plate of crispy, real-deal fried chicken, tender pot roast, and yummy meatloaf accompanied by mashers, fresh green beans, and collard greens. Of course it's all swimming in gravy so you may want to request it on the side. For dessert, opt for s'mores—where else can you enjoy the exotic taste of crunchy graham crackers, dripping chocolate, and golden melted marshmallows prepared for you without the hassle and smell of a fire pit? Before leaving check out the adjoining Tune-In Lounge for a highball complete with glowing ice cubes.

> **CARA'S TIP**: Ask to sit in one of the restaurant's "TV kitchens" for a close up of the monitors, although all seats have a fairly good view of several. If you didn't make advance dining reservations consider having a meal at Tune-In Lounge's bar where the full menu is served.

SAMPLE MENU ITEMS

Lunch and dinner entrées: Vegetable lasagna; grilled pork chop topped with arugula, fennel, and apple salad; old-fashioned pot roast; chicken pot pie; Caesar salad with chicken or salmon; olive oil poached salmon with mushroom ragout, bacon, and Swiss chard.

The Hollywood Brown Derby

Contemporary American cuisine. Lunch and dinner.

The best food at Disney's Hollywood Studios is to be found at the illustrious Brown Derby, perfectly re-created right down to the collection of celebrity caricatures hanging on just about every square inch of wall space. The glam of 1930s Hollywood is seen everywhere from the rich mahogany walls and furnishings to the sway of potted palms. Massive cast-iron chandeliers, crisp white tablecloths, snug ruby-red banquettes, and derby-shaped art deco lamps all set the mood for a sentimental waltz through the heyday of Hollywood. The cuisine here, however, is nothing but 21st century.

Begin in true Hollywood style with a round of martini flights—a trio of tasting-size gems—then a tantalizing appetizer or two, the best being the cheese and prosciutto cake, a savory and smoky wedge composed of a mixture of brie, Midnight Moon goat cheese, and prosciutto, made perfect by the accompanying antipasto salad and cheese petals of thinly sliced *Tete de Moine* soft Swiss. Or maybe the over-the-top blue lump crab spring rolls served with a touch of fresh mint, ready to dip in a slightly spicy miso aioli.

After that it's on to the pan-seared, coriander-spiced grouper with balsamic reduction and fennel oil or whatever the seasonal flavoring may be. Vegetarians as well as non-vegetarians will love the spicy noodle bowl spiked with coconut-crusted tofu, edamame, snap peas, bok choy, and shiitake mushrooms in a red curry broth. Carnivores should think about the succulent grilled filet of beef with a side of Zellwood corn and pancetta risotto and just a splash of arugula pesto; or perhaps the moist mojo-marinated pork chop enlivened with a bubbly crust of golden brown smoked Gouda served over a rich potato hash peppered with smoky bacon.

Now, you absolutely must order a slice of the not-too-sweet but oh-so-perfect grapefruit cake or your meal just isn't complete. Not your typical cake, this one is juice-infused with chunky grapefruit filling, cream cheese frosting, and a candied grapefruit ring piercing the top.

CARA'S TIP: The restaurant's lounge offers both indoor and outdoor patio seating serving wine, beer and cocktails as well as martini flights, wine, Scotch and Grand Marnier flights. Enjoy small plates of artisanal cheeses; charcuterie; duck confit tacos; steamed Prince Edward Island mussels; Derby Cocktail with jumbo lump blue crab, black tiger shrimp, avocado and a horseradish-tomato juice; and two Derby Sliders: Wagyu beef slider with cognac mustard aioli, smoked gouda cheese, bacon and avocado; and a house-made chorizo slider with chipotle mayo, Manchego cheese, pickles, and crispy onions. Even dessert is available with Chocolate Three Ways (praline milk chocolate cream, crunchy ganache, and orange-chocolate mousse); a banana-white chocolate toffee tower on a cocoa-almond cookie and bananas Foster; or strawberry Champagne cheesecake.

SAMPLE MENU ITEMS

Lunch and dinner entrées: *Duck Two Ways,* sautéed confit with Swiss chard over an herb and goat cheese polenta cake finished with a pan-seared maple bourbon, and duck Margret in a sun-dried cherry sauce; seafood cioppino; free-range roasted breast of chicken served over house-made spiced chorizo, yellow plantain hash, and an avocado and heirloom tomato purée; Hollywood Brown Derby's famous cobb salad;

spit-roasted American bison over wilted greens, tossed in an herb shallot vinaigrette with roasted fingerling potatoes, and a cocoa espresso
barbecue sauce; grilled Loch Duart salmon with black beluga lentil stew,
roasted purple cauliflower, olive tapenade, and a lemon thyme sabayon.

Sci-Fi Dine-In Theater Restaurant

American cuisine. Lunch and dinner.

Anyone lonesome for the drive-ins of their youth will go mad for this
place. Load into sleek, 1950s-era convertibles to watch B-movie sci-fi
and horror trailers and waiters who carhop the darkened, starlit theater.
Speaker boxes hang on the side of your car and, of course, popcorn and
hot dogs dance on the screen during intermission. One gladly overlooks the so-so food for the ambience when the likes of Godzilla is your
entertainment!

> CARA'S TIP: If you want to be seated quickly let the host know
> you're willing to dine at one of the flying-saucer tables or in a
> table and chair car (a full-size table surrounded by the sides of a
> car instead of one that faces forward). Stop in during nonprime
> hours for dessert only and soak up the surroundings in one of
> Disney's best themed restaurants.

SAMPLE MENU ITEMS

Lunch and dinner entrées: Famous All-American picnic burger, a
flame-broiled Angus burger patty topped with a grilled hot dog, sau-
erkraut, and sautéed onions; salmon BLT served on a French roll with
arugula, tomatoes, bacon, red onion, and chili-chive aioli; Reuben sandwich; smoked St. Louis-style ribs basted in BBQ sauce served with baked
beans and coleslaw; vegetable burger with cucumber, vine-ripened tomatoes, grilled red onions, and arugula, drizzled with balsamic vinegar;
shrimp or chicken pasta, whole wheat penne with garlic, basil, cream,
and fresh tomatoes; vegetarian shepherd's pie, fresh vegetables and a
vegetable patty topped with garlic mashed potatoes and melted cheddar.

Best Animal Kingdom Dining

Tusker House Restaurant

African cuisine in the Animal Kingdom's Africa area. Breakfast, lunch, and dinner.

One of Disney's better buffets, Tusker House offers a wide variety of healthy fare, an emphasis on whole grains, and many vegetarian choices, all with an African twist. Accompany your meal with a nice glass of South African wine and save room for the plethora of savory desserts served in tasting portions perfect for trying just a bite of everything. Better yet, Donald, Daisy, Mickey, and Goofy are on hand to spice up the atmosphere for breakfast and lunch.

SAMPLE MENU ITEMS

Breakfast buffet: Fresh fruit, cereals, oatmeal, *mealie pap*, biscuits and sausage gravy, scrambled eggs, oven-roasted potatoes, bacon, sausage, vegetable frittata, ham and cheese frittata, spiced corned beef hash, cheese blintzes, beef *bobotie* quiche, sweet potato casserole, carved rotisserie honey-glazed ham, warm cinnamon rolls, warm banana-cinnamon bread pudding with vanilla sauce, muffins, whole-grain breads, turnovers, cheese-filled and apple danish, croissants.

Lunch and dinner buffet: Marrakesh couscous, green bean and red onion salad, Tunisian couscous salad, curried rice salad with golden raisins, apple and endive salad with blue cheese crumbles, tomato and cucumber salad with mint yogurt dressing; seasonal fresh fruit, hummus, *tabbouleh*, cold cuts and cheeses, whole grain breads and rolls, *mealie* corn bread, lavosh; ham and bean soup, samosas, saffron infused root vegetables and cabbage, basmati rice with toasted almonds, pearl couscous with sweet basil, oven roasted red skin potatoes, mashed potatoes, spiced vegetable and tofu tandoori; Peri Peri baked salmon, seafood stew with tamarind BBQ sauce, spiced spit roasted chicken, spit roasted beef top sirloin, Kenyan coffee BBQ pork loin, curried chicken; hot cobbler, chocolate chunk cookies, oatmeal raisin cookies, coconut macaroons, lemon bars, pecan chocolate tart, passion fruit tart, chocolate volcano cake, carrot spiced cake, baklava, warm banana cinnamon bread pudding with vanilla sauce (their best dessert), strawberry mousse. *Children's buffet:* corn dog nuggets, spit-roasted chicken, macaroni and cheese, roasted corn medley, fresh green beans, mashed potatoes.

Best Walt Disney World Resort Dining

The best dining experiences in the "World" are to be found at Disney's Deluxe Resorts. Back in 1996 the California Grill set the pace when it opened to rave reviews with an ever-changing menu of New American cuisine. One by one the deluxe hotels launched a new breed of dining venues offering innovative cuisine and superior wine lists, one of which, Victoria & Albert's, boasts a AAA Five-Diamond Award rating, the only such restaurant in central Florida.

Artist Point

Pacific Northwest cuisine at Disney's Wilderness Lodge. Dinner only; resort casual dress. Open nightly 5:30 to 9:30 p.m.

The rustic, U.S. National Park theme of Disney's Wilderness Lodge continues here at Artist Point where the intoxicating aroma of cedar wafts among the expanse of fat ponderosa pine columns, vaulted ceilings, and Bierstadt-inspired Old West murals. Oversized windows offer views of sparkling Bay Lake and the hotel's enchanting courtyard of giant boulders and cascading waterfalls. Service, while friendly, lacks the polish of some of Disney's other signature restaurants. The wine list, however, is an awesome representation of the Pacific Northwest and is one of Disney's best so don't neglect to request a recommendation from the restaurant's sommelier.

Starters are divine, in particular the rich and smoky portobello soup (really one of the best things on the menu). And then there's the sourdough bread served with an incredible fennel-infused olive oil; I normally don't rant about oil, but I tend to down at least three slices and almost the entire baby pitcher of the concoction before moving on to the almost equally delicious butter topped with lava salt.

Entrées have always been exceptional here, so imagine my surprise on one of my last visits when overcooked fish and meat with surprisingly ho-hum presentations seemed to be the norm. Minimalism was taken to new heights when a filet mignon arrived looking lost on its large plate with only a dollop of mushroom ragout and a lonely donut filled with a strange hazelnut crunch sweet potato puree. A side of Yukon potato gratin was the only saving grace for the Kurobuta pork tenderloin, cooked to an unappealing gray. A flavorless halibut, which actually tasted as if previously frozen, was nicely crisped but overcooked; once again, a side of sweet corn and *chevre* porridge and confit of mushrooms was its only salvation.

But then a surprise winner, an excellent airline-cut chicken breast with oh-so-crispy skin accompanied by house-made whole-wheat pasta, micro greens, and a light but earthy, mushroom fondue sauce. And on my latest visit I was treated to a stunning cedar-planked Copper River wild salmon, simply cooked to a smoky medium prepared with only a lemon-butter sauce. Served with a brilliant dab of applewood bacon jam and, of all things, an uber rich short rib strudel wrapped in just a smidgen of phyllo, it was absolute perfection! So I'll chalk the problems up to hopefully what was an off night since Artist Point seems to be back on track and living up to its normally great reputation.

Berry cobbler here is really a must-have so just go ahead and order it. Or if you insist on branching out, try the Café Macchiato cake with pistachio crumble and sea salted caramel-vanilla *panna cotta*, a worthwhile departure from the norm.

CARA'S TIP: Before dark, ask for a view of Bay Lake. After dark, ask for one of the tables that sits off to right side of the restaurant with views of the resort's illuminated waterfall; it makes all the difference to move out of the central area's hustle and bustle. There are quite a few unacceptable tables here, including several wedged in corners behind giant Ponderosa pines, so request a move if your placement does not suit your fancy. After dinner take a romantic walk through the property to the edge of Bay Lake for a gander at the resort's geyser which erupts every hour on the hour until 10:00 p.m.

SAMPLE MENU ITEMS

Dinner entrées: Crusted big-eye tuna, stir-fry of udon noodles, baby bok choy, and shiitakes with yellow miso aioli; seared diver scallops with jumbo asparagus risotto, blistered tomatoes, citrus *pisto*, and sweet onion-chardonnay nage; truffle pasta ribbons with English peas, black and white truffle, pea puree, wild mushrooms, black figs, pearl onions, and Fontina cheese; slow-roasted buffalo strip steak, truffle mac 'n' cheese, rainbow chard, and blackberry Pinot Noir reduction; wild caught prawn and crab "hot pot" with mussels, crispy pork, jasmine rice, and spiced Thai coconut broth.

FOODIE ALERT!

Those looking for a unique experience should plan on an evening at one of these special Walt Disney World venues:

Chef's Tasting Wine Dinner at Flying Fish Café. Take your place at one of nine seats at the chef's counter located directly in front of the exhibition kitchen affording a perfect opportunity to interact with the chef. Five inventive courses, created and delivered by the chef himself using the freshest ingredients of the season, are each served with a wine that perfectly complements each course. Only for guests ages 14 and older, two seatings per night at 5:45 p.m. and 8:15 p.m., Sunday through Thursday. Groups of up to six can be accommodated, and reservations must be made at least one day in advance.

Chef's Domain at Citricos. Meet the chef during dinner in a glassed-in dining room seating up to twelve guests. You may either choose from the restaurant's menu or, better yet, have the chef create a multi-course meal just for you and your group. The restaurant's sommeliers will suggest wine pairings from the award-winning list, and there's even a direct view into the show kitchen in order to watch the preparation of your meal. Only one seating per evening on Friday, Saturday, Sunday, and Monday with a minimum $650 per party requirement. So gather up a few friends and let the fun begin! On Wednesday is a non-private, five-course Wine Tasting Dinner with a rotating roster of featured wineries for up to ten guests for $155 per person.

California Grill

New American cuisine at Disney's Contemporary Resort. Dinner only; resort casual dress. Open nightly 5:30 to 10:00 p.m.; lounge open 5:30 to 11:30 p.m.

Over the course of almost two decades California Grill has attained cult status and is consistently one of the toughest tickets in the "World" to obtain reservations. I am a view fanatic, and the drop-dead-gorgeous setting on the 15th floor of the Contemporary Resort enjoys Disney's best—period. From its lofty heights diners can see the Magic Kingdom, the sparkling Seven Seas Lagoon, and, best of all, the Wishes fireworks. An inventive approach to seasonally focused food goes along with the restaurant's coveted position, and now that it is newly remodeled in a mid-century look with modern touches, everything is better than ever. White walls mix with warm fabrics and carpeting in sunset colors of yellow, red, and orange, and the massive picture windows are perfect for peering out at that spectacular view. The open kitchen is still the restaurant's central focus, but lines are cleaner and the views more expansive now that windows are floor to ceiling with virtually no interruption except for minimal framing.

Upon entering the restaurant you are greeted by a massive cabinet featuring 1,600 bottles of mostly California wine. Offering everything from boutique wines to those of South Africa or Oregon, there is absolutely something for everyone. If your table isn't yet ready on arrival nab a seat in the lounge area where some of the best views are to be had.

Begin with the dangerously delicious, crusty bread in several varieties including whole-grain sourdough and lavender focaccia served with a salty slab of butter (I still prefer the old sourdough slices). As for appetizers, I'm a easy target for meatballs; so when California Grill's new menu was presented with wood-fired, three-meat (pork, lamb, and veal) varieties flavored with *harissa* and salty olives and crusted with a lemony *chimichurri*, it met with absolutely no resistance and proved to be as good as it sounds. With its bed of orzo and outstanding flavor I think it might be one of my new favorites. Or perhaps Duck in all its Glory to start your meal, housemade duck sausage, rillettes, duck prosciutto, and duck liver pate served with garnishes of housemade pickles and tart cranberry compote. But you can never go wrong with the Sonoma goat cheese ravioli, one of my absolute favorite appetizers ever, thin-thin pasta in it's pool of tomato-fennel broth and slivers of fresh basil. And a good bet is always the restaurant's flatbreads with perhaps the best choice the tart and tasty sundried beefsteak tomatoes with chewy mozzarella *di bufala* and a sprinkling of aged balsamic. Can you tell I like the appetizers here almost better than the entrées?

The ever-present grilled pork tenderloin, perfectly pink in the center with a zinfandel glaze accompanied by renowned goat cheese polenta (if you're smart you'll order a side of this for the table to leave plenty for yourself) has always been a favorite, but now it is served "two ways" along with a braised lacquered pork belly with country applesauce. The oak-fired filet is still on the menu but with what I consider a much-improved presentation now with heirloom tomato risotto and tomato butter. But a wild Columbia River salmon had a fishy taste and was a bit undercooked although the accompanying crispy salmon cake was phenomenal. Skip the 24-hour short rib "filet". It either needs to be cooked longer to make it more fork-tender, or chef has come up with one of his worst recipes ever.

And while great sushi and sashimi might be the last thing one would expect at Walt Disney World, here only the best is served along with ten varieties of sake. There's even a 12-course *omakase* menu available only at the 9-seat sushi bar, leaving the selection up to the chef with some unusual presentations you might not taste otherwise. Reserving this experience should and can be done online or with Disney Dining.

Finish with warm fritters, banana stuffed and cinnamon dusted with dipping sauces (peanut butter *crème anglaise*, chocolate, and caramel) and even toasted caramel marshmallow. The sundae sampler with a tiny Coke float and diminutive caramel corn sundae, while cute, is way too sweet for my taste. Better yet try something lighter such as the no-sugar-added lemon meringue cheesecake. Honestly, who needs the sugar when you can have this?

Procuring a window seat can be tough but don't be discouraged; time your meal around the fireworks and head outside to not one but two super observation platforms for a bird's-eye view of the extravaganza.

CARA'S TIP: Reservations here go quickly so plan ahead. Check-in is on the 2nd floor where you'll then be escorted upstairs.

SAMPLE MENU ITEMS

Dinner entrées: Georges Bank scallops with homemade potato gnocchi, smoked pork, grilled onions, rapini, and parmesan foam; Bell & Evans chicken with teriyaki barbecue glaze, truffle macaroni & cheese, glazed vegetables, and chicken sausage; roasted squash ravioli, root spinach, parsnips, petite herb salad, sage brown butter, 12-year balsamic; Pacific halibut with parsnip silk, roasted heirloom beets, arugula, macadamia vinaigrette, beet syrup.

Citricos

Contemporary Mediterranean food at Disney's Grand Floridian Resort. Dinner only; resort casual dress. Open nightly 5:30 to 10:00 p.m.

This restaurant only seems to improve over the years with an ambitious menu that is a delight to the senses, an ultra-friendly staff, and superb management. These attributes, combined with an exhibition kitchen where chefs actually walk your entrée to your table and refuse to let you depart without a wave goodnight, makes for one of Disney's very best places to dine. All is enhanced by starched white linens, rich silk curtains, mosaic tiles, swirling wrought iron railings, and immense windows affording views of the charming resort courtyard and, for just a few tables only, the Magic Kingdom fireworks in the distance.

Almost large enough to make it an entrée, everyone's favorite appetizer is the lemony sautéed shrimp peppered with feta and tomatoes; but don't let its deliciousness allow you to neglect ordering a platter of *arancini,* crispy fried risotto balls stuffed with Italian sausage and mozzarella and served with a tart tomato coulis. Or mull over ordering the superb tomato salad with slices of delicate fresh mozzarella—a variety of perfectly ripened heirlooms, mixed greens tossed lightly in vinaigrette, and a drizzle of aged balsamic tomato emulsion, all sprinkled with toasted garlic *gremolata.*

While the hearty braised veal shank, Citricos signature entrée, is raved about and rightly so, the question is how to resist the intensely flavored, Madiera-braised boneless short ribs made even more sinful by a truffle *crème fraiche?* Or the oak-grilled filet with an intense Cabernet demi-glace and standout potato and Vidalia onion gratin, even a fried

Vidalia onion ring with a spoon of remoulade sauce—perfection! For a lighter touch there's Florida grouper in a broth of blistered tomatoes, basil, and fettuccini, simple but welcome after days of rich dining. Even chicken is exceptional here . . . an organic, airplane-cut breast, pan roasted to a golden brown with a light peach glaze served with roasted fingerling potatoes and ice root spinach. Dessert should be the warm chocolate banana torte, a definite winner, topped with a dramatic Belgium Couverture chocolate crown, or the berry gratin swimming in the best sabayon sauce imaginable (it doesn't hurt that it has Champagne and Grand Marnier in it!).

Wine lovers are attracted to the extensive list of global vintages including almost 50 by the glass along with iconic, epic wines available by the ounce for tasting. For special occasions The Chef's Domain, a small private dining room, is available for you and up to eleven family and friends. Here you may either choose from the restaurant's menu or, better yet, have the chef create a multi-course meal just for you and your group.

SAMPLE MENU ITEMS

Dinner entrées: Oak-grilled swordfish, roasted fennel, and Vermouth risotto with black garlic aioli; seared tofu with zucchini and eggplant ratatouille, roasted mushrooms, lentils, and sun-dried tomato puree; Berkshire pork two ways, rotisserie pork tenderloin and roasted pork belly, with hominy cheddar puree, rainbow Swiss chard, and pork consommé.

Flying Fish Café

Seafood at Disney's BoardWalk. Dinner only; resort casual dress. Open 5:30 to 10:00 p.m.

Parachuting flying fish, sparkling sea blue mosaic floors, cloud-painted ceilings, and golden fish scale pillars literally cry out "Great Seafood!" and great seafood you can certainly find at the lively Flying Fish Café. With friendly yet polished service and an award-winning global wine list strong on California vintages, along with an entire page of by-the-glass wine, this is one Disney restaurant that needs to be on your radar.

Elsewhere a salad tends to be just a salad, but Flying Fish Café's sweet bibb and red oak lettuces from the Epcot Land pavilion gardens is exceptional, made slightly crunchy with strips of radishes, slightly bitter with radicchio and frisée, and slightly sweet with nicely ripened pears and candied walnuts, along with touches of creamy Gorgonzola, all tossed in a light, walnut oil vinaigrette. Or instead, a Caprese salad—fresh mozzarella paired with an unbelievable assortment of tomatoes drizzled with a rich aged balsamic—would be a nice substitute. The signature crab cake appetizer has a bit too much filler for my taste but comes with a tasty red pepper coulis and ancho chili remoulade.

The menu will cause dizziness since it lists just about every ingredient for each dish; nevertheless, entrées here are quite exceptional. Gorgeous grilled diver scallops sit atop a bed of English pea, pecorino, and mascarpone risotto, all sprinkled with crispy prosciutto; and the luscious Faroe Island sustainable salmon is married to a Vermouth, dill, caper, and butter emulsion for even more flavor. But it's mainly the ever-changing Chef's Thunder fish entrée that is what you should focus on. On my last visit the featured fish was, of all things, tilapia from Epcot's fish farm in The Land. With an Asian touch, sesame and horseradish crust, and the pairing of tasty gulf shrimp along with a bed of exotic and savory rice, crunchy sunchokes, a barely there and to-die-for ginger, butter sauce, and slightly bitter wilted greens, onions, and mushrooms, this proved to be one near-flawless dish.

If its steak you're yearning for, the excellent New York strip served with sauce *foyot* (a version of Béarnaise sauce) is delectable. Or the signature potato-wrapped snapper is always a temptation on its bed of creamy leek fondue. The only problem here is the accompanying red-wine butter sauce, something, in my estimation, that doesn't go well with the delicate fish. Or, if you simply can't decide between the two, there's a duo platter on the menu with both the steak and the snapper!

Dessert is best spent eating the caramelized banana napoleon with layers of crispy phyllo and banana mousse drizzled with crème caramel, fruit coulis, and a touch of bitter chocolate.

CARA'S TIP: If traveling solo ask to sit at the bar where there always seems to be a spirited group of diners ready and willing to chat.

SAMPLE MENU ITEMS

Dinner entrées: "Char-crusted" yellow fin tuna with bok choy, lotus root, mushrooms, snap and snow peas, and tiny asparagus stir-fry with Thai green curry, cucumber, coconut, Kaffir lime, and lemongrass infusion; asparagus and mushroom pasta, forest mushrooms, pecorino, arugula, porcini cream, crispy shiitakes, and Amaretti crumbs; trio of Heritage Berkshire Kurobuta pork, grilled pepperberry and wattleseed-dusted tenderloin, slow-cooked belly, and braised shoulder-mushroom ragout with a Zellwood corn "pudding" and rich pork jus.

Il Mulino New York Trattoria

> Italian cuisine at the Walt Disney World Swan. Dinner only; resort casual dress. Open daily, 5:00 to 11:00 p.m.

First opened in New York's Greenwich Village more than twenty-five years ago, this restaurant offers some of the best Italian on Disney property. It's Abruzzi-style Italian food in a trendy, contemporary setting with fashionable lighting, leather seating, exposed brick, and wood floors. Glass partitions section off the kitchen as well as smaller, more intimate nooks, but I prefer the open, more lively dining area.

Nothing much ever changes on the menu here so don't worry that a favorite dish will somehow disappear. Savor an order of *arancini*, succulent rice balls stuffed with ground meat perched on a bed of tasty marinara, or a Caprese salad with creamy, fresh buffalo mozzarella and the addition of roasted peppers all sprinkled with extra virgin olive oil and aged balsamic.

Pasta lovers will adore the brothy rigatoni *con funghi*, al dente pasta with an assortment of garlicky wild mushrooms and just enough truffle oil to make it nice and decadent. *Pollo Aromatico* is certainly your best choice for something light, a beautifully roasted, airplane cut breast served in a pool of rich white wine sauce over wilted escarole. A surprisingly great *costolette di maiale*, a thick pork chop cooked pink in the middle, is topped with mounds of chopped mushrooms and spicy cherry vinegar peppers. And if you crave fabulous shrimp but don't mind intensity, the *gamberi francese* fits the bill with its lightly battered, giant, succulent shrimp swimming in a bed of creamy, white wine lemon sauce.

DISNEY'S FINEST LOUNGE FOOD

It was my final evening of a weeklong trip to Walt Disney World and my planned dinner at Narcoossee's just took too much energy expenditure to contemplate, even though I was only a monorail ride away from my villa at Bay Lake Tower. So on a whim I walked across the skybridge to the Contemporary Resort and down the escalator to the California Grill's 2nd floor podium where I asked for a seat in the restaurant's 15th-floor lounge. The hostess on duty cheerfully complied, and in a matter of minutes I was seated with a prime view overlooking the Seven Seas Lagoon and the Magic Kingdom.

I mean seriously, where else can you find lounge food like this! The restaurant's entire menu is available in the lounge so I had a multitude of choices. Of course I had to start with a Napa Valley Groth Chardonnay chosen from an amazing list of wines by the glass. And then there's the dangerously sinful, golden-crusted and grainy breads served with a slab of salty butter that I totally overindulged in. Then to add insult to injury after downing the entire basket of bread, out came a chewy heirloom tomato flatbread sprinkled with smoky applewood bacon. Never mind, I will diet later.

My entrée was perhaps the best I've had here, a superbly crisp Florida red snapper atop slices of waxy fingerling potatoes, crisply cooked yellow and green beans, all sprinkled with frisée and a tangy mustard vinaigrette . . . almost like a warm salad. And believe it or not I actually found room for the peaches and cream dessert—Florida peaches spooned over a dense olive oil cake with scoops of creamy vanilla *panna cotta* and luscious peach ice cream. And the best part of this indulgence is that it was a no-sugar-added dessert. It didn't do much to redeem my excess, but I did feel a bit saint-like in ordering it. So I trudged, luckily not very far, back to my villa in a total food coma so glad that I opted for a night at the top of the town.

An impressive international wine list boasting a Wine Spectator Award of Excellence is heavy on Italian vintages.

CARA'S TIP: Those traveling with small children should take advantage of the two hours of complimentary childcare at Camp Dolphin (one child per adult entrée). Valet parking is complimentary when dining at Il Mulino. Cigar aficionados will enjoy the smoking courtyard just off the lounge with cigars available for purchase.

SAMPLE MENU ITEMS

Dinner entrées: *Manicotti*, baked pasta stuffed with ricotta and spinach with a tomato sauce; *costoletta dentice*, seared red snapper with cherry tomatoes, garlic, pancetta, and white wine, served over broccoli rabe; *costoletta di vitello*, single cut veal chop with sage and garlic over a bed of potatoes; *bistecca* ribeye, 14-oz. grilled boneless ribeye served with fried onion, sautéed spinach, and Chianti sauce; *risotto ai frutti di mare*, Arborio rice with mixed seafood.

Jiko—The Cooking Place

Contemporary cuisine with an African flair at Disney's Animal Kingdom Lodge. Dinner only; resort casual dress. Open daily, 5:30 to 10:00 p.m.

Jiko richly deserves kudos for its innovative and consistently great cuisine, seductive atmosphere, and an amazing array of South African wines. The handsome dining room is furnished with massive mosaic tile columns surrounded by floor-to-ceiling windows, blue leather banquettes, honey-colored walls, and gleaming wood floors. Warm, contemporary lighting shaped in the guise of bird wings hangs from a rich blue ceiling, giving the feeling of open space. Giant, twin clay ovens draw the eye to the open kitchen where an eclectic blend of creations, prepared with an African flair in terms of spices and ingredients, is turned out in attractive presentations. The food veers towards the exotic, but you can't go wrong with most anything on the menu.

You'll be impressed with the restaurant's breadbasket of flax seed focaccia and Ethiopian honey bread with its accompanying spiced tandoori butter. The ridiculously good Taste of Africa appetizer offers four types of exotic spreads and, you guessed it, more fabulous breads like *naan*, *pappadam*, and *lavosh*. The beet salad is the starter ticket here topped with Serrano ham and blackberry vinaigrette with a dollop of creamy pistachio-crusted goat cheese. Then succumb to Jiko's tantalizing version of fall-off-the-bone short ribs, surprisingly devoid of any kind of starch accompaniment, something not even necessary so rich is the pile of roasted vegetables and spicy tomato sauce that goes along with them. Giant *chermoula*-spiced Nigerian prawns atop saffron rice are also pretty delectable, surrounded by a pool of pea nage and an interesting orange and olive salad. Now, if you would like to partake of the restaurant's famous oak-grilled filet with red wine sauce, the standard side of mac 'n' cheese is no longer on the menu, but don't despair. Simply ask your server to substitute it for the potatoes or rice it's now served with and they will be happy to oblige. For an after-dinner treat you really must try Jiko's seasonal bread pudding, my last go-round a coconut-flavored version with rum sauce and caramel ice cream.

Those who want to learn more about South African wine should keep an eye out for Jiko Wine Dinners offered at various dates throughout the year. A multi-course meal with wine pairings hosted by renowned South African winemakers in Jiko's private Wine Room makes for one memorable evening. Call 407-939-3463 for reservations or 407-938-7149 for specific information.

SAMPLE MENU ITEMS

Dinner entrées: Pan-seared yellowtail snapper with tea-smoked lentils, South African lobster, and citrus-curry beurre blanc; curry-rubbed lamb loin with cauliflower puree, eggplant artichoke *zaalouk*, and red olive-walnut tapenade; seared Barbarie duck breast, potato and spinach masala, royal trumpet mushrooms, and port emulsion; "bunny chow" and falafel, Durban curry vegetables with *naan* bread, mango ketchup, *harissa* mustard, and chickpea lentil cake with cilantro yogurt, wilted greens, and olive tapenade; guinea hen *Doro Wot*, braised leg and *berbere* roasted breast, sweet potato, wilted greens, and ancho glaze.

Narcoossee's

Seafood at Disney's Grand Floridian Resort. Dinner only; resort casual dress. Open daily, 5:30 to 10:00 p.m.

Views of Cinderella Castle and the Magic Kingdom fireworks anyone? Nestled on the shore of the Seven Seas Lagoon this restaurant offers a pleasant if not exciting nautical ambience along with wriggling fresh seafood. A good start to your meal is butter soft Prince Edward Island mussels served with garlicky toast in a fennel, chorizo, and saffron broth, or crispy calamari made interesting with the addition of spicy pepperoncini and olives. A welcome summer salad offered baby lettuces, slices of just-ripened local peaches, dabs of Flore Belle blue cheese, slivers of dried apricots, and a scattering of roasted cashews tossed in a light, white peach vinaigrette.

There's always a nice variety of seasonal fish choices, but my last visit's Alaskan halibut, seared a golden brown and accompanied by Narcoossee's version of "chowda" sauce, superbly smoky with bacon and crunchy with celery and sweet corn was exceptional. Known for the steamed whole Maine lobster, that's a clever choice if you're prepared to spring for the high price tag; but better yet go with a house-made scampi fettuccine loaded with Maine lobster and wild shrimp dotted with beautiful heirloom tomatoes in a lemon-Chardonnay-garlic sauce. And can we talk about the scallops? Georges Bank day boat beauties in a pool of lemon-thyme-mustard jus with a pile of al dente trofie pasta tossed with string beans, almonds, and herb crème all scattered with arugula: simply superb. If seafood isn't your thing then order the tender filet mignon served with a creamy gruyere cheese and caramelized red onion risotto with roasted wild mushrooms, red wine reduction, and just the right touch of white truffle oil.

The cheesecake here, enlivened with a solid crust of thinly sliced almonds, is a sure bet with its mouthwatering Lambert cherry sauce; but I wish the key lime crème brûlée, a permanent fixture on the menu for years, were still a choice. Time moving on isn't always easy, although the yummy coconut and chocolate crème brûlée runs a pretty close second. For a perfect culmination of your evening step outside to the restaurant's verandah or the adjoining boat dock for prime fireworks viewing. Then stick around for an after-dinner drink in the bar and a performance of the Electrical Light Parade.

CARA'S TIP: Request a window table with a view of Cinderella Castle on arrival.

SAMPLE MENU ITEMS

Dinner entrées: Sustainable *Togarashi*-spiced seared ahi tuna with spring vegetables, sesame sticky rice, and ginger-soy-*hijiki* broth; house-made mushroom, spinach, and cheese ravioli with organic baby carrots, marinated semi-dried tomatoes, arugula *pistou*, Parmigiano-Reggiano, mushroom-black tea consommé, and aged balsamic; "chicken and dumplings," Ashley Farms chicken breast with potato dumplings, baby carrots, English peas, caramelized red pearl onions, and peppered soubise sauce; two-pound steamed Main lobster, whipped boniato potatoes, broccolini with hazelnut *gremolata*, and spiced rum-vanilla sauce.

WHAT I LOVE ABOUT WALT DISNEY WORLD DINING!

After more than two decades enjoying Walt Disney World's restaurants I wanted to compose a list of my all-time favorite dishes. They might possibly become your favorites too!

- *Yachtsman Steakhouse's Prime New York Strip Steak*, cooked to perfection and served with yummy potato gratin made with Carmody cheese, topped with a rich and creamy peppercorn-brandy sauce.

- *50s Prime Time's Sampling of Mom's Favorite Recipes*. Yes, I'm a child of the 50s and nothing is more nostalgic than a platter filled with fall-off-the-bone pot roast, good old-fashioned meatloaf served with sides of mashed potatoes and gravy, and the very best, real-deal, fried chicken around.

- *California Grill's Grilled Pork Tenderloin*, perfectly pink in the center and spiked with a zinfandel glaze. But the dish's pièce de résistance is the accompanying and renowned goat cheese polenta.

- *Via Napoli's Carciofi Bianca White Pizza* with freshly grilled artichokes sprinkled with heady truffle oil. Wood-fired, thin yet chewy, and cooked to smoky excellence, it's topped with a tasty blend of pecorino and mozzarella cheese and just a touch of garlic. This is the stuff dreams are made of.

- *Portobello's Rigatoni Calabrese*, a dish I fell in love with on my first visit over 20 years ago, is still my favorite and features Italian sausage, kalamata olives, mushrooms, tomatoes, and escarole. The pasta is perfectly al dente and the sauce is just the right touch of richness without being overwhelming.

- *Artist Point's Cedar Plank Roasted Salmon*, always fantastic, topped with ever-changing sauces. Try it in late spring when the offering is Copper River, the most delectable salmon ever!

- *Florida Snapper at California Grill.* A superb portion of golden-seared fish placed on slices of waxy fingerling potatoes, crisply cooked yellow and green beans, all topped with frisée and a tangy mustard vinaigrette. Almost like a warm salad and oh so savory!

- *Epcot's Coral Reef's Pan-seared Sustainable Seasonal Catch.* Golden brown with basil risotto studded with bay scallops atop a pool of white wine butter sauce and sprinkled with lightly sautéed yellow and red baby tomatoes. Delish!

Sanaa

African and Indian cuisine at Disney's Animal Kingdom Villas–Kidani Village. Lunch and dinner. Open daily, 11:30 a.m. to 3:00 p.m. and 5:00 to 9:30 p.m.

This charmer of a restaurant has the advantage of full-length picture windows overlooking the resort's savanna, something not available next-door at Jiko's dining room. In the tradition of an African lodge it's as if you are dining under the trees with the rich palette of nature displayed by the basket light fixtures, cement flooring, adobe walls, thatch ceilings, *krall* fencing, tree trunk posts, and African shield chairs. And for once the lighting is somewhat subdued, overcoming one of my Disney pet peeves.

At Sanaa you will find a variety of tastes all vibrating with unusual spices woven into the small but interesting menu. Order a glass or bottle of wine from the restaurant's mostly South African list along with the bread service and your choice of delectable spreads and dips. The appetizer sampler is also a good way to try a bit of everything, all of which includes crispy curried potato and pea samosas with a touch of heat, chunky *chana tikki* chickpea cakes, and somewhat dry lamb *kefta* sliders topped with a dab of goat cheese and red peppers all accompanied by mango chutney, cucumber *raita* sauce, and an *atchara* of green papaya pickled in vinegar. If you want to try a salad or vegetarian dish no need to order the sampler; simply ask for a side serving of whatever you wish, a good choice being the Indian spiced seasonal greens and tomatoes (spinach and mustard greens with a colorful mélange of cherry tomatoes).

The sustainable fish is seared to a golden brown and prepared in a brothy citrus saffron bath with a bed of crisp seasonal vegetables accompanied by scallops and perfectly plump shrimp; on my last visit the featured fish was a luscious corvine and before that king salmon. Or choose two of five small dishes (butter chicken, spicy Durban chicken or shrimp, bison masala, and sustainable fish with Goan curry) with the curries tasting a bit superior and less sweet than their typical Asian counterparts. Now when it's described as Durban, please beware because the scotch bonnet chilis push it as spicy as it can go! Skip the lamb *kefta*, more like a hamburger instead of the delicate grilled versions found in most Moroccan restaurants, as well as the lunchtime *naan* sandwiches, so huge that they are almost impossible to eat even with a fork. A must dessert is the incredible chai cream, now part of a dessert trio also featuring Tanzanian chocolate mousse and carrot halva cake.

> **CARA'S TIP:** Arrive early and request a table facing the wall of windows overlooking the resort's savanna, and while you wait have a drink in the restaurant's tiny gem of a bar.

SAMPLE MENU ITEMS

Lunch entrées: Bison burger, tandoori chicken, lamb *kefta*, or tandoori shrimp—your choice, served open-faced on *naan* bread with minted greens, tomato, onion, and cucumber-yogurt *raita*; *vegetarian sampler*, choice of two (seasonal greens and tomatoes, lentil *dhal*, *paneer tikka*, seasonal vegetable *wat*, or potato *masala*) served with basmati rice or five-grain pilaf; roasted turkey sandwich served on ciabatta with avocado, smoked bacon, pickled red onion, lemon mayonnaise, and choice of chickpea salad or fruit; chicken *chaat* and *bhatura*; sustainable fish of the day.

Dinner entrées: Tandoori chicken, lamb, or shrimp served with apple-raisin chutney and basmati rice or five-grain pilaf; New York strip, roasted potatoes, peppers, and onion, and your choice of coriander chutney, cucumber *raita*, or garlic pickle; sustainable fish of the day; vegetarian sampler.

DINE WITH AN ANIMAL SPECIALIST OR AN IMAGINEER

Feast on a delicious four-course lunch with an animal specialist at Sanaa restaurant in the Animal Kingdom Villas–Kidani Village. Your table offers a prime view of the resort's savanna in a group of no more than twelve guests as one of the resort's animal specialists fills you in on all that goes on behind the scenes in the Animal Kingdom Resort's menagerie. The chef even stops by for a visit. After your meal venture into a secured area for an up-close encounter with the radiated tortoises, one of the most endangered animals cared for at the resort. Offered every Wednesday and Saturday. Call 407-938-6922, option 3 for reservations or reserve online at Disneyworld.disney.go.com/dining/dine-with-an-animal-specialist/.

At Disney's Hollywood Studios' Hollywood Brown Derby at the lunch hour, and Disney's BoardWalk's Flying Fish Café at dinner, guests enjoy a four-course meal along with a mealtime discussion with a Disney Imagineer, the creative minds that bring Disney magic to life. You can also purchase a souvenir plate personalized by the Imagineer. Guests must be at least 14 years of age to attend.

Shula's Steak House

Steaks at the Walt Disney World Dolphin. Dinner only; business casual dress. Open daily, 5:00 to 11:00 p.m.

This masculine restaurant's theme, based on the Miami Dolphins' 1972 undefeated season, is depicted in attractively framed black-and-white photos embellishing the rich wood-paneled walls. The dimly lit, dark-hued interior is comfortably outfitted in elegant cherry wood, loads of shiny brass, cushy high-backed chairs, leather banquettes, and white linen-covered tables. The menu is short on fuss and long on prime ingredients, but the presentation printed on a football (yes a football!) along with a tray of raw meat explained in detail (a la Morton's) seems a bit overkill. But you don't have to be a quarterback to enjoy the sensational Angus beefsteaks, unbelievably tender and cooked to perfection, accompanied by mouthwatering sourdough bread.

True aficionados should consider only the 22-ounce Cowboy, a huge hunk of bone-in ribeye that never disappoints. The French onion soup is perhaps the best starter while a double baked potato studded with aged white cheddar and chives, or the crab macaroni and cheese are the best sides. Order a bottle from Shula's outstanding California wine list, winner of the Wine Spectator's Best of Award of Excellence, to round out the evening ending with a decadent chocolate soufflé served with *crème anglaise*, vanilla ice cream, and whipped cream.

CARA'S TIP: Those traveling with small children should take advantage of two hours of complimentary childcare at Camp Dolphin (one child per adult entrée). Be sure to reserve ahead and enjoy time on your own. Valet parking is complimentary when dining here.

SAMPLE MENU ITEMS

Dinner entrées: *Steak Mary Anne,* two filet medallions prepared in a demi glace; 12-ounce filet mignon; 24-ounce porterhouse; 24-ounce prime rib; twin 11-ounce lamb porterhouse; 4-pound Maine lobster; French-cut chicken breast; jumbo lump crab cakes; pan-seared sea scallops.

Todd English's Bluezoo

Contemporary seafood at the Walt Disney World Dolphin. Dinner only; resort casual dress. Open daily, 5:00 to 11:00 p.m.

Todd English's outpost at the Walt Disney World Dolphin is really just *too-cool-for-school*. It's worth the cost of dinner simply to check out this stunning, underwater-like fantasyland adorned with air bubble light fixtures, gauzy swaths of silver-blue organza curtains, and carpet mimicking an expanding drop of water. Seductive seating of chocolate brown leather booths interspersed with mango orange chairs completes the picture.

The menu, as captivating as the surroundings, is fresh, inventive, and ultramodern with much of the ingredients brought in from small farms and handled with tender loving care. Meals here begin with a basket of savory house-made bread with nice, salty butter. It's hard not to love the amazingly fresh sashimi, but for a starter I just can't seem to pass up the irresistible tempura *haricot verts* served with truffle aioli, or the smoky jumbo shrimp with savory white cheddar grits and tiny slices of pickled okra.

Entrées here are hit-or-miss. The best choice on the menu really is the miso-glazed Hawaiian sea bass updated with trendy black garlic and sticky soy. So imagine my surprise when I tasted a new preference—super-flavorful, Cajun-style swordfish rubbed with spicy seasonings sitting atop a delish Tasso and rock shrimp-spiked risotto surrounded by plump littleneck clams. Skip the simply fish . . . even the warm crabmeat and Dijon mustard sauce can't save it from blandness. And tell the chef to go light on the salt—a scallop pasta special was inedible due to over salting. Those that prefer meat can't go wrong with the filet, charred on the outside, juicy and tender on the inside, a dab of horseradish *crème fraiche*, and an amazing side of ultra-caramelized potatoes.

CARA'S TIP: For a light meal and cocktails head to Bluezoo's svelte bar with its mellow vibe where you'll pick your choices from a touchscreen menu. Those traveling with small children should take advantage of two hours of complimentary childcare at Camp Dolphin (one child per adult entrée). Be sure to reserve ahead and enjoy your time alone. Valet parking is complimentary when dining here.

SAMPLE MENU ITEMS

Dinner entrées: Pork collar, creamed corn, country ham, and tomato cornbread salad; char-grilled chicken, *pomme fondant*, garlic spinach, celery root, and chicken jus; beef tenderloin, marble potatoes, charred dandelion greens, and horseradish *crème fraiche*; fish grilled on a *teppanyaki* grill with your choice of sauce; tuna *di calabria*, polenta, artichoke mushroom ragout, and *calabrese* chili vinaigrette.

Victoria & Albert's

Contemporary American cuisine with classical influences at Disney's Grand Floridian Resort. Dinner only with reservations mandatory; call (407) 939-7707. Jackets for gents (tie optional) and dinner attire for women. Open daily with two seating times in the dining room: 5:45 to 6:30 p.m. and 9:00 to 9:45 p.m.; July and August one seating daily, 6:45 to 8:00 p.m.; one seating only for Chef's Table and Queen Victoria's Room.

It might be surrounded by theme parks but Victoria & Albert's offers only perfectly refined cuisine. Overseen by the brilliant Chef de Cuisine Scott Hunnel and awarded the AAA FiveDiamond 14 years in a row and the Wine Spectator Best of Award of Excellence year after year, this is Disney's true gastronomic temple. And better yet, it seems to keep reinventing itself, raising the bar even higher each and every year.

Tables are set with only the finest in Frette linens, Royal Doulton and Wedgewood china, and Italian Sambonet silver, and a seasonal prix fixe menu includes six sumptuous courses, all small, served by an ultra-professional waitstaff while a harpist performs (although the harp music sometimes feels a bit over the top). Over the course of two and a half hours indulge in one exemplary dish after another, every morsel with its own distinct flavor, no one ingredient overwhelming another—food here is simply a work of art. And those non carnivore-eaters will swoon over the six-course vegetarian menu, a rare find. The menu changes on an almost weekly basis so don't ever expect to have the same of anything on a return visit, but this I can promise you, your meal will be nothing but sigh-inducing perfection.

Those seeking a truly special evening should book the Chef's Table set in an alcove in the kitchen, a spot perfect for an up-close, behind-the-scenes look at Disney's top chef in action. Or for a more formal and intimate experience with the same outstanding menu as the Chef's Table try the Queen Victoria's Room where up to twelve spectacular courses are served, each more fantastic than the last. Add the wine pairings to make it a meal of a lifetime.

CARA'S TIP: Children younger than ten are not allowed so be sure to pre-book a sitter.

SAMPLE MENU ITEMS

Appetizers and first course: Masago-crusted gulf shrimp with *ponzu* vinaigrette; roasted Long Island duck with pomegranate, pistachios, and hearts of palm; onion ash-crusted black grouper with Zellwood corn ragout; braised oxtail and cherry ravioli with roasted red peppers; roasted quail with parsnip puree and fig *gastrique*; diver scallop, Maine mussel, and lobster cioppino with fennel nage.

Entrées: Marcho Farms veal tenderloin with baby tomatoes and artichokes; *poulet rouge* with chanterelle mushrooms and gnocchi; herb crusted lamb with caramelized turnips and Swiss chard; Australian Kobe beef tenderloin with smoked garlic potato puree (additional $35).

Desserts: Meyer lemon and blood orange purse with blackberry violet sherbet; Tanzanian chocolate timbale with orange scented milk chocolate gelato; Hawaiian Kona chocolate soufflé; caramelized banana *gâteau*; vanilla bean crème brûlée; Grand Marnier soufflé.

Vegetarian menu: Chiogga beet carpaccio with peaches and Burrata cheese; vegetable ravioli with tomato broth; porcini mushroom soup with wild mushroom bread pudding; red cabbage tart, bamboo rice blend, and chef's garden vegetables; Colston Bassett stilton, Sottocenere *al tartufo*, Gouda Reypenaer XO and Flagship Reserve cheddar.

Yachtsman Steakhouse

Steak at Disney's Yacht Club Resort. Dinner only; resort casual dress. Open daily 5:00 to 9:30 p.m.

Not the most atmospheric restaurant, but white linen-topped tables, red leather chairs, and walls of framed pictures depicting the cattle drives of the Old West set the scene for a Disney-style, unfussy steakhouse. The in-house butcher can be seen next to the hostess stand hand cutting chops in a glassed-in dry aging room, and just around the corner is the open kitchen where you can watch the wood-fired grill sizzling away with aromatic steaks. After being seated you must take care not to eat so many of the melt-in-your-mouth onion popover rolls that you ruin your dinner, although they are awfully hard to resist as is the soft and spreadable roasted garlic.

Begin your meal with an interesting house-made charcuterie composed of tasty morsels like lamb sausage, suckling pig, veal sweetbread terrine, and steak tartare. You might decide to accompany that with a Caesar salad, nothing exciting unless you count the addition of thin-sliced and flavorfully cured Coppa Secca.

Please take my work on this—go ahead and order the restaurant's specialty steak, an incredible New York strip. Dry-aged for seven days this is one flavorful piece of meat, served with a brandy peppercorn sauce and stacked potato-cheese gratin loaded with Carmody, a buttery cheese, and studded with thyme. Actually, it may be the most perfectly cooked steak I've ever tasted. Now if you prefer a juicier cut of meat then definitely go with the char-grilled ribeye covered with melting red wine butter. Although it tends to be a winter offering, another favorite is the braised beef, giant-sized ravioli sprinkled with interestingly crisp wild mushrooms and surrounded by a luscious cheddar fondue.

For sides it's pretty hard to resist the truffled macaroni and cheese, this version made with orecchiette and creamy Reypenaer gouda; for something a bit less caloric go with the roasted Brussels sprouts. It seems that the must-try dessert here is habanero-infused flourless chocolate cake, and it certainly had a zing to it although cooled a bit by mango compote and an icy lime sorbet; not exactly my cup of tea but guests love it. The international wine list, strong on California selections, is a Wine Spectator Award of Excellence winner.

CARA'S TIP: Ask to sit in the circular dining room overlooking Stormalong Bay, the Yacht Club Resort's lovely pool, as well as distant views of Epcot's Illuminations fireworks.

SAMPLE MENU ITEMS

Dinner entrées: 28-oz. Porterhouse with herb fries and roasted garlic butter; New England striped bass with salsify, persimmon, fennel, and broccoli rabe; braised short rib with baby root vegetables, heirloom apple, and natural jus; beef hangar steak with herb butter and truffle frites; handmade ricotta *cavatelli* pasta of wild mushrooms, fall squash, root spinach, and truffles.

Best Downtown Disney Dining

Fulton's Crab House

Seafood at Downtown Disney Marketplace. Lunch and dinner; call (407) WDW-DINE, or (407) 934-8888, for advance reservations. Open daily 11:30 a.m. to 11:00 p.m.

To dine here you literally have to walk the gangplank to the moored riverboat restaurant dominating the waterfront at Downtown Disney Marketplace. The concept is finding fresh, seasonal seafood from worldwide ports and serving them in traditional, appetizing ways. Begin your feast with sourdough bread, a perfect accompaniment to the dramatic, double-decker chilled seafood tower of Alaska king crab, seasonal oysters, jumbo shrimp, and Maine lobster served with cocktail and remoulade sauces. Or maybe the lobster corn dogs (sounds too good to pass up, doesn't it?), but skip the crab and lobster bisque; too much thickening agent for my taste.

If you can't decide on which delicacy to order as an entrée try a sampler of blue crab-stuffed shrimp and pan-roasted scallops with lemon beurre blanc. While crab cakes are always a temptation, and these are served with an exceptional remoulade sauce and fried green tomatoes, they really do have a bit too much filler. And although the fish and chips are made with authentic cod, they probably should be skipped; too thickly battered and too greasy. All in all I think the fresh, seasonal fish is the ticket, always good and certainly a no-brainer choice, or at least a side order of the not-to-be-missed fried gulf shrimp. Lobster mac 'n' cheese is sort of a natural choice whenever it's on just about any menu, but I miss the twice-baked potato which now seems to have vanished.

As for dessert there really isn't a better option than the key lime pie with its almond-studded graham cracker crust, rich center, and lightly browned meringue topping.

BREAK FOR LUNCH

If you're looking for a mid-day escape from the Walt Disney World theme parks, here are some great options:

- **Kona Café** at Disney's Polynesian Resort, just a monorail or boat ride away from the Magic Kingdom, for Pan Asian food overlooking the lobby's tropical profusion. Try the traditional Hawaiian plate lunch with your choice of pan fried chicken or teriyaki steak served with sticky rice and pasta salad, or the brothy Asian noodle bowl.

- **Whispering Canyon Café** at Disney's Wilderness Lodge, a boat ride over from the Magic Kingdom, for a slow-smoked pulled pork sandwich or Kansas City-style slow-smoked pork ribs. At lunchtime the hootin' and hollerin' is at a minimum.

- **The Wave** at Disney's Contemporary Resort, only one monorail stop from the Magic Kingdom, where healthy, whole grain options and a relaxed atmosphere are on the menu. Choose the fresh, sustainable fish on a bed of luscious edamame stew.

- **Grand Floridian Café** at Disney's Grand Floridian Resort, a boat or monorail ride from the Magic Kingdom, for super salads and oversized sandwiches, not to mention a chance to check out Disney's flagship resort. If you're not dieting try the Grand Sandwich, an open-faced hot turkey and ham wonder topped with rich Boursin cheese sauce and fried onion straws.

- **Fulton's Crab House** at Downtown Disney where fresh seafood is served in a docked Mississippi riverboat. Good choices include lobster corn dogs, a crab club BLT sandwich, or a cold seafood platter with Alaska king crab legs, Maine lobster, shrimp, and Apalachicola Bay oysters served with cocktail and remoulade sauces.

- **T-Rex Café** at Downtown Disney for roaring dinosaurs, Ice Cave dining, and a fantastic, fun atmosphere that can't be beat. Try the tomato basil soup followed by tribal fish tacos.

CARA'S TIP: Outdoors under the stars or indoor dining are the choices, but ask to sit in the bow of the boat for perfect sunset views.

SAMPLE MENU ITEMS

Lunch entrées: Ahi tuna Cobb salad; lobster/shrimp roll; crab cake BLT; Florida grouper sandwich; blackened fish tacos; fried seafood combination of beer battered cod, shrimp, and fries; steakhouse burger.

Dinner entrées: Key West yellowtail snapper; cedar planked and roasted North Atlantic salmon; ultimate crab and lobster experience; Narragansett Rhode Island lobster; snow crab legs; cowboy ribeye with *chimichurri*; ratatouille pasta; lobster ravioli.

Portobello

Italian cuisine at Downtown Disney Marketplace. Lunch and dinner; call (407) WDW-DINE, or (407) 934-8888, for advance reservations. Open daily 11:30 a.m. to 11:00 p.m.

A bit of a gem in the midst of many Downtown Disney so-so restaurants has always been Portobello. Starters such as the too-simple arugula and fennel salad or the ho-hum Caprese should be skipped in lieu of a thinly sliced, wood roasted portobello mushroom on a bed of rich, rosemary-balsamic reduction atop creamy polenta sprinkled with a light touch of Gorgonzola. Then again, others might argue that the Sambuca shrimp is the first course ticket, nice and garlicky with a hint of anise.

The old standard here is rigatoni *calabrese*, a dish I fell in love with on my first visit over twenty years ago, one that is still my favorite. Featuring Italian sausage, kalamata olives, mushrooms, tomatoes, and escarole with perfectly al dente pasta, the sauce has just the right touch of richness without being overwhelming. Now, I wish I could say the same for the chewy and undercooked gnocchi, and worse, topped with an overwhelming shredded pork *ragù*. Much better would have been a basic Bolognese sauce or perhaps tiny pork meatballs instead of a heavy and unappetizing dish.

The grilled fish of the day, whatever it might be, is crispy-skinned with a side of chunky oregano-flavored roasted potatoes topped with a vinaigrette-tossed arugula and pickled red onions. Chicken *pizzaiola*, an updated version of the traditionally heavy chicken parmesan, is made fairly healthy with a flour-dusted and sautéed chicken breast in a light, garlicky broth with a hint of oregano and anchovies topped with freshly chopped tomatoes, slivers of garlic, a dusting of capers, and just a touch of melted cheese. Order a side of sautéed zucchini, red onions, and green peppers to go along with it and you'll be pleased as punch. Then again, there are the paper-thin crusty pizzas brought out bubbling hot from the restaurant's wood burning ovens. Decisions, decisions.

The super rich cappuccino gelato is still amazing after years on the menu (used to be espresso gelato, but little has changed), so just go for it and save yourself the trouble of deciding. On pleasant evenings ask to dine on the outdoor patio overlooking the lake.

SAMPLE MENU ITEMS

Lunch entrées: Penne pasta Bolognese, slow cooked beef and pork meat sauce; house made artisan lasagna with spinach, ricotta, mozzarella, and spicy tomato; chicken farfalle pasta with snow peas, asparagus, tomatoes, and Parmigiano cream sauce; *quattro formaggi* pizza with mozzarella, gorgonzola, Parmigiano, Fontina, and sun dried tomatoes; meatball sub sandwich; mozzarella stuffed beef and veal burger.

Dinner entrées: Flat iron steak with grilled arugula, olive oil, and wood-roasted tomatoes; grilled pork chop with polenta and Florida sweet pepper vinegar; mahi mahi and polenta with zucchini ribbons in tomato seafood broth; grilled pork tenderloin with poached Tuscan beans and farmer's market vegetables; handcrafted ricotta and spinach filled ravioli, tomato, basil, and toasted garlic; black fettuccini with shrimp, garlic, tomatoes, and asparagus.

The Dining Room at Wolfgang Puck Grand Café

Contemporary cuisine at Downtown Disney West Side. Dinner only; resort casual dress; call (407) WDW-DINE, or (407) 938-9653, for advance reservations. Open daily 6:00 p.m. to 10:00 p.m.

This is Downtown Disney's most upscale dining choice, where great food comes with lovely views through giant picture windows of Village Lake and much of the surrounding complex. Located upstairs in a four-restaurant complex, a quiet, hushed atmosphere prevails, much different than its downstairs sister café although some of the same menu items are to be found at both restaurants, including Wolfgang Puck's famous smoked salmon pizza and butternut squash soup.

Dive into the divine, creamy oyster chowder, super smoky with bacon and Pernod, swimming with cubes of potatoes and giant, plump oysters, all topped with a hefty sprinkling of herbs; rich, but not overwhelming and quite the pleaser. Long on the menu here is an organic baby beet, arugula salad adorned with Humboldt Fog goat cheese and crunchy toasted pistachios, the pistachios the icing on the cake so to speak, drizzled with a light and tasty vinaigrette. Nicely seared to a golden brown the firm, plump scallops come with an Asian slant and a bit of spice, with zingy roasted and charred eggplant and a smidgen of Thai coconut broth. Now if you choose the butternut squash soup think about saving it for dessert, so rich and sweet it is with cinnamon and, believe it or not, a swirl of maple syrup and brown sugar (forget that it more than likely also has a quart of cream in each and every bowl).

A filet mignon arrived overcooked, was promptly returned, and arrived at the correct temperature the second go-round. While it was made ever tastier if not a bit overpowering with its port wine reduction, it didn't light a candle to the best garlic mashed potatoes on the planet. A hickory smoked pork chop was savory with a bourbon honey mustard glaze, but again, it was somewhat overcooked making it drier than necessary although an accompanying sweet potato puree was a perfect match with only a mere hint of sweetness.

While a bit passé, the warm lava cake served with a scoop of vanilla ice cream and a dollop of fresh cream is the favored dessert in my opinion; although the somewhat cloying carrot cake, whose claim to fame is batter that has been stirred for an hour before baking, is what is touted as the restaurant's signature dessert.

SAMPLE MENU ITEMS

Dinner entrées: Steamed seasonal fish "Hong Kong Style" with bok choy, shiitake mushrooms, snap peas, and chili oil with jasmine rice; spicy beef goulash, braised beef with sautéed *spaetzle* and parsley; *wiener schnitzel*, a breaded pork cutlet with warm potato salad, fresh arugula, and mustard-caper sauce; seared salmon with lobster butter and seasonal vegetables; grilled Ecuadorian mahi with citrus fennel salad and cherry tomato vinaigrette.

Best Restaurants Near Walt Disney World

Bull & Bear

Steaks at the Waldorf Astoria Orlando. Dinner only; call (407) 597-5500 for reservations or online at opentable.com; smart casual dress. Open daily, 6:00 to 10:00 p.m.

Not surprisingly, the décor at the Waldorf Astoria's signature restaurant is old world and pretty sensational. From the dark mahogany and rich leather banquettes to the starched white tablecloths, gleaming goblets, and stellar service, it's sure to please if atmosphere is what you are seeking. A stylish and roomy bar is the place to begin where fine wine and high-end cocktails are de rigueur.

Move on to the restaurant proper for dazzling presentation and food (forget the cocky waiter I had last go-round who was just a bit too full of himself). Tender and tasty is the signature Veal Oscar with crisp asparagus and Maryland lump crab in a pool of béarnaise. Or try the phenomenal lamb loin with a porcini crust served with a rich lentil cassoulet and rosemary mustard sauce. Steakhouse traditionalists shouldn't resist the Tomahawk, a 36 ounce beauty, dry-aged 32 days, perfectly cooked, and sliced tableside; to add excitement to perfection, four sauces are served along with the cut: peppercorn cognac, roasted shallot bordelaise, *béarnaise*, and Bull and Bear steak sauce.

In true Waldorf fashion there's something for everyone, and although it is a steakhouse, fish entrées certainly do not disappoint; try the nice, crispy rockfish with a flavorful roasted corn and crab medley and an unusual corn *spaetzle*. And if you're really feeling decadent order the side of macaroni and cheese with pancetta, or the amazing au gratin potatoes, wrapped in a crispy coating of shredded potatoes, much like a bird's nest. I still have dreams about the hot beignets with two dipping sauces of chocolate and Madagascar custard, while my dining companions feel you really can't visit a place like this without ending with a chocolate soufflé.

✦ WALT DISNEY WORLD FOR THE WINE AFICIONADO

There's an amazing array of restaurants at Walt Disney World with truly impressive wine lists. Here are the best of the lot:

- **Victoria & Albert's at Disney's Grand Floridian Resort.** The diverse and quite extensive array of global wine is also available in pairings with a glass served for each of six courses ($65 additional per person).

- **Jiko at Disney's Animal Kingdom Lodge.** Here you'll find the most exclusive South African wine list in the country with the bonus of a rich Reserve list.

- **Citricos at Disney's Grand Floridian Resort**. An acclaimed global list includes Californian and French vintages. Wine flights and an accompanying wine suggestion is listed for every item on the menu, and iconic, epic wines are available by the ounce for tasting.

- **Artist Point at Disney's Wilderness Lodge**. An exclusive Pacific Northwest wine list is this restaurant's claim to fame with many choices available by the glass. You'll even find Oregon *sake* offered.

- **California Grill at Disney's Contemporary Resort**. Eighty wines offered by the glass, all accompanied by spectacular views. With 248 wines on the list and ten varieties of *sake*, it requires a team of 20 sommeliers to handle it all.

- **Shula's at the Walt Disney World Dolphin**. Offering a great selection of champagnes, single vineyard wines, and a big, bold list heavy on California vintages.

- **Todd English's Bluezoo at the Walt Disney World Dolphin**. Here you'll choose from a list heavy on California and French wines. Love the selection of Opus One.

- **Il Mulino at the Walt Disney World Swan**. The best selection of Italian wine on property, but California wine lovers need not despair since they represent a respectable portion of the list.

CARA'S TIP: Those wanting a nice view should ask for a table in the glassed-in front room with vistas of the golf course. And plan on a long meal here where service sometimes is excruciatingly slow.

SAMPLE MENU ITEMS

Dinner entrées: Pan roasted Loch Duarte salmon; pan-roasted Dover sole with lemon butter, capers, and roasted mushrooms; chicken confit and cheese mashed potatoes; 16 oz. Delmonico rib eye; beef Syrah wine-glazed short rib; Allen Brothers Prime, 45-day dry aged, 16 oz. New York sirloin.

La Luce

Italian cuisine at the Hilton Orlando Bonnet Creek. Dinner only; call (407) 597-3600 for reservations or online at opentable.com; smart casual dress. Open daily, 5:00 to 11:00 p.m.

If you're looking for Orlando's best Italian cuisine, look no further than this sleek restaurant at the Hilton Bonnet Creek, just a 5-minute drive from Disney's Hollywood Studios and Disney's BoardWalk. The pizza has a cult following with my top choice the Quattro Formagio with crispy prosciutto. Or for lighter fare try the olive *fritte*, lightly fried nuggets of battered olives paired with sautéed Marcona almonds, almost too unusual to pass up. Accompany this with a salad of delicate beets, green beans, shaved fennel, and avocado tossed in Roquefort vinaigrette.

Follow with the insanely delicious lasagna con *polpettine* prepared with basil, ricotta, Parmigiano, and tomato sauce, dotted with tiny, tender meatballs. Or the fettuccine *all lina* with a rich porcini and pork *ragù* sauce tossed in tender, homemade pasta. If it's fish you're craving, opt for an unfussy wild salmon filet simply seared with a chive butter sauce and pureed potatoes.

SAMPLE MENU ITEMS

Dinner entrées: Grilled Berkshire pork chop with roasted potatoes, garlic, broccolini, and aged balsamic; *bistecca tagliata*, sliced porcini-rubbed ribeye with shaved Reggianno; braised lamb shank with Tuscan bean *ragù* and mint *gremolata*; roasted half chicken with polenta;

saltimbocca, prosciutto, sage, Fontina, and sherry jus; ricotta ravioli with pesto and lemon cream or tomato sauce; farfalle con *funghi* pasta with wild mushrooms, artichokes, thyme, and truffle cheese.

SECTION TWO

DISNEY CRUISE LINE

Honored as the #1 Large-Ship Cruise Line For Families by the readers of Travel + Leisure and all four ships among the top large cruise ships in the world by Condé Nast Traveler readers, you just can't make a better decision to sail on Disney Cruise Line for a family-oriented vacation at sea. While there are four ships in Disney Cruise Line's repertoire, for luxury I suggest choosing from the two newest ships, Disney Dream and Disney Fantasy, both of which offer the very best Disney Cruise Line has to offer.

Parents seeking time alone while still enjoying a quality family vacation will absolutely go crazy for this cruise line where there are many shared family experiences as well as adult exclusive activities. And children will adore the supervised Youth Clubs providing an amazing array of interactive programs where kids have fun each and every day of their vacation. Where else can you find Disney characters at every turn and entertainment Disney-style galore around every corner while enjoying a vacation at sea?

While mostly geared toward adults traveling with children, both ships offer many adults-only experiences for those 18 and older (note the drinking age onboard is 21) including their very own beach area at Disney's Castaway Cay (Disney's 1,000-acre private Bahamian island), adults-only restaurants, an exciting nightclub area, adults-only pool, and a relaxing spa. There are also singles socials, a variety of seminars on wine tasting, art, and health, Disney's Art of Entertaining seminars, as well as tours of the ship. And I haven't yet mentioned a casino have I? If I did then I was sorely mistaken; you'll find nothing of the sort onboard a Disney cruise ship. I must say that adults without children would probably be better off finding a different kind of cruise, unless that is, you really love all things Disney in which case this cruise line would be a perfect fit. Regardless, do come prepared to vacation with hordes of little ones; it just can't be avoided, although Disney does such a great job in keeping children happy that you won't see too many misbehaved children onboard.

Combining a Walt Disney World land package with a Disney cruise gives you the best of both worlds. Departing from nearby Port Canaveral are three- and four-night cruises to the Bahamas (with occasional variations offered) on the Disney Dream as well as seven-night cruises to both the western and eastern Caribbean on the Disney Fantasy, a perfect way to extend your Walt Disney World vacation.

For reservations call your travel advisor, Disney Cruise Line at (800) 951-3532, or go online to DisneyCruise.disney.go.com for more information and reservations.

PLANNING YOUR DISNEY CRUISE LINE VACATION

Planning a Disney cruise, just like a land vacation, requires forethought as well. You'll need help choosing the perfect stateroom, something that is a true art form. You'll need to know when your shore excursions, spa treatments, adults-only dining, etc. is available to reserve. You'll want to be sure to bring along proper documentation. A travel advisor who specializes in Disney cruises can prove invaluable. They will keep track of what needs to be done when, saving you plenty of stress along the way. An Authorized Disney Vacation Planner agency can make the difference between a mediocre vacation and an excellent one. For your Disney Cruise Line vacation call Glass Slipper Concierge at (866) 725-7595 or go online at GlassSlipperConcierge.com.

Disney Cruise Line Reference Guide

Alcoholic Beverage Policy. The drinking age aboard ship is 21 and a valid photo I.D. is required.

Gratuities. Gratuities can be paid ahead of your cruise or automatically added to your account on embarkation day. The suggested amounts are assessed for your Server, Assistant Server, Head Server, and Stateroom Host/Hostess. If you like you can modify or add gratuity amounts or pay in cash at the Guest Services Desk onboard. In addition, a fifteen percent gratuity is automatically added to any bar, beverage, wine, and deck-service receipt.

Dietary requests. Dietary requests such as kosher and low-sodium, as well as special requests regarding allergies to gluten or wheat, shellfish, soy, lactose or dairy, peanuts, tree nuts, fish, eggs, corn, or other foods can be accommodated at table-service restaurants. Detail any dietary requests at the time of booking.

Flowers and such. Flowers, gift packages, and bon voyage wine can be delivered to your stateroom if pre-ordered at least 48 hours prior to sailing. Call (800) 601-8455 or go online at DisneyCruise.disney.go.com/gifts-and-amenities.

Guests with disabilities. All ships offer accessible staterooms and suites equipped with 32" (minimum) doorways, ramped bathroom thresholds, open bed frames, additional phones in the bathroom and on the nightstand, bathroom and shower handrails, fold-down shower seats, hand-held showerheads, emergency call buttons, and lowered towel and closet bars.

Most guest areas aboard ship—including theaters, restaurants and shops—are accessible. In some cases such as on tender services or in pools, guests may need to transfer from their wheelchairs. This will require the assistance of a member of their party, so it is a good idea for guests to plan to sail with someone who can physically assist them when necessary. There will be times where it may be impossible for guests using wheelchairs to transfer to the tenders due to rough water.

Special viewing areas for scheduled onboard activities are available for guests using wheelchairs. Contact a crew member outside the *Walt Disney Theatre* at least 10 minutes prior to show time for assistance with accessible seating.

Assistive listening systems are offered in theaters and other performance venues, show scripts are available at Guest Services, and communication kits containing open captioning on a guest's stateroom TV may be activated by contacting Special Services prior to sailing or contacting Guest Services once onboard the ship. Common area video monitors may also be available with captions, but due to satellite limitations, not all video sources or television signals are available with a caption playback option. On Castaway Cay are paved pathways throughout the main promenade, sand wheelchairs available free of charge and on a first-come, first-served basis, wheelchair equipped trams, and accessible restrooms.

ECV rentals can be arranged with Special Needs At Sea. SpecialNeedsAtSea.com or call 800-513-4515.

Internet and Phone Services. Guests traveling with a laptop or notebook can utilize wireless Internet at the Vista Café and Cove Café (adults only). While slower, Internet connectivity also sometimes works in your stateroom. A fee is accessed for Internet services.

In addition to dedicated locations where you can take advantage of ship-to-shore calling, Cellular at Sea, available from most cell phone carriers including AT&T, Sprint and T-Mobile, works throughout the ship and in staterooms; beware that international roaming rates apply. Check with your carrier before traveling to see if a roaming package is available for your cruise. To avoid the unwanted costs associated with data downloads it's best to keep your wireless devices turned off during your cruise.

Each stateroom is equipped with a pair of Wave Phones that allows you to call and text your fellow travelers both onboard and at Disney's Castaway Cay. From your Wave Phone you can call any shipboard phone, stateroom phone, or other Wave Phone. Additional phones are available for a fee.

Laundry and dry cleaning. Self-service, coin-operated washers and dryers are located on most passenger decks along with detergent and ironing equipment; personal irons cannot be brought aboard. In addition, same-day dry cleaning and laundry service is available with stateroom pickup.

Medical care. A physician and nurse are on call 24 hours a day to provide basic medical services with standard prevailing fees charged.

Money matters. Guest Services offers foreign currency exchange and personal check cashing up to $100.

Parking. Operated by the Port Canaveral Port Authority, the gated Port Canaveral parking facility is staffed from 10:30 a.m. to 3:30 p.m. for guest parking. Parking costs are $60 for a 3-night cruise; $75 for the 4-night cruise; and $120 for a 7-night cruise. Preferred parking, located inside the secured area next to the vehicle drop off area, is also available for $25 per day.

Pets. No animals or pets except for assistance dogs licensed to guests are permitted onboard. Assistance dogs brought onboard must comply with National Regulations including the Regulations at the various ports of call.

Security. All bags are checked prior to entering the cruise terminal and at each port prior to embarkation.

Smoking. Smoking is not allowed in guest staterooms or verandahs and is prohibited in all interior spaces throughout the ship. Smoking is permitted at outside designated areas throughout the ship.

What Should I Pack?

Disney Cruise Line daytime attire is very casual with shorts, capri pants, and t-shirts the norm. Even though the weather might be chilly in Port Canaveral, it warms up quickly once your cruise is underway. Only in mid-winter will you need to bring a combination of summer and somewhat warmer clothes for the sail-away party and those chillier nights on deck. For the most part pack shorts, light-colored short-sleeved or sleeveless shirts, comfortable walking shoes for shore excursions, sunglasses, hat, a couple of bathing suits and a cover-up, flip-flops, water-resistant footwear, exercise clothing, and a rain jacket for daytime hours.

Most evenings dinner in the main dining rooms is cruise casual dress with women wearing a simple dress or casual pants and a stylish blouse with sandals, and men in comfortable khakis and a short-sleeve collared shirt with loafers or sandals. Even shorts are now allowed in the dining room. Seven night cruises have one formal night with the dress code a jacket or suit for men, and a gown or a dress for women, and one semi-formal evening with a suit or jacket for men and a dress or pantsuit for women.

Palo requires dress pants and a dress shirt–jacket is optional–for men, and a dress or pantsuit for women; no jeans, shorts, capri pants, flip-flops or tennis shoes. Only at Remy is a jacket required for men and a cocktail dress, pantsuit, or skirt/blouse for women; here too no jeans, shorts, capri pants, flip-flops or tennis shoes allowed.

Weddings and Vow Renewals at Sea

A growing number of couples are tying the knot on cruise ships with their entire wedding party in tow to take part in the celebration. Disney Cruise Line's Weddings and Vow Renewals can be performed either onboard or on Disney's private island, Castaway Cay. Included is the marriage license, on-site wedding coordinator, officiant, solo musician, flowers for the bride and groom, cake and champagne reception, dinner for two at Palo (the adults-only dining room) the night of the ceremony, and a $100 onboard credit. To book your Disney Cruise Line ceremony contact your travel advisor or call (321) 939-4610.

DISNEY CRUISING 101

- **Best Dining Experience:** *Remy* as the best adults-only choice with its multi-course, French-inspired cuisine although *Palo* runs a very close second. *Animator's Palate* as the best Main Dining Restaurant for dinner and a show that only Disney knows how to throw.

- **Best Nightclub**: You've gotta love *Skyline*, the adults-only cocktail lounge found on both the Dream and the Fantasy, where photographic views of the world's most famous cities magically transform before your very eyes.

- **Best Quiet Spot**: The *adults-only sun deck*, expanded on the Fantasy; and quiet *Cove Café* on both ships for specialty coffees and a comfy, quiet place to read and work.

- **Best Spirited Spot**: *Evolution* on the Dream and *The Tube* on the Fantasy, both great late-night dance scenes.

- **Best Activity**: Hands-down it has to be a wet and wild ride on *AquaDuck*!

- **Best View**: From the Royal Suite's huge wrap around verandah presenting gorgeous ocean vistas—simply paradise!

- **Best Value Experience**: The best deal around for a mere $16 per day is The Rainforest Room at Senses Spa, a coed thermal suite with steam bath, steam room, and sauna along with four sensory showers. In the solarium relaxation area soak in one of two hydropools and relax on heated ceramic lounging beds, all with gorgeous ocean views.

- **Best show**: *Disney's Aladdin—A Musical Spectacular* on the Fantasy, one of the most entertaining shows at sea.

- **Best Wow Experience**: An evening at *Remy* where the cuisine is as great as any 5-star restaurant back on shore.

- **Best Disney-only Experience**: Pirate Night culminating with spectacular fireworks at sea.

- **Best Splurge**: A concierge stateroom or suite with upgraded décor and a private lounge and sun deck just for concierge guests.

- **Best Room For Improvement**: As much as I hate to say it, the food in the main dining rooms, something that could use a major revamp

- **Best Thing to Skip**: Such seminars as "Secrets of a Flatter Stomach" and "Detox For Health" which are simply come-ons to sell products.

Disney Cruise Itineraries

The Disney Dream sails 3- and 4-night Bahamas itineraries from Port Canaveral, and, on rare occasions, special 5-night itineraries. Three-night itineraries come with a stop in Nassau and at Castaway Cay. Four-night sailings the same but with the additional day spent at sea.

On the Disney Fantasy are 7-night Caribbean itineraries also sailing from Port Canaveral where you'll either cruise the Western or the Eastern Caribbean. Western Caribbean sailings include ports of call in Grand Cayman, Cozumel, Mexico, Castaway Cay, and either Costa Maya, Mexico or Falmouth, Jamaica. Eastern Caribbean sailings stop in St. Thomas/St. John U.S. Virgin Islands, Castaway Cay, and either St. Maarten or San Juan, Puerto Rico.

Castaway Cay

Both ships include a stop, and on rare occasions even two stops, at Castaway Cay, Disney's private, 1,000-acre island paradise. I can think of nothing better than an entire day dedicated to fun in the sun, and that is exactly what Castaway Cay is all about. Here you'll find crystal-clear turquoise water, powdery white sand beaches, and swaying palm trees, a place where guests can swim, sail, sea kayak, snooze in a hammock, shop a Bahamian marketplace, dine at a barbecue buffet, and snorkel in special Disney-created "shipwrecks."

Four separate beaches cater to the needs of children, families, teens, and adults. Kids have their own supervised area, *Scuttle's Cove*, an extension of the onboard children's program for kid's ages 3-10, where a program of activities is sure to please; there's even a water play area for the little ones with a soft wet deck complete with pop jets, geysers, and bubblers. *Serenity Bay* is the adults-only beach for those age eighteen and older where there are private cabana massages, a fun tropical bar, and yet another barbecue buffet. The *Family Beach*, recently expanded to more than 700 feet, offers not only a huge expanse of sand but also *Pelican Plunge*, a floating platform in the lagoon just off shore with two water slides, loads of spray cannons, and a giant-size "bucket dump," plus *Spring-a-Leak*, a water play area featuring a washed-away beach dwelling theme of broken plumbing and dripping pipes, all concocted to help young guests cool off in the hot sun. *Hideout* is a teens-only activity area on the beach where they can hang out and soak up the sun while listening to music, or participate in the nearby beach volleyball and soccer areas; teens can also explore Castaway Cay during The Wild Side excursion designed just for them with snorkeling, biking, and kayaking.

For the fitness-minded there are trails and bike paths, Yoga on the Beach, Island Power Walks, and the popular Castaway Cay 5K, all designed to keep you moving for much of the day. Super shore excursions are on tap with such choices as *Captain Ray's Stingray Adventure*, parasailing, fishing charters, glass bottom boat voyages, a WaveRunner Adventure, and a catamaran snorkeling trip. For water sport devotees water cycles, paddleboats, kayaks, sailboats, and snorkel gear are available for rent. Those just wanting to kick back will find plenty of hammocks, beach chairs, and umbrellas, and several bars scattered throughout the island sell alcoholic and non-alcoholic tropical drinks. In-Da-Shade Games pavilion is the place for complimentary table tennis, billiards, foosball, and basketball, and most importantly, character greetings are in full force with plenty of opportunity to meet your favorites dressed out in beach regalia.

YOUR VERY OWN BEACH SHACK

Have you ever dreamed of your very own shack on a beach complete with access to a private stretch of white sand and a comfy hammock in which to while away the time? Then look no further. Castaway Cay offers 325-square-foot beach cabanas for rent on the far side of the Family Beach as well as at Serenity Bay, the adults-only beach. Accommodating up to six guests, cabanas offer shade and sun, comfortable lounge furnishings and a sofa, a swinging hammock, outdoor fresh water shower, plush beach towels, the use of floats, sand toys, and snorkel equipment, a bountiful fruit tray, an array of snacks, and a refrigerator stocked with soft drinks and water. Missing anything? Not to worry; just ring up your ever attentive attendant.

CARA'S TIP: If you book a beach cabana I would forgo planning an excursion for that day. By the time you are finished with your excursion much of the day is gone with very little time to enjoy your cabana. If having a beach cabana is a must on your list then it's almost mandatory you reserve a concierge stateroom whose guests get that advantage, along with Platinum Castaway Club members, of the ability to reserve beach cabanas 120 days prior to sailing with the others following behind at 105, 90, and 75 days respectively.

THE DISNEY DREAM
AND DISNEY FANTASY

The much anticipated Disney Dream came aboard the Disney Cruise Line fleet in January 2011, followed closely by the Disney Fantasy in March 2012, both fabulous additions built on the same classic style but with more contemporary amenities, public rooms, and staterooms. Both ships hold up to 4,000 passengers making them quite a bit larger than Disney's classic ships, the Disney Magic and Disney Wonder, which hold up to 2,700 passengers.

The Dream is a wow of a ship featuring an Art Deco atrium accentuated by a one-and-a-half story chandelier made of 24-carat gold and over 1,000 Swarkvski crystals. At the bottom of the atrium's curving staircase sits a bronze Admiral Donald ready to welcome each and every guest. Nice crisp lines define the look with decorative bronze friezes featuring favorite Disney characters edging the balconies of three atrium decks. Outstanding additions differentiating it from the Disney Cruise Line classic ships: an exciting nightclub concept, The District; two unique main dining restaurants as well as a second adults-only restaurant, Remy, one of the best dining rooms at sea; concierge stateroom and suite options located in a private, keyed access area with a concierge lounge and private sundeck; virtual portholes for inside staterooms; and the water coaster, Aqua Duck, one of the Dream and Fantasy's most popular features.

The equally gorgeous Fantasy is more Art Nouveau style whose décor includes peacock flourishes and flora and fauna patterns in vibrant shades of blue, green, and pink. A bronze Mademoiselle Minnie, dressed to the nines in 1930s evening attire, poses next to her steamer trunk in the towering atrium where fluted columns, a cascading chandelier of stained glass and crystal beads, the sweeping grand staircase, and Carrera marble floors make quite the impression. The new additions integral to the Dream are also onboard the Fantasy with even more enticing options: a Bibbidi Bobbidi Boutique where young princesses and princes are transformed into their favorite characters; an adults-only area, Satellite Falls, on the top deck; AquaLab, a children's water fun playground; and Europa, an all-new concept nightclub area.

Staterooms

Disney Dream and Disney Fantasy offer 1,250 staterooms and suites (70 percent with verandahs), among the first in the industry to be designed especially for families. In all except concierge staterooms and suites you'll find a nautical décor in a palette of blue and red with light wood furnishings. Standard stateroom baths are decorated in white tile with blue and red accents and most offer a bath-and-a-half design: one bath with a vanity, sink, and full tub/shower; and second bath with a vanity, sink, and toilet. The split-bath configuration makes all the difference when the entire family is trying to get ready at once, and many staterooms have a round tub/shower with a built-in seat perfect for giving little ones their bath.

Luggage fits nicely under the bed, there's loads of drawer and shelf space, and even the coffee table opens to reveal a hidden storage area. Closet space is sufficient but not as large as perhaps it could be.

Staterooms have crown molding, teak accents, and nice wood finishes. Super comfort queen beds are adorned with padded leather headboards and made with soft Frette linens and duvet along with plush pillows. All feature a 22" flat-screen TV, iPod docking station clock, mini fridge, H2O toiletries, electronic safe, and two Wave Phones for onboard, wireless communication.

Non-concierge Staterooms

Category 4, Deluxe Family Oceanview Staterooms with Verandah. Located on Decks 5 through 10 sleeping three to five with 299 square feet including the verandah. Queen bed with single sleeper sofa, wall pull-down bed (in most), and upper berth pull-down bed in some. Split bath with round tub and shower in most.

Category 5 and 6, Deluxe Oceanview Stateroom with Verandah. Located on Decks 5 through 10 sleeping three to four with 246 square feet including the verandah. Queen bed and a single sleeper sofa; pull-down bed in some.

Category 7, Deluxe Oceanview Stateroom with Navigator's Verandah. This stateroom's navigator's verandah is somewhat enclosed, typically smaller than other verandahs, and may have an obstructed view. Located on Decks 5 through 9 sleeping three to four with 246 square feet including the verandah. Queen bed and a single sleeper sofa; pull-down bed in some.

Category 8, Deluxe Family Oceanview Staterooms. Located on Decks 5 through 10, sleeping three to five with 241 square feet. On the upper decks you'll feel as if the ocean is practically inside the room due to their massive porthole window (no verandah) which takes up almost the entire ocean-side wall of the stateroom with in-porthole seating (Decks 5 and 6 have two smaller, less dramatic portholes). Baths have the bonus of a round tub/shower. Staterooms on Deck 6 have the lifeboats beneath you; not blocking the view but a bit distracting. Queen bed, single sleeper sofa, and pull-down bed in most; upper berth pull-down bed in some.

Category 9, Deluxe Oceanview Stateroom. Located on Decks 2, and 5 through 8 sleeping three to four with 204 square feet. Categories 9C and 9D have an obstructed view. Here portholes are smaller than those in a Deluxe Family Oceanview Stateroom. Queen bed and single sleeper sofa; pull-down bed in some.

Category 10, Deluxe Inside Stateroom without a verandah located on Decks 5 through 9 sleeping three or four with 204 square feet. I'm not much for inside staterooms, but those on the Fantasy and

Dream are the exception, each featuring a Magical Porthole providing a real-time view of the outside of the ship that reflects the actual stateroom's location, port or starboard. High-definition cameras placed on the exterior of the ship feed live video to an LCD flat-screen monitor with a stylized nautical frame cleverly disguised as a porthole. Be on the lookout for Disney animated characters that make cameo appearances, and when you want to sleep just turn it off with a flip of a switch. There's even an astrological night sky light option when the bunk is dropped down. Queen-size bed and single sleeper sofa; upper berth pull-down bed in some.

Category 11 Standard Inside Staterooms without a veranda are located on Deck 2 and 5 through 10 sleeping three or four with 169 square feet. These staterooms also feature a Magical Porthole, but do not have a split bath. Queen-size bed and single sleeper sofa; upper berth pull-down bed in some.

Concierge Staterooms and Suites

Shiny teak hallways, a dreamy palate of sea blue and chocolate brown, elegant furnishings, deep balconies . . . this is what concierge guests, located on Deck 11 and 12, have to look forward to on their Disney Dream or Disney Fantasy cruise. Those ensconced in the ship's twenty-one suites will also enjoy your choice of pillows as well as TVs integrated into bathroom mirrors. All suites come with two baths with the master featuring a giant-size whirlpool tub, rain shower, double sinks, and separate toilet area. Closets are walk-in, living areas feature a Blue-ray DVD player, and both the living and the master have a 42" HDTV. Balconies in all concierge staterooms and suites are deeper than standard staterooms and some balconies in the largest suites are absolutely gigantic, wrapping the front of the ship.

Reserving a concierge stateroom or suite on the Dream and the Fantasy also comes with the following extra special amenities: concierge lounge with continental breakfast, lunch of sandwiches and beverages, afternoon snacks, evening cocktails and appetizers, and after dinner dessert; 100 megabytes of complimentary Internet per stateroom; access to the concierge sun deck from 7:00 am to 10:00 pm which features misters, lounge chairs, and refreshments, open to guests age 18 or older;

in-stateroom breakfast, lunch or dinner available from any of the main dining rooms (guests of the Royal Suites have the additional choice of Palo in-stateroom dining); concierge pre-arrival services; priority tendering in applicable ports; and priority check-in.

Category R, Royal Concierge Suite with Verandah (also known as the Walt Disney and Roy Disney Suites). Enter these two art-deco-styled suites through a marble foyer to the living room where you can't help but notice sweeping views off the bow of the ship through floor-to-ceiling windows. Furnished in lovely burled wood, a curved chenille sofa in shades of gray, gold and green, an easy chair with ottoman, media library, 8-person circular dining table, wet bar, and oversized flat-screen TV, there are also two pull-down beds, a double and a single. In the kitchen are full-size refrigerator, sink, microwave, wine refrigerator, and cappuccino machine. The bedroom has a TV that raises and lowers at the foot of the queen bed, twinkling star lighting in the ceiling, reading nook, vanity, and walk-in closet as well as a master bath with double sinks, a rain/steam shower and whirlpool tub, a TV built into the mirror, and separate toilet area. Another full-size bath with a single sink and shower is found just off the entry. The massive, wrap-around verandah comes with a Jacuzzi tub and plenty of cushy lounge chairs. Located on Deck 12. Sleeps five in 1,781 square feet including the verandah.

For a splendidly luxurious family reunion it's possible to connect these two top suites with a central one-bedroom suite and two Family Concierge Staterooms to accommodate up to 25 guests with three suites and two staterooms basically wrapping the bow of the ship (the verandahs all open to each other if requested).

Category T, One-bedroom Concierge Suite with Verandah. This is a superb choice if a bit of additional room, a separate bedroom, and additional bath is what you crave. The entry hall features two closets and a full bath with shower, a queen-size bed and walk-in closet in the master, and a master bath offering two above-sink basins, whirlpool tub, separate shower, separate commode area, and TV built into the mirror. In the living area you'll find a four-person dining table, desk, double convertible sofa, and a single pull-down bed. This can connect to a Concierge Family Oceanview Stateroom to become a 2-bedroom suite.

Located on Decks 11 and 12 sleeping five in 622 square feet including the verandah.

Category V Concierge Family Oceanview Stateroom with Verandah. Much like the non-concierge, Category 4 stateroom, but with upgraded décor and a deeper balcony, these accommodations offer a queen bed, double sleeper sofa and upper berth pull-down bed in the living area, and a split bath featuring a round tub/shower. Located on Decks 11 and 12 sleeping five in 306 square feet including the verandah.

INTERACTIVE GAMING AT SEA

As at the Disney theme parks the interactive gaming craze continues at sea. Here is what's on order: The Midship Detective Agency, offered on both the Dream and the Fantasy, is an interactive game involving twenty-two pieces of enchanted art taking you from one end of the ship to the other in search of clues.

While the Dream has two different scenarios, "The Case of the Stolen Puppies" and "The Case of the Plundered Paintings" that the Fantasy also shares, the Fantasy adds a third mystery, "The Case of the Stolen Show" hosted by none other than the Muppets gang. Pick up your unique game card at the kiosk on Deck 5, Midship, and you are ready to begin work on this one-of-a-kind, self-paced journey.

Disney Cruise Line Dining

Disney's dining system, which rotates through each of three restaurants, is a unique one not found on any other cruise line. Seating is assigned and although you'll be moving to a different place each evening, your servers as well as table guests will travel with you. There are two seating times: Main Seating at 5:45 p.m. and late seating at 8:15 p.m. With so many children onboard the earlier Main Seating is always the most popular, so reserve your preference as soon your cruise reservation is made. Disney tries to put adults traveling without children together or at tables for two and families with children at their own table or with other families, but it doesn't always work out quite that way; if you are unhappy with your table assignment speak to the maître d' immediately and see what can be done about a table reassignment.

Evening attire changes nightly, but most if not all evenings are resort casual. Aboard cruises five nights or longer there are also semiformal and formal or black-tie-optional attire evenings.

Food in the standard dining rooms is fairly mediocre, something I feel Disney could work on; for goodness sakes, drop a line and get fresher fish for the table (lol)! There is an occasional exceptionally good dish, but again, note the word "occasional." That said, beyond the rotational dining restaurants are two terrific adult-exclusive restaurants choices, Palo and Remy. At the very least you should plan on one meal per restaurant or more per sailing. Only one dinner per restaurant can be pre-reserved, but if you want additional evenings head straight to the restaurant's podium after embarkation to make another night or two of reservations. I also recommend reserving at least one of the brunches offered on at-sea days at both Palo and Remy; both are truly extraordinary.

Main Dining Restaurants

Animator's Palate. Pacific Rim-inspired food with an American twist is just one of the specialties here at this one-of-a-kind restaurant where the entire dining room is transformed as the meal progresses. With more than 100 video monitors that change into virtual "windows," this is one fun place to dine. On both the Dream and the Fantasy animated Crush from *Finding Nemo* fame entertains guests with his own brand of "cool" craziness. But an additional dinner show, Drawn to Magic, takes place on the Fantasy where guests create their own animation drawing that just might become part of the show, all overseen by an animated Sorcerer Mickey.

Favorite appetizers are pasta "purses" filled with truffle cheese in a Champagne sauce, smoked salmon tartare, or the goat cheese tomato tart. Interesting entrées include the vegetarian black bean chipotle cakes topped with a tomato-cilantro salsa, ginger-teriyaki-dusted Angus beef tenderloin with wasabi mashed potatoes and a tamarind-barbecue reduction, and a veal chop brushed with Dijon mustard and dusted with

herbed breadcrumbs and a Barolo wine sauce. End with a white chocolate brownie cheesecake. Located on Deck 3, Aft; open only for dinner.

Sample Menu Items: Baked potato and cheddar cheese soup; creamy
butternut squash soup; seared red snapper with scallops and salsa *verde*;
white shrimp *pennette* Bolognese; jumbo shrimp salad; cookies and cream
sundae; crunchy walnut cake; no-sugar-added dense chocolate cake.

Enchanted Garden. Changing from a "daytime" garden setting to a
"nighttime" evening garden, this is one charming restaurant. The décor
is one of painted frescoes reminiscent of the French countryside, flower-
shaped lighting that blooms and changes color, an ever-transforming
sky, and a sparkling centerpiece fountain. Serving breakfast and lunch
buffets on select days and dinner each evening, good starters are golden
and red beet carpaccio with rice wine vinaigrette or the lobster ravioli.
Skip the pan-seared sea bass with fava beans and pea risotto in favor of
entrées such as caramelized sea scallops with a veal jus reduction and the
New York strip steak with a creamy double-baked potato. Located on
Deck 2, Midship.

Sample Menu Items: Ahi tuna and avocado tower; thyme and garlic
brioche filled with lobster, morels, and porcini mushrooms; cream of
asparagus soup; spinach and raspberry salad; roasted pork tenderloin
seasoned with smoked salt and served with citrus flavored polenta cakes;
pearl-barley cakes with shallots, leeks, and rosemary on a light saffron
sauce; sushi grade seared tuna on organic field greens with a wakame
and squid salad; steamed lemon buttermilk pudding; *sacher* chocolate
torte; banana foster sundae.

Royal Palace and Royal Court. Royal Palace on the Dream and Royal
Court on the Fantasy both offer French-inspired cuisine. Royal Palace
is a glamorous dining room with a resplendent chandelier made of glass
slippers and enchanted roses surrounded by portraits of Disney princesses and princes. The Fantasy's Royal Court features handcrafted Italian mosaics of the Disney princesses, marble columns, and throne-style
chairs. Both are open for dinner nightly with breakfast and lunch available on select days. Probably my favorite cuisine of the three main dining restaurants, such appetizers as the garlicky escargot and the bubbly
French onion soup are certain to please. A horseradish crusted salmon
or the flavorful double-cut rack of lamb with Dijon crust are both safe

Quiet Cove Pool. Kick back in quiet comfort at the adults-only pool and whirlpool on Deck 11, Forward. Plush lounge chairs and the adjoining Cove Bar and Cove Café add to the entertainment. Poolside massages are available if desired. My only issue is that it's located just off the entry to the Deck 11 concierge staterooms virtually requiring children to walk through it to and from their stateroom from the Mickey and Donald pools.

Satellite Falls. Found only on the Fantasy and wrapping around the forward Deck 13 is this very popular, adults-only sundeck. Its centerpiece is a circular splash pool topped with a gentle curtain of rain emitting from the ship's satellite transmitter. Much to the concierge guests dismay, this area has taken up part of the concierge sundeck which, only on the Fantasy, also lacks the forward view off the bow of the ship.

BIBBIDI BOBBIDI BOUTIQUE ON THE HIGH SEAS

Uber popular at Walt Disney World and Disneyland, the Bibbidi Bobbidi Boutique is also on the Disney Fantasy. Here too boys and girls get the full treatment with princess and pirate makeovers and unbelievably great costumes. Along with a bevy of princess do-overs and an Under the Sea transformation with swimsuit and "mermaid tail" for the girls, boys can opt for a Royal Knight package with hair gel, sword, and shield.

On Pirate Night this place is really hopping with swashbuckler transformations. Beards and bandanas, eye patches, fake teeth, swords, earrings, and scars are a kid's delight with several costumes to choose from. This is one popular place so reserve your space as soon as it becomes available.

Entertainment

Some of the best entertainment at sea is to be found on Disney Cruise Line. Broadway-caliber live musical shows have the added advantage of featuring many of your favorite Disney characters and music from beloved Disney feature films. And adding to the excitement are first-run movies, most of which are shown in 3-D, seen at the exceptional Buena Vista Theater.

For All Ages

Buena Vista Theater. Disney classics and first-run feature films are shown in this Art Deco-style, state of the art theater. 3-D is the ticket here along with an astounding Dolby Surround 7.1 sound system and dual-level stadium seating. If only the movies were this great at home!

Character Greetings. This is a highlight of the cruise for the young and young-at-heart. A bevy of characters is available at every turn (including on Castaway Cay) with your Personal Navigator listing their designated meeting places each day. Even occasional character surprise appearances are to be had. You can also dial 7-PALS from your stateroom phone or check the message board in the Lobby Atrium for more details. Get that autograph book ready!

D Lounge. Family lounge and nightclub offering a dizzying list of quality activities such as game shows, karaoke, dance parties, and fiestas.

Pirate Night. An entire evening dedicated to pirates. During the dinner hour wait staff are dressed as pirates (as are many enthusiastic guests), and pirate-themed dishes are offered with plenty of "ahoy matey" and "arrr!." On deck there are games, pirate tales, dancing, and skits with Mickey, Minnie, Goofy, and Captain Hook. The grand finale is Captain Jack Sparrow rappelling down the funnel with a Buccaneer Blast of fireworks at sea. Bring along your pirate attire from home if you're the type that likes to participate.

Walt Disney Theater. Three-level, 1,022-seat theater offering original live productions most evenings. On the Dream are super shows like *Villains Tonight*, a comic revue starring some of Disney's most beloved scoundrels; *Disney's Believe*, an enchanting journey into the world of Disney stories; and *The Golden Mickeys*, my favorite, featuring songs and characters from classic Disney films. On the Fantasy guests enjoy *Disney's Aladdin—A Musical Spectacular*, featuring Aladdin and his very funny genie, even a flying magic carpet scene; *Disney Wishes* where three best friends go on a magical journey down a wishing well; and, like on the Dream, *Disney's Believe*. Other evenings are filled in with comedians, magicians, and such. When you'll see the show depends on your dining time. Those with Main Seating attend the later show at 8:30 p.m. and those with Second Seating the earlier show at 6:15 p.m.

Adult Exclusive Entertainment

After the sun goes down the adults are ready to rock and roll sans children, and Disney offers a surplus of nightclub and lounge opportunities for those age 18 and older (note the drinking age onboard is 21). You might find family fun games and activities in these locations during the day, but after 9:00 p.m. it's for grownups only.

Meridian. On both the Dream and the Fantasy and located between Palo and Remy on Deck 12, Aft is this classy bar. Offering both indoor and outdoor seating and classic as well as contemporary cocktails, wine, champagne, single malt scotch, specialty coffees, and cognacs, it is one of the most sophisticated place for drinks onboard. In a clubby atmosphere where travel is the theme, décor here is one of leather club chairs, wood flooring, and overhead a constellation map lit with twinkling stars. Cigar lovers can partake in the outdoor seating area where there are superb ocean vistas. Martini, whiskey, and rum tastings often take place here in the afternoon hours on days at sea; check your Personal Navigator for details. A dress code is in place with dress pants and shirt for men and a dress or pant suit for women.

The District. The District nightclub area is specific to the *Disney Dream* with five different venues to choose from, each possessing its own unique theme, look, and signature drinks.

- **687.** A contemporary sports bar with multiple LED screens, colossal plasma TV, and digital surround sound, perfect for live sports broadcasts. A stamped metal ceiling, leather seating, warm wood finishes, and a circular bar along with ocean views that can be seen from the giant porthole windows is the perfect setting to enjoy a pint or two. Be forewarned, this place is at a high frenzy when a big game is on the agenda.

- **District Lounge.** Relaxing piano bar where soft music and vocals allow for conversation. Cozy, yet modern, it's a sophisticated stop where I always like to begin the evening.

- **Evolution.** If it's loud dance music you're looking for this is your place; just don't expect to carry on a conversation. DJ music including contemporary hits as well as classics with large video screens and special lighting effects add to the nightspot atmosphere.

- **Pink.** Here bubbles are the word, and the menu of champagne favorites takes the cake as do the champagne flute light fixtures, pink velvet sofas, and backlit glass "bubbles" with dancing pink elephants. Inspired by French champagne, a profusion of pink and gold in blown glass reminiscent of bottles bursting with bubbly explode from the ceiling behind the bar. The Elder-bubble should be your cocktail of choice mixed with raspberry vodka, elderflower syrup, and, of course, champagne.

- **Skyline.** Furnished like a lavish penthouse, this, my favorite place for a cocktail, features high-tech LED "windows" of an ever-changing, bird's-eye-view simulation of the world's great-est city skylines: New York, Chicago, Paris, Hong Kong, and Rio. Watch the traffic on city highways, a Ferris wheel spin-ning on a pier, and a sparkling Eiffel Tower as day transforms to night in real time and with amazing detail. As the skyline changes so does the music—one moment a Frank Sinatra song, the next a Brazilian samba with the drink menu reflecting signature concoctions from each of the feature cities. During daytime hours mixology classes are offered here on select days.

Europa. On the *Disney Fantasy* adult guests enjoy Europa nighttime entertainment district featuring sophisticated bars and trendy lounges inspired by European travel.

- **La Piazza.** This central lounge is reminiscent of Italy's outdoor plazas with a vintage carousel theme. It's a great place for cock-tails around the bar or in a cozy booth for two. There's even a classic Vespa with a sidecar for decoration.

- **O'Gill's Pub.** The ship's sports bar is fashioned after an Irish neighborhood pub with an atmosphere of dark woods, brass ac-cents, and great Irish beers. Enjoy a pint while catching the big game on high-def televisions.

- **Ooh La La.** A whimsical French boudoir ambience with velvet-tufted walls, Victorian furniture, and Louis XIV-style chaise lounges, this hot spot puts on the sparkle along with champagne and fun cocktails. Much like Pink on the Dream, it's a gal's dream-come-true with a "jewel box" feature bar mimicking diamond facets. During daytime hours wine and champagne tastings are offered here on select days; there's even a chocolate tasting one day at sea.

- **Skyline.** Much like the Skyline Bar on the Dream only a bit larger, the ever-changing city skylines featured are: Paris, London, Athens, Barcelona, Florence, St. Petersburg, and Budapest. Here too the music changes by city, and the drink menu reflects signature concoctions from each. During daytime hours mixology classes are offered on select days.

- **The Tube.** It's 1960s London where guests lounge on mod furniture, hang out in the red English phone booths, dance the night away on an illuminated Union Jack dance floor, and sip on London-inspired drinks. This is definitely the most hopping place onboard.

CELEBRATE AT SEA ON A DISNEY CRUISE

The holiday season is a popular time to enjoy a Disney cruise with all sorts of happenings onboard to celebrate.

- **Halloween on the High Seas Cruises.** It's a real scream aboard the Disney Dream between late September and October 31st. Spooky events and trick-or-treating with favorite Disney characters throughout the ship are on tap along with super special Halloween décor including a gigantic pumpkin tree in the atrium that magically sprouts up overnight! Don your costumes then dance the night away with Disney characters at Mickey's Calling All The Monsters Mouse-Querade Deck Party. There's even a Jack and Sally at the Nightmare Before Christmas—Sing Along and Scream!, and spooky movies at the Buena Vista Theater. Mask making and pumpkin carving are also on the agenda. Adults can join in the fun by entering a costume contest at a dance party where villains take over in Evolution Night Club. As you can see there is something for the entire family!

- **Thanksgiving at Sea.** A bountiful turkey feast and Disney characters dressed in traditional Thanksgiving attire makes for a festive day onboard. And don't worry about missing the traditional NFL football games. They will broadcast live on the giant Funnel Vision screen at the pool deck.

- **Very MerryTime Cruises.** Beginning in mid-November through early January both the Dream and the Fantasy transform into winter wonderlands with a nautical bent (yes, even in the sunny Caribbean!). The celebration kicks off with King Triton's tree lighting ceremony the first evening of your cruise, then fun galore with a tropical Deck the Deck Holiday Party featuring some favorite Disney characters. Holiday storytellers recite tales of Christmas, Hanukkah, and Kwanzaa; special meet and greets feature Disney characters in festive holiday outfits; and a midnight mass is held Christmas Eve with Christmas services the following day. Santa and his elves are on hand to greet young and old alike with surprises for the children on Christmas morning followed by caroling from the crew along with a traditional Christmas dinner. Even Castaway Cay gets into the act with a festive Christmas tree, "snow flurries," and tropical holiday music.

Disney Cruise Line Spa and Fitness

Senses Spa & Salon. After a few days of fun in the sun where better to head for relaxation than the ship's impressive spa? With a total of twenty-one treatment rooms you might be in luck and receive one boasting an ocean view. With a long list of luxurious services including many types of massage, body treatments, facials, and hydrotherapy, the usual suspects such as a Swedish Massage, Hot Stone Massage, and Elemis Facial are always available. But something unusual like the Bamboo Massage just might fit the bill. While you soak in essential oils, warmed bamboo sticks are rolled, slid, and massaged over your muscles, and, depending on your preference, done in either a deep tissue technique or with gentle strokes. There is a bit of awkwardness here and there when the bamboo just doesn't work well on certain parts of the body, but all in all a great massage. And since I've heard it can be slightly uncomfortable if you're on the thin side, I recommend scheduling your massage like I do after a few days of indulgence onboard.

Other good choices are wrap treatments performed on a dry float bed (you've got to try this!) for a feeling of weightlessness. Showers available in each of these treatment rooms are ideal preparation for an additional massage. The Ionithermie Cellulite Reduction treatment comes with a guaranteed inch loss, another perfect choice after days of overeating.

For the ultimate in pampering book a Spa Villa, where couples enjoy a private treatment room for side-by-side massages and an outdoor veranda complete with whirlpool tub and shower, strawberries and champagne, a tea ceremony, and grand ocean vistas. Or for a more run-of-the-mill retreat there's a 50-minute Couple's Swedish Massage in a standard room with two treatment tables. Don't forget that a Couple's Massage can also be had in one of the Castaway Cay cabanas on the adults-only beach.

The best deal around for a mere $16 per day is The Rainforest Room, a coed thermal suite where guests luxuriate in a Hammam (Turkish steam bath), a Caldarium (steam room), and Laconium (dry sauna). In the solarium relaxation area soak in one of two hydropools and relax on heated ceramic lounging beds, all with gorgeous ocean views. There are even four sensory showers, each with their own theme, scent, and sound (Rainforest, Water Fun, Tropical Thunder, and Cool Mist). Better yet, because it's limited to only thirty-five people per day, it's quite often practically empty of people.

Even the younger set gets in on the action at *Chill Spa*, an area of Senses specifically for teens with two treatment rooms offering such indulgences as a Hot Chocolate Wrap, Surfer's Scrub, Fabulous Fruity Facial, and Ice Cream Manicure and Pedicure. And if you want to find something to do with your teenager think about reserving either a Mother/Daughter or Father/Son massage.

Both the men's and women's locker rooms have a sauna room and a before and after-treatment relaxation room. Salon and nail services are available as is barbershop services. Even teeth whitening can be performed at Smile Spa. Reservations can be made online at Disneycruise. disney.go.com (concierge guests 120 days prior with the other following behind at 105, 90, and 75 days respectively).

> **CARA'S TIP:** If you have more than one treatment then you need to check out and pay after each one, a somewhat ridiculous policy. And tell me why there aren't brushes or combs in the locker room, something that is standard in most spas?

Fitness Center. The ocean view Fitness Center, located adjacent to Senses Spa, offers a nice variety of state-of-the-art equipment including ellipticals, treadmills, spinning machines, weight machines, and free weights. Also offered are group classes such as Sunrise Stretch, Fab Abs, Group Cycling, and, for the teen set, Fitness Frenzy. For a small fee try the Body Sculpt Boot Camp. Personal training is available for $75 per hour.

Disney Cruise Line Youth Clubs

With nearly an entire deck dedicated to children, it's a kid's (and parents!) dream-come-true. We all know what Disney does best, and that is catering to the needs of children. And when children are happy, so are parents. The youth activities and programs run from 9:00 a.m. to around midnight and are complimentary (with the exception of It's a Small World Nursery). Both lunch and dinner are provided if desired. Families with Second Seating dining will be happy to know that counselors come to the restaurants each evening at 9:00 p.m. to pick up children interested in a quick meal with their parents before heading over to the Youth Clubs for the evening.

Pre-registering online will eliminate the need to fill out paperwork later, but it is still necessary to complete final paperwork and obtain a wristband to participate on arrival. This can be done either in the cruise terminal while waiting to board, or once onboard in the Youth Club area. Children have the ability to move back and forth between *Disney's*

Oceaneer Club and *Disney's Oceaneer Lab* in order to experience all activities making it easy for friends and siblings to have fun together.

It's a Small World Nursery. This is the place for children ages three months to three years with a fee of $9 per hour per child ($8 per hour for each additional child in the same family). It's best to make advance reservations (the same schedule as shore excursion reservations) because only a limited number of infants and toddlers are accepted at one time.

Activities are unscheduled but include movie time, story time, and naptime; there is a separate room for naps. Children with special needs are welcome. Open from 9:00 a.m. to 11:00 p.m.

Oceaneer Lab and Oceaneer Club. Children ages three to twelve enjoy this incredible children's area, both interconnected to the other.

In Oceaneer Club is a central rotunda featuring a giant-screen TV for movie watching and magical interactions with Crush, and a stage for theatrical productions and special appearances by Disney characters. Branching off from the rotunda are four themed areas: Andy's Room filled with larger-than-life characters from *Toy Story* including a giant-size Slinky Dog for climbing; Monster's Academy where an immersion into Monstroplis is possible along with computers featuring interactive games; Pixie Hollow, a peaceful fairy world with a pixie dust tree adorned with twinkling lights and acorn and mushroom stools for storytelling; and Explorer Pod featuring a Nemo Sub containing interactive computer stations.

A workshop and laboratory for experimentation, honing culinary skills, and hands-on activities connects the Oceaneer Club to the Oceaneer Lab where there are more toys than you can imagine along with individual computer stations and plenty of room to explore. Branching off from the Oceaneer Lab's main room with Magic PlayFloor is the Media Room where the kids can relax in bean bag chairs, watch a movie, read a book, or play video games; Animator's Studio allowing creation of hand-drawn artwork and sketching; Craft Studio for arts and crafts projects; The Wheelhouse, a Pirates of the Caribbean simulator game; and Sound Studio for creation and appreciation of music.

Days in both the Oceaneer Lab and Club are filled with special activities including a Monster's Inc. Open "Mike" Night, a comedy show that the children put on for their parents; Get the Hook, a three-day search for clues around the ship in search of Captain Hook's favorite dress hook; Puzzle Playtime with Mickey and Friends; Tinker Bell's Talent Show; Stitch's Adventure Squad; Pluto's Pajama Party; Super Sloppy Science–Flubber; ESPN Dream Team Draft Day; So You Want To Be A Pirate?; and Journey to Neverland.

Edge. A super 'tween club is available for those children ages eleven to fourteen located in the ship's forward funnel. Here are an illuminated dance floor, notebook computers with an onboard social media application, and best of all a video wall over 18 feet long and 5 feet tall with 18 individual screens. Pre-teens enjoy a day consisting of video games, listening to music, watching movies and TV, and participating in a number of social activities geared just for them such as Disney Animation–Cartoon Physics; Anyone Can Cook; Animation Cells; A Pirate's Life For Me; That's Hilarious improv show; Ghost Voyages equipped with ghost-hunting gear; and Flubber.

Vibe. A key-card-access-only spot for teens age fourteen to seventeen, this trendy and inviting place is a combination coffee shop/nightclub with a dance floor, multi-screen video wall for gaming and movies, a stage for talent shows and karaoke, computers, giant-screen TV, even individual nooks for relaxing. An exclusive outdoor sun lounging area adjoins the club with two hot tubs, splash pools, misters, and deck games.

The club's super cool counselors are experts at helping teens feel at ease and part of the program. Special activities include Disney Animation–Creating a Character; Pump It Up in the fitness center; Zombified; and ESPN Dream Draft Day; pool parties and pizza making.

DISNEY DREAM AND DISNEY FANTASY'S VERY BEST SHORE EXCURSIONS

At each port of call a variety of shore excursions are available through Disney Cruise Line, and the good news is that they can be pre-reserved online (concierge guests and Platinum Castaway Club members 120 days prior, 105 for Gold Castaway Club repeat guests, 90 days prior for Silver Castaway Club members, and all other guests 75 days prior). No prepayment is necessary; your excursions are charged to your onboard account.

While it might be less expensive to plan some of these excursions on your own, remember if your return to the ship is delayed the cruise line will not wait for you unless you are with a ship-sponsored shore excursion. It's usually worth it for the peace of mind to book your shore side activities through Disney. Now if all you wish to do is look around in places such as Cozumel and Grand Cayman where town is literally down the gangplank or just a tender away, do so without worry. It's almost impossible to miss the ship when it is so conveniently docked or just a tender ride away.

Castaway Cay

Although Disney's private island will keep you busy enough for the day, there are a few interesting shore excursions that you might not want to miss.

Castaway Ray's Stingray Adventure. It seems as if those guests interested in stingrays usually plan for a trip to Stingray City in Grand Cayman, a spot that can be very crowded and a bit intimidating. Here in Castaway Cay you're acclimated slowly into touching and feeding the stingrays in shallow water before actually donning snorkel gear and getting a bit more up close and personal with the rays that call the island home.

Parasailing. If I am going to parasail it's certainly going to be with a company that has safety first and foremost in their mind, which makes Castaway Cay my preferred choice. From heights of 600-1000 feet there's an excellent birds-eye-view of the island and the crystal clear waters below, although it's a short ride at only 5-7 minutes per person. Minimum weight is 90 pounds, maximum 375 pounds. Because of weather conditions guests may be required to fly tandem with a single ride not guaranteed.

Seahorse Catamaran Snorkel Adventure. Board a 63-foot power catamaran and anchor at a reef brimming with tropical fish native to the Abacos. Enjoy about 75 minutes of snorkel time before returning to Castaway Cay. Another option is to rent snorkel gear at Gils' Fins and Boats or Flippers 'n Floats for the day to enjoy the waters just off the Family Beach. With 22 acres of underwater beauty to discover including a beginner snorkel trail, there are also a few hidden surprises along the way.

Costa Maya, Mexico

A faux village built specifically for the cruise ships sits next to the pier at Costa Maya. If you just want to get off for a bit to explore you'll find swimming pools, restaurants, bars, and shopping within minutes of the ship. Another option is a 5-minute cab ride into Mahahual, a nearby fishing village where there's a clean beach offering a shallow surf, but beware the overabundance of beach vendors. I would definitely avoid the Dolphin Swim here located just off the pier in not-very-clean water.

Dzibanché & Kohunlich Mayan Ruins. It's pretty tough to find ruins that aren't overrun with hoards of tourists, but I think you'll find these to be the exception. Available on selected sailings only when there is enough time allocated in port, this is a definite time commitment at over eight hours, but one I found to be well worth it particularly if you are interested in the Mayan culture. Completely surrounded by tropical jungle, these interesting ruins have the additional bonus of howling monkeys and exotic birds, and the unique 10-feet-tall, stucco masks at Kohunlich are worth the entire trip.

Chacchoben Mayan Ruins. If the long trip to Dzibanché and Kohunlich ruins seems too daunting or if your ship isn't in port long enough to take advantage of that particular shore excursion then visit Chacchoben instead, only a one-hour bus ride from port. Interestingly this ruin was not even explored until 1999 and is still not completely excavated. The highlight is the ascent up the steep stairs of El Gran Basamento.

Jungle Beach Break. Beach bums will enjoy a day here via a 40-minute bus trip up the coast. At the Uvero Beach Club are beach chairs, hammocks, kayaks, sand toys, and full bar, all included in the cost of the tour. A fast food restaurant is on site for an additional cost. You might even take part in a salsa lesson or a game of beach volleyball.

Costa Maya Beach Snorkel. Same as the above Jungle Beach Break but with snorkeling equipment and instruction included.

Cozumel, Mexico

Long known for its excellent coral reef diving and snorkeling this bustling island has grown by leaps and bounds because of the cruise industry. You'll more than likely be docked in town where it's simply a short walk to a myriad of shops, restaurants, and bars. And from Cozumel you are just a ferry ride away from the mainland where top Mayan ruins await.

Those of you who are in need of supplies will be glad to know that a large Chedraui grocery store is within walking distance from the pier. Just hang a right as you exit the pier on the main drag and walk about one block; you can't miss it.

For lunch seek out Pancho's Back Yard on the main drag at Avenue Rafael Melgar between Calles 8 and 10 where there's Mexican food in a charming setting—try the regional Veracruzana fish or the plump garlic shrimp. A bit further off the main drag but within fairly easy walking distance is La Choza at Avenue 10 Sur where tasty, traditional Mexican food is served in an open air, thatch-roofed restaurant—choose the *sopa* Azteca, a soup of chicken, tortilla strips, melting white cheese, and avocado in a smoky chicken-chili broth.

Certified Scuba Tour. Certified divers should not miss outstanding diving in the second largest reef system in the world. Led by a PADI certified dive master, you'll boat to two sites: first to a wall dive with depths of 70 to 80 feet; then a second reef for a dive of 50 to 60 feet. Be sure to bring along your dive card!

Three Reef Snorkel. If you don't have diving certification then settle for the second best thing, snorkeling. Sail for 30 minutes to the first of three snorkeling reefs. You'll spend about half an hour at each one, but which particular reefs visited will depend on the winds and the weather; popular choices include Paraiso Bajo, Paraiso Profundo, and Dzul Ha.

Tulum Ruins. If you want to visit a Mayan ruin that sits on a stunning site overlooking the crystal clears waters of the Yucatan then *Tulum* is your very best bet. Do expect, however, hordes of tourists at this very popular site, and do expect to spend time on a 45-minute ferry in each direction that will take you to and from Cozumel to the mainland, then a 70-minute bus ride in each direction to reach the site. But the climb up El Castillo and that view overlooking the Caribbean Sea is phenomenal. You'll even have time to take a swim from the beach below if you like.

Xel-Ha Park & River Tubing. Another great option for a shore excursion to the mainland is Xel-Ha. Once almost unknown except for its beauty, you'll snorkel and tube in a crystal clear lagoon and through a collection of caves and inlets where you'll view tropical fish and coral formations. There's also the option of relaxing on the beach or taking a stroll through the jungle-like area surrounding the park. You'll still have to take a 45-minute ferry in each direction to and from the mainland, but the drive is a bit shorter than Tulum at 45 minutes in each direction. Also included is lunch at one of several restaurants as well as drinks and beverages at Xel-Ha's bars.

Falmouth, Jamaica

Falmouth is Jamaica's fourth and newest cruise stop located on the north coast of the island. The Fantasy docks just a few minutes walk from town, a place that is worth an hour or two stroll to check out the Georgian plantation-style homes and authentic atmosphere, although the port complex is filled with plenty of shops and handicraft vendors. Most visitors to Jamaica know Falmouth as the starting point for bamboo raft excursions on the Martha Brae River, but not too far away is Ocho Rios for zip line adventures and the super popular Dunn River Falls shore excursion. Just west is Montego Bay and the beaches of Negril. In other words a wealth of places to visit and discover.

Rafting on the Martha Brae. It's a 25-minute drive to the rural village of Martha Brae where you'll board a two-person raft for a peaceful 3-hour journey down a meandering river. A good choice for all but the youngest children, this is an excursion that the entire family can enjoy.

Falmouth By Private Vehicle. Enjoy the freedom of discovering this port on a private tour providing you with a customized day of your choosing. Either a 4- or 6-hour tour can be reserved in a sedan or van seating anywhere from three to ten people.

Dunn's River Falls Express With Lunch. Take a 70-minute drive to the famous Dunn's River Falls where you'll climb a 600-foot waterfall. This is a rightly renowned excursion so expect to climb with plenty of others, and don't forget to bring along a good pair of water shoes. After your climb enjoy a Jamaican-style jerk chicken lunch (you simply must partake of a jerk dish of some sort while you are in Jamaica, so here's your chance).

Chukka Zipline Canopy and River Tubing. For those adventuresome folks out there who would like to try ziplining in a jungle atmosphere combined with a cooling river float, this super two-in-one excursion fits the bill. Take a 25-minute drive to Good Hope Estate where you are outfitted for your hour-long river tubing trip along the Martha Brae River. Enjoy a jerk chicken lunch then get ready for a wild ride through the jungle canopy of treetops. Only for the brave of heart!

George Town, Grand Cayman

Known for tidy little George Town, excellent scuba diving, and almost 300 banks, this place is also a bit overrun like in many Caribbean ports. Nevertheless it's a favorite stop, but one that you'll need to access via tender. The water here is exceptional, so if possible plan an activity that includes a dip in its crystal clear beauty.

Your tender will drop you right smack in the middle of town where you'll find shops galore. If there's time consider lunch at Rackam's Waterfront Bar and Grille, just a half block past the pier (hang a left). Nothing fancy, but you can't go wrong with the views or the food; favorites include the fresh snapper *escovitch*, fish 'n' chips, and conch fritters.

Aquaboat and Snorkel Adventure. The most fun I've had in years was on my last stop in Cayman skippering my own 2-person inflatable powerboat following guides to two different snorkeling spots. Your first snorkel is at Governor's Reef where there's a variety of tropical fish, then blast off to a sunken shipwreck just offshore in George Town. It's totally a kick of an excursion!

Cayman Luxury Yacht Private Charter. One of Disney Cruise Line's luxury series shore excursions. You and up to 14 guests enjoy a 3-hour cruise around Grand Cayman aboard a private 52-foot Searay Sundancer yacht. Visit snorkeling reefs, Starfish Point, then Starfish Beach for sun and sand. Cruise through the Mangrove Reserve Environmental Park for a glimpse at some of Cayman's wildlife before heading back to shore. Sandwiches and non-alcoholic beverages are provided along with snorkeling equipment.

Two-tank Dive Tour. Like Cozumel, Grand Cayman is a must for those certified to dive. Experience the Cayman Wall, famous for its variety of colorful coral and marine life, as well as a second dive site that may include a shipwreck or another reef. Be sure to pack and bring along your dive card.

Catamaran, Reef, and Kittiwake Snorkel Sail. Board a catamaran from the Seven Mile Beach area and sail to two snorkeling spots. First the *USS Kittiwak* shipwreck, sunk off the coast to become a dive and snorkel spot, then a shallow reef where there are schools of tropical fish and marine life. Relax later on the beach at Sea Grape Beach Club.

Nassau, Bahamas

Nassau is a mandatory stop on any Bahamian cruise. The pier is located right in town so it's easy to walk over to explore the town, visit the traditional Straw Market and duty-free shops, maybe have a drink or lunch somewhere, then head back to the ship. The main attraction is Atlantis Resort where you'll enjoy dolphin swims or Aquaventure, the resort's exciting water park, both easily arranged through the ship's shore excursion division.

Aquaventure. Take a bus ride to Atlantis Resort on Paradise Island for a self-guided tour of The Dig, an aquarium viewed from underground passageways. Then dive into Aquaventure, a 141-acre waterscape of wild slides, river rapids, waterfalls, and sparkling pools. A light lunch is included. Take time to visit the casinos before catching your shuttle back to the ship.

Atlantis Snorkel The Ruins and Aquaventure. Basically the same excursion as Aquaventure above but with the addition of a 30-minute snorkel through the Ruins Lagoon where there are over 20,000 fish and other marine life amid artifacts inspired by ancient Atlantis. Wet suits are provided for the chilly water, and the tour is limited to only eight guests.

Nassau By Private Vehicle. Tour Nassau with your own private guide on your own schedule customized for you and your group. Vehicles hold from 3 (sedan) to six (SUV or limo) people on either a 4-or 8-hour tour of the island.

Ardastra Gardens and City Tour. Fun for all ages is this visit to the tropical gardens of Ardastra teeming with birds, reptiles, and mammals. The flamingos are a big draw and the kids will love watching the fun show they put on for guests. There is an opportunity to hand-feed parrots and have your photo taken with a cockatoo, a snake, and a peacock. The city tour is a bit arduous, but it's an easy way to see some of the historical buildings to and from the ship. You'll be dropped off back in town where it's an easy walk back to the ship.

San Juan, Puerto Rico

The charm of Old San Juan makes this a very worthwhile port with its cobbled streets, colorful 16th- and 17th-century buildings, and tasty cuisine. Of course, while the Old Town is a destination in itself, getting out and about on the island is a true highlight so it's a tough choice to make. If the ship stops long enough take a half-day tour of the island and then walk into the city for a double-dipper day.

Hopefully the ship will dock right in the heart of town (there are two piers, one a bit further out requiring a taxi into town). Enjoy lunch at one of Old Town's exceptional restaurants such Toro Saleo for Spanish/ Puerto Rican food at 367 Calle Tetuan or La Fonda del Jibarito on 280 Calle Sol for solid Puerto Rican cuisine.

El Yunque Rainforest Tour and Hike. It's tough to resist visiting the only rain forest in a U.S. National Forest where it rains up to 200 inches each year. Walk along designated park trails to view waterfalls, giant ferns, and tropical birds then climb to the top of Yokahu Tower for panoramic views of the park and the beach far below. Remember that this is a rainforest so bring along a waterproof jacket.

Castillo San Cristóbal Walking Tour. Take a walking tour of Castillo San Cristobal, a UNESCO World Heritage Site (actually part of the US National Parks Service) led by a heritage guide dressed in 1797 period clothing. Hear the legends of the Devil's Sentry Box, see the dungeons, prisoner graffiti, tunnels, and more.

San Juan By Private Vehicle. Do as you like on your own private tour of San Juan and Puerto Rico. Either in a sedan holding up to three people, an SUV for 6, or a van for 10 for either 4 or 8 hours, your tour will be customized to your preferences.

Philipsburg, St. Maarten

This has become one bustling stop over the years, and the streets of Philipsburg are now filled with many shops geared toward cruise passengers. From the pier it's about a mile to town requiring a bit of a walk, a cab, or a water taxi (the dock is a 5-minute walk from the pier with the boat dropping you in the heart of Philipsburg).

For good French food including lobster thermidor along with great views, stop at Antoine Restaurant on 119 Front Street on Great Bay Beach. Or for a hip atmosphere try Ocean Lounge at Holland House Beach Hotel on the Boardwalk in Philipsburg at 43 Front Street.

The Ultimate Charter Choice. Reserve your own private 4-hour trip on a 65-foot catamaran for a cruise around St. Maarten. Sail down the coast to a white sand beach or stop to snorkel at one of the island's nature parks. The boat will take on 10 guests, a perfect choice for a family and friends excursion. Includes unlimited champagne, beer, rum punch, and beverages as well as French baguette sandwiches.

Twelve-Metre Regatta. This is a popular shore excursion where everyone gets to be part of the action. No previous sailing experience is required for you to become a crewmember and learn to trim a sail or turn a winch as you race on an America's Cup participant yacht.

Afternoon Beach Bash Tour. If you just want to hang out in the sun with the sand between your toes this is the place for you. On the shore of Orient Bay, a 30-minute drive from the ship, relax in a lounge chair and enjoy a few hours of beach time with complimentary fruit and rum punch included. Those traveling with children should be advised there will more than likely, in true European fashion, be some nudity on the beach.

St. Thomas, U.S. Virgin Islands

This is probably the best place to duty-free shop in the Caribbean, but don't neglect the beautiful waters here just to bring home a trinket or two. And with St. John just a hop, skip, and a jump away where there's even more water-based activities, it's always a tough decision which excursion to take.

Your ship will dock a 5-10-minute taxi ride from Charlotte Amalie where it's possible to walk, but know that the road is hot and busy. Over fifty shops are located pier-side as well as a marina and restaurants, but it's probably best to head into town to experience the true essence of St. Thomas as you shop the historic streets and alleyways. For an authentic

Virgin Island lunch try Cuzzin's Caribbean Restaurant on Back Street where conch stew, curried chicken, and freshly-caught fish is on order, or Gladys' Café, a cozy spot for jerk pork chops, pan-fried Creole style grouper, and conch in lemon butter sauce, located in the Royal Dane Mall historical buildings.

Magen's Bay Beach Break. The island's most picturesque beach is Magen's Bay, a 25-minute ride from the pier in an open-air taxi. Stop along the way at Drake's Seat for a panoramic view then enjoy the beach, swim, and sun for your three and a half-hour stay. This is not a beach club so there are limited facilities, although you are entitled to beach chairs and will be able to purchase food and beverages at a bar and snack bar.

St. John Champagne Catamaran Sail and Snorkel. Sail on a catamaran to lovely St. John (a 1-hour trip) where you'll anchor off a pristine beach. Snorkel the reef from the boat, or take a dingy ride to the beach for sand and sun. Onboard are bread and cheese, fruit, champagne, beer, and beverages.

Water Island Mountain Bike Adventure. Take a 15-minute harbor cruise to Water Island and prepare yourself to explore over five miles of winding trails on a mountain bike experiencing the unspoiled scenery. There's time to swim on Honeymoon Beach before boarding the boat heading back to the ship.

Full Day Caribbean Sail & Snorkel to Turtle Cove & Honeymoon Beach. Those who want a full day of sail and sun will enjoy this all-encompassing excursion. Board a schooner for a 3-mile sail to Turtle Cove on famous Buck Island where you'll stop for a snorkel in amazing, crystal-clear water among coral and tropical fish. Then it's on to a second destination, Honeymoon Beach, accessible only by boat, for a swim, snorkel, or beach relaxation. A barbecue lunch is served before heading back to St. Thomas.

SECTION THREE

DISNEYLAND® RESORT

Disneyland Park, opened in 1955, is a place where generations of families have created countless, beloved memories. Wedged in the middle of busy Anaheim with its numerous hotels and convention facilities, Disneyland Resort itself is composed of two theme parks, Disneyland Park and California Adventure Park, three hotels, and a thriving Downtown Disney District area. Needless to say, the feel is very different from Walt Disney World's 30,000-acre metropolis. Many vacationers travel to Orlando countless times without a thought of visiting Disneyland Park, but believe me when I say there really is life after Walt Disney World!

You'll be shocked to realize that at this walker-friendly destination neither bus nor even monorail are required to reach the parks (although a monorail is conveniently located in Downtown Disney just outside the Disneyland Hotel). At most it's an easy 10-minute stroll to either Disneyland Park or Disney California Adventure Park from any Disney resort. The ease of transportation (or lack of the need for it) is incredible! So different from Walt Disney World where traveling via bus, monorail, or boat from most resorts to a park is almost a requirement. And even better, if you want to switch between the parks it's just a matter of strolling across a broad plaza. How refreshing!

At Disneyland Park you'll need to gear up for the shock of that first glimpse of Sleeping Beauty Castle that, while enchanting, is just a fraction of the size of the Magic Kingdom icon. However, you'll quickly discover that this entire park is an absolute charmer. Wander through narrow, winding streets in New Orleans Square, stroll throughout the Castle en route to the nostalgic attractions in Fantasyland; even Main Street has a special kind of magic that is sure to please.

The remarkably transformed California Adventure Park has created more excitement than ever with the new, atmospheric Buena Vista Street and sensational Cars Land, real bonuses to your experience.

Disneyland Resort's nighttime shows and attractions are re-markable with World of Color perhaps the most incredible spec-tacular of all. The Magical fireworks show at Disneyland is oh-so-nostalgic with the addition of Tinker Bell and Dumbo literally flying around Sleeping Beauty Castle. And the shock of seeing a full-size pirate ship and the Mark Twain riverboat as part of the Fantasmic! show is worth the entire trip.

Oh, wait . . . did I mention the fabulous weather, incredible beaches within minutes of the parks, and a vibe that you'll never find in Florida? Maybe I shouldn't push it too far.

PLANNING YOUR DISNEYLAND RESORT VACATION

There's nothing quite like a *true* Disney expert when it comes to choosing a travel advisor. An Authorized Disney Vacation Planner agency can make the difference between a mediocre vacation and an excellent one. For your Disneyland Resort vacation needs call Glass Slipper Concierge at (866) 725-7595 or go online at GlassSlipperConcierge.com. Glass Slipper Concierge is the brainchild of this book's author, Cara Goldsbury, originating from a desire to offer a client-centric option to those who want an exceptional and unforgettable Disney vacation. Cara has gathered an exclusive team of luxury concierge advisors whose knowledge of Disney Destinations can only be matched by their passion for delivering white-glove service.

When Should I Travel?

Disneyland Resort is quite different from Walt Disney World in that the locals come out in full force each and every weekend. So a calm weekday vacation can totally change once Friday night rolls around, continuing into craziness on Saturday and sometimes even into Sunday. The busiest times of year are the summer months (Memorial Day through Labor Day), the Christmas and New Year holiday period, Thanksgiving weekend, Presidents Week, various spring breaks around the country in March and April, and the weeks before and after Easter Sunday.

To avoid large crowds opt for just after New Years until the first week of March avoiding Presidents Week, the week following Easter week until Memorial Day, the month of September after Labor Day until the second week of October, and usually the week or so after Thanksgiving. Do remember that slower times of year mean shorter park hours and more attractions closed for refurbishment, but absolutely worth it to avoid the huge swell of crowds during the most popular times of year. Of course events such as conventions, marathons, and such will vary from year to year making what should be a slow time of year a busy one, so it's always best to check the calendar of events and plan accordingly.

As for weather, except for summer during the daytime hours when temperatures are in the 90s and rain chances are slightly higher, weather in Southern California is pretty fabulous all year 'round with its moderate days and cool but not bitterly cold evenings and very little rainfall. Even in summer the nights will be in the 60s and 70s.

What Should I Pack?

Think casual! Park attire is appropriate throughout Disneyland Resort with the exception of Napa Rose and Steakhouse 55 where resort casual dress is requested. Definitely leave the coat and tie at home. Park attire should consist of shorts or capri pants, t-shirts, comfortable walking shoes (bring two pairs to switch off), cushy socks, sunglasses, and a hat. Bring along warmer clothing in the winter months, including a jacket for evenings when temperatures drop. It's always best to check the Internet for a weather forecast before beginning your packing. Don't forget a bathing suit and cover-up, and it's not a bad idea to throw in a rain jacket just in case. Women should take a light purse or backpack to the parks; nothing is worse than lugging a heavy bag around all day.

How Long Should I Plan on Staying?

You could easily spend three days or more exploring the Disneyland Resort theme parks. It does, however, seem a shame to miss visiting the surrounding Southern California area. With a five night or longer vacation you could base yourself at a Disney hotel for your entire stay spending three days at Disneyland Park and California Adventure, then two or three days choosing from a variety of local options such as Universal Hollywood, LEGOLAND, SeaWorld San Diego, or perhaps even a day at the beach. Of course if all you can spare is a long weekend plan on spending the entire time at the Disneyland Resort theme parks with a return trip in mind to pick up what you've missed.

Should I Rent a Car?

If the only place you plan on visiting is the Disneyland Resort then take a taxi, private transfers, or a shuttle from the airport and forget about renting a car. There's really no need to have a car given that everything is in walking distance.

Now if you want to visit some of the surrounding Southern California attractions a car might be a good idea; however, driving here is oftentimes nerve-wracking so it just depends on your personality. Transportation can be arranged and even added as part of your resort package, so don't think it's mandatory to have a car.

ARRIVAL AT
DISNEYLAND RESORT

Getting to Disneyland Resort

Airports

The closest airport to Disneyland Resort at 16 miles away is John Wayne Airport (SNA), with Long Beach (LGB) then Los Angeles International Airport (LAX) in order of proximity. Of course if non-stop flights are important then LAX is more than likely your best choice, but do expect to spend at least 45 minutes or longer driving in overwhelming traffic during the rush hours.

Airport Transportation

For personalized service book private car or limousine transfers prior to your arrival with South Coast Limo (SouthCoastLimo.com or 866-725-4667). Your driver will meet you at baggage claim. Reservations are mandatory.

Taxis are available from all airports to Disneyland Resort. The average cost of a taxi from John Wayne Airport is $45, from Long Beach $56, and from LAX $94.

The Disneyland Resort Express (Southern California Gray Line) provides transportation to Disneyland Resort area hotels between John Wayne Airport ($17 per adult and $14 per child one way) and Los Angeles International Airport ($22 per adult and $19 per child one way), an option that can be added to your resort reservation. Or, make reservations directly by calling (714) 978-8855 or online at Grayline-Anaheim.com/shuttles.shtml.

Disneyland Resort Express buses from LAX depart hourly between 7:30 a.m. and 10:00 a.m. and again from 4:30 p.m. and 10:30 p.m. and every 30 minutes between 11:00 a.m. and 3:00 p.m. Buses from SNA depart hourly between 7:00 a.m. and 11:00 a.m. and again from 3:00 p.m. and 10:00 p.m., and every 30 minutes between 10:30 a.m. and 4:00 P.M. Reservations are not required. Buses only depart once an hour and not on a set schedule for the return to the airport so for convenience you might consider another mode of transportation for your return.

Super Shuttle also provides the same service for $16 per person one-way to and from Los Angeles Airport, $10 for John Wayne Airport, and $35 for Long Beach Airport. Reservations can be made online at SuperShuttle.com or by calling 800-BLUEVAN or 800-258-3826. Super Shuttle may also be added as an option on your resort reservations.

Car Rental

On-site rental cars at John Wayne Airport are Alamo Rent-A-Car, Avis, Budget, Enterprise, National, and Thrifty with rental cars located in the airport's parking structure. At Los Angeles Airport are Advantage, Alamo Rent-A-Car, Avis, Budget, Dollar Car Rental, Enterprise Rent-A-Car, Hertz Car Rental, Fox, Payless, National, and Thrifty, all with shuttle service to their respective vehicle rental sites. At Long Beach Airport are Avis, Budget, Enterprise, Hertz Car Rental, and National/Alamo located directly across from the terminal.

For something more luxurious try the Hertz Prestige and Dream Collection offering Infiniti QX56 and G37, and Mercedes C Class, GL 450, and GLK350 at John Wayne Airport with the addition of a Corvette Convertible and Porsche Boxter, 911, and Panamera at Los Angeles Airport. Specific models may be reserved, and Sirius/XM and a complimentary NeverLost GPS system are included. Avis has Signature Series rentals including a BMW 528 and BMW X5.

Midway Car Rental will deliver their exotic rental cars to either the airport or your hotel, and in addition to standard types offer Rolls Royce Phantom or Ghost, Range Rover Sport and HSE, BMW sedans, SUVs, and convertibles, Mercedes convertibles and sedans, Mini Cooper Countryman, Lamborghini LP550, Fiat 500C convertible . . . the list goes on. For reservations call your travel advisor or 866-717-6802.

Disneyland Resort Transportation

Because Disneyland Resort is so compact and a pedestrian resort, a bus or shuttle system is unnecessary as long your stay is at a Disneyland Resort Hotel. The Disneyland Monorail, the first transportation system of its kind in America, makes a 2.5-mile loop from just outside the Disneyland Hotel in the Downtown Disney complex to Tomorrowland in Disneyland Park. Because you disembark inside the park, bags and park tickets are checked before boarding.

Disneyland Resort Reference Guide

Alcoholic beverages. Alcohol is served throughout the Disneyland Resort except for Disneyland Park. The legal drinking age in California is twenty-one; however, Disney's lounges allow minors as long as they do not drink alcohol or sit at the bar.

ATMs. Chase automated teller machines (ATMs) are located at each theme park, in Downtown Disney, and in or near the lobby of each resort.

Business centers. All Disneyland Resort Hotels offer a business center with personal computers, high-speed Internet, printing and fax services, office equipment rental, office supplies, and shipping.

Childcare. Pinocchio's Workshop at the Grand Californian Hotel is the only childcare facility at the Disneyland Resort. Available only to registered guests of a Disneyland Resort Hotel, the facility is open from 5:00 p.m. until midnight for children ages 5 to 12. The cost includes dinner and snacks; call (714)-956-6755 for reservations.

For in-room childcare, nanny, or mother's helper services visit your Disney resort Guest Services desk after check-in to receive a list of

non-Disney agencies to contact on your own. A waiver must be signed
to receive the list.

Dietary requests. Dietary requests such as kosher, no sugar added,
low-carb, or low-fat as well as special dietary requests regarding allergies
to gluten or wheat, shellfish, soy, lactose, peanuts, or other foods can be
accommodated at select table-service restaurants by calling (714) 781-
DINE (3463) at least 24 hours in advance. Most table-service and many
quick-service restaurants offer at least one vegetarian choice, something
I have tried to reflect in my entrée examples in the restaurant section.

Guests with Disabilities. Parking for guests with disabilities is available
at Mickey and Friends parking structure and the Toy Story parking area
off Harbor Boulevard. Transportation is provided from the Mickey and
Friends parking structure and the Toy Story parking area to the Main
Entry Plaza. Oversized wheelchairs and Electric Convenience Vehicles
may be too large for some transportation vehicles.

Each resort offers special equipment and facilities for guests with
disabilities. Features vary by resort but may include wider bathroom
doors, roll-in showers, shower benches, handheld showerheads, accessible vanities, portable commodes, bathroom and bed rails, bed shaker
alarm, text typewriter, strobe-light fire alarm, and phone amplifier. Other features include double peepholes in doors, closed-captioned television, and braille on signage and elevators.

A guide for guests with disabilities is available at Guest Services in
each theme park. Wheelchairs and ECVs are available for rent on a first-
come, first-served basis. Most restaurants and shops are accessible to
guests with disabilities, although some quick-service locations have narrow queues with railings (ask a host or hostess for assistance). Companion-assisted restrooms are located at both theme parks. Many attractions provide access through the main queue while others have auxiliary
entrances for wheelchairs and service animals along with as many as five
members of your party. Certain attractions require guests to transfer
from their wheelchair to a ride system. Parade routes and some shows
have designated viewing areas on a first-come, first-served basis.

Braille guidebooks, handheld captioning receivers, digital audio
tours, and assistive listening devices are available at Guest Services in
each theme park for a $25 refundable deposit. Reflective captioning is

provided at many theater-type attractions and video captioning at others. A sign language interpreter is provided at specific live shows on a rotating basis on certain days of the week. For more information call (714) 781-6176 or (714) 781-7292 (TTY), or online at Disneyland. Disney.Go.com/guest-services/guests-with-disabilities.

Internet services. Complimentary in-room high-speed Internet access is available at all Disneyland Resort Hotels. Additional access is found at the business centers of each resort.

Laundry and dry cleaning. Self-service, coin-operated washers and dryers are located at each Disney resort in addition to same-day dry cleaning and laundry service.

Lost and found. Located in the Guest Services Building outside and to the left of the Main Entrance to Disneyland Park or call (714) 817-2166.

Medical care. Both theme parks offer first aid during park hours. Emergency medical needs are met by Western Medical Center at 1025 S. Anaheim Boulevard, or the U.C. Irvine Medical Center at 101 The City Drive South in the city of Orange.

Money matters. Disneyland Resort accepts cash, traveler's checks, Disney Dollars (available at Disney Stores, Guest Services, and Resort Services), and Disney Gift Cards as well as six types of credit cards: American Express, MasterCard, Visa, Discover, Japanese Credit Bureau, and Diners Club.

Guests of a Disneyland Resort Hotel may charge throughout Disneyland Resort by using their room key as long as a credit card is given at check-in. ATMs are readily available throughout Disneyland Resort in each resort and theme park, and in Downtown Disney.

The Disneyland Resort offers currency exchange through Travelex Exchange Services. Foreign currency may be exchanged for U.S. dollars at City Hall in Disneyland Park, the Guest Services Lobby just inside the Disney California Adventure Park Main Entrance, the Guest Relations Window located to the left of the Disney California Adventure Park Main Entrance, Travelex in the Downtown Disney District, and the front desk at Disneyland Resort Hotels.

Parking. Theme park parking is $16 per day. There are two parking areas: the Mickey & Friends structure the closest, located next to the Downtown Disney parking lot; the Toy Story lot further away off Harbor Boulevard, closer to the Convention Center. Remember to make a note of the section and aisle, and board the tram to the drop off area for the theme parks. Parking for guests with disabilities is available at both Mickey & Friends parking structure and the Toy Story parking area off Harbor Boulevard; valid disability parking permit is required.

Parking is free for the first three hours in the Downtown Disney lot although in the evening hours it can be quite difficult to find a spot. Two additional free hours are added with validation at AMC Theatres or at Downtown Disney table-service restaurants. Each additional hour is $6, charged in 20-minute increments with a maximum parking fee of $30. From the Downtown Disney lot there is easy access to the monorail entrance which deposits you in Disneyland Park's Tomorrowland.

Downtown Disney valet parking is available from 5:00 p.m. to 2:00 a.m. for $6. The valet price is in addition to any parking fee, bringing the maximum fee to $36.

All Disneyland Resort Hotels charge $15 for self-parking and $22 per day for valet parking to registered guests. Non-registered guests pay $15 for self-parking and $22 for valet parking the first hour plus $9 for each additional hour with a maximum of $51 for self-parking and $58 for valet parking.

Pets. Only service dogs for guests with disabilities are allowed inside Disney's theme parks and resorts. Kennel facilities are located east of the Disneyland Park Main Entrance. First-come, first-served basis; no reservations accepted. For information call (714) 781-4565. Proof of vaccination is required with no overnight accommodations allowed.

Rider Switch Service. Parents traveling with young children who don't meet height restrictions should consider utilizing the Rider Switch program. One parent waits with the child while the other rides, then the second parent hands off the child and goes to the head of the line. Just speak to the Cast Member on duty.

Safety. Disneyland Resort is a relatively safe environment; still, caution must be taken. Be alert at all times, particularly at night. Always lock your guest room door, and make sure you verify who is knocking before allowing entry. Use the safe provided in your room to store money and valuables. Park in well lighted areas, lock your car, and be aware of your surroundings when leaving the car.

Security. All bags are checked prior to entering the theme parks by uniformed Security Cast Members; allow yourself extra time if you've booked Advance Dining Reservations.

Smoking. All Disneyland Resort Hotel guest rooms, including room balconies, restaurants, and public areas, are smoke-free environments. In the theme parks and Disneyland Resort Hotels smoking is limited to designated outdoor areas; look for the cigarette symbol on the guide maps.

Strollers and wheelchairs. Rentals are located outside the Disneyland Park next to the Pet Kennel. Single strollers are $15 per day, $25 for two strollers. Wheelchairs are $12 per day, electric convenience vehicles $50.00 per day; both require a $20.00 refundable deposit. Rental strollers are permissible in both theme parks but are not allowed in Downtown Disney.

Taxi service. Taxis are found in front of all resorts and at Downtown Disney.

Important Disneyland Resort Phone Numbers

Glass Slipper Concierge—Travel Advisors (866) 725-7595

General information (714) 781-INFO or (714) 781-4636

Advance Dining Reservations (714) 781-DINE or (714) 781-3463

Park tickets (714) 781-INFO or (714) 781-4636

Fantasmic! Premium Viewing (714) 781-SHOW or (714) 781-7469

Behind-the-Scenes tours (714) 781-TOUR or (714) 781-8687

VIP Tours (714) 300-7710

Children's Activity Center reservations (714) 635-2300

TTY Line (714) 781-4569

ANNUAL DISNEYLAND RESORT
CALENDAR OF EVENTS

- **January:** Tinker Bell Half Marathon—mid-January; Happy Lunar New Year at California Adventure Park—end of the month

- **March:** New Orleans Bayou Bash at Disneyland Park and Mardi Gras at Downtown Disney; St. Patrick's Day Celebration

- **August:** Disneyland Half Marathon—last weekend of the month

- **September:** Mickey's Halloween Party at Disneyland Park—end of the month.

- **October:** Mickey's Halloween Party at Disneyland Park continues

- **November:** Holidays at Disneyland Resort begins

- **December:** Holidays at Disneyland Resort continues

DISNEYLAND
RESORT LUXURY
ACCOMMODATIONS

Disneyland Resort offers three hotel choices: Grand Californian Hotel, Disneyland Hotel, and Paradise Pier Hotel. For the purpose of this luxury guide we will only be reviewing the Grand Californian and the Disneyland Hotel. While both are super convenient to the theme parks with only Downtown Disney separating the two resorts, Grand Californian is the closest, although there's only perhaps a 10-minute difference in stroll time.

When choosing your resort accommodations consider whether or not a standard guest room is all you'll need; you may want to think about a room on the concierge level or perhaps a suite. Luxurious suites at both hotels come in various sizes, some as large as 2,000 or more square feet and certainly the most extravagant option. Of course budget together with how much time may be spent in your room are major considerations and will play a large part in your decision.

If hanging out at your resort for part of the day sounds appealing, the concierge rooms are a smart idea. These accommodations come with the use of a private lounge offering complimentary continental breakfast, snacks throughout the day, before-dinner hors d'oeuvres and cocktails, and late evening cordials and desserts. These amenities are in addition to private check-in and checkout and the assistance of a concierge staff ready to help you with Advance Dining Reservations or anything else within their power; definitely a nice plus to your vacation.

BENEFITS OF STAYING AT A DISNEYLAND RESORT HOTEL

- Easy access to the parks making midday breaks and naps possible plus allowing parties to effortlessly split up to go their independent ways

- Exclusive Entrance into the California Adventure Park through Disney's Grand Californian Hotel & Spa

- Charge privileges to your resort account for purchases throughout Disneyland Resort

- Extra Magic Hour each day whereby Disneyland Resort Hotel guests gain admission into select attractions one hour ahead of the general public (Disneyland Park opens early on Tuesday, Thursday, and Saturday, and Disney California Adventure Park on Sunday, Monday, Wednesday, and Friday.)

- Package delivery from anywhere on-property directly to your resort

- Access to Disney's childcare facilities available only to resort guests

Disneyland® Hotel

975 rooms (including 65 suites). 1150 W. Magic Way, Anaheim, CA 92802; phone (714) 778-6600, fax (714) 520-6099. Check-in 3:00 p.m., checkout 11:00 a.m. For reservations contact your travel advisor or call (714) 956-6425.

Talk about nostalgia! Disneyland Hotel originally opened in 1955 with only 104 rooms. In its new incarnation there are 975 rooms in three recently renamed themed towers—Adventure Tower, Frontier Tower, and Fantasy Tower—spread out over this fun, fun resort. Each tower embraces a theme from the original "lands" of Disneyland Park, each a time capsule of sorts filled with memorabilia and classic Disney artwork. A complete renovation was completed in 2012 with contemporary guest rooms offering touches of magic, an expanded pool area, and new dining and entertainment options, making this remarkable hotel better than ever.

You'll find the lobby and front desk located in the Fantasy Tower, most of the concierge rooms and exciting Signature Suites in the Adventure Tower, and many of the standard suites in the Frontier Tower (the only tower offering balconies in some of its rooms and suites).

Outside are three sparkling pools (not to mention fabulous So Cal weather), a welcoming fireplace area with comfortable and cozy seating, and Trader Sam's terrace, a favorite gathering spot with live Hawaiian music nightly.

Claim To Fame. Its sheer sense of nostalgia says it all.

Rooms to Book. Concierge Premium View Room located in the Adventure Tower with a spectacular view of the Disneyland Resort including the nightly fireworks show.

The Wow Factor! A Signature Suite where you'll live out your dreams in your very own storybook a la Disney style!

REST

Guest rooms. Not your normal cookie-cutter size, these rooms offer anywhere from 364 to 415 square feet depending on the configuration with every room a bit unique throughout the hotel. Headboards are the highlight with a carved Sleeping Beauty Castle motif and fiber optic fireworks; flip the switch and it lights up and plays *When You Wish Upon a Star*. Fireworks motif bed runners in a navy blue and gold color scheme along with "A Dream Is a Wish Your Heart Makes" velvet bolster pillows decorate fluffy white duvets on either two queen beds or one king. The same blue/gold color scheme continues into the drapery and carpeting. Walls are covered in subtlety-striped wallpaper, and additional furnishings include a beige corner easy chair, small desk and chair, entertainment center containing a flat-screen TV, and a vintage framed photograph of Disneyland in the '50s.

Our particular guest room came with a split configuration bath on either side of the entry hall with a tub and commode on one side, and a small closet and single sink in a black granite vanity on the other (remember that there are many bath layout variations). Mickey-gloved light fixtures and sleek Mickey-eared sink and shower hardware are fun surprises in all the rooms. Additional amenities include an undercounter refrigerator, super comfortable mattresses and pillows, and high quality linens along with robes, H2O spa bath products, full length and makeup mirrors, hairdryer, iron and ironing board, and electronic safe. Guest rooms here can accommodate up to five people with a daybed.

Views vary and your options are: *Standard View* of either the front or the back of the resort and a parking area; *Resort/Pool View* of the central pool courtyard; or the *Upper Level Resort/Pool View* also looking at the central pool courtyard but on a higher floor.

If you want a balcony request one in the Frontier Tower on the 14th (top) floor and/or the sides of the building in the corner rooms. Our 14th floor room was considered a Standard View overlooking the parking lot but also offered an incredible view of the Grand Californian Hotel, California Adventure and Cars Land, and the surrounding area.

Concierge Rooms. Guests with concierge level service have access to the *E-Ticket Club* located on the 11th floor of the Adventure Tower. From this lovely vantage point are spectacular vistas of the entire Disneyland Resort, including a view of all five "mountains" in both parks. And better yet, it's a picture perfect location for watching the fireworks show complete with music. Additional amenities include DVD players with complimentary DVDs available for checking out, nightly turndown service, and priority check-in and checkout processed regrettably at the front desk instead of inside the concierge lounge. Concierge guest rooms have either a *Pool View* or a *Premium View* overlooking Downtown Disney and the parks in the distance.

Breakfast offers fresh fruit, juice, cereal, bagels, muffins, pastries, oatmeal, cold cuts and cheeses, hard-boiled eggs, and yogurt. Snacks throughout the day include a variety of beverages, fruit, homemade potato chips with dips, breakfast bars, goldfish crackers, Smucker's Uncrustables, and trail mix. Evenings bring cold appetizers of cheese, breads, and crudités as well as two hot entrées such as empanadas, spring rolls, potstickers and the like. Beer and wine are served by the lounge hosts with the choices of BV Chardonnay, BV Cabernet, BV Merlot, and Woodbridge White Zinfandel. Bottled water is available for the asking, and there is also an espresso machine. After dinner enjoy cordials along with cookies, brownies, rice crispy treats, and mini tarts.

Suites. The most exciting suites at the Disneyland Resort are the fantastically themed *Signature Suites*, all found on the Adventure Tower's 11th floor. By contrast the standard suites here, some of which come with balconies, are located in each of the three towers with some offering far superior layouts than others; you never quite know what you will receive until check-in. Only the Signature Suites automatically have concierge access. Concierge in standard suites is by request only with confirmation on arrival and for an additional fee.

Don't jump when the doorbell rings in the *Adventureland Suite*—it's only the sound of drums in deepest, darkest Africa! Its décor includes a mix of tribal masks lining the walls leading to a living room with Oriental rugs upon rich wood flooring, a leather-tufted sleeper sofa, monkey and elephant-themed curios, drum-style cocktail tables, a cozy draped sleeping alcove, a TV hidden behind a painting hung above a gas fireplace, even a hidden closet behind the faux bookcase, all evoking the idea of a British Colonial safari. In the adjoining dining area a six-person table sits on a zebra rug next to a striking wet bar boasting a gorgeous tiger's eye countertop. Nearby is a bonus full bath with a copper pot sink and a nice-sized shower.

In the master bedroom a delightful safari theme reigns with walls decorated in expedition helmets and explorer maps, a four-poster king bed draped in mosquito netting, slate floor covered with Oriental rugs, crocodile-stamped leather easy chairs, luggage-style end tables, even a claw-foot tub in the sleeping area. And you won't even believe the master bath with its dual sinks in a marble vanity, a TV built into the mirror, and, best of all, a rock-lined steam/rain shower/whirlpool tub complete with rain forest sound effects.

The suite's guest room is reminiscent of a safari tent with camp desk, luggage-strapped bureau and side tables, canvas curtains and wall coverings, and rustic king bed. Yet another gorgeous bath features natural stone, above-counter basins, trough-like faucets, tribal mirrors, and a tub/shower with a separate commode area. The suite has lovely pool views but alas no balcony. 1,800 square feet sleeping five.

The *Fairy Tale Suite* is a princess' dream come true. At only 725 square feet what it lacks in size it makes up in pure charm. Who greets you on arrival? None other than Tinker Bell with a sprinkling of pixie dust in the suite's entry hall (just you wait and see!). Two steps down the bedroom adorned with silver and shimmery sage fabrics and carpeting holds a luxuriously draped and oh-so-romantic canopy bed as well as a silky chaise lounge, the perfect spot for resting royalty. At the touch of a button a wall of curtains opens to reveal a magical view of the Disneyland Resort and the nighttime fireworks shows. Not even the TV will spoil your view since is can be raised and lowered within the bureau remotely.

In the massive white marble bath a mosaic of Sleeping Beauty Castle is spread over a fantasy whirlpool tub flanked by Corinthian columns. Shooting stars twinkle above double sinks with a makeup vanity nestled in-between; mosaics adorn the marble flooring; a luxurious steam shower is encased in frosted glass; and a separate room houses the bidet and commode. To top it all off, the vanity mirror disguises a built-in, almost magical TV. This dreamy hideaway fittingly sleeps only two guests.

The Old West is alive and kicking at the *Big Thunder Suite*. This two-bedroom beauty has a doorbell that rings like the howl of a wolf, a foyer with sounds effects from a runaway mine train, stone columns, repurposed barn wood flooring and paneling, and Navaho-style rugs. A mixture of rustic and luxury is on display in the suite's living area with a stone gas fireplace centerpiece with hidden TV above. A cowhide covered armoire, leather sleeper sofa, and two oversized chairs mix with antique mining tool accessories. The eight-person dining table is lit by a wagon wheel chandelier, and a nearby wet bar has an unusual trough-style copper sink over which hangs a "magical" gold miner photo. A half bath is found off the living area with a copper bucket sink, lantern light fixtures, and pull-chain commode. There's no balcony, but lovely views of the resort pools are seen from the oversized windows.

The master bedroom has a king bed with a leather and wood headboard, Nubuck spread, leather pillows and bolsters, desk, leather easy chair, and entertainment center with TV. It is, however, the master bath that really stands out. You enter through a sliding barn door to find a freestanding copper tub set in a stone surround alcove, pebble-lined steam shower, above-counter copper sinks, a magical TV concealed within the vanity mirror, and a separate commode area. On the other side of the living area is the second bedroom decorated 50s-style cowboy with a queen bed topped in a plaid spread, boot lamps, and single sink bath. 1,450 square feet sleeping six.

The whimsical two-bedroom *Pirates of the Caribbean Suite's* doorbell (are you catching on that doorbells are a big thing here?) rings with "Yo Ho, Yo Ho, A Pirate's Life For Me." Tough enough to get this ditty out of your head after a ride on the Disneyland Park attraction, even tougher when the kids are ringing it over and over again! It features wooden beams and planked floors with Spanish colonial-style furniture, rich oriental rugs, a fireplace with a Jolly Roger painting above hiding the TV, leather sofa, two high-back easy chairs, dining room table for eight, and wet bar, all inspired by the *Pirates of the Caribbean* films and attraction. Scattered throughout is a treasure trove of pirate memorabilia, including a replica of Davy Jones's dead man's chest, pirate maps and figurines, model pirate ships, even Jack Sparrow's revolver.

In a smallish master bedroom, a.k.a. Captain's Quarters, a half-canopied bed is draped in royal red and gold brocade. There's an entertainment center, easy chair and ottoman, and the master bath features ornate vanity mirrors, red brocade-like wallpaper, double sinks, whirlpool tub, and steam shower all in one area. For the mateys is the guest room with a pair of twin beds, pirate-ship motif spreads, and treasure chest bureau. There is a 3rd bonus bath, and views from the suite are of the pool via stand-up French balcony. Sleeps four guests with 1,770 square feet.

Talk about a big cheese, you won't believe the *Mickey Mouse Penthouse*! This suite, with 1,725 square feet, two bedrooms and two- and a half baths, is certainly a colorful affair. The modern look is not for everyone; its black, white, red, and yellow color scheme and Mickey Mouse memorabilia in every nook and cranny is different indeed. The oversized living room pops with hardwood floors covered with wacky area rugs, contemporary furnishings including an armless sofa and red leather easy chairs, and a wall of animator pencil drawings of the mouse himself. Overhead is glowing Mickey cutout lighting. If you are a media buff then you'll adore an entire wall of TVs and a state-of-the-art stereo system. An adjoining dining room seats eight people and has the bonus of a wet bar with three stools.

The master bedroom has a king bed with red leather headboard surrounded by Mickey maquettes (scale models) and a bath featuring a steam shower, whirlpool tub, and a double vanity with a magic TV in the mirror. And don't be shocked when the shower heats up and an image of Mickey appears on the tiled wall! The second bedroom is fun, fun, fun with a round bed, Mickey Mouse motif armoire, puffy Mickey-hand pillows, TV and PlayStation, and even an animator's station perfect for hours of playtime; the adjoining single sink bath is an accessible one. Views are of the Disneyland Resort and yes, you can see the fireworks from the suite.

Regal Suites are non-themed, one-bedroom affairs that can connect to make either a 2 or a 3-bedroom suite. A nice-size living area with sleeper sofa and half bath connects to standard-type guest rooms with two queen beds.

Many standard *One-bedroom Suites* are located on the 14th floor of the Frontier Tower and come with a balcony. In this Tower views vary of either the pool or the parking area and California Adventure theme park. Near the entry is a half-bath with black granite countertop and wet bar with sink, under-counter refrigerator, and three white leather barstools. In the parlor area is a sleeper sofa, easy chair, desk, and flat-screen TV as well as access to the Plexiglas-enclosed balcony. The suite's master bedroom offers a king bed with lighted castle headboard, easy chair, and entertainment center, and in the bath are double sinks and a separate tub/shower and commode area.

Ambassador Suites are located in the Frontier Tower and are corner units, each with 1,400 square feet. A long entry hall leads to the living/dining area with sleeper sofa, two easy chairs, desk, entertainment center with TV, and 6-person dining table. Off this area is a wet bar similar to that of the one-bedroom suite. Bedrooms are located behind the wet bar area down a long, strange hallway. The master has a king bed, easy chair, another balcony, and single sink bath with a separate tub/shower and commode area; the small guest room also has a king bed and bath. A half bath is in the hallway off the guest room.

DINE

The Coffee House. Stop in here for quick breakfast items, salads, and desserts along with specialty coffees.

Goofy's Kitchen. Character buffet restaurant open for breakfast and dinner. Goofy is always the chef, but his friends vary with Pluto, Chip 'n' Dale, Rafiki, Sleeping Beauty, and the Mad Hatter some of the usual suspects. *Breakfast:* a bountiful buffet of Mickey-shaped waffles and pancakes, French toast, create-your-own omelet station, eggs benedict, sausage, bacon, muffins, pastries, and fruit. *Dinner:* the buffet features a carving station, fresh catch of the day, pasta of the day, fried chicken, seasonal vegetables, tossed salads, assorted pizzas, and a dessert station.

Steakhouse 55 & Lounge. Fine dining in a Hollywood setting with exceptional steaks, chops, salads, and seafood. Open for breakfast and dinner. (See full description in Dining in Style at Disneyland Resort.)

Tangaroa Terrace. South Seas-style quick-service restaurant with indoor and wraparound terrace seating overlooking the pool. In the evening hours sit outside to enjoy Trader Sam's live entertainment nextdoor. Open 7:00 a.m. to 11:00 p.m. *Breakfast:* French toast topped with warm banana-caramel sauce, breakfast whole wheat wrap, scrambled egg platter, grilled cinnamon spiced oatmeal cake with fruit compote and Greek yogurt, egg white and vegetable/tofu bake. *Lunch and dinner:* cheeseburger, barbecue chicken sandwich, panko-crusted fish and chips, Asian chicken salad, crispy tofu salad, Kalua pork flatbread, Angus Hawaiian cheeseburger with teriyaki sauce and fresh grilled pineapple; prepackaged cold sandwiches and sushi; brownies, cupcakes, apple pie, muffins, croissants, cookies. *Children's menu:* grilled salmon, hamburger, chicken nuggets.

SIP

Steakhouse 55 Lounge. Stop in here for a mellow vibe and a heyday of Hollywood experience. Order a serious cocktail along with something from the appetizer menu such as a trio of cheese, Dungeness crab cake, smoked ahi, Mediterranean pizzetta, chicken and brie pizzetta, soy-glazed barbecue short ribs, fried calamari with spicy aioli, and a charcuterie plate.

Trader Sam's Enchanted Tiki Bar. My favorite place for a drink! Located poolside, stop in for Polynesian cocktails and live Hawaiian music on the torch-lit verandah. Inside, the interactive bar is also a kick. Tropical drinks (the best mai tai this side of Hawaii) and light meals such as panko-crusted Chinese long beans with Sriracha aioli (don't miss these), sweet 'n spicy Asian wings, ahi poke (wasabi-yuzu-marinated tuna), Angus Hawaiian cheeseburger, fish tacos, chicken lettuce wraps with Hoison ginger sauce, barbecued chicken sandwich, Asian chicken salad, and Kalua pork flatbread.

PLAY

Activities. The resort offers complimentary activities such as Trivia Challenge, Learn to Draw, Get Up & Go Power Walk, poolside games.

Swimming. Three pools for water play fun galore: the original Never Land Pool, now the E-Ticket Pool, has a fresh new look and whirlpool tub, even three cabanas featuring lounge chairs and sofa, refrigerator, flat-screen television, wireless Internet, safes, and fans—call (714) 778-6600 for reservations; the new Monorail Pool features a re-creation of the original Disneyland Park entrance sign, two water slides (one slide is 187 feet long, the other 112), three cabanas for rent (see above), and an immersive water play area and mini slide for the little ones; and the four-foot-deep D-Ticket pool, the most laid back choice with a soothing waterfall surrounded by fun geysers. Cushy, padded lounge chairs can be found around each pool.

WORK, MOVE, SOOTHE

Business Center. Located in the Convention Center offering Internet access, printing, office equipment rental, office supplies, and shipping.

Fitness Center. Goofy About Health Club with Life Fitness ellipticals, treadmills, and bicycles, free weights, and a small set of strength training equipment that has seen better days. Complimentary to resort guests; age 14 or older for admittance.

LOOKING FOR THE BEST OF BOTH WORLDS?

Are you torn between a Disney Destination and a trip to the beach? Then definitely consider a visit to the Disneyland Resort followed by a few days at the nearby Orange County beach area just a 40-minute drive away.

Lovely beaches, unbelievable weather, and quaint towns such as Newport Beach or Laguna Beach are a dream come true. If luxury is what you are looking for then you can't go wrong at one of the area's renowned resorts, like Montage Laguna Beach, the Ritz Carlton Laguna Nigel, or Newport Beach's Resort at Pelican Hill. Or, if boutique hotels are your thing then opt for Surf and Sand Resort in Laguna where the ocean is right outside your window and the hotel's on-site restaurant, Splashes, offers the very best of views along with outstanding food.

Spend the daytime hiking the canyons, shopping Newport's Fashion Island, or relaxing on a strand of sand like Crystal Cove whose historic cottages wax nostalgia, and lunch at The Beachcomber is an absolute must. In the evening enjoy dinner at one of Laguna's premier restaurants such as Watermarc (go for paella or whatever fresh fish is on the menu), 230 Forest Avenue (pray that king salmon is in season), or Studio at the Montage (panoramic ocean views and a world-class menu).

Use nearby John Wayne Airport for total convenience, and start scheming for any excuse to return to "Sunny Cal" within hours of arriving home. I'm telling you, it's the perfect vacation.

Disney's Grand Californian Hotel® & Spa

1,019 rooms (including 40 suites) and 50 villas. 1600 S. Disneyland Drive, Anaheim, CA 92802; phone (714) 635-2300, fax (714) 300-7300. Check-in 3:00 p.m., checkout 11:00 a.m. For reservations contact your travel advisor or call (714) 956-6425.

Claim To Fame. An entrance from the hotel directly into Disney California Adventure Park.

Rooms to Book. Preferred Concierge rooms with a California Adventure view.

The Wow Factor! Disneyland Resort's very best restaurant, Napa Rose.

Location, location, location. It doesn't get much better than this with a back-door entrance leading straight into Disney California Adventure Park. Nature is the theme at this 6-story hotel fringed by pine trees and constructed of cedar and redwood, an accolade to turn-of-the-century Craftsman style. The jaw-dropping lobby hung with Mission-style chandeliers and strewn with comfy seating is a favorite meeting place for guests. Each afternoon and into the evening is storytelling and live entertainment in and around the great hearth where there's a fire lit year round.

REST

Guest rooms. Standard guest rooms here are a bit small at 353 square feet and, in my opinion, ready for renovation. An Arts and Crafts-style headboard with a carved Tree of Life motif is adorned with lantern lighting, and beds (either a king bed and sleeper sofa, two queen-size beds, or a queen bed and bunk beds) are made with white duvets and red and cream floral bed runners. The double-decker bureau features not only drawer space but also a built-in under-counter refrigerator and overhead flat-screen TV. Because the rooms are small you won't find a sofa or daybed . . . there's only room for a small table and two dining chairs. But unlike the Disneyland Hotel rooms, these do have a balcony with varying views: *Standard View* of the front of the resort; *Wood's, Garden, Courtyard View* of the courtyard, pool, or gardens; *Downtown Disney District View,* a somewhat noisy option; or a *Premium View* of California Adventure Park which can also come with quite a bit of noise from the park.

Double sinks in a black marble vanity sit outside of a commode and white-tiled tub area. The nature theme of the resort carries over into a Bambi motif shower curtain and an accent bear tile inside the tub/shower. Unattractive brown leaf wallpaper, low water pressure, old-style showerhead, and dim lighting does little to improve the aesthetics. Additional amenities include H2O spa bath products, robes, hairdryer, non-lighted makeup mirror, full-length mirror, coffeemaker, DVD player, turndown service, and keyed safe.

Concierge rooms. Guests of concierge may access the comfortable *Craftsman's Club Lounge* located on the 6th floor of the resort, a perfect spot to just hang out and enjoy the multiple food services available. Specialty Presidential and Vice Presidential suites as well as concierge guest rooms include access to concierge; standard one, two, and three-bedroom suites do not although concierge can be added at time of check-in for an additional fee.

Breakfast consists of luncheon meats and cheeses, hard-boiled eggs, bagels, croissants, muffins, fresh fruit, cereal, and juice. Afternoon snacks are fresh fruit, tea cookies, PBJ sandwiches, scones and jam, chocolate-covered strawberries, and goldfish crackers. In the evening enjoy cheese and crackers, focaccia bread, crudités and dip, and one hot dish such as crab cakes, chicken teriyaki on sugar cane skewers, black bean empanadas, jerk chicken brochette with sweet chili garlic sauce, Southwest chicken spring rolls with salsa, and Kalua pork. Beer and wine are served by the lounge hosts with choices of BV Chardonnay, BV Cabernet, BV Merlot, and Woodbridge White Zinfandel. Bottled water is available for the asking, and an espresso machine adds to the enjoyment. Evening desserts served from 8:00 until 10:00 p.m. include chocolate chip and oatmeal cookies, macaroons, petit fours, and chocolate-covered strawberries.

One of the most enjoyable aspects of the lounge is the balcony that runs the length of it with a view of the monorail zipping through the hotel courtyard as well as the Disneyland fireworks. Bedtime storytelling and songs along with milk and cookies are offered in the lounge each evening at 8:15 p.m. Additional amenities includes nightly turndown service, DVD players, Bose Wave music system, and in-room check-in.

Suites. The *Arcadia Suite* on the 6th floor, one of two Vice Presidential Suites at the Grand Californian, comes in one, two, or three-bedroom options sleeping either four, eight, or twelve guests. It is a tribute to Frank Lloyd Wright with such nice touches as the living/dining area's centerpiece brick fireplace and a wall of windows that fill the room with natural light, etched in Frank Lloyd Wright's Tree of Life pattern. A half bath is found off the entry hall. In a separate area is the dining room seating eight adjoining a service kitchen with sink, microwave, and full-size refrigerator. Relax on two smallish verandahs overlooking the Redwood Pool and California Adventure, one off the dining room, the other off the master bedroom. In the master is a king bed, and the adjoining bath has a whirlpool tub. Optional connecting rooms have either two queen beds or a king bed with queen sleeper sofa.

The *Mt. Whitney Suite*, one of two Presidential Suites at the Grand Californian (the other is the El Capitan Suite), is embellished with warm tones of green, brown, and gold reminiscent of nature and strongly suggestive of the Mission style seen throughout the resort. Off one side of the entry hall is a half bath, and on the other side an office with an oversized desk and credenza. In the massive living room is rich hardwood flooring, fireplace, forest green sofa, and four easy chairs, two of which are Morris-style leather chairs, all flanked by amber-hued Craftsman standing lamps. As part of this "great space" the dining table seats eight, and above it hangs a stained glass light fixture. A service kitchen adjoins the dining area with full-size refrigerator, sink, and microwave.

The grandeur of the living area outshines the somewhat low-keyed master bedroom bedecked in moss green and lilac hues. The furnishings of king bed, easy chair, desk, bureau, and entertainment center seem a bit lost in such a spacious room. Pass through the bedroom to a small walk-in closet where a vanity area divides a two-part master bath: on one side is a single sink, whirlpool tub, bidet, and commode; on the other side, an oversized marble shower, single sink, and a separate commode area, all enhanced with Carrera marble and mosaic flooring. An additional bedroom with two queen beds can be added to make a 2-bedroom suite sleeping eight guests.

My favorite aspect of the suite is its outdoor space with a balcony the entire length of the suite as well as a gem of an eating porch (even an outdoor fireplace!) perfect for al fresco dining. And even more perfect is the superlative view of the resort's pools and California Adventure Park with semi-views of the World of Color show.

Also on the 6th floor the *El Capitan Suite* comes in one, two, or three-bedroom options sleeping four, eight, or twelve guest respectively. With a wall of floor to ceiling etched glass windows in the living area, an office, dual-sided rock fireplace, and kitchen, it's a haven in the midst of theme park craziness. The arched living area's furnishings include a sofa and four easy chairs; on the other side of the fireplace a dining table seats eight. The furniture in the sizeable master bedroom, like the

Mt. Whitney Suite, feels a bit lost. In the bath are three rooms, all with marble flooring: one with two single sink marble vanities; another with a large shower and whirlpool tub; the third with a commode and bidet. A balcony the length of the dining room, living room, and office comes with splendid views of California Adventure Park.

Standard one, two, and three-bedroom suites are also available with standard-size guest rooms attached to a small parlor area the size of a guest room with sofa, easy chair, entertainment center, and wet bar.

The Villas at Disney's Grand Californian Hotel. The successful Disney Vacation Club villas are also available at the Grand Californian Hotel with studio, and one, two, and three-bedroom options. Designed as part of the existing hotel, the newest wing houses these Deluxe Villas where the hotel's Mission-style architecture and nature theme continues, much in the same manor and décor as the guest rooms. Views vary and are of either the Paradise Pier area of California Adventure Park or the pool.

Studios are 379 square feet with a queen bed and a queen-size sleeper sofa, balcony, and kitchenette with microwave, under-counter refrigerator, and coffeemaker. Sleeps four.

One-bedroom Villas sleeping five with 865 square feet have a full kitchen with granite countertops, small kitchen island, and a dining alcove booth. In the living area are a queen sleeper sofa, pull-down bed, and entertainment center. A stacked washer and dryer as well as a bonus bath with shower and pedestal sink are just off the kitchen. In the bedroom are a king bed, desk, and entertainment center, and the adjoining bath has a single sink, whirlpool tub, and oversized shower with separate toilet. The villa's balcony is accessed from either the living room or bedroom.

Two-bedroom Villas are the same as One-bedroom Villas with the addition of a studio-size guest room with two queen beds, entertainment center, and desk. The guest bath has a single sink in one area, and the toilet and shower/bath in the other area. Dedicated two-bedroom units do not have a mini-kitchen in the guest room. Sleeps nine with 1,257 square feet, two balconies, and three baths.

Three-bedroom Grand Villas are enormous with 2,426 square feet sleeping twelve. Spread over two stories, downstairs is the kitchen, living area with sleeper sofa, dining room with balcony, and master bedroom/ bath. Upstairs are two bedrooms, each with two queen beds and each with its own bath and balcony. An additional bonus bath is located off the entry hall, making a total of four baths.

DINE

Napa Rose Restaurant. Disneyland Resort's most illustrious restaurant. (See full description in Dining in Style at Disneyland Resort.)

Storyteller's Café. Open for breakfast, lunch, and dinner. Join Chip and Dale and their critter friends for *breakfast* only with either a buffet choice or a la carte options such as a classic Denver omelet, Spanish omelet, huevos rancheros, steak and eggs, eggs benedict, Mickey-shaped waffle, and banana-stuffed French toast. *Lunch* offers a la carte entrées of salmon with artichoke tapenade, grilled albacore tuna sandwich, grilled New York steak with steamed vegetables, cobb salad, four cheese ravioli, salmon spinach *panzanella* salad, *margherita* flatbread, and spaghetti with meat sauce. *Dinner*: sake-infused sea bass with ponzu sauce, lemon prawns tossed in a low fat citrus sauce, New York strip steak with garlic mashed potatoes and a mushroom demi-glace tossed with crispy leeks, lobster cobb salad, and Sonoma Valley chicken in a red wine sauce topped with diced bacon.

Whitewater Snacks. Quick-service restaurant open for breakfast, lunch, and dinner. *Breakfast:* buttermilk biscuit sandwich, California breakfast burrito, French toast sticks, American breakfast plate, Mickey-shaped waffle, and oatmeal. *Lunch and dinner: carnitas/*Angus cheeseburger, veggie burger, pesto chicken sandwich on herb focaccia, turkey sandwich on a honey-fig baguette, tuna sandwich on ciabatta bread, hot dog with chili and cheddar, personal pizza, charbroiled chicken sandwich with Ortega chilis and guacamole, and chicken or shredded beef nachos.

SIP

Hearthstone Lounge. After a day in the parks you'll more than likely find me here winding down with a nice glass of chardonnay in hand. A popular gathering spot, it's a bit too large for a cozy atmosphere. But if you're in luck you'll be able to nab the nook table in front of the fireplace. Offering a Californian and global wine list, international beers, and cocktails, there are also light meals such as an artisan cheese selection, pan-seared crab cakes with lemon-basil mayonnaise and arugula salad, Bloody Mary shrimp cocktail, chicken quesadilla with Anaheim chili, mini Wagyu sliders topped with Cabrales bleu with garlic skinny fries, "sticky" spare ribs served with soba salad, margarita flatbread, and the specialty *robusto* flatbread topped with fingerling potatoes, chorizo, Burrata cheese, and Romenesco sauce. A continental breakfast and coffee is served in the morning hours.

Napa Rose Lounge. If you can't get a table at the adjoining restaurant then consider its atmospheric lounge instead. Almost a full menu is served with such delectables as beet salad with Cara Cara oranges, endive and mizuna; The Sizzling Beach Rock with garlic seared shrimp, soy glazed spare ribs, and lemon grass chicken skewers cooked on a hot beach stone; pan-roasted diver scallops; portobello mushroom bisque "cappuccino"; wood-fired pizzetta of the season; and braised spring rabbit with portobello mushroom *ragù*. There's a wide range of desserts, too. Grab a seat in the outdoor fire pit area, perfect for enjoying the Southern California weather as you sip on fine wine or specialty cocktails.

PLAY

Activities. Get Up & Go Power Walk led by a Guest Activity Coordinator through Downtown Disney, a non-impact Morning Fitness Fusion at the outdoor fireplace alcove, washcloth creations lessons at Hearthstone Lounge, or Learn to Draw Mickey classes. Weekly outdoor movies are scheduled at the outdoor fireplace alcove. For family fun stop by the Guest Services Desk and pick up instructions for The Grand Quest, a scavenger hunt held throughout the hotel.

Arcade. Grizzly Game Arcade is located across from the Mariposa Pool.

Swimming. Three pools are located in the resort's courtyard area all surrounded by cushioned lounge chairs: the peaceful Fountain Pool with hot tub; the adjacent Redwood Pool with its waterslide; and the Mariposa Pool with another hot tub and four cabanas with comfortable lounge furniture, fruit basket, TV, ceiling fan, safe, refrigerator, and the services of a pool attendant (half day rental $110; full day $185). Call (714) 635-2300, option 5 for reservations.

Tours. Art of the Craft Tour, a complimentary one-hour guided walking tour showing the influence of the Arts and Crafts Movement on the architecture and design of the Grand Californian Hotel.

WORK, MOVE, SOOTHE

Business Center. Located in the Convention Center offering Internet access, printing, office equipment rental, office supplies, and shipping.

Childcare. Pinocchio's Workshop, the only childcare facility at the Disneyland Resort, is located next to the Grizzly Game Arcade across from the Mariposa Pool. Open from 5:00 p.m. until midnight for children between ages 5 and 12, the agenda consists of video and board games, computer stations, arts and crafts, air hockey, Disney DVDs, and even a view of the Disneyland fireworks. Cost includes dinner and snacks; open only to registered guests of the Disneyland Resort Hotels.

Fitness Center. Adjacent to the Mandara Spa, this small fitness room offers LifeFitness stair steppers, treadmills, bicycles, and ellipticals as well as free weights, Cybex strength training equipment, and a cable crossover machine. Open 6:00 a.m. until 8:00 p.m. daily, it is complimentary to registered guests age 14 or older.

Mandara Spa. Offering a variety of soothing and exotic Balinese-inspired treatments, this small spa has eight treatment rooms, including a couple's pavilion, with Balinese Massage as their signature treatment. Locker rooms have steam and sauna and a coed tea lounge. The spa's retail store sells Mandara brand, Bliss, and Elemis products. Open 8:00 a.m. until 8:00 p.m.

SAMPLE SERVICES

Elemis Tri-Enzyme Resurfacing Facial. The layering of three enzymes stimulates and accelerates exfoliation process by up to 75% leaving the skin smooth and radiant with a new level of clarity and evenness.

Mandara Stone Therapy Massage. Customized massage using aromatic oils and heated stones for deep relaxation.

Ionithermie Cellulite Reduction Program. A noninvasive way to detoxify, reduce fluid retention, and tone muscles. Lose up to eight inches after a single treatment.

Elemis Aroma Spa Seaweed Massage. Combining sea plants and marine algae with aromatherapy, begin with a warm seaweed body mask containing essential oils, then become wrapped in a foil cocoon. While the active ingredients work to detoxify receive a scalp and foot massage. Follow with a full body massage.

THE VERY BEST OF DISNEYLAND RESORT THEME PARKS AND DOWNTOWN DISNEY

At Disneyland Resort there are two exciting theme parks, Disneyland Park and Disney California Adventure. Disneyland was Walt's dream and his creation, as wonderful as ever, continues on for yet another generation to love and enjoy. Who can resist zipping down Splash Mountain, that charming pink Sleeping Beauty Castle, or the sentimental Fantasyland attractions that we remember as kids? "The Happiest Place on Earth" remains in many aspects as it was in the '50s—nostalgic, enchanting, and enduring. I think nothing can beat this glorious theme park.

California Adventure has evolved—particularly in the last year or so after a billion dollar expansion—into an exciting and interesting destination. Here the theme is The Golden State, beginning with early 20th century Los Angeles as it was when Walt first arrived in Los Angeles. After adding a sensational new "land," entirely updated and revised areas, and re-"imagineered" attractions, California Adventure has finally come into its own, fit to stand across the plaza from its sister park, Disneyland.

General Information

First I'll go over what you need to know about getting into and around the parks; then I'll examine the best of each park. You'll find important information on only the best attractions and dining, the most anticipated special events, and the most memorable entertainment.

Disneyland Resort Theme Park Admission

Several options are available for Disneyland Resort theme park passes. Choose the number of days you wish to purchase and then consider your options. Purchase tickets by consulting a Disney specialist travel advisor (see page 10 in the Planning Your Walt Disney World Vacation chapter), online at Disneyland.Disney.Go.com/tickets, or by calling (714) 781-4636. No matter which ticket plan you opt for, children ages two or younger have complimentary theme park entrance.

Base Tickets. Choose the number of days you'll need, allowing entrance to one theme park each day. Base Tickets are offered from one to five days, and you'll save with each extra day added. Tickets expire thirteen days after first use.

Park Hopper Option. Allows park-hopping privileges for a flat rate of $45 for a 1-day ticket or $35 for a multi-day ticket regardless of the number of days.

Deluxe Annual Passport. Valid for a full year with access to both Disneyland Resort theme parks for 315 pre-selected days. Also included is a 10% dining discount at select restaurants and special rates at Disneyland Resort Hotels. An annual parking pass can be added for $139. If you plan to return within a year this is the way to go. You may even consider this type of pass for shorter stays simply to receive the great savings available to Annual Pass holders; only one person in your party must have an annual pass to obtain the discount. If you make an annual trip to Disneyland Resort you should plan your return trip a few weeks shy of the expiration date of your pass and your park admission will already be paid. At press time Annual Pass rates were $499 for guests age 3 and older.

Premium Annual Passport. The same as the Deluxe Annual Passport, but for 365 days without blackout dates. It also includes a free annual parking pass, 20% merchandise discount at select retail stores, and up to a 15% dining discount at select locations. At press time Premium Annual Pass rates were $669 for guests age 3 and older.

Southern California CityPASS. If visiting other area attractions is part of your vacation plans consider purchasing this pass which comes with admission to: one day at Universal Studios Hollywood; one day at Sea-World Adventure Park; and one 3-Day Disneyland Resort Park Hopper ticket for Disneyland Park and Disney California Adventure Park. At press time the price was $319 for adults and $279 for guests ages 3 to 9.

Disney FASTPASS® Service

FASTPASS is a free computerized service offered to all Disneyland Parks visitors as a way of reducing time spent waiting in line. Here's how it works. As you approach a FASTPASS attraction you'll see two time clocks on display: one estimating the wait time in the normal line, the other the return time for the FASTPASS issued at the moment. If the normal wait time is less than thirty minutes, by all means get in line. If not, just insert your park pass in one of the machines located at each individual FASTPASS attraction and receive a ticket printed with a designated one-hour window in which you may return and enter a special line with little or no waiting.

In most cases only one FASTPASS at a time is issued. To find out when you can receive another FASTPASS ticket look on your current FASTPASS. Each person must have a FASTPASS to enter the line and must show it to the cast member (Disney's name for park employees) at the beginning of the line and the cast member waiting at the boarding area. There is usually no need to use FASTPASS for the first hour or so after the park opens, but it is a good idea to pick up one right away for one of the big attractions if you wish to ride it more than once later in the day. Note that on the most popular attractions, particularly in the busier seasons, those seeking a FASTPASS late in the afternoon may find there are none left for the remainder of the day.

Touring Advice

Just as at Walt Disney World a bit of planning is necessary. Determine which attractions are the most desirable in each park, hit them first thing in the morning, and after you have lost your lead and the park begins filling up, simply see the rest of the attractions as you encounter them.

In the busier seasons be in place at park opening and immediately head to the most popular rides in the park. In Disneyland Park this means Space Mountain, Indiana Jones Adventure, and Splash Mountain; in California Adventure beeline it directly to Radiator Springs then to 'Soarin. After that you'll have lost your edge on the latecomers, so simply explore each attraction as you come to it utilizing FASTPASS when necessary.

At the very least plan a loose itinerary for each day and make Advance Dining Reservations for any table-service restaurants. Find out before leaving home the park hours for the days of your vacation and what special events are happening during your stay by going online at Disneyland.Disney.Go.com/calendar. The worst thing you can do is wake up each morning and then decide what you want to do that day. That's best left for free days when you plan to just relax by the pool.

DISNEYLAND RESORT'S VIP TOUR SERVICES

Those wishing to make their visit to the theme parks as seamless and easy as possible should consider Disney's personalized tours. For $315-355 per hour ($340-380 for non-Disney resort guests) with a minimum of six consecutive hours, a Disney VIP tour guide will completely customize your experience and maximize your time by assisting you and up to nine others with a day at the parks and plenty of Disney trivia along the way. You'll have flexibility of start time, valet parking at the Grand Californian Hotel, the option of visiting both theme parks if you wish, meet and greet at your resort, expedited entry to FASTPASS attractions, and VIP seating for parades, select shows, and nighttime spectaculars. Even if your guide is no longer with you in the late evening, your entrance to a VIP viewing area will still be arranged. Make reservations at least forty-eight hours in advance by calling (714) 300-7710 or your travel advisor.

Failure to plan at least a bit could mean losing out on a great restaurant like Napa Rose or miss special seating arrangements for a show like Fantasmic! because they're totally booked. That said, do try and plan for at least some spontaneity in your day.

The best advice I can give is if at all possible come during the slower times of the year by avoiding holiday periods, Saturdays, and the height of summer.

Rider Switch Service

Disney extends this option at all attractions to parents with small children with a height restriction. Just advise the cast member on duty upon entering the line. Your entire party will wait in line as usual until you reach the loading area. Then one adult rides while the other stays behind with the children. When the first adult returns, the second adult rides without delay.

Parking

Theme park parking is $16 per day. There are two parking areas: the Mickey & Friends structure next to the Downtown Disney parking lot and closest to the theme parks; and the Toy Story lot further away on Harbor Boulevard near the Convention Center. Remember to make a note of the section and aisle then board the tram to the Main Entry Plaza drop off area. Parking for Guests with Disabilities is available at both parking areas; a valid disability parking permit is required.

Disneyland Park

The only theme park designed and built under the direct supervision of Walt Disney, Disneyland Park still offers tried-and-true experiences such as watching Mickey Mouse leading the marching band down Main Street, vintage cars full of characters zipping by, the quintessential Emporium for shopping, even a walk through Sleeping Beauty Castle filled with dioramas of the story. Nostalgia reigns supreme, and there's excitement around every corner with plenty of surprises along the way. Expect to have the time of your life!

Operating Hours

Typically parks open from 10:00 a.m. to 8:00 p.m. Monday through

Thursday, 9:00 a.m. to 10:00 p.m. on Friday and Sunday, and 8:00 a.m. to 11:00 p.m. on Saturdays with extended hours during holidays and busy seasons. Call (714) 781-INFO (4636) or log on to Disneyland. disney.go.com/calendar/ for updated park hours along with parade and fireworks information.

If you are driving to the parks get a jump on the crowds by arriving about 45 minutes early, allowing plenty of time to park, ride the tram, buy tickets, and be one of the first to hit the big attractions. Those staying on property can stroll over and be ready to hit the parks about 15 minutes prior unless they are enjoying Extra Magic Hour, available only to resort guests, with one of the parks opening an hour early just for them each day of the week. I recommend heading straight to Space Mountain, Indiana Jones Adventure, or Splash Mountain. However, if little ones are with you make a beeline to Fantasyland.

FASTPASS Attractions

Autopia

Big Thunder Mountain Railroad

Indiana Jones™ Adventure ©Disney/Lucasfilm Ltd.

Roger Rabbit's Car Toon Spin

Space Mountain

Splash Mountain

Star Tours—The Adventures Continue ©Disney/Lucasfilm Ltd.

See the introduction to this chapter for FASTPASS details.

Park Services

ATMs. Five ATMs operated by Chase Bank are located at the park: just outside the park entrance to your left; at Bank of Main Street; at the entrance to Frontierland; at Starcade in Tomorrowland; and outside Fantasy Faire.

Baby Care Center. Found at the northeast end of Main Street next to First Aid, here you'll find comfortable facilities for diaper changing, nursing, and bottle feeding. All restrooms throughout the park are outfitted with changing tables.

First aid. The First Aid Center is located on Main Street right behind the infamous Red Wagon corn dog cart.

Guest Relations. City Hall on Main Street houses Guest Relations where a knowledgeable staff is ready to assist with dining, ticket upgrades, messages for separated parties, information for guests with disabilities, and international guests.

Guests with disabilities. Parking for Guests with disabilities is available at Mickey and Friends parking structure and the Toy Story parking area off Harbor Boulevard. Transportation is provided from the Mickey and Friends parking structure and the Toy Story parking area to the Main Entry Plaza. Please note: oversized wheelchairs and Electric Convenience Vehicles may be too large for some transportation vehicles. A guide for guests with disabilities is available at Guest Relations. Wheelchairs and ECVs are available for rent on a first-come, first-served basis.

Most restaurants and shops are accessible to guests with disabilities, although some quick-service locations have narrow queues with railings (ask a host or hostess for assistance). Companion-assisted restrooms are located at First Aid, Frontierland at Rancho del Zocolo, and Tom Sawyer Island. Many attractions provide access through the main queue, while others have auxiliary entrances for wheelchairs and service animals along with as many as five members of your party. Certain attractions require guests to transfer from their wheelchair to a ride system. Parade routes and some shows have designated viewing areas on a first-come, first-served basis.

Braille guidebooks, handheld captioning receivers, digital audio tours, and assistive listening devices are available at City Hall for a $25 refundable deposit. Reflective captioning is provided at many theater-type attractions and video captioning at some attractions. A sign language interpreter is provided at specific live shows on a rotating basis on Mondays and Saturdays. For more information call (714) 781-6176 or (714) 781-7292 (TTY).

Lockers. Located outside to the left of the main entrance as well as inside the park behind Main Street Cinema. The cost for unlimited access is $7, $10, $11, $12, and $15 per day depending on the size of the locker.

Lost and Found. Located in the Guest Services Building which is outside and to the left of the Main Entrance to Disneyland Park or call (714) 817-2166.

Lost children. Locate lost children at the Baby Care Center at the end of Main Street or at City Hall.

Package pickup. Shop and send your purchases for pickup later in the day to Newsstand at the Main Entrance, The Star Trader in Tomorrowland, or Pioneer Mercantile in Frontierland. Disneyland Resort Hotel Guests may send packages directly to Bell Services at their hotel for next-day arrival.

Pet kennel. Kennel facilities are located to the right of the Main Entrance of Disneyland Park. First-come, first-served basis with no reservations accepted. For information call (714) 781-4565. Proof of vaccination is required, and no overnight accommodations are allowed.

Strollers and wheelchairs. Rentals are located outside the Disneyland Park next to the Pet Kennel. Single strollers are $15 per day, $25 for two. Wheelchairs are $12 per day, electric convenience vehicles $50.00; both require a $20.00 refundable deposit. Rental strollers are permitted in both theme parks but not allowed in Downtown Disney.

The Lay of the Land

Disneyland Park consists of eight enchanting areas accessed from the central hub in front of Sleeping Beauty Castle. Travel down Main Street to reach the hub from the front entrance. Moving counterclockwise around the hub, you first encounter Tomorrowland then Mickey's Toontown (accessed via a walkway located between Tomorrowland and Fantasyland), Fantasyland, Frontierland, Critter Country and New Orleans Square (both accessed via Frontierland or Adventureland), and Adventureland. Travel the Disneyland® Railroad on a 20-minute loop around the park exiting at one of four stops: Main Street U.S.A, New Orleans Square, Mickey's Toontown, and Tomorrowland.

The Very Best Attractions in Disneyland Park

BIG THUNDER MOUNTAIN RAILROAD

Take a peek at the Old West mining town of Rainbow Ridge in Disneyland's Frontierland. The queue is a kick as you snake through an old mining town complete with hotel, dance hall, and the requisite saloon (listen closely) while overhead the train goes zipping by. Board a "runaway" mining train led by a puffing and chugging engine for a wild journey through creepy caves, rushing waterfalls, hazardous rockslides, rumbling earthquakes, a natural arch bridge, and more. For those who like speed but not big drops, this is your coaster; there are plenty of curves and small dips, but all in all you'll find it fairly tame and loads of rip-roarin' fun. And keep an eye out for those rattlers! **Minimum height 40 inches (3 feet, 4 inches). Not recommended for expectant mothers or those with back or neck problems. FASTPASS. 3 ½-minute ride.**

DISNEYLAND PARK'S BEHIND-THE-SCENES TOURS

Call (714) 781-TOUR or (714) 781-8687 for reservations.

- **Walk in Walt's Footsteps**. Traveling through Disneyland you'll learn how Walt wove his personal history and interests into the creation of the park. Tour his Town Square apartment, peek in the exclusive, members-only Club 33 lobby, ride two classic 1955 attractions, and end with a private, quick-service-type lunch on Main Street. Theme park admission is required to attend the tour. This three-hour tour is available twice a day at 9:30 a.m. and 2:30 p.m. for $109.

- **Cultivating Magic**. Enjoy select attractions while gaining a fresh perspective on the plants used in that particular area of Disneyland Park. Tour the lush landscape and gardens and find out how important plants have been to the design of the park. This two-hour tour is offered on Saturday and Sunday at 9:00 a.m. and Monday at 10:00 a.m. for $49; theme park admission is not included in the price.

- **Discover the Magic**. Enjoy an interactive scavenger hunt for hidden treasure through Disneyland Park. Along the way you'll learn things you might not have known about the park as you hunt for clues, solve puzzles, and hunt for hidden treasures. You'll even ride an attraction or two. Perfect for the entire family. The tour is 2.5 hours long, offered on Friday, Saturday, and Sunday at 10:00 a.m. for $59, and does not include theme park admission.

- **Disney's Happiest Haunts**. Join your "ghost host" to search for Disney Villains, experience thrilling attractions, and hear spooky stories in both theme parks on this seasonal fall tour offered mid-September through the end of October. Ride Tower of Terror and Big Thunder Mountain ending at the "Haunted Mansion Holiday." The tour is $68 and does not include theme park admission.

- **Holiday Time at Disneyland.** Hear tales of the holidays from around the world, enjoy two popular holiday themed attractions, receive reserved seating for A Christmas Fantasy Parade, and enjoy a holiday treat and warm beverage as well as a collectible pin and tour button. Theme park admission for Disneyland is required to attend the $65 tour; approximately three hours long. Offered only seasonally mid-November through early January.

- **Welcome To Disneyland.** Perfect for the Disneyland Resort first-timer, learn tips and trivia about the attractions, entertainment, and services of both theme parks. Ride two attractions, receive two FASTPASS to enjoy after the tour, and a World of Color FASTPASS to use the evening of your tour. 2.5 hours offered Sunday, Monday, Friday, and Saturday at 10:30 a.m. for $25; does not include theme park admission.

HAUNTED MANSION

Board a "doom buggy" in New Orleans Square inside the 19th century mansion of a long-gone sea captain who met an untimely end courtesy of his newlywed bride. The estate is now inhabited by plenty of friendly ghosts who are "dying" to meet you. Filled with terrific special effects and hair-raising sounds you'll take part in a séance, travel through the ballroom where a wild party is in progress, move down the creepy hallways and into the attic where secrets are hidden, then outside through the graveyard where ghosts come out to socialize, all the while entertained by 999 ghosts and ghouls who manage to always pull a prank or two. If this sounds frightening, don't worry. It's nothing but fun, and only the smallest of children might become alarmed. **9-minute ride.**

> CARA'S TIP: If you're prone to allergies, don't worry. The "dust" used here is an artificial, non-allergenic material.

INDIANA JONES ADVENTURE

Here is one ride that you won't find at Walt Disney World although its track is the same layout as the Animal Kingdom's Dinosaur attraction. After working your way through an archeology site and winding your way through The Temple of the Forbidden Eye's numerous passageways, you'll board a 12-passenger military transport vehicle that tips and pitches its way through a wild Indiana Jones expedition. Now, whatever you do, don't gaze upon the Forbidden Eye! You did it . . . you looked into the Forbidden Eye! Get out, get out before the temple crashes around you, but not before encountering creepy crawly creatures, hissing snakes, scrambling rats, collapsing bridges, and, in true Indiana Jones fashion, a gargantuan granite ball a la *Raiders of the Lost Ark*. **Minimum height 46 inches (3 feet, 10 inches). Not recommended for expectant mothers or those with back, heart, or neck problems. FASTPASS. Single-rider line. 3.5-minute ride.**

> CARA'S TIP: This is one popular attraction so head here first thing in the morning before or after Space and Splash Mountain. Although it may seem like the attraction is packed in the first hour or so after park opening with the line snaking outside the entrance, it's probably best to ignore it and just get in line. You'll more than likely find that the queue inside the temple is almost

non-existent, and you'll be patting yourself on the back that you avoided what could have been a ridiculous wait in line later in the day. The attraction breaks down quite often so come prepared.

PETER PAN'S FLIGHT

This is one of the most endearing attractions in Fantasyland, sure to steal your heart. Though old-fashioned and certainly not a thrill a minute you'll find it hard to resist "flying" with Peter Pan, Wendy, and the boys on gently soaring pirate ships. Your adventure begins in the Darling nursery, "and off we go," flying over the twinkling lights of London with Big Ben and the London Bridge standing out against a starry, moonlit night (definitely the best part of the ride). Next stop Never Never Land where far below are glistening waterfalls, glowing volcanoes, sunning mermaids, an Indian Village, the Lost Boys, and Captain Hook's ship. All the while the movie's theme song tells us "you can fly." The sight of Wendy walking the plank is hair-raising, but of course Peter Pan saves the day. This ride is a real charmer; perfect for all ages. **FASTPASS. 3-minute ride.**

PIRATES OF THE CARIBBEAN

The tune "Yo Ho, Yo Ho, a Pirate's Life for Me" will ring in your ears for hours after leaving this likable ride. Drift through a magical nighttime bayou where fireflies twinkle and a banjo strums out a sentimental tune as you pass quaint shacks perched on the bank. Enjoy the wonderful sense of contentment because soon the action begins as you drop and float through caves filled with the skeletal remains of scurvy pirates and hoards of gold and jewels with the constant chant "dead men tell no tales." Enter the darkened bombardment of a Caribbean town at the merciless hands of rowdy pirates where hundreds of shouting, singing, and grunting Audio-Animatronics buccaneers chase women (some women chase the men), pillage and burn the town, and party through the night. It may sound a bit rough, but it's quite a charmer and executed in nothing but good humor. You'll find music from the *Pirates of the Caribbean* movie and Captain Jack Sparrow's lifelike image lurking throughout. **16-minute ride.**

JUST FOR THE LITTLE PRINCESS

Young girls will not want to miss the *Bibbidi Bobbidi Boutique*, a beauty salon for little ones, where they'll be transformed into the perfect princess. Located behind the Castle in Fantasyland, multiple hairstyles, nail color, make-up, and a total package including a Disney princess costume and photographs are offered. It's simply irresistible. Call (714) 781-7895 for reservations.

Afterward head to *Fantasy Faire*, a medieval village square next to Sleeping Beauty Castle, to meet the Disney princesses at Royal Hall followed by a show in the Royal Theater (check your daily schedule for showtimes).

SPACE MOUNTAIN

The 180-foot, conical-shaped "mountain" in Tomorrowland is one of the most popular attractions in the park, a cosmic roller coaster shooting through the darkest depths of the solar system. Sit two across on shuttle transporters and blast into orbit, plunging through a dark interior of sparkling comets, shooting stars, and glowing planets. Moving along at only 28 miles per hour you encounter only small drops and no loops or twists; it's just the darkness and the addition of an amazing onboard sound system that makes it such a thrill. **Minimum height 40 inches (3 feet, 4 inches). Not recommended for expectant mothers, those with back or neck problems, or those prone to motion sickness. FASTPASS. 3-minute ride.**

CARA'S TIP: Lines are sometimes extremely long. Come first thing in the morning or before park closing. And hang onto your valuables or risk losing them in the deep, dark vastness of space. Those of you who have experienced Magic Kingdom's Space Mountain will be shocked at how much more exciting this same attraction is here at Disneyland.

SPLASH MOUNTAIN

This is one ride guaranteed to put a smile on your face. Who can resist the charms of Brer Rabbit, Brer Fox, Brer Bear, and the rest of the gang, even if it culminates in one heck of a plunge? Float in a hollowed-out log through Audio-Animatronics scenes from Disney's classic film *Song of the South*, splashing and dropping through Brer Rabbit's Laughin' Place. Drift 'round the briar patch while toe-tapping music plays among the pumpkin and watermelon patches as you pass the lairs of Brer Fox and Brer Rabbit. Inside the mountain Brer Fox and Brer Bear cause plenty of commotion along the way as Brer Rabbit outwits them at every turn. As you float through bayous, marshes, and caverns, all is a delight to the eye, ear, and heart with loads of colorful detail and too-cute characters cavorting to the tune of the addictive theme song "Time to Be Moving Along." When the ride creeps upward, heed the doomsday warnings of a gloomy pair of buzzards ("It's turning-back time" and "We'll show you a laughing place") just before the final doozy of a splashdown over a five-story waterfall and into an oversize briar patch. It's pretty tough to keep your eyes open (at least for first-timers), but try to grab a peek of the park from the top. And don't think you missed the cherished "Zip-A-Dee-Doo-Da" tune; you'll hear it on the way out. **Not recommended for expectant mothers or those with back or neck problems. Minimum height 40 inches (3 feet, 4 inches). FASTPASS. Single-ride line. 11-minute ride.**

> CARA'S TIP: The drop's really not as bad as it looks, so don't let it keep you from experiencing one of the best rides Disney has to offer.

STAR TOURS—THE ADVENTURES CONTINUE

Just when you think a Disney attraction is so outdated it's too far gone, they up and make it more fun than ever. Pick up a pair of 3-D glasses before boarding your interstellar space vehicle flight simulator from the Star Tours spaceport. Unfortunately your launch isn't going to be a standard one; this go-round C-3PO inadvertently is your pilot on a wild voyage through the depths of the galaxy. Hang tight as he navigates you through jagged rocks on Tatooine, maneuvers around AT-AT's in a crazy battle on the icy planet of Hoth, hyperspaces to Naboo, and flees inside the Death Star in an attempt to escape Darth Vader. All this before nearly crash landing back in the hanger bay! And believe it or not, this is only one of over fifty scenarios, each with different storylines. So ride again and again if you would like to attempt to experience them all. This is certainly one instance that you had better hope the "Force" is with you. **Minimum height 40 inches (3 feet, 4 inches). Not recommended for expectant mothers; those with back, heart, or neck problems; or those prone to motion sickness. FASTPASS. 5-minute ride.**

CHARACTER GREETING SPOTS AT DISNEYLAND PARK

The pointing Mickey gloves on your guide map will help you find the following locations:

- Disney princesses at Fantasy Faire
- Tinker Bell and her Fairy Friends at Pixie Hollow in Fantasyland
- Mickey Mouse and Minnie Mouse at their respective houses in Mickey's Toontown
- Winnie the Pooh and his Friends in Critter Country
- Merida and her three wee bear cubs in Fantasyland near "its' a small world" attraction
- Woody and the Gang at Big Thunder Ranch Jamboree
- Snow White near her wishing well alongside Sleeping Beauty Castle
- Princess Tiana in New Orleans Square near the French Market Restaurant

The Very Best Dining at Disneyland Park

Blue Bayou. The park's most popular restaurant where you'll actually dine inside the Pirates of the Caribbean attraction. (See full description in Dining in Style at Disneyland Resort.)

Carnation Café. A Main Street institution, hearty all-American food with a few updated twists is on the menu. Ask for a table outside in the courtyard for great people watching. *Breakfast:* apple granola pancakes, huevos rancheros, steel cut oatmeal cakes, Mickey-shaped waffle with strawberry topping, spinach and tomato egg white frittata, ham and cheese omelet, and fruit parfait. *Lunch and dinner:* delicious baked potato soup, Walt's chili, warm spinach salad with grilled chicken and warm pancetta-mustard seed vinaigrette, green chili cheeseburger topped with a fried egg on toasted brioche, romaine salad with shrimp, and a vegan burger with chipotle mayo.

Plaza Inn. One of Disneyland's original landmarks, this Victorian-themed restaurant offers Disney's best character breakfast, Minnie & Friends–Breakfast in the Park, offering a bountiful buffet along with a fun mix of Disney characters. A quick-service, cafeteria-style lunch and dinner is famous for the signature golden fried chicken. *Breakfast:* cereals, made-to-order omelets, scrambled eggs, sausage, bacon, biscuits and gravy, Mickey-shaped waffles, pastries, muffins, and fruit. *Lunch and dinner:* fried chicken, pot roast, penne pasta with Bolognese, penne chicken-pesto Alfredo, and cobb salad. Dine inside or out on the terrace.

Little Red Wagon Corn Dog Cart. I know you're thinking that this is not your idea of luxury, but you must stop in for one of these gems at least once during your vacation. It is absolutely mandatory!

Special Entertainment

Mickey and the Magical Map. The Fantasyland Theatre is once again the home of live entertainment with the introduction of this show. The wise sorcerer, Yen Sid, tells of a wondrous map with the power to take dreamers to any place imaginable. When his young apprentice, Mickey Mouse, tries to paint the map's one unfinished spot, he is off on a fantastic adventure. There's music and characters from *Tangled*, *The Jungle Book*, *Pocahontas*, and *Mulan*, and a grand finale with Tiana and her showboat. **22 minutes.**

Mickey's Soundsational Parade. Jam with bandleader Mickey and his friends along with a chorus of live musicians, energetic dancers, thrilling percussion bands, a slew of Disney characters and fun floats accompanied by favorite Disney classic movie tunes. It all ends with a float brimming with Disney princesses. **23 minutes.**

CARA'S TIP: The most popular place to watch the parade is on Main Street, so if you're smart you'll find another place on the route. If there are two parades scheduled always opt for the later one.

Fantasmic! A similar show to its Walt Disney World counterpart (see full description on page 186), this rendition wins the grand prize. Disneyland's show is bigger than life and much more three-dimensional; the reason being, its staging is smack dab in the middle of the park set on Tom Sawyer's Island with the Rivers of America serving as the backdrop for the water screens. The sight the Sailing Ship Columbia cruising by with the swashbuckling Peter Pan and Captain Hook, a 40-foot fire-breathing dragon from *Sleeping Beauty*, and the impressive Mark Twain riverboat filled to the brim with just about every Disney character imaginable is worth the sometimes considerable wait to see the show. **25-minute show.**

CARA'S TIP: For the best view of Fantasmic! without having to go through the drudgery of saving a seat sometimes hours before the start of the show, book a Fantasmic! Premium Viewing package. Included is a front row seat along the waterway and a snack box filled to the brim with cheese, crackers, fruit, and several mini desserts (key lime tart, jam-stuffed cookie, cheesecake, macaroons) along with a non-alcoholic beverage such as soda, coffee, bottled water, or hot chocolate. Call (714) 781-7469 for reservations beginning 30 days prior. You'll need to pick up your tickets from Guest Relations, either at the park or at one of the Disney resorts, before arriving at the podium about two and half hours prior to showtime. Here you'll choose your seat assignments, then you can roam the park until about 30 minutes prior when you'll need to return for the show.

If you want to combine Fantasmic! and the fireworks it's just about impossible to see the early Fantasmic! show and still make it through the crowd to watch the fireworks from in front of the Castle or on Main

Street. Don't let them sell you on the idea of watching the fireworks from the Rivers of America area, not the best of views. If the little ones can stay up late or if you are traveling with older children, opt for the first fireworks show and then head to the second Fantasmic! show. And don't try to walk the impossible upstream battle from the Main Street/ Castle area to Fantasmic! after the fireworks; hang out for a bit on the Fantasyland side of the Castle and wait for the crowds to funnel out of the park first.

Fireworks. Two fireworks shows rotate on a seasonal basis.

Magical! celebrates the magic of life accompanied by sparkling fireworks and oh-so-nostalgic Disney classic songs. With music and narration from *Pinocchio*, *Mary Poppins*, *Cinderella*, *Beauty and the Beast*, and much, much more, nothing can beat the sight of Tinker Bell and Dumbo literally flying around Sleeping Beauty Castle!

Remember: Dreams Come True is a celebration of Walt Disney's dream. What begins as Disney World's Wishes show's soundtrack morphs into something very different with Julie Andrews narrating and even Walt's voice popping in at one point. The soundtrack is so nostalgic including the music of Main Street Electrical Parade, *Indiana Jones*, Haunted Mansion, *Pirates of the Caribbean*, *Davy Crockett*, and *Star Wars*, and the fireworks sequences are spectacular. They certainly know how to do it right at Disneyland!

> **CARA'S TIP**: Stay away from walkways if you plan on watching from the hub area. The constant cast member "move along" policing to those who decide to sit in the walkways can be very distracting. Just as at Walt Disney World, I think the best place to stand is in the hub area near the Walt and Mickey's statue. Fireworks are only a nightly event during the summer months; other months the show takes place only on weekends.

Special Events

Mickey's Halloween Party. What can be better than trick-or-treating in the perfect neighborhood of Disneyland Park? Main Street boasts over 300 pumpkins (one of them giant-size and looking strangely like a certain mouse we know), and the Haunted Mansion is decorated with over 400 flickering candles and 100 Disney character Jack-O-Lanterns.

Try out Space Mountain with its touch of Ghost Gallery eeriness then rock the night away at Monsters U Dance Party at Tomorrowland Terrace while Disney characters and villains costumed out for the occasion roam the streets. Special events such as Mickey's Costume Party Cavalcade parade and a special edition fireworks show, Halloween Screams, are the evening's highlights. This is a separate ticketed event occurring on selected nights mid-September through October 31st with many attractions also open to enjoy. For information and ticketing go online to Disneyland.disney.go.com/events-tours/disneyland/mickeys-halloween-party or call (714) 781-4400.

Christmas at Disneyland. From the enormous decorated tree at the head of Main Street and a holiday-trimmed and lighted Sleeping Beauty Castle whose towers are topped with "snow," the holidays are a fabulous time to visit. There's also a Christmas Fantasy parade, a nightly special holiday fireworks culminating in "snowfall," a retrofitted Haunted Mansion in "A Nightmare Before Christmas" theme, and Big Thunder Ranch Jamboree where you can meet Santa Claus and enjoy holiday games, music and crafts, all included in the cost of admission.

Disney California Adventure Park

The Golden State is the theme at Disneyland's sister park, California Adventure. Opened in 2001 it has been a real work in progress over the years, but the park's newest incarnation completed in 2012 is a definite keeper due to the addition of one of the most popular areas of all Disney parks, Cars Land, and it's excellent main attraction, Radiator Springs Racers. Buena Vista Street, an exemplary re-creation of Los Angeles in the 1920's and 30's complete with a bronzed statue of Walt and Mickey to greet you on arrival, is a sure winner. Hop on the Red Car Trolley, L.A.'s transportation system until the early '60s, at the park's entrance and travel all the way to Hollywood Land's Twilight Zone Tower of Terror, passing a replica of the Carthay Circle Theater along the way which houses the only 5-star restaurant in a theme park. A flight high above California on Soarin', a good soaking on Grizzly River Run, a wild spin on Toy Story Mania, and one heck of a scare on California Screamin' are just a few of the exciting thrills you'll find in this kick of a park.

Operating Hours

Generally open from 10:00 a.m. to 8:00 p.m. Monday through Thursday and 10:00 a.m. to 9:00 p.m. Friday, Saturday, and Sunday with extended hours during holidays and busy seasons. Call (714) 781-INFO (4636) or log on to http://disneyland.disney.go.com/calendar/ for updated park hours along with parade and fireworks information.

Those driving to the parks should get a jump on the crowds by arriving about 45 minutes early allowing plenty of time to park, ride the tram, buy tickets if necessary, and be one of the first to hit the big attractions. Those staying on property can stroll over and be ready to hit the parks about 15 minutes prior unless they are enjoying Extra Magic Hour, available only to resort guests, with one park opening an hour early just for them each day of the week. I recommend heading straight to Cars Land for Radiator Springs Racers.

FASTPASS Attractions

California Screamin'

Goofy's Sky School

Grizzly River Run

Radiator Springs Racers

Soarin' Over California

The Twilight Zone Tower of Terror™

World of Color

See the introduction to this chapter for FASTPASS details.

Park Services

ATMs. Five ATM cash-dispensing machines are located inside the park: at the Main Entrance near the lockers, on the walkway between Paradise Pier and Grizzly Run just past The Little Mermaid attraction, Pacific Wharf District near the restrooms, outside Off the Page in Hollywood Pictures Backlot, and near Sideshow Shirts at Paradise Pier.

Baby Care Center. Found next to the Bakery Tour in the Pacific Wharf area are comfortable facilities for diaper changing, nursing, and bottle feeding. All restrooms throughout the park are outfitted with changing tables.

First aid. The First Aid Center is located next to the Bakery Tour in the Pacific Wharf area.

Guest Relations. Guest Relations is located on Buena Vista Street where a knowledgeable staff is ready to assist with dining, ticket upgrades, messages for separated parties, information for guests with disabilities, and international guests.

Guests with disabilities. Parking for guests with disabilities is available at Mickey and Friends parking structure and the Toy Story parking area off of Harbor Boulevard. Transportation is provided from the Mickey and Friends parking structure and the Toy Story parking area to the Main Entry Plaza. Please note: oversized wheelchairs and Electric Convenience Vehicles may be too large for some transportation vehicles.

A guide for guests with disabilities is available at Guest Relations. Wheelchairs and ECVs are available for rent. Most restaurants and shops are accessible to guests with disabilities, although some quick-service locations have narrow queues with railings (ask a host or hostess for assistance). Companion-assisted restrooms are located at First Aid, A Bug's Land at Flik's Fun Fair, and at the restrooms located on the walkway between Paradise Pier and Grizzly Run just past The Little Mermaid attraction. Many attractions provide access through the main queue, while others have auxiliary entrances for wheelchairs and service animals along with as many as five members of your party. Certain attractions require guests to transfer from their wheelchair to a ride system. Parade routes and some shows have designated viewing areas on a first-come, first-served basis.

Braille guidebooks, handheld captioning receivers, digital audio tours, and assistive listening devices are available at Guest Relations for a $25 refundable deposit. Reflective captioning is provided at many theater-type attractions and video captioning at some attractions. A sign language interpreter is provided at specific live shows on a rotating basis on Sundays and Fridays. For more information call (714) 781-6176 or (714) 781-7292 (TTY).

Lockers. Lockers are located outside the main entrance as well as on Buena Vista Street immediately on your right just after entering the park. The cost for unlimited access is $7, $10, $11, $12, and $15 per day depending on the size of the locker.

Lost and Found. Located in the Guest Services Building outside and to the right of the Main Entrance or call (714) 817-2166.

Lost children. Locate lost children at the Baby Care Center next to the Bakery Tour.

Package pickup. Shop and send your purchases for pickup later in the day to Fly n' Buy. Disneyland Resort Hotel Guests can send packages directly to their hotel for next-day arrival.

Pet kennel. Kennel facilities are located to the right of the Main Entrance of Disneyland Park. First-come, first served basis; no reservations accepted. For information call (714) 781-4565. Proof of vaccination is required, and no overnight accommodations are allowed.

Strollers and wheelchairs. Rentals are located outside the Disneyland Park next to the Pet Kennel. Single strollers are $15 per day, $25 for two. Wheelchairs are $12 per day with electric convenience vehicles $50.00; both require a $20.00 refundable deposit. Rental strollers are permitted in both theme parks, but are not allowed in Downtown Disney.

The Lay of the Land

Enter the park on Buena Vista Street and stroll down to a hub of sorts, Carthay Circle. Forking off to the left of Carthay Circle is Hollywood Land also leading to "a bug's land." To the right of Carthay Circle is Condor Flats, home of Soarin', leading also to Grizzly Peak. Walk straight through Carthay Circle and slightly right to proceed to Cars Land on your left and Pacific Wharf and Paradise Pier straight ahead (Grizzly Peak can also be accessed from the walkway on the right just past Pacific Wharf).

The Very Best Attractions at California Adventure

CALIFORNIA SCREAMIN'

The centerpiece of the Paradise Pier area is this thrill-a-minute coaster. It's designed to look like an old-fashioned wooden variety, but don't let it fool you. This baby is all steel, adding up to one smooth and high-powered ride. Accelerating from zero to 55 miles per hour, you blast down a lagoon-level track and up the first of two hills with the second one offering a 107-foot drop on the other side. Screech through a progression of embankments, camelbacks, and scream tubes, and watch out for that 360-degree doozy of a loop-de-loop! **Minimum height 48 inches (4 feet). Not recommended for expectant mothers or those with back or neck problems. FASTPASS. Single Rider Line. 2.5-minute ride.**

CARA'S TIP: Ride after dark when the coaster and the park are exquisitely lit.

IT'S TOUGH TO BE A BUG!
INSPIRED BY DISNEY·PIXAR'S A BUG'S LIFE

It's always twilight in the underground waiting area where chirping crickets sing Broadway tunes from such insect shows as The Dung and I (featuring the hit song "Hello Dung Lovers"), Beauty and the Bees, and A Cockroach Line. Flik (the star of *A Bug's Life*) is the host of this creepy-crawly 3-D movie of assorted bugs who only want humans to understand them. But much to the glee of the audience seated in the theater, they just can't help misbehaving.

A favorite opening act is the stinkbug who accidentally lets his smelly, gaseous fumes rip into the crowd. As the show progresses you'll be doused with bug spray, stung sharply in the back, and showered with termite acid, all innocently achieved through special effects. Receive one final surprise as the beetles, maggots, and cockroaches exit safely ahead of you. This is one super show, a highlight of the park! **FASTPASS. 8-minute show.**

CARA'S TIP: Definitely one attraction too intense for young children, particularly when Hopper, the despicable grasshopper from *A Bug's Life,* scares the dickens out of every child under age five. If you'd like to sit in the center of the auditorium, hang back a little in the waiting area and allow some of the audience to enter ahead of you. And try not to sit on the far sides of the theater where the 3-D effects are slightly minimized.

THE LITTLE MERMAID—ARIEL'S UNDERSEA ADVENTURE

Immerse yourself in the music and wonder of one of Disney's best-loved animated movies, *The Little Mermaid*. California Adventure's version of this attraction lacks the terrific queue found at Walt Disney World, but you'll love it all the same. Board your clam-mobile on a journey through Ariel's undersea world where famous songs combined with Audio-Animatronics tell the story of everyone's favorite mermaid. **6-minute ride.**

RADIATOR SPRINGS RACERS

The best road trip around and certainly the most popular ride at Disneyland Resort, this headliner attraction is sure to stay that way for years to come. Similar in some ways to Epcot's Test Track, board a 6-passenger convertible complete with a grinning face on the grill and off you go on what seems like a peaceful and serene journey through the stunning Ornament Valley of *Cars* fame. But it's race day in Radiator Springs, and the peace and quiet abruptly ends just after passing sparkling Radiator Falls when you swerve to avoid Mac. Then it's a bit of a run-in with the Sheriff who passes you off to Mater who talks you into detouring through the fields for tractor tipping. Several familiar faces (*Cars* faces that is) cheer you on and offer a few pointers before your final fine tune at either Luigi's Casa Della Tires or Ramone's House of Body Art. Then hit the start line and head out on the track for a high speed race with another vehicle as you speed through the red rock formations, around banked curves, and over a few hilarious dips and bumps before ending up where you began, wishing you could do it all over again. **Minimum height 40 inches (3 feet, 4 inches). Not recommended for expectant mothers or those with back or neck problems. FASTPASS. Single Rider Line. 4-minute ride.**

> CARA'S TIP: This attraction should be your top priority first thing in the morning. Either head straight to the FASTPASS distribution machines near It's Tough to be a Bug! or beeline it to the attraction itself. FASTPASSes are sometime gone within the first hour or so after park opening. If you want to save time opt for the Single Rider line, but don't expect to sit with other members of your party.

SOARIN' OVER CALIFORNIA

Hang glide over California in an attraction guaranteed to leave you speechless. After rising 40 feet inside a giant 80-foot projection screen dome, you're completely surrounded with phenomenal bird's-eye views of the Golden State. Soar over the Golden Gate Bridge, towering redwood forests, hot air balloons drifting over the Napa Valley wine country, a golf course in Palm Springs, the majesty of Yosemite, and more, ending high above Disneyland just in time for a fireworks display. Smell the aroma of the orange groves and feel the wind in your face, all the while listening to a stirring musical score. This is one fantastic ride! **Minimum height 40 inches (3 feet, 4 inches). Not recommended for expectant mothers or those with motion sickness, or heart, back, or neck problems. FASTPASS. Single Rider Line. 10-minute ride including the pre-show.**

> CARA'S TIP: Ask for the first row; if not you'll be a bit distracted with dangling feet above you.

TOY STORY MIDWAY MANIA!®
INSPIRED BY DISNEY·PIXAR'S TOY STORY FILMS

While the queue here isn't nearly as interesting as at Disney's Hollywood Studios—the only entertainment is from a Mr. Potato Head boardwalk barker—the ride portion of this attraction is an exact replica. And, thankfully, the attraction's popularity is not quite as enthusiastic either.

Don your 3-D glasses and board a carnival tram to embark on a 4-D virtual version of midway-style game play. Use your spring-action shooter to plug away at a series of giant-size video screens, each hosted by a member of the *Toy Story* gang and featuring virtual spinning plates, tossing cream pies, bursting balloons, and funny little green aliens as you zip through game after game, each lasting 30 seconds, each more fun than the last. Adding to the entertainment is a 4th dimension of air shots and water spritzers while *Toy Story* characters yell hints and cheer you along. Watch out for bonus targets and simply have a blast (no pun intended)! **5.5-minute ride.**

THE TWILIGHT ZONE TOWER OF TERROR

On this free-falling adventure you'll certainly feel you've entered the twilight zone or at the very least a brand-new dimension of fright. The waiting line snakes through the crumbling grounds of the deserted, thirteen-story Hollywood Tower Hotel with its rusty grillwork, cracking fountains, and overgrown, unkempt foliage before proceeding through the spooky, abandoned lobby, dusty with forgotten luggage and dead flower arrangements. Step into the gloomy hotel library for a message from *Twilight Zone* TV show host Rod Serling (on a black-and-white television, of course) who relays the tale of a stormy night in 1939 when an elevator full of guests was struck by lightning and then disappeared. A bellhop invites you into a seemingly old, rusty service elevator that ascends and moves horizontally through several remarkable special effects in pitch-black space and, without warning, plummets almost thirteen stories to the bottom. Up you go again, then down, and up, and down, during which you'll be treated to dazzling views of the park. If you can stand the thrill, don't miss this one; just be sure to ride it with an empty stomach. **Minimum height 40 inches (3 feet, 4 inches). Not recommended for expectant mothers; those with back, heart, or neck problems; or those prone to motion sickness. FASTPASS. 5-minute ride.**

> CARA'S TIP: If you chicken out there's an escape route immediately before entering the elevator; just ask a bellhop for directions.

WILDERNESS EXPLORER REDWOOD CREEK CHALLENGE TRAIL

At Disney's very best children's play area, inspired after Russell in the Pixar film *Up*, kids will want to spend hours enjoying all it has to offer. Pick up an activity map at the entrance and search forested paths on your way to earning a Senior Wilderness Explorer Badge with completion of six tasks: tracking, bravery, wolf howl, animal spirit, rock climbing, and puzzle solving. Find each on your map as you romp and play in a woodland setting filled with pine trees, tire slides, rocks for climbing, rope bridges, lookout points, tree tunnels, and training towers.

CHARACTER GREETING SPOTS AT CALIFORNIA ADVENTURE PARK

The pointing Mickey gloves on your guide map will help you find the following locations:

- Lightning McQueen and Mater at Cars Land's Cozy Cone Motel

- Green Army Men from Toy Story on Paradise Pier

- Mickey, Goofy, Chip and Dale dressed in 1920's and 30's style on Buena Vista Street

- Stewardess Minnie near Soarin' Over California

- Sophia the First in Hollywood Land near Disney Junior: Live on Stage!

- Duffy the Disney Bear at Paradise Pier

- Russell and Dug at Redwood Creek Challenge Trail

The Very Best Dining at California Adventure

Ariel's Grotto. If dining with the Disney princesses is on your agenda then this is your place. Characters only at breakfast and lunch. (See full description in the Dining in Style at Disneyland Resort chapter.)

Carthay Circle. Chefs Andrew Sutton and Gloria Tae of Napa Rose fame bring California cuisine to Disney California Adventure Park. Open for lunch and dinner. (See full description in the Dining in Style at Disneyland Resort chapter.)

Flo's V8 Café. Cutesy 1950's style, Route 66-inspired roadside diner with views of Radiator Springs; open for quick-service meals at breakfast, lunch, and dinner. Start your day at *breakfast* with brioche French toast topped with salted caramel and banana, chicken tamale breakfast with scrambled eggs and *salsa verde*, American scrambled egg breakfast, or a fruit platter with yogurt and a blueberry muffin. *Lunch and dinner* include roast beef with gravy, pork loin with Coca-Cola BBQ sauce, citrus turkey breast with old-fashioned turkey gravy, and veggie tater bake; desserts are apple-cheddar pie, chocolate mud pie, seasonal fruit pie, and milk shakes.

HEYDAY OF HOLLYWOOD ANYONE?

On the ground floor of Carthay Circle restaurant you'll find a sophisticated lounge, the ideal place to get away from the hustle and bustle of the park. High bar stools surround tall tables where updated retro cocktails and small plates are in order. Think about selecting a Brown Derby with bourbon and fresh grapefruit juice or the Carthay Manhattan with small batch American whiskey, bitters, vermouth, and maraschino cherries. Favorite bites are the Vietnamese twice cooked beef taco with a pineapple mint salsa and the Moroccan lamb meatballs with a cooling *tzatziki* sauce. If those choices don't suit your fancy then go for lobster pad Thai imperial rolls, duck confit sliders, even Santa Monica deviled eggs with smoked salmon and lemon crème fraiche. You'll forget that you're in the middle of a theme park (well almost, if only it weren't for tourists wearing Mickey ears!).

Special Events

Christmas at California Adventure. Yes, even in sunny California you can get in the Christmas spirit with Buena Vista Street, Cars Land, and "a bugs land" decked out for the holiday, a wintertime Mad T Party, Phineas and Ferb's Rockin' Rollin' Dance Party holiday edition, and a special "Winter Dreams" World of Color show, all included in the price of admission.

Special Entertainment

Pixar Play Parade. Phineas and Ferb host this afternoon parade with the gang from *Monster's University*, *A Bug's Life*, *Toy Story*, *Cars*, and more.

World of Color. Disney's most amazing nighttime show is quite the spectacle, honestly worth the trip to California just to see it. Shimmering mists project Disney and Pixar characters on jets of sky-high water combined with exploding fire, color wheels of light, and exciting orchestral music. Mickey's Fun Wheel and California Screamin' are even part of the action. Many of Disney's most famous movies are represented including scenes from *Finding Nemo, The Little Mermaid, The Lion King, Up, Brave*, even an explosive *Pirates of the Caribbean*. A daytime Bellagio-style fountain show is in the works for this area.

CARA'S TIP: There are three ways to obtain a great spot to view the show:

#1. Get a FASTPASS ticket early in the day available at Grizzly River Run distribution area. Registered guests of a Disneyland Resort Hotel can take advantage of Extra Magic Hour on select days to enter California Adventure Park one hour early, a perfect time to grab a FASTPASS before non-resort guests even enter the park. Remember that all members of your party must enter the park and present their park tickets first before heading over to receive a FASTPASS.

#2. Dine at Wine Country Trattoria (lunch or dinner), Carthay Circle (lunch or dinner), or Ariel's Grotto (dinner only) and receive a ticket for a preferred viewing area. You'll view the show from either near the water where you will more than likely get wet but have a great view, or on a level higher with a lesser but drier view (stand on the stairs to get a view above everyone's heads).

#3. Take a Disney VIP Tour. Even if your guide is no longer with you that late in the evening VIP viewing entrance for you and your party can still be arranged.

Downtown Disney

Conveniently located between the theme parks and the Disneyland Hotel this high-energy shopping, dining, and entertainment district is the ideal addition to a day in the parks. Street performers and live music liven up the action in the evening hours, and you'll find an ESPN Zone along with a 12-screen AMC® Theater. Go online to DowntownDisney.com/Anaheim to find out what's happening during your stay.

Downtown Disney's Best Shopping

Apricot Lane Boutique. Apparel and accessories geared toward younger women including Miss Me, Rock Revival, Lucky Brand, and AG Jean.

Studio 365. Transform into your favorite Disney Channel super star selecting from five different makeovers—including a Rock Star makeover for boys—and three wardrobe packages. And while you are there shop for girls of all ages from a variety of cute clothing. Call (714) 781-7895 for reservations.

LEGO® Imagination Center. Marvel at giant LEGO models both inside and outside the store with every LEGO set imaginable for sale.

RIDEMAKERZ®. Customize a 1:18 scale model car with your choice of body, color, rims and more. Choose from a wide variety of vehicles then decide whether you want your racer to be radio-controlled or "free wheel." Pick colors, paint details, rims and tires, real working lights, sounds, accessories, and decals with over 649 million combinations possible. Once it's ready, take it out for a spin on the store's test track.

World of Disney® Store. With the largest selection of Disney merchandise on the West Coast, this superstore offers room after room of all things Disney. Girls will love the Build Your Own Charm Bracelet Station, and Disney art buffs will want to order something from the self-service Art of Disney kiosk where hundreds of digital images can be perused before choosing paper or canvas, picking your desired size, and even adding a frame.

Downtown Disney's Very Best Dining

Catal Restaurant. Chef Joachim Spichal's delectable Mediterranean food is Downtown Disney's best dining option. (See full description in Dining in Style at Disneyland Resort.)

Napolini. The oven here turns out chewy-crispy Naples-style pizza by the slice, perfect if you want something on the go.

Uva Bar & Café. A circular centerpiece bar and sidewalk café associated with Catal Restaurant sits smack dab in the midst of the hustle and bustle of Downtown Disney, the best place for people watching and enjoying Anaheim's fantastic weather. On the Barcelona-inspired menu: *Appetizers* of street fries with chorizo Bilboa, spicy *crema*, pickled garlic, and cheese curds; crispy calamari; sweet potato flatbread; spicy-sweet chicken wings; tuna tartare tacos; *Entrées* of lamb burger with *piquillo* peppers, feta, arugula, lemon dill aioli, and pickled red onion; grilled market fish with roasted artichoke hearts, preserved lemon puree, and blistered tomatoes and olives; shrimp salad a la Grecque; fish and chips; savory *Sides* of sea salt garlic fries; asparagus *a la plancha* (grilled) with applewood bacon and 6-minute egg; Shishito peppers with sea salt and lemon garlic emulsion.

14

DINING IN STYLE
AT DISNEYLAND RESORT

While gourmet dining is somewhat limited at Disneyland Resort, you will be more than content if your only meal is at Napa Rose, one of Orange County's very best restaurants. If time is short or making advance reservations simply slips your mind, you'll easily find a great meal at one of the resort and theme park lounges such as Napa Rose Lounge, Steakhouse 55 Lounge, and Carthay Circle Lounge where excellent menu items are to be found.

Dining with the Disney Characters

Dining at least once with the Disney characters is a must if you are traveling with children. Character appearances at restaurants tend to vary at Disneyland Resort, so if a particular character is tops on your list don't count on them always being in attendance. That is unless your favorite character happens to be Goofy at Goofy's Kitchen, Mickey at the Surfs Up! Breakfast, Ariel at Ariel's Grotto, or Minnie at the Plaza Inn. They are the hosts, after all!

Chip and Dale Critter Breakfast at Storyteller's Café. Chip and Dale host this popular breakfast at the Grand Californian Hotel along with their critter friends. Breakfast buffet as well as a la carte choices.

Surfs Up! Breakfast with Mickey & Friends. If Mickey is on your bucket list then reserve this character breakfast buffet at Disney's Paradise Pier Hotel where he's the host along with a bevy of friends.

Minnie & Friends–Breakfast in the Park. This popular breakfast buffet set in Disneyland Park is perhaps the most lively and interactive of them all. Join Minnie and her friends for a great start to your morning.

Ariel's Disney Princess Celebration. This family-style meal at California Adventure Park has the distinction of the only Disney princesses character meal and the plus of spectacular Paradise Pier views. Characters are in attendance only for breakfast and lunch.

Goofy's Kitchen. Goofy hosts this breakfast and dinner buffet at the Disneyland Hotel along with his pals.

Best Disneyland Park Dining

Blue Bayou

Cajun and creole cuisine. Lunch and dinner.

It's tough to find a more enchanting setting than Blue Bayou, and better yet it's smack dab in the middle of the Pirates of Caribbean attraction. A dreamy, moonlit terrace overlooking the bayou is strung with Chinese lanterns and surrounded by live oak trees dripping with moss. Louisiana-style cuisine is on the menu, totally overpriced, but who cares when there's scenery like this?

Begin your meal with a basket of sweet potato biscuits and luscious sourdough rolls along with your choice of salad or a spicy gumbo, both good options. The fiery jambalaya is respectable but can be a bit on the dry side. Nevertheless it is studded with fish, shrimp, chicken breast, and Andouille sausage (this is one huge dish so do consider splitting). Probably the best entrée is the Cajun-spiced salmon prepared with a light dusting of spices, a touch of citrus *mousseline* and *salsa verde*, and a side of corn risotto, although (sigh!), healthy as it may be, I do miss the previous recipe stuffed with goat cheese and topped with buerre blanc sauce. Or just opt for a Monte-Cristo sandwich, always a popular if not overly rich choice.

CARA'S TIP: Request a waterside table on arrival, but don't fret if you don't get it or the wait is just too long; you'll still enjoy the restaurant's atmosphere nonetheless. If you forget to make reservations at Blue Bayou and there are none to be had on arrival, no problem. You'll find Monte Cristo sandwiches as well as Cajun/Creole specialties, even pommes frites tossed with parmesan and garlic served with remoulade (yum!) around the corner at Café Orleans, a much easier place to get a seat.

SAMPLE MENU ITEMS

Lunch entrées: Portobello mushroom and couscous *macque choux* marinated in a balsamic vinaigrette, broiled and served with roasted corn, bell pepper Israeli couscous and sautéed spinach; slow roasted beef strip loin over rock salt with crispy shoestring onions, au gratin potatoes, and Armagnac green peppercorn sauce; Tesoro Island chicken breast, pan-seared with Boursin cheese mashed potatoes and fennel confit with roasted shallot reduction; boneless beef short ribs, Boursin cheese mashed potatoes, and Cabernet reduction.

Dinner entrées: much the same as lunch with the addition of herb panko-crusted rack of lamb with cassoulet of cannellini beans, feta cheese, and rosemary jus; surf & turf of petite Pacific Northwest lobster tail and broiled filet mignon served with au gratin potatoes and béarnaise sauce; broiled filet mignon with au gratin potatoes and béarnaise sauce.

Best Disney California Adventure Dining

Ariel's Grotto

Disney princesses character dining (breakfast and lunch only).
Breakfast, lunch, and dinner.

If you're keen on dining with the princesses then this is the place. A cute and sassy Ariel is the star (in fact, you'll meet her for a photo op at the entry) in this light-filled restaurant featuring an under-the-sea theme and views of Paradise Pier. At breakfast and lunch only, an assembly of Disney princesses mingle with diners, pose for photos, and sign autograph books for the little ones while music from *The Little Mermaid* plays in the background.

Club 33

Who doesn't want to be part of an exclusive club? Needless to say, Disneyland guests are no exception. Opened in 1967 at Walt's request Club 33 is located upstairs and above Café Orleans in Disneyland Park's French Quarter area. With a limited membership of only 487 it is indeed exclusive. Membership is virtually never advertised and is tough to secure. Its two dining rooms, the more formal Main Dining Room and a casual and fun-filled Trophy Room, are filled with antiques and mementoes. But Club 33 will be temporarily closing in early 2014 for an extensive six-month renovation. What this legendary club will look like after it reopens is unknown and greatly anticipated.

If you are lucky enough to be accepted, a Platinum membership requires a hefty initiation fee in the tens of thousands and a sizeable annual fee. Full membership benefits are extended to the member and up to three others, including access to Club 33 and its dining, Club 33 special events, valet parking at the Grand Californian Hotel when dining, access to any Disney U.S. theme park, the exclusive Club 1901 in California Adventure Park, and more. Also included is up to 50 complimentary theme park passes per membership to be distributed to the member's guests. And better yet, members may arrange for friends and associates to dine at the club. I suggest you form a steadfast friendship with at least one of these 487 privileged members.

Lunch and dinner are three-course, prix fixe meals beginning with pull-apart sourdough bread and a tasty, family style antipasto tower and green salad followed by your choice of an entrée. A chicken breast meal, airplane-style cut with the drumette attached, is not only crispy skinned and golden brown but also tender and juicy with a light and creamy pineapple chutney, a side of vegetable medley, and memorable cheddar mashed potatoes. The pasta choice, while a bit too al dente, is tasty with Italian sausage and a rich *ragù* sauce. Perhaps the best option is the simply prepared, ever-changing sustainable fish, nicely grilled and served with pineapple chutney, wild rice, and grilled asparagus. Dessert is where this meal falls flat with a family-style platter filled with gooey, neon-colored cupcakes, M&M's-studded cookies, a too-sweet white chocolate conch shell, and an overly dense chocolate cake.

CARA'S TIP: There's outdoor seating if you so desire with fantastic views of Paradise Pier. For those dining in the evening hours a World of Color Dinner Package can be purchased including dinner and a ticket to a reserved viewing area for the show. Book your meal about two and a half hours prior to show time in order to finish dinner and still arrive in time for a good viewing spot.

Upstairs is the open-air Cove Bar with great views of the World of Color show ($10 cover charge), fun cocktails, and tasty appetizers such as fish tacos, lobster nachos, spinach and artichoke dip, buffalo wings, citrus-marinated shrimp cocktail, tri-tip sliders, and barbecue chicken pizza. But take note that you'll need to show up mighty early for a seat to the show.

SAMPLE MENU ITEMS

Breakfast entrées: Begin your meal with a tower of fresh fruit, assorted cheeses, and pastries. Follow that with a family-style platter of Belgium waffles, scrambled eggs, bacon, turkey sausage, and breakfast potatoes.

Lunch and dinner entrées: Spinach and ricotta agnolotti (a type of ravioli) topped with spinach, sun-dried tomatoes, julienne onions, and asparagus served in a light mushroom broth; cioppino with lobster tail, scallops, sustainable fish, green-lip mussels, shrimp, and Bilboa chorizo in a fire-roasted tomato broth; Santa Maria-style tri-tip, slow-roasted and smoked over red oak wood served with cheddar-herb mashed potatoes; pasta with Italian sausage tossed in Piemonte-style *ragù*.

Carthay Circle

Contemporary Southern Californian cuisine. Lunch and dinner.

Housed in a replica of the original Carthay Circle Theatre where *Snow White and the Seven Dwarfs* premiered in 1937, this lavish, second-story restaurant exudes classic luxury with an emphasis on seasonal, locally sourced ingredients. No dowdy décor here. Instead there's a masculine, old-Hollywood look with heavy drapery, hardwood flooring, rich wood paneling, a frescoed *Snow White and the Seven Dwarfs* ceiling, inlaid tables (sans tablecloths), loads of banquettes, and candelabra-style chandeliers. The first restaurant in the world to open its doors with 92 sommeliers, here you'll find 250 international wines on its prestigious menu with thirty available by the glass in both the restaurant and downstairs lounge. But after all the publicity, what has been touted as the best theme park food in the world does have its up's and down's.

The Carthay house biscuits really are a must and worth the somewhat hefty calories—balls of delight loaded down with white cheddar, bacon, and spicy jalapeno accompanied by yummy apricot honey butter. A first-course beet salad was quite ho-hum with a promised blue cheese ingredient that was nowhere to be found. As for Carthay Circle's duck wings, they do have a cult following and managed to live up to their glorious reputation—giant things, slightly crunchy, superbly tender, and enlivened with an aggressively spiced glaze of soy and Sriracha.

Now what promised to be truly great lamb *cavatelli* pasta, a dish that has endured through several seasonal menu changes, was almost boring. The pasta, while nicely grabbing the rich jus, was totally overcooked, and the lamb lacked the zing that a bit of spice might have added. If it's lamb you are wanting better to go with the lamb duo of Colorado rack and osso buco, a much more satisfying choice. The saving grace as far as entrées are concerned proved to be short rib ravioli, flecked with slightly wilted sage leaves and a sprinkling of sautéed mushrooms swimming in a rich Cabernet jus; pity that its bed of carrot puree hindered rather than enhanced.

For intimate dining worlds away from the theme parks you MUST request to be seated in either the Hyperion or the Buena Vista room, single-table private rooms seating up to five and waited on by the upper echelon of wait staff—a true treat for any diner. However, no matter how posh this restaurant is purported to be it's still in a theme park and thus subject to those who ignore the business casual dress code and believe shorts, Mickey Mouse ears, and tennis shoes are *de riguer*. More polished wait staff assistants would be an immense improvement, too; I had to ask with each and every course for a new set of flatware. But if you seek the bliss of a quiet respite and the promise of food a few notches above that of the usual run-of-the-mill park restaurants, then Carthay Circle is a perfect choice.

CARA'S TIP: Choose an outdoor terrace seat if you want to catch the action on Buena Vista Street or have a primo view of the Disneyland fireworks show, but realize that the tradeoff is missing the ambience of the inside dining room. World of Color Dinner Packages are also available here.

If you are looking for a lighter meal head to the restaurant's jewel box lounge where signature classic cocktails match with small plate appetizers.

SAMPLE MENU ITEMS

Lunch entrées: Grilled Angus flank steak "cobb" salad, Mine Shaft blue cheese, bacon, avocado, arugula, and Cabernet essence; roasted organic chicken and Ruby Red grapefruit salad tossed in grapefruit mustard vinaigrette; udon noodle bowl with shrimp and black mussels, red Thai curry broth, shiitake mushrooms, bok choy, mint, cashews, and cilantro; Kobe beef cheek sliders, horseradish sour cream, red bell pepper marmalade, and crispy onions; pan-roasted lamb *rolitini* with parmesan stuffing, baby artichokes, leeks, sun-dried tomatoes, and roasted garlic cloves.

Dinner entrées: Vegetable risotto; sautéed tiger prawns on a broth of fingerling potatoes, leeks, applewood bacon, and thyme; sautéed Skuna Bay salmon with almond couscous, dried cranberry, and lemon vinaigrette; grilled Angus rib-eye with mushroom *ragù*, red flame grapes, and blue cheese; Santa Maria braised pork pot roast with sour cream smashed potatoes and dried cherry Zinfandel sauce; whole roasted petit chicken with squash puree, sautéed chanterelles, and sage essence.

Wine Country Trattoria

Italian cuisine. Lunch and dinner.

Not the very best restaurant around but one that offers atmospheric al fresco dining in a Tuscan villa setting and acceptable Italian fare. Perhaps best on the menu is a flavorful roasted chicken breast crusted with herb-infused breadcrumbs served with a light white wine sauce tossed with pasta studded with asparagus and red peppers. Or choose the beef filet made extra flavorful with blue cheese butter and the addition of golden brown roasted potatoes and crisp-tender green beans. You can book a World of Color prix fixe dinner package that includes a ticket to a reserved viewing area for the show which comes with either soup or salad, your choice of six entrées, and a nice dessert platter. But book your meal for about two and a half hours prior to show time in order to finish dinner and still arrive in time for a good viewing spot.

> **CARA'S TIP:** If you are in the mood to nosh then forget the full meal and enjoy a nice glass of Californian wine along with a fritto misto platter of fried calamari, mussels, green beans, and artichoke hearts served with a piquant pepperoncini aioli. Or take a seat on the patio at the restaurant's Mendicino Terrace where a cheese platter and a nice glass of vino from their global list are available.

SAMPLE MENU ITEMS

Lunch entrées: Tuscan salad with sautéed shrimp or grilled chicken; arugula salad with smoked chicken, fennel, spiced walnuts, goat cheese, and fig-balsamic dressing; pasta with clams; shrimp scampi; roasted vegetable panini; lasagna *rustica*; sustainable fish of the day.

Dinner entrées: Pasta bolognese; balsamic braised short ribs with cannellini bean stew; broccolini aglio olio tossed with spinach, arugula, tomatoes, garlic, chili flakes, and olive oil; braised lamb shank served with polenta, Pinot Noir reduction, and *gremolata*.

Best Disneyland Resort Hotel Dining

Napa Rose

California farm-to-table cuisine at the Grand Californian Hotel. Dinner only.

For more than a decade the Grand Californian Hotel has been known for innovative cuisine at this exceptional restaurant. Chef Andrew Sutton's contemporary cuisine is its claim to fame making it a must-do on your Disneyland list. Focusing only on what is fresh and seasonal, guests dine in a lovely Arts and Crafts-style room with murals of the California wine country, an exciting exhibition kitchen, and massive windows over-looking the California Adventure park.

Begin by ordering the ridiculously delicious Smiling Tiger Salad composed of greens tossed with baby radishes, spicy diced filet mignon, and a rich coconut milk vinaigrette topped with savory lobster tem-pura—definitely lives up to the hype. And even if pizza isn't your idea of California cuisine, Napa Rose's luscious signature version with smoked prosciutto, red grapes, caramelized onions, and oh-so-creamy Cambo-zola cheese hits the mark. However, on a subsequent visit the seasonal lamb and cherries pizza's center was undercooked and the cheese not bubbly and brown enough for my taste. Salmon served three ways: roasted with Meyer lemon, *escabeche*-style (like a ceviche), and tanger-ine cured sashimi with dill (much like gravlax) was a big hit as was the sublime seared diver scallop appetizer bathed in a bed of lemon sauce with diced tomatoes, just a hint of vanilla, and accompanied by chive potatoes speckled with lobster.

Delicious essentials: wild striped bass arriving crispy-skinned, bathed in flavorful tomato broth, surrounded by Manila clams and tender hari-cot verts; or a perfectly pink duck breast with a rhubarb orange mar-malade, thankfully lacking in what could have been cloying sweetness, served in a simple au jus with nice spring onions and kale. You could also go with the tender filet mignon, its preparation changing with the seasons; ours was served with a highly flavored braised oxtail *ragù* in a vibrant Cabernet jus with precious baby corn fritters. And speaking of another must, it's the truffled mac and cheese served piping hot in a miniature copper pot!

If you love to watch the action in the kitchen, consider the restau-rant's Chef's Counter accommodating up to eight people with two seat-ings per evening. At the counter are three menu options: the regular dining room menu, a four-course Vintner's Table pre-fixe menu that changes weekly . . . or simply have Chef prepare a multi-course meal according to his whim and your taste. Feel free to chat up the kitchen staff, asking any questions that might come to mind.

If you arrive without a reservation it's possible to dine in the restau-rant's spacious lounge where a full menu is served along with cocktails and the award-winning California wine list. And don't hesitate to heed your server's wine suggestion since, believe it or not, every server in the restaurant is also a sommelier.

SAMPLE MENU ITEMS

Dinner entrées: Sustainable fish of the day with golden cauliflower, almond couscous, grilled tangerine relish, and blood orange sauce; sage grilled American Red King Rock dove with summer squash, golden cauliflower, and Santa Rosa plum marmalade; Angus beef short rib slowly braised with summer blackberries, roasted country corn, and grilled Yukon potatoes; grilled Colorado lamb porterhouse and rack chop, kalamata olive, and Sangiovese jus.

Steakhouse 55

Steakhouse at the Disneyland Hotel. Breakfast and dinner.

Ditch your park clothes and take a step back to the glamour of classic Hollywood at this clubby hot spot. The décor is art deco with the addition of framed vintage photos of Walt Disney and the heyday of Disney Studios. Begin with a super-sized loaf of hot, chewy sourdough with plenty of creamy butter; but for me there is no other choice except to start with the Steakhouse 55 salad, romaine tossed with bacon, cucumber, tomato, red onion, and flavorful Tillamook cheddar. If you prefer something lighter try the spring greens with sweet pecans and raspberry vinaigrette.

I'm a filet kind of gal, and it did not disappoint. But I have to say that the food presentation here leaves much to be desired. A full size plate arrives with a small mound of parsley accompanied by a plain, somewhat dry looking steak. Sauces, if ordered, arrive on the side. Purists should order the juicy bone-in ribeye seasoned with the restaurant's special rub and ask for the garlicky 55 butter (skip the disappointing peppercorn sauce). On one visit a New York strip was chewy and tough (maybe an off night?)—good flavor and the "Oscar" style topping of crab cake and béarnaise sauce was a great choice—but tough all the same.

Super sides include the sharp cheddar potato gratin stack or the fat asparagus spears with rich hollandaise. But the star is the four-cheese macaroni topped with crispy bacon. For dessert a root beer baked Alaska served with a miniature root beer float proved to be awfully cute but overly sweet. Perhaps a better choice would be the crème brûlée, a traditional yet delicious option.

One of Disneyland Resort's best-kept secrets is the 55's breakfast. It's as if no one knows about it, but it's the perfect place for a bit of serenity in the morning hours before heading out for the parks.

SAMPLE MENU ITEMS

Breakfast entrées: Buttermilk stack or French toast with warm bananas foster or warm berries; eggs benedict; build-your-own omelet; New York steak and eggs; huevos rancheros; sunrise burrito with scrambled eggs, chorizo, potatoes, and cheese in a flour tortilla with *pico de gallo*, guacamole, and sour cream.

Dinner entrées: 14 oz. New York strip; 12 oz. roasted prime rib; 20 oz. porterhouse steak; pistachio crusted rack of lamb; free range double breast of chicken; broiled salmon; sustainable fish; cold water lobster tail.

Best Downtown Disney Dining

Catal

Mediterranean cuisine. Breakfast, lunch, and dinner.

Chef Joachim Splichal of the Patina Restaurant Group has a definite crowd pleaser at this Downtown Disney eatery, one that has remained a popular and well-thought-of choice for many years. The two-level restaurant features a mish-mash of dining rooms with intriguing cuisine offering a variety of small plates as well as creative specialty entrées. Start with goat cheese-stuffed *piquillo* peppers, really a must, with its scattering of toasted pine nuts and golden raisins, although a touch of additional spice might make this dish even more interesting. But truly, the very best appetizer is the Spanish cheese (aged Manchego, soft Mahon, and Valdeon blue) and charcuterie (Iberico *jamon* and *sobrasada*), a savory selection accompanied by crusty bread, Marcona almonds, dried apricots, and a seasonal fruit compote; you'll be fighting over every morsel.

Follow with one of the earthy paella options, the lobster probably the best and actually as good as it sounds, tender yet not overcooked rice, spicy chorizo, a nice portion of Maine lobster, and plenty of paprika; the only thing missing was perhaps a bit more saffron. Better yet it is beautifully presented in a piping hot paella pan! Another great entrée choice is the *a la parrilla* (barbecued) gulf shrimp, huge, plump, garlicky beauties perched on roasted fingerling potatoes and grilled Brussels sprouts, all doused in green, fruity olive oil. The hangar steak is loaded with flavor made even better with the addition of blue cheese and a green peppercorn sauce and the same delicious sides as the a la parrilla shrimp. The bold-flavored, shredded lamb Bolognese with al dente house-made *cavatelli* peppered with bright green Castelvetrano olives topped with a dollop of ricotta is a super pasta choice; again, a bit of spice would have been a nice compliment to the dish.

Probably the best dessert is the butterscotch bread pudding with caramelized bananas and cinnamon gelato. The chocolate *ardiente* ganache cake (ardiente meaning hot or burning) is overly dense and the addition of habanero peppers not really appealing. A topping of orange curd helped to cool it down a bit, but I just don't understand the gimmick of a spicy dessert.

> CARA'S TIP: You might want to request the rotunda room if super views of the Downtown Disney complex is what you are seeking. I think the best view is from the outdoor terrace, that is, if you don't mind the Downtown Disney hubbub. For a quicker, lighter meal opt for the open-air Uva Bar just outside the main restaurant located in the middle of Downtown Disney's walkway.

SAMPLE MENU ITEMS

Breakfast entrées: Eggs benedict; smoked salmon hash; shrimp and grits with bacon lardons, fried egg, and pickled Thai chilis; Virginia ham and cheese omelet; spinach and fresh egg white omelet; berry pancakes.

Dinner entrées: Suckling pig, tart apples, quinoa, wild arugula, *chicharrones*, pickled onion, and smoked cider jus; seared jumbo diver scallops, sunchoke puree, citrus segments, and truffle vinaigrette; Skuna Bay salmon pan-seared and served on a bed of beets, farro, corn, and soft pickled garlic; lamb shank slow cooked and served with pepper and squash ratatouille with braising jus; gnocchi with rapini, Moroccan olives, smoked mozzarella, pancetta, and fried capers.

SECTION FOUR

ADVENTURES BY DISNEY

Who knows families better than Disney and who better to show you the world and lead you on a unique travel experience? With close to thirty itineraries across the globe guests can choose from a trip to Macchu Picchu in Peru, the Scottish Highlands, exotic Southeast Asia, or somewhere closer to home such as America's National Parks. In the summer months there's even the chance to combine a Mediterranean or Alaskan cruise with a shore side Adventures By Disney vacation, the best of both worlds.

Adventures By Disney vacations connect you to the destination in unforgettable ways. You actually become participants in the story of the country you are visiting. For instance, while strolling through the labyrinth of streets in Venice you suddenly bump into "Marco Polo" in a charming courtyard. The children gather 'round and listen in rapt attention as he speaks of his adventures traveling the world. Or, while adults take in the sites of the Roman Colosseum, children learn about gladiators and even try out a sword and shield in a mock fight. In Cambodia adults explore the wonders of Ankor Wat's temples while the kids take a treasure hunt in a traditional tuk tuk vehicle. At Paris's Louvre museum children join their Adventure Guide on a detective mission in search of clues among the masterpieces while their parents explore in a more traditional fashion.

Not only will you see the famous sites but you'll meet the locals as well. In Florence participate in a pasta or pizza-making class; in Venice make your very own carnival mask. You can even stroll in Merida's shoes and learn archery in Scotland's Glamis Castle, ride a pony through the forest, and compete in Disney's version of the Highland Games.

Local guides lead you through each destination, but two very entertaining Adventure Guides are always on hand to sweat the details throughout the trip. They take photos ad infinitum, and you'll not only end up with personalized postcards but also a DVD mailed to you at the end of the trip—perfect reminders of your fabulous vacation. Another nice touch is that parents and children get a break from each other at least one evening when Junior Adventurers enjoy a special event with their Adventure Guides while the adults sneak off for a romantic meal on their own. And better still, the children return with both fond memories of their destination as well as memorable bonds formed with their newfound friends.

For each Adventures By Disney vacation there is a minimum age for participation and also a "recommended" age that Disney feels is the "sweet spot" where a child will truly enjoy this type of trip. Included in the cost of your vacation are airport transfers (such welcome conveniences for arrivals and departures in unknown destinations), accommodations, luggage service, entrance and activity fees, daily breakfast, most lunches, and several dinners. Gratuities are included with the exception of your two Adventure Guides left to your discretion. Your mode of transportation is a luxury motorcoach where you might even catch a Disney movie on one of your long-haul days traveling from one city to another.

So get ready, you're about to embark on an amazing adventure of discovery, learning, and the sheer joy of traveling the world!

PLANNING YOUR ADVENTURES BY DISNEY VACATION

There's nothing quite like a *true* Disney expert when it comes to choosing a travel advisor. An Authorized Disney Vacation Planner agency can make the difference between a mediocre vacation and an excellent one. For your Adventures By Disney vacation needs call Glass Slipper Concierge at (866) 725-7595 or go online at GlassSlipperConcierge.com. Glass Slipper Concierge is the brainchild of this book's author, Cara Goldsbury, originating from a desire to offer a client-centric option to those who want an exceptional and unforgettable Disney vacation. Cara has gathered an exclusive team of luxury concierge advisors whose knowledge of Disney Destinations can only be matched by their passion for delivering white-glove service.

Another option is to go online at AdventuresByDisney.com or call 800-543-0865.

CARA GOLDSBURY'S ADVENTURE IN ITALY, DISNEY-STYLE

I've never been much of a group player. In fact anything even remotely hinting of the word "group" makes me run in exactly the opposite direction: group sports, group therapy, Groupons. But the most frightening two words for me have always been "group tours."

Adventures By Disney proved to be the big exception to my rule.

A travel advisor for over thirty years I've always prided myself for arriving in a major European city with a stack of guidebooks, a great map, and a carefully prepared itinerary in hand with each day planned in minute detail. Seriously, who needs a guide? Never mind that I arrived exhausted from all that research and came home exhausted from trying to maneuver around a strange and bewildering city. But with the holidays looming and nothing presenting itself as even remotely exciting I couldn't resist the opportunity to join, along with my husband, an Adventures By Disney Italy guided tour. I mean running away to Venice, Florence, and Rome over Christmas and escaping the craziness at home . . . it was just too exciting to resist!

Days 1 and 2

After four days in Paris on our own (I just couldn't stand it; I had to experience at least a few days with map in hand) we landed in Rome before most of the group, over jetlag, and ready to go. I know the drill. Gather our luggage then wander around the airport until I find the taxi stand. But wait, is that someone with a sign reading "Adventures By Disney?" Could it be? Yes! And that someone is ready and willing to help with the luggage and place us in a comfortable van that whisks us away to the Hotel Bernini Bristol. Way, way too easy.

The hotel, while touted as five-star, is nice enough although a bit worn around the edges in a few places (note: this hotel has since been replaced by the Gran Meliá Rome Hotel). But it is also one of those places you know you'll come to love after a few days of pleasant service and easy sleep. Right on the Piazza Barberini and just a 10-minute walk to the Spanish Steps it is one of Rome's better locations.

Our first evening was on our own with a hearty feast of rabbit *ragù* pasta at Ditirambo near the Campo De' Fiori followed by grappa at our favorite spot overlooking the Parthenon and the piazza's beautiful fountain.

Tomorrow, after a perfect day wandering the oh-so-charming and intimate streets of Rome, a city brimming with fabulous dining spots, gorgeous piazzas, and bubbly fountains around every corner, we would meet our Adventures By Disney travelers at a cocktail reception and dinner at the hotel. Another group travel concern about to be completely shot down!

Day 3

After only one day with the group I ventured to admit, there can't be a better choice for family travel. "Junior Adventurers" were treated like royalty, and Marco, our Italian Adventure Guide, had the children in giggles half the day. After 10-year-old Bryce accidentally dropped and broke his Colosseum souvenir statuette on our walk through Rome, I caught Courtney, our U.S.A. Adventure guide, buying a replacement for him in a shop along the way. Bryce's giant-size smile was her reward when she handed him a replica of the one he lost!

The pace was perfect. No rushing through important sites, something I had thought was a given on group tours. Our local Roman guide, Christina, was unbelievably informative yet so entertaining. She really made the ancient world come alive for us all. And sure enough, before the day was out we all felt like one big happy family. Best of all, it was even more thrilling to see Rome through all the little ones' eyes.

Proof of the adage that small things do make a big difference: a bag full of coins for each person to throw in the Trevi Fountain, lunch

in a *pizzaria* with a jovial and entertaining owner hosting the feast, a stop for a gelato treat at the end of a long day. It was a memorable day with the glories of the Colosseum, the Forum, the Spanish Steps, the Pantheon, and the Piazza Navona. Next, the Vatican!

Day 4

Our tour of St. Peter's Basilica and the Vatican Museums was a hit. Parents could listen to the guide without interruption as the Junior Adventurers were given their own talk prior to entering the Sistine Chapel, Michaelangelo's most famous work of art which captivated Adventurers of all ages. Lunch was a festive affair featuring anti-pasto and saltimbocca. The group had livened up, and the children paired off in natural age groups, having the time of their lives.

Traveling in off-season certainly has its benefits. The weather was cold but also sunny, and winter light is always spectacular. You can actually move without someone's elbow in your ear at the Sistine Chapel, and some of the lesser-known museums are so quiet I could actually hear the floor creaking beneath my feet.

On our last night in Rome my husband and I wandered the en-chanting backstreets near the Piazza Navona and decided to have a drink before dinner at a fun and festive trattoria. But we couldn't resist just a little something to go along with the wine and ordered appetizers of grilled artichokes and the local specialty of *filetti de baccala*, fried cod. As plates of steaming pasta passed by filling the air with their appetizing fragrances we had to give in. What the heck—we went for a complete dinner and loved every minute of it. It was a perfect ending to a fabulous three days.

But the topper of the evening was the hundreds of Santa Clauses we ogled rollerblading down the Italian flag-lit Via Corso on our way back to the hotel. We could not believe our eyes!

Day 5

Off to Umbria and Tuscany in the morning. Setting luggage out-side our room, having it picked up during breakfast, and then taken to the bus with not even a thought about it until our arrival in Florence that evening seemed something of a miracle. My usual modus operandi is to lug it off to the station, figure out the schedule to the next destination, drag myself down the platform, and hope for the strength of Hercules to get it up and into the train. It's either that or paying a small fortune for private transfers, which I must confess is oftentimes my choice. What, I ask myself now, was I trying to prove all those years of doing it on my own?

And I'm still in shock that the pace was just about the same as what I would have set for myself. We had yet to depart before 8:30 a.m. This, my strongest argument against a group tour, had been shot down in a matter of days.

Our stop in Orvieto was a charmer, and a lunch of wild boar pasta (a local specialty) with a glass of dry Orvieto white wine was perfection. It's a picture-postcard town and once again the streets were almost empty, although the stores were open and welcoming. Our favorite stop was an amazing cheese and meat shop where wild boar is featured in every fashion—wild boar prosciutto, wild boar salami, wild boar truffled sausage—the list goes on and on. We decided on a slab of pecorino cheese and truffled sausage to take with us to Florence. The missing ingredients were a nice bottle of Tuscan red and gourmet crackers which we picked up on arrival in Florence, preparatory to a sumptuous feast in our room the next evening.

The only aspect of the trip that I'm a bit stuck on is the hotels. Our hotel in Florence was an A-plus location just off the Pizza Signorina with a charming lobby and lounge area. But I swear our room was the size of a large closet. Our request to be moved was met with more spacious accommodations, but no more than 50 square feet larger. In truth, however, most of the other travelers in the group described their room as huge, so thankfully this isn't the norm for everyone. Next day—Christmas Eve and its special aura cast upon the sights of Florence.

My husband and I really did feel an amazing sense of camaraderie

with our fellow travelers after a few days of seeing the world together. And what a perfect group! The children were all a joy; the adults gracious, fun, and incredible travel partners. I kept asking myself, "where is that one pain in the rear that I've always heard is a mandatory part of any tour group"? Definitely missing in action, at least on this occasion.

Day 6

Our Adventure Guides, Courtney and Marco, were extraordinary in making every day so easy-going and pleasurable. It's obvious that they love their work, and it truly made all the difference. The previous day in Florence Courtney took a group over to the leather and gold market on her afternoon off. Seriously? I so would have been in my room with my feet up watching a good movie instead! Disney dedication, I guess.

Christmas day found us all making pasta at a local restaurant (I mean, come on, doesn't everyone make pasta on Christmas Day?). What a riot—a demonstrative Italian chef explaining the process, Marco translating, plenty of laughs, and flour everywhere . . . in our hair, up our nose, covering the floor! We followed our pasta frenzy with a festive meal featuring, what else, more pasta. Fortunately, it was chef-made and not composed of our creative and oddball-shaped raviolis. Lunch ended with panettone, a delicious Italian Christmas cake, and a hearty toast of Prosecco.

I think my favorite thing about this holiday trip was the sounds and sights of an Italian Christmas. It's certainly more low key than in the U.S. and so charming with its *italianesque* decorations and nativity scenes around every corner, church bells ringing, big, floppy trees decorating the *duomos* . . . all of it adding up to a nostalgic and wonderful time of year. It's definitely not as commercial as home but rather more reminiscent of the Christmas of my youth when it was all about family and what I thought was the most beautiful tree in the world sitting smack dab in the middle of our living room.

Dinner was at a restaurant outside of Florence concluded by a

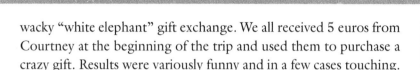

wacky "white elephant" gift exchange. We all received 5 euros from Courtney at the beginning of the trip and used them to purchase a crazy gift. Results were variously funny and in a few cases touching.

Day 7

Ahh Venice! Honestly, I think it might possibly be the most beautiful place in the world. My third time there and awesome as ever, maybe more. We caught the Eurostar from Florence, so simple with Adventures By Disney handling our luggage by bus. Our only requirement was to step onboard for the two-hour train ride in first class comfort.

Just a short walk from the station we hopped aboard gondolas for a dreamy ride through the canals of Venice to meet our local tour guide for a walk through the narrow streets and beautiful piazzas that make up this wonderful city. Upon stopping in an enchanting courtyard, who awaited us but none other than "Marco Polo," whereupon the Junior Adventurers were given a personalized history lesson of his exploits and the daily trading pins (each one cuter than the last). We ended our excursion at St. Mark's Square with the bells ringing out the hour. True magic!

Our hotel in Venice was the lovely Luna Hotel Baglioni in a primo location just a one-minute walk off St. Mark's Square. This time our room is palatial with rich red carpeting, Old World style furnishings, roomy bath, and even a stand-up balcony with a side view of the Grand Canal. Heaven! Couldn't ask for much better (and certainly did not).

Day 8

The day dawned gorgeous and sunny but with a definite chill in the air, the winter light phenomenal. Had we not overslept we could have participated in Venetian mask making which followed a walk led by Courtney and Marco through the Rialto fish and vegetable market. Sorry to have skipped one of the highlights of the trip but wandering the streets of Venice on our own instead was a great option. Exciting new discoveries around every corner and getting lost

in the ambience is exactly what is so marvelous about this charming city.

The last day of our Adventures journey was bittersweet, as, alas, all good things do come to an end. We had a farewell dinner, said our goodbyes. It had been fun, informative, and surprisingly delightful. I doubt if I'll ever buy another Groupon, or sign up for group therapy, and certainly never consider the thought of group sports. But this trip got me thinking that another group tour might be somewhere in my future. Maybe it was sheer luck that the group got along so well, but Disney really does that to you sometimes. It's part of the magic!

THE VERY BEST ADVENTURES BY DISNEY VACATIONS

While all the Adventures By Disney guided vacations are tempting, here are the best of the best, ones I think are the most intriguing.

Europe

Scotland: A Brave Adventure

What could be more fascinating than following the adventures of a big screen heroine through incredible highland scenery? In Disney's first adventure themed around one of their animated movies, *Brave*, the focus is on family bonding. Over eight nights explore Edinburgh, Inverness, Loch Ness, the Isle of Lewis, and the Isle of Skye, some of the most beautiful places on the planet, overnighting at the historic Balmoral Hotel in Edinburgh, the Cullin Hills Hotel on the Isle of Skye, and The Kingsmills Hotel in Inverness.

Begin with a private tour of historic Glamis Castle where archery lessons are on tap, then on to Dunnottar overlooking the North Sea, the actual castle that was the inspiration for the movie. That evening adults enjoy a whiskey tasting while Junior Adventurers are busy with the guides.

Take a boat (or a canoe if you're brave—pun intended) out on the loch in search of the infamous Loch Ness monster, then tour the eerie Urquhart Castle back on shore. Each day is progressively more exiting: ride through the moors on Highland ponies, just like Merida but hopefully at a slower pace; visit a tapestry maker where guests can try their own hand at weaving; and end the vacation with a private evening at Edinburgh Castle to see Scotland's Crown Jewels and enjoy a candlelit meal in the Queen Anne room. There's even a traditional Scottish dinner, including haggis (again, only for the brave) accompanied by a bagpiper and topped off by single malt whiskey tasting.

Austria, Germany & Czech Republic

In one of Adventures by Disney's newest European itineraries visit Central Europe and the countries of Austria, Germany, and the Czech Republic. In Prague your hotel is the Marriott, just steps away from Gothic Old Town Square. Tour famous landmarks such as St. Vitus Cathedral, Charles Bridge, and the medieval Astronomical Clock followed by lessons in marionette making. Dinner at Folklore Gardens with traditional singing and dancing concludes your time in Prague.

Next, bustle off to quaint Berchtesgaden, Germany, nestled in the Bavarian Alps and check in at the Intercontinental Hotel. A private tour of the Salzbergwerk Salt Mines and the Eishole Ice Cave are trip highlights; later join in and learn the art of pretzel making. End the day with a visit to a schnapps distillery with plenty of tasting included. The following day travel through scenic *Sound of Music* locations with lunch at Helibrunn Castle. At dinner that evening you're entertained by Mozart violinists at St. Peter's Stiftskeller, a UNESCO World Heritage Site in operation since 803 A.D.

En route to Vienna your entourage stops for a privately guided tour of Hohenwerfen Castle where you also catch a falconry demonstration, strudel making, and a private marionette show. After check-in at the Ritz Carlton, dine that evening in Austria's oldest restaurant. Next morning enjoy the renowned Royal Spanish Riding School in the ornate Hofburg Castle and a guided tour of the Old Quarter. During the grand finale of your trip learn to waltz at a private dinner in the Emperor's Pavilion at the Vienna Zoo.

Italy & Amalfi Coast

Some of the most romantic places on earth can be found in Italy. Of course, fabulous food, places steeped in history, fascinating ruins, and lovely beaches simply go without saying. On arrival in Naples you're whisked off to Sorrento to begin a uniquely charming vacation. The Grand Hotel La Favorita welcomes you with a reception and dinner the first evening. On day two wind your way along Italy's spectacular coastal region for an exploration of the charming cliff side village of Postino before boarding a private boat to yet another charming place, Amalfi. The following day take a ferry to the magical isle of Capri and ride a funicular to the heights of Capri town, followed by a private cruise around the island and a chance for a dip in the sapphire blue water. That evening back in Sorrento visit a farm for mozzarella cheese and pizza-making lessons, then dinner and a folkloric dance.

A visit to ancient Pompeii with a private guided tour of the ruins is truly a highlight. After lunch in Naples take the train trip to Florence and the Hotel Bernini Palace which is just steps from the main piazza. Next day, walk the streets of Florence on a guided tour, see Michelangelo's "David" and the Duomo, then embark on a tour of the Uffizi, one of the most famous art museums in the world.

The subsequent morning's excursion to Monteriggioni, a wonderfully preserved hilltop town, follows with a visit to Sienna to relish the historic medieval square and learn about the famous Palio horse race. During your stay travel out of the city on a daytrip to Lucca for a bicycle ride atop the famous walls of the city, then to Pisa for views of its leaning tower. End your spectacular trip with a farewell dinner perched high above Florence overlooking a nighttime view of the sparkling city.

France

Discover art, history, and culinary delights on this enchanting jaunt through France. Begin just outside of Paris in the woodland retreat hotel of Trianon Palace. Visit the magnificent palace of Versailles, the historic home to France's kings and queens, then off to Claude Monet's home in Giverny followed by an enjoyable art activity. Move on to your home for the next three nights, Normandy's Royal Barrière Hotel on the beach of Deauville.

During the next day's excursion to the island fortress of Mont Saint-Michel wander the cobblestone streets and feast on enormous omelets at the historic La Mère Poulard. Late afternoon savor the delights of cider and Calvados tasting. Other highpoints include a visit to the famous Bayeux tapestry and Omaha Beach to see the historical sites commemorating D-Day. More excursions offer a trip to Honfleur, a town made famous by the Impressionist painters and then on to the "city of lights"—Paris. Stay at the Hotel Napoleon just off the Champs Elyseés, tour the Eiffel Tower, shop the markets, and learn to cook French cuisine. An unforgettable *bon voyage* dinner at the Louvre overlooking the glass pyramid entrance concludes your adventure *extraordinaire*.

Greece

There's nothing quite like the flavor of Greece, and this tour certainly hits the highlights. Your odyssey begins in Athens where your home will be the Hotel Athenaeum Intercontinental. Visit the iconic sites of the Acropolis, the Parthenon, and the Panathenaic Stadium, site of the first modern Olympics where Junior Adventurers take part in a mini marathon. Dine that night in the heart of the exciting Plaka district in a *taverna* with traditional Greek music and dancing. Next day tour the ancient site of Delphi to see the stunning Temple of Apollo and the Delphi Museum, followed by lunch overlooking the Gulf of Corinth.

Then off to the Greek Isles. Your first stop is Santorini with its famous caldera and a stay at the Vedema Resort. Enjoy a local winery where Junior Adventurers become grape crushers i.e. *stompers*. Next day sail the caldera on a charter with stops for a volcano hike and a dip in the blue Mediterranean with lunch at a fishing village on the water's edge. A guided walking tour introduces you to the captivating cliffside village of Oia, followed by a visit to the Bronze Age archeological site of Akrotiri, often referred to as the Minoan Pompeii. That evening dine at a local *taverna* in a delightful mountain village.

In the morning board a high-speed ferry to Crete and the seaside resort of Porto Elounda, your base for kayaking to the Venetian island fortress of Spinalonga, touring the Palace of Knossos, and soaking up the Cretan culture and its art of *tsaziki* making. You can even ride a donkey, hike in a mountain village, and learn how to make cheese. Your last evening's farewell dinner takes place in an olive grove with entertainment by Greek musicians.

Norway

On Adventures By Disney's newest guided vacation the Kingdom of Norway, setting of Disney's animated adventure, *Frozen,* is revealed in all its magical beauty. Convene in Bergen, a storybook village that was the inspiration for Arendelle where Anna and Elsa live. The Radisson Blu Royal Hotel is your home for the night. Located in the heart of the 700-year-old Bryggen area it's an absolutely charming UNESCO World Heritage Site. Meet your fellow travelers for a welcome dinner overlooking the waterfront.

Adventure begins in full force the next morning with river rafting in Voss amid stunning mountain vistas. Have lunch in a grass-roofed cabin before departing for Flam. From the historic Fretheim Hotel launch your excursions to dramatic fjords on RIB (rigid inflatable boat), a visit to a 12th century Stave church, and lessons in cheese making.

The next day it's off to Geiranger for some of the most spectacular scenery in Norway. Along the way visit the famed Borgund Stave Church. Upon arrival begin to enjoy activities such as rainbow trout fishing, row boating, a glacier safari, hiking, a farm visit, a ferry tour past the town's Seven Sisters waterfall, and a stunning viewpoint of the fjord of Geirangerfjord. Continue to Oslo via train to enjoy Norway's capital city where a farewell dinner with traditional Norwegian folk dancers and musicians tops off your last evening.

Germany

Talk about magic: touring Germany's castles and quaint villages amid gorgeous scenery! Begin with a private visit to Heidelberg Castle and dinner in a traditional *biergarten.* Then on to medieval Alsfeld to walk in the footsteps of the brothers Grimm and discover what inspired their charming stories before picnicking in an outdoor courtyard, visited by none other than Little Red Riding Hood.

Spend two nights in a real castle (maybe *the* trip highlight) with evening dinners overlooking incredible vistas of Lake Edersee from within the hotel's 800-year-old walls. Next day takes you to Lowenburg Castle and a royal welcome by a real German princess, followed by lunch at a manor house. After which you'll journey to Rothenburg, one of the most picturesque places in Germany. That evening walk with a night watchman through cobblestone streets. The following day princesses dress up in princess costumes at a Medieval Shop, and everyone learns how to pretzel twist (and taste!) and savor authentic German cuisine at the oldest hotel in town.

On the way to Munich stop at the Steiff Bear Museum for a tour and lunch, then travel south along the scenic Romantic Road to the historic Hotel VierJahreszeiten Kempinski Munchen. A side visit to the awe-inspiring Neuschwanstein Castle, the inspiration for Disneyland's Sleeping Beauty Castle, comes complete with a horse-drawn carriage ride through the countryside and lunch with picture perfect views of the palace. This memorable trip ends with a traditional dinner accompanied by oompa music, song, and dance.

The Americas

Costa Rica

You can't get much closer to nature than on this adventure. And you don't even have to travel half way around the globe to explore such wonders as rain forests, smoking volcanoes, and wildlife galore.

After one night at the Costa Rica Marriott Hotel in San Jose board a private charter plane in the morning to Tortugero and reside in rustic Laguna Lodge located smack dab in the middle of a tropical rainforest. This is the perfect place to learn about endangered sea turtles. At Tortugero National Park you'll be able to spot sea turtles, toucans, sloths, even white-headed capuchin monkeys as you travel by boat through the flora and fauna (be on the lookout for swinging monkeys!).

Your next Costa Rican sojourn takes you to Arenal Volcano and a visit to a working pineapple plantation. Your stay at Hotel Arenal Manoa in La Fortuna offers impressive views of the resident volcano. The most exciting day of the trip comes the next morning on a zip line, followed by a welcome soak in nearby hot springs heated by the volcano itself!

Even more adventure awaits you along the way before commencing your beach vacation at Guanacaste and the Villas Sol Hotel & Beach Resort: white water rafting on the Tenorio River. Next morning board a catamaran and enjoy snorkeling off secluded beaches. Your high-spirited Costa Rican farewell consists of a lesson in mojito making and a final dinner with live regional music.

Arizona & Utah

If you love to fantasize about the Old West this adventure to Arizona and Utah will fit the bill. Enjoy the canyon lands of the American Southwest as well as the pine trees of the surrounding mountains. Begin in Sedona, Arizona with a stay at lovely Enchantment Resort, perfect for launching your explorations of fascinating red rock canyons by day via jeep and by night under the star-studded sky guided by a local astronomer. And then . . . the mother of all canyons, the Grand Canyon, as seen from the jaw-dropping South Rim, followed by a feast of BBQ with prime views.

Next stop, Monument Valley, easily recognizable from old Hollywood westerns (think John Ford). Take a Navaho-guided, off-road excursion through the magical mesas of the valley before checking into The Red Cliffs Lodge on the banks of the Colorado River, your home for the next two nights. A jaunt to Arches National Park and its thousands of sandstone arches follows with jet-boating on the Colorado River. Spend your last day enjoying white water rafting and grand finale cowboy cooking on the banks of the river.

Peru & Machu Picchu

After a night in Lima fly to captivating Cusco high in the Andes Mountains. Proceed to the Sacred Valley and your hotel, the Sol y Luna Lodge & Spa. Watch master weavers demonstrate the art of traditional Peruvian textiles and partake in a welcome Andean feast accompanied by dances and stories of the Incas. The next few days brings an exciting raft trip down the Urubamba River as well as visits to the salt pan terraces of Maras, where salt has been mined for over 500 years, and the ruins of Moray with its fascinating circular terraces.

Next day take a motor coach to Machu Picchu, one of the most magnificent structures in the world, and have lunch at Sanctuary Lodge located right next to the site. On your way to Cusco the next morning shop a Pisac market for local crafts, then view llamas, alpacas, and the rare vicuna at the Awana Kancha Camelida Center. Your hotel that evening is the luxurious Libertador Palacio Del Inka Hotel Cusco just blocks from the main plaza.

The following day, visit the remarkable fortress of Sacsayhauman where 200-ton stones were moved miles without modern machinery, then explore Cusco on your own in the afternoon. Your adventure ends back in Lima and a farewell lunch at a 16th-century colonial mansion before boarding your plane for home.

Alaska

See some of the world's most stunning landscapes and majestic scenery on your discovery of the 49th state. It all begins in Anchorage with a welcome seafood feast at Bridge Restaurant spanning a salmon stream. Next morning bicycle around Cook Inlet and get up close and personal with bald eagles, then visit the Alaska Native Heritage Center for an interesting look at Native Alaskan cultures with a demonstration by the Native Junior Olympians.

From Anchorage motorcoach to Talkeetna located at the edge of Denali National Park where you reside at the Grand Denali Lodge perched dramatically above the Denali Valley. Along the way a jet boat cruise shows you the sights of the Susitna River and the Alaskan wilderness. Your stay includes a breathtaking trip deep into Denali National Park, a hike and picnic lunch in the wilderness, and a mountain climber presentation.

On the road to Girdwood and the Hotel Alyeska experience Iditarod at Happy Trails Kennels, including a sledding demonstration and a visit to meet the racing dogs and their litters of puppies. That evening the adults take a tram to the Seven Glaciers Restaurant for jaw-dropping views of Cook inlet and the surrounding glaciers while the children enjoy a Junior Adventurers dinner and games back at the hotel. Next day board the Scenic Alaska Railroad to Seward and take in the spectacle from rail cars with outdoor viewing decks.

In Seward a cruise of Resurrection Bay takes you on a search for whales, and the Alaska Wildlife Conservation Center demonstrates how the resident bears, moose, and bison are rescued and rehabilitated. Savor one last taste of wild Alaska salmon accompanied by traditional native dancers and drummers at your farewell dinner.

Asia and More

China

Immerse yourself in the rich history and traditions of mysterious China, one of the world's oldest civilizations. Explore the mysterious Forbidden City and the breathtaking Great Wall of China during your stay at the Peninsula Palace Beijing. Lunch on Peking duck, take part in a traditional tea-pouring ceremony, enjoy a noodle making demonstration, visit Beijing's historic neighborhoods by pedicab, and try your hand at ancient arts (kids love attempting the Chinese yo-yo). Then it's off to the Shangri-La Hotel in Chengdu with visits to the giant pandas and the Sichuan Face-Changing Opera.

Fly to Xian to see the famous Terra Cotta Warriors, then on to Guilin and a stay at the Shangri-La Guilin with its views of the Li River. Try your hand (and the rest of your body) at Tai Chi, later cruising the Li River where a magical landscape of formations awaits you.

What can compare with the excitement of Shanghai and Hong Kong? Find out as you explore these exhilarating cities. The Peninsula Shanghai on the Bund River and the waterfront district is the perfect base for exploring old Shanghai, the 300-year-old Yu Gardens, and the multitude of outdoor markets. End your stay at the Shangri-La Kowloon, Hong Kong, with an exploration of Stanley Market, lunch on Victoria Peak, and a special farewell dinner at Hong Kong Disneyland!

Cambodia, Vietnam & Laos

Ho Chi Minh City (formerly Saigon) is your first stop in this land of many contrasts. Prearranged excursions include a Saigon River cruise, lunch at a river lodge, and a visit to the fascinating Cú Chi Tunnels. Then off to Da Nang for a stay at the Hoi Ann Beach Resort with a visit to the town of Hoi Ann, a UNESCO World Heritage Site. From here fly to Hanoi to stay at the historic Sofitel Legend Metropole and experience a sunrise tai chi class, visits to the Ho Chi Minh's stilt house and his mausoleum, and a spin through the infamous Hanoi Hilton.

Next stop Laos and the ancient capital of Luang Prabang, a step back in time at this fascinating UNESCO World Heritage Site. Visit the Royal Palace Museum along with several of the town's many gilded temples. Nothing is more fascinating than the sight of monks strolling the streets in their marigold robes, and the colorful and exciting night market with its local crafts (talk about bargains galore!) are sure to please. Your hotel is the Le Palais Juliana, with dinner poolside on the first evening. Rise early the next morning to witness, and even participate if you wish, in the traditional gathering of the morning alms by Luang Prabang's monks. Then visit a rice farm and try your hand at rice production before stopping at Kuang Si Falls, famous for its turquoise cascades.

End your vacation in Cambodia, one of the most fascinating spots on earth, where temples, temples, and more temples are on the agenda. After check-in at the 5-star Sofitel Angkor Phokeethra board your gondola for a trip around the mystical moats of the Ankor temple complex. Next day explore Ankor Wat in depth, then enjoy a treasure hunt by tuk-tuk through several different temples as you work your way to Ta Prohm, a complex literally overgrown by thick, sinewy jungle tree trunks. Visit even more temples by elephant until your farewell dinner with Cambodian cuisine and dancing.

Australia

If you love nature as well as history and are looking for a wide variety of experiences, then this is the vacation for you. Begin in Cairns at the beachside Sea Temple Resort & Spa and sail away on a catamaran for a glorious day on the water with a visit to the Great Barrier Reef. Accompanied by a marine biologist, it's your chance to snorkel in the largest coral reef system in the world with the option of viewing the reef from a semi-submersible vessel. Back on land visit a crocodile adventure park and go "croc-spotting" on a lagoon cruise followed by a traditional Australian "barbie" dinner.

Immerse yourself in the aboriginal culture of the land "down under" with the Tjapukai tribe where spear and boomerang throwing lessons add to the fun. Then off to the outback to explore the spectacular Ayers Rock in Australia's red desert and a stay at the Desert Gardens Hotel. Follow that with a flight to the cosmopolitan city of Sydney to visit famous sites such as the Opera House and Harbour Bridge, take a bike ride along the harbor, and even learn to surf at Bondi Beach.

Next stop, Tasmania and the Freycinet Lodge, surrounded by dramatic pink granite peaks. Explore Tasmania's fascinating nature reserves, zip-line in an ancient eucalyptus forest, sea kayak on Coles Bay, and visit a wildlife sanctuary to see the Tasmanian devil, koalas, and wallables. End with a visit to Port Arthur and its penal colony with a farewell dinner in, of all places, a prison asylum!

South Africa Safari

Begin this trip of a lifetime in gorgeous Cape Town and Table Bay Hotel on the waterfront. Hop the aerial cableway up the landmark Table Mountain for breathtaking views and a nature walk through the indigenous *fynbos*, one of the world's largest floral kingdoms. See the District Six Museum, a sensitive exposure to South Africa's Apartheid Era followed by lunch. Then embark on a city walking tour and craft shopping at Greenmarket Square. That evening your welcome dinner at the 17th-century Castle of Good Hope is accompanied by traditional South African song and dance.

Next day visit the Cape of Good Hope, have lunch with a stunning seaside view, and see Boulders Beach for an encounter with a colony of African penguins. The day after it's on to Cape Dutch wine country for an Afrikaans pastry making class then make your way through the countryside to Spier Winery. Lunch at Moyo is set among Bedouin tents and garden gazebos for a pan-African buffet. Then adults enjoy wine tasting while Junior Adventurers learn the ancient art of falconry.

Fly to George for a two-night stay at Pezula Resort Hotel and trips to the sanctuaries of Monkeyland, the world's first primate refuge, and Birds of Eden. Lunch is at the Bramon Wine Estate overlooking the vineyards and an elephant sanctuary. Next day ferry across the Knysna Lagoon to see the lush Featherbed Nature Reserve where lunch is held under the shade of the Milkwood trees.

Fly to Kapama River Lodge near Kruger National Park. Your first evening at the Lodge includes a game drive in Big Five country followed by dinner in the bush. Subsequent days are filled with both morning and evening game safari drives. Your last game drive occurs at the crack of dawn on your final morning in South Africa before boarding a plane bound for home.

SECTION FIVE

AULANI

Disney in Hawaii? You bet! Set in Ko Olina on Oahu's west coast seashore and a 45-minute drive from either Waikiki or the North Shore, Aulani is perfect for finding the true flavor of Hawaii in every nook and cranny. From the authentic, hand-carved details to the dreamy pool and winding waterways to traditional storytelling and Hawaiian music at sunset . . . there is something unique and amazing around every corner.

On arrival in the open-air lobby you are welcomed by a friendly staff with a lei for the women, a *kukui* nut necklace for the men, and a Menehune (the mythical "little people" of Hawaii) necklace for the children. Three carved *ki'i* ("tiki" elsewhere in Polynesia) grace the entry of the lobby where twin pools of water in lava rock represent the balance of the feminine and masculine side of the resort—one calm and gently flowing, the other wilder with rushing water through large boulders. Arched ceilings supported by massive timbers illuminated with clusters of basket lighting soar overhead, and a story-telling mural of Hawaiian life wraps high above the flagstone flooring. Throughout the lobby is decorative banding inspired by Hawaiian kappa cloth representing land, sea, and sky. Behind the check-in desk you'll find an interesting 200-foot long "Rainbow Wall" of photos taken by local students capturing the essence of the islands. With plenty of seating areas both inside and on the verandah outside, the lobby is a great place to gather or relax. And you can't beat the views that spread across a wide expanse of gorgeous scenery and welcoming pools of water highlighted by the resort's volcanic outcropping and the sparkling blue ocean in the distance.

While I'm not particularly enamored with the Ko Olina area, it does offer a golf course, marina, a few shops and restaurants, and over a mile of seashore pathways. But if it is a resort family experience you are looking for you can't do much better than Aulani. Don't expect a theme park atmosphere or characters wherever you go (although you will certainly have the opportunity to hang with Mickey and the gang at various times each day), but do expect an authentic Hawaiian atmosphere with a few obvious Disney touches. For instance, the elevator music is classic Disney songs translated into the Hawaiian language. However, step outside and you'll find gorgeous swimming pools on par with a 5-star resort.

Local artisan touches are just about everywhere you look. In fact, Aulani houses one of the world's largest collections of contemporary Hawaiian art. Realistic faux aboriginal petroglyphs adorn the rocks, and there's even a lava tube for the kids to explore. And get ready to see plenty of Aunty and Uncle on hand to educate guests about the lore and tradition of the Hawaiian culture through their storytelling.

PLANNING YOUR
AULANI VACATION

There's nothing quite like a *true* Disney expert when it comes to choosing a travel advisor. An Authorized Disney Vacation Planner agency can make the difference between a mediocre vacation and an excellent one. For your Aulani needs call Glass Slipper Concierge at (866) 725-7595 or go online at GlassSlipperConcierge.com. Glass Slipper Concierge is the brainchild of this book's author, Cara Goldsbury, originating from a desire to offer a client-centric option to those who want an exceptional and unforgettable Disney vacation. Cara has gathered an exclusive team of luxury concierge advisors whose knowledge of Disney Destinations can only be matched by their passion for delivering white-glove service.

When Should I Travel to Aulani?

Hawaii's weather is pretty darn perfect year round. Of course most visitors come to Hawaii when the weather is snowy and cold back home. So expect winter to be a busy and a more expensive time of year particularly over the Christmas and New Year holidays.

If low crowds and less expensive resort and airline rates are to your liking plan on visiting Hawaii in the off season, generally mid-April to mid-June (with the exception of the last week of April and early May, a traditional holiday time in Japan when Japanese tourists flock to Hawaii) and then again September through mid-December. Coincidentally low season is some of the best weather of the year.

What Is The Weather Like in Ko Olina?

Luckily the Ko Olina area is located on the Leeward side of the island and basks in almost year-round sun with very little rain and moderate temperatures. So just about any time of the year will be pleasurable. There are actually two seasons, dry and rainy, with dry season in the summer (April-October) and a rainier season in winter (November-March) although it's never terribly wet at Aulani. If weather strikes the Ko Olina area, don't worry. Just change to a different part of the island; there's just about always sun somewhere on the island.

What Should I Pack?

Hawaii and Ko Olina is very casual with not a suit or tie anywhere in site. Throughout the year bring shorts, light-colored short-sleeved or sleeveless shirts and t-shirts (darker colors really attract the heat), flip flops, sandals, comfortable outdoor shoes for those that want to walk or hike, sports socks, sunglasses, hat, several bathing suits and a cover-up, water-resistant footwear, and maybe a rain jacket in the wetter months. For evenings dress is resort casual: women should plan on wearing a simple sun dress, dressier shorts, or casual pants with a summery blouse, and sandals; men will be comfortable pretty much anywhere in dressier shorts or khakis, and a short-sleeved collared shirt with sandals. The only place a jacket might be required is for one of the few upscale restaurant in Waikiki. For the cooler months bring along a wrap, sweater, or sweatshirt for the evenings or early morning although it usually isn't necessary. Check the Internet for a weather forecast before beginning your packing.

How Long Should I Plan on Staying?

Unless you live on the West Coast it seems a shame to fly such a long way for only a few days. Plan on six or seven nights at the least and even more if you wish to visit another Hawaiian island. Each island has it's own distinct flavor and a stay at Aulani combined with perhaps Kauai or

Maui is a perfect vacation plan. Just another good reason to use a travel advisor to plan your trip.

Should I Rent a Car?

If you plan on spending all of your time at Aulani then by all means take a shuttle or private transportation from the airport to Ko Olina and enjoy the resort to it's fullest. But you really should plan on a day or two to get out and see the beauty of Oahu or spend the day in Waikiki. I would arrange for airport transportation to and from the resort then rent a car on-site (an Alamo Car Rental desk is located at the resort) for a day or two to explore. Or reserve one of the Adventures By Disney excursions, a perfect way to see the island.

General Information

ATMs. An ATM machine is located in the lobby area.

Internet services. High-speed Internet access is complimentary in all guest rooms and throughout the resort.

Business center. Luana Lounge features two computers—one for browsing the Internet and one for printing boarding passes. It's perfect for hanging out if you need somewhere to wait before a late flight. Here you'll find comfortable sofas and chairs, TVs, and locker facilities with restrooms, showers, even a spin dryer for wet swimsuits.

Car rental. An Alamo Car Rental desk can be found just off the resort's lobby area.

Childcare. In addition to Aunty's Beach House, a supervised kid's club for children ages 3 to 12, in-room babysitting can be arranged with Kama'aina Kids Sitters. Available for children ages 6 weeks to 14 years; call (808) 372-5992.

Driving Directions. It's a easy 17-mile drive to Aulani from Honolulu International Airport: Head east 0.3 miles, take the left ramp to I-H-1 W 0.3 miles, keep left at the fork and follow the signs for Interstate H1 W/Waianae and merge onto I-H-1 W for 17.1 miles; I-H-1 W becomes Farrington Hwy/HI-93 W in 1.9 miles, take the ramp toward Ko Olina

0.3 miles, take a slight right at Ali'inui Drive for 1.6 miles to Aulani located on your right.

Guests with disabilities. Aulani offers accommodations for guests with disabilities including wheelchair and hearing accessible rooms. TTY equipment is available upon request at check-in.

For Guests in wheelchairs both Waikohole Pool and Waikohole Stream have zero-entry access points; water wheelchairs are also available to use. All other pools and whirlpools are equipped with a pool lift to assist guests in transferring into and out of the water. A limited number of sand wheelchairs are available on a first-come, first-served basis for use on Aulani's beach area.

Groceries. A small selection of groceries can be found onsite at Kālepa's Store in the lobby area. Four outdoor grills are available for use behind Aunty's Beach House.

Laundry and dry cleaning. Self-service, coin-operated washers and dryers are located in each of the two resort wings in addition to same-day dry cleaning and laundry service.

Parking. $35 per night for self and valet parking (high but in line with other resorts in the area). Disney Vacation Club Members enjoy complimentary parking for up to two vehicles.

Shopping. Round-trip transportation is available for a fee to Waikiki with stops at the Ala Moana Center, DFS Galleria (duty free) and Waikele Premium Outlets. The shuttle runs 3 days a week. For reservations visit the Holoholo Tour Desk in the lobby.

Tour Desk. Visit the Holoholo Tour Desk in the lobby area to arrange for off-site excursions around the island such as a visit to Pearl Harbor, snorkeling, luaus at Paradise Cove or Polynesian Cultural Center, surfing lessons, jet-skiing, parasailing, fishing charters, and dolphin encounters at Sea Life Park. This is also where you can arrange for the special Adventures By Disney excursions (see the Aulani Special Excursion section for more details).

Transfers. Pre-arrange for shuttle transfers between Aulani and Honolulu International Airport through SpeediShuttle via SpeediShuttle.com or (877) 242-5777.

Transportation. The complimentary Ko Olina intra-resort shuttle runs every half hour from 6:00 a.m. to 11:00 p.m. from Aulani's porte cochere.

Aulani Accommodations

359 hotel rooms (including 16 suites), and 481 Disney Vacation Club villas. 92-1185 Ali'inui Drive Kapolei, HI 96707; phone (808) 674-6200, fax (808) 776-5763. Check-in 3:00 p.m., checkout 11:00 a.m. For reservations call (714) 520-7001, or contact your travel advisor specializing in Disney Destinations.

Comprising 16 floors spread over two towers in a "U" shape, the Ewa Tower and Waianae Tower are centered upon the lobby area. Hotel rooms are found only in the Waianae Tower with villas located in both towers.

Guest rooms. Guest rooms in the hotel section at Aulani offer 382 square feet adorned with earth tone colors and fabrics. Beds, either two queens or a king, are covered in white duvets and festooned with pineapple patterned Hawaiian quilt bed runners in either royal blue or cherry red. Headboards are reminiscent of outrigger canoe posts and beams; the beds are conveniently high enough to slide your luggage underneath. King-bedded rooms also have a retro queen sleeper sofa in buttercup yellow embellished with a tangerine and royal blue print depicting birds of paradise and other flowers. A wall mirror is cleverly framed in what looks like carved interlocking fish hooks, and built into the bureau is a 37" flat-panel TV, an undercounter refrigerator, and a nice amount of drawer space. Even more storage can be found within the padded coffee table. Upon a two-person table is a 'ukulele-playing Surfer Mickey lamp, and Hawaiian themed artwork decorates the walls. The Hawaiian theme even extends to the carpet with taro leaf motif done in tones of cream and beige. Standard are Blu-ray DVD players, laptop-size electronic safe, hairdryer, iron and ironing board, coffee maker, tea kettle, robes, ceiling fan, H2O Sea Salt products, pack 'n' play, and nightly turndown service. My only complaint is how dark the guest rooms are with lighting that is totally inadequate.

In the bath are a single sink set in a black granite countertop and a bathtub/shower. Cream-colored porcelain tile resembling stone and a ribbon of pebbled tile encircle the tub, and you'll enjoy the luxury of both a hand-held and a rain showerhead. The commode is in a separate area behind louvered doors.

All rooms offer either a patio or nice-sized balcony with two rattan outdoor chairs and a small cocktail table offering the following views: *Standard View* of the parking garage, conference center, or parking lot; *Island Garden View* of the spa's hydrotherapy garden, mountains, or resort landscaping; *Poolside Garden View* with a partial view of the pool, courtyard, or water features; *Partial Ocean View* of the ocean and possibly the pool; or *Ocean View* with a full view of the ocean. All sleep four plus an infant.

Villas. Decorated in virtually the same fabrics and décor as the hotel rooms, Aulani's Disney Vacation Club villas offer a wide range of accommodation choices including studios, one-, two-, and three-bedroom options.

Deluxe Studios are 356 square feet sleeping four plus an infant. In the entry hall is a black granite mini-kitchen with sink, microwave, and undercounter refrigerator, and off the entry is a single sink bath with a shower/tub combination featuring both a rain shower and standard showerheads as well as a separate commode area. A queen bed and queen sleeper sofa are accompanied by an entertainment center with flat-panel TV, coffee table with storage, and two-person table and chairs.

One-bedroom Villas come with 750 square feet and although they are just about the same size as Aulani's Parlor Suite, you'll find they are less expensive. Just past the entry hall is the villa's kitchen featuring wood floors, black granite countertops, sink, full-size refrigerator, dishwasher, microwave, and stove. A dining booth is just off the kitchen, and the adjoining living room offers a queen sleeper sofa as well as a murphy bed (it actually pulls out from the entertainment center) or a sleeper chair along with a coffee table, easy chair, and flat-panel TV. A half-bath and stacked washer/dryer are located next to the entry hallway. Off the living area is an angled balcony.

In the bedroom are a king bed, desk, entertainment center, and second balcony. The bath has a shuttered window opening into the master bedroom and includes a large shower, whirlpool tub, and single sink with separate toilet area. Sleeps up to four guests plus an infant.

The *Two-bedroom Villa* with 1,100 square feet is basically a studio combined with a one-bedroom villa. In it are two bedrooms, two and a half baths, kitchen, and living area. There's a king bed in the master, and either two queen beds or a queen bed and a sofa sleeper in the guest room. The guest room and living area share a balcony, and the master has its own. Dedicated Two-bedroom Villas have a half-bath off the entry, but the master bath does not offer a split-bath configuration, and the guest bedroom does not offer a mini-kitchen. Non-dedicated Two-bedroom Villas (in other words the second bedroom is considered a "lock-off" Deluxe Studio) have a door off the entry into the master bedroom bath's commode/shower area, part of a two-part bath. Sleeps up to nine guests plus an infant.

Grand Villas are three-bedroom beauties flanking each of the resort's two towers, offering a full ocean view. These one-story villas have almost a suite feel to them. The living, dining, and kitchen are all together in a "great room" of sorts done in bamboo flooring and partially divided by columns. In the living area are a queen sleeper sofa and sleeper chair along with two easy chairs, coffee table, and entertainment center. The dining area has an eight-person table accessing a nice sized kitchen with black granite countertops and a three-person bar stool counter, side-by-side refrigerator with ice and water in the door, stove, dishwasher, microwave, and all the accouterments necessary for preparing meals.

The master bedroom sits off the dining area; a hallway and separate entrance between the two has a closet with a stacked washer/dryer. In the master is a king bed, entertainment center, and easy chair with an adjoining bath featuring a whirlpool tub, single sink, shower, and separate commode area with a Toto Washlet. Built into the vanity mirror is a "magic" TV.

On the opposite side of the living area are two guest rooms, each with two queen beds. One has a bath in the hallway with double sinks; the other is a bath within the bedroom with a single sink. Sleeps up to twelve guests plus an infant.

Suites. *Parlor Suites (One-bedroom Suites).* With 764 square feet these suites sleep up to five people and are a perfect choice for families. Very similar to a One-bedroom Villa minus the kitchen, each is named after a constellation. In the parlor area is a four-person dining table and wet bar, a queen sleeper sofa, two grasscloth occasional chairs, and a pull-down single bed that is stored in the entertainment center. Off the entry is a half-bath. Carpeting has a taro leaf motif just as in the guest rooms but in a moss green color. There's a king bed in the master and an entertainment center with TV, desk, and occasional chair. In the bath you'll find a shuttered window opening into the bedroom, single sink, whirlpool tub, vanity, and shower in one area; and a commode and sink in the other. All is done in a green porcelain tile resembling stone with mosaic tile trim in the shower. A balcony runs the length of the suite offering either ocean or partial ocean views. Sleeps up to five guests.

Lei Hulu Suite (Deluxe 1-bedroom Suite). Located on the resort's 16th floor in the Waianae Tower the one-bedroom Lei Hulu Vice Presidential Suite offers an absolutely stunning Hawaiian-style contemporary look. With 1528 square feet sleeping up to five people, extra touches include integrated lighting controls, wood flooring throughout the entry, living, and dining areas, and a somewhat feminine ocean theme (the Hawaiians believe that the ocean possesses feminine qualities). The living area contains an oversized sleeper chair covered in buttercream and chocolate hued leather, leather topped coffee table, queen sleeper sofa in royal blue and moss green with a *honu* (turtle) motif, and occasional chair. One entire wall consists of a sumptuous wood entertainment center with a 42" flat panel TV and Blu-ray DVD player. The full bath adjoining the living area has a single, above-counter sink and a shower sparkling with blue glass tile. A credenza partially divides the living area from the dining room and its eight-person table. Above it all is a dramatic curved ceiling with recessed lighting. Near the dining area is a service kitchen that includes a full-size refrigerator, dishwasher, sink, and microwave. It features a pass-through bar with two bar stools and separate catering access. A balcony runs the length of the suite with pool and partial ocean views.

In the beautiful bedroom sea foam green carpeting mimics the ocean waves. On one side of a dramatic contemporary pillar of wood is a wet bar and desk area; on the other side is a king-size bed adorned with a sea foam green spread accented in white and surrounded by white curtain sheers flowing from a modern four-poster frame. There is also an additional 42" flat-panel TV and Blu-ray DVD player, a chaise lounge, a